DOES
FOREIGN DIRECT
INVESTMENT PROMOTE

DEVELOPMENT?

INSTITUTE FOR INTERNATIONAL ECONOMICS
CENTER FOR GLOBAL DEVELOPMENT

DOES FOREIGN DIRECT INVESTMENT PROMOTE DEVELOPMENT?

EDITED BY THEODORE H. MORAN, EDWARD M. GRAHAM,

AND MAGNUS BLOMSTRÖM

WASHINGTON, DC
APRIL 2005

Theodore H. Moran holds the Marcus Wallenberg Chair at the School of Foreign Service, Georgetown University, and is founder and director of the Landegger Program in International Business Diplomacy. In 1993–94, he was senior adviser for economics on the Policy Planning Staff of the State Department. Among his recent books are *Parental Supervision: The New Paradigm for Foreign Direct Investment and Development* (2001) and *Foreign Direct Investment and Development* (1998).

Edward M. Graham, senior fellow at the Institute for International Economics, was associate professor in the Fuqua School of Business at Duke University (1988–90), associate professor at the University of North Carolina (1983–88), principal administrator of the Planning and Evaluation Unit at the OECD (1981–82), international economist in the Office of International Investment Affairs at the US Treasury (1979–80), and assistant professor at the Massachusetts Institute of Technology (1974–78). He is author or coauthor of *Fighting the Wrong Enemy: Antiglobal Activists and Multinational Enterprises* (2000) and *Foreign Direct Investment in the United States* (3d ed., 1995).

Magnus Blomström is professor of economics and president of the European Institute of Japanese Studies at the Stockholm School of Economics. He was assistant professor, University of Gothenburg (1985–87) and a research fellow at the Institute for International Economic Studies, University of Stockholm (1982–84). He is coauthor or coeditor of *Scandinavia and the EU* (Stockholm: SNS Förlag, 1994; in Swedish) and *Foreign Direct Investment: Firm and Host Country Strategies* (MacMillan, 2000).

INSTITUTE FOR INTERNATIONAL ECONOMICS
1750 Massachusetts Avenue, NW
Washington, DC 20036-1903
(202) 328-9000   FAX: (202) 659-3225
www.iie.com

C. Fred Bergsten, *Director*
Valerie Norville, *Director of Publications and Web Development*
Edward Tureen, *Director of Marketing*

CENTER FOR GLOBAL DEVELOPMENT
1776 Massachusetts Avenue, NW, Suite 301
Washington, DC 20036
(202) 416-0700   FAX: (202) 416-0750
www.cgdev.org

Nancy Birdsall, *President*

Typesetting by Circle Graphics
Printing by Automated Graphic Systems, Inc.

Printed in the United States of America
07 06 05   5 4 3 2 1

Library of Congress Cataloging-in-Publication Data

Does foreign direct investment promote development? / Theodore H. Moran, Edward Graham, Magnus Blomström, editors.
  p. cm
  "April 2005."
  Includes bibliographical references and index.
  ISBN 0-88132-381-0
  1. Investments, Foreign—Evaluation. 2. Investments, Foreign—Developing countries. 3. Economic development. I. Moran, Theodore H., 1943- II. Graham, Edward M. (Edward Montgomery), 1944- III. Blomström, Magnus, 1952-

HG4538.I4654 2005
338.9—dc22   2005043298

Contents

Preface

Does foreign direct investment (FDI) promote development? For decades, the attempt to answer this question has been controversial. With this volume, the Institute for International Economics and the Center for Global Development bring together new research that shows why earlier investigations came to diverse conclusions, demonstrates how novel analytic techniques can provide rigorous answers, presents new results, and draws policy conclusions for developing and developed countries alike.

Part I asks why the search for "universal" effects from FDI in manufacturing and assembly has produced highly differing results. A systematic assessment of previous research suggests that the key lies in how competitive the conditions are into which FDI is introduced—in particular, the extent of openness to trade and investment. The degree of competition in the host economy determines the ability of foreign investors to enhance productivity, introduce new production possibilities, and generate positive spillovers that benefit host economies.

New data from industry surveys document many examples of positive spillovers (or externalities)—that is, benefits to the host economy beyond what can be captured by the foreign investors themselves. At the same time, it shows why the use of econometric techniques to identify and measure them—whether in a horizontal direction among competitor firms or in a vertical direction among suppliers—is particularly difficult. Part I offers new approaches to unscrambling the subtle and sometimes contradictory impacts of FDI and presents exemplary research to show how this can be done. This research controls for factors that have confounded previous econometric efforts, rigorously demonstrates the presence of externalities, and shows how these externalities diffuse throughout the host economy, generating welfare benefits to both firms and consumers.

Part II turns from the impact of FDI on host welfare to the particular relationship between FDI and host-country growth. One study fails to find any indication that FDI accelerates growth as a general proposition. A second study disagrees, suggesting that inappropriate pooling of evidence from developed and developing countries, as prevalent in most previous research (including the first study), is responsible for the failure to find a significant relationship. This second study argues that when developed- and developing-country data are kept segmented, FDI does have a significant impact on per capita growth in less developed countries. When the first study makes this adjustment, however, the results again show no positive correlation.

Can these opposing findings be reconciled? Part II concludes with a synthesis showing that the solution lies in examining whether increases in FDI and trade take place together in the countries included in the sample. The results reported by both studies converge in demonstrating that when increases in FDI and increases in trade coincide, the result is a significant expansion of host-country growth.

The powerful interaction between trade and investment is particularly prominent within firms that are organized to trade internally. Part II presents novel research demonstrating that firms organized to trade intrafirm differ systematically from those that are not, transferring best practices in technology and management across borders in a larger and more dynamic fashion between home and host country.

Research reported in part III demonstrates that FDI has two distinct impacts on the host economy: positive and negative. FDI in which local affiliates operate within a relatively open trade and investment policy framework greatly benefits the host country. FDI in which local affiliates produce for the domestic market behind trade barriers, with joint-venture and domestic-content requirements, has a much less positive impact and often subtracts from host-country welfare. New data from China and Africa, as well as Latin America and Asia, make this distinction clear, both in the past and the present.

Part III shows how industry case studies, carefully structured to avoid selection bias, and survey research can be combined with econometric studies (using the controls introduced in part I) to advance understanding of how FDI affects host-country development. Part III identifies the principal challenges in conducting future research and proposes major areas where further investigation is needed: For example, what steps poor developing countries can take to benefit from FDI the way middle-income developing countries have and how backward linkages and supplier relationships can be enhanced across all developing countries. These areas are prominent in the research agenda of the Center for Global Development.

Part III concludes with the policy implications for developing and developed countries. Developing countries can serve their own interests best through vigorous trade and investment liberalization and by turning away from the suggestion of some of their members that performance requirements (like mandatory joint ventures, technology sharing obligations, and domestic-content targets) should regain legitimacy in the World Trade Organization. At the same time, developed countries have no business allowing their political risk-insurance agencies to support and subsidize import-substitution FDI that stifles trade and detracts from host-country welfare—as the United States, Canada, the United Kingdom, Germany, France, Japan, and others currently do.

Finally, despite the evidence of externalities from FDI, the escalation of incentives and subsidies offered to international corporations by both developed and developing countries needs to be capped and brought under multilateral discipline to maximize the benefits that flow from investor operations, a topic treated in the Institute's 2003 book by John H. Mutti, *Foreign Direct Investment and Tax Competition*, as well as this volume.

This volume continues in a long tradition of cutting-edge work on FDI at the Institute for International Economics. In 1989, Edward M. Graham and Paul R. Krugman first produced *Foreign Direct Investment in the United States*, which is now in its third edition. Graham followed with *Global Corporations and National Governments* (1996) and *Fighting the Wrong Enemy: Antiglobal Activists and Multinational Enterprises* (2000). Theodore H. Moran focused on FDI and development in *Foreign Direct Investment and Development: The New Policy Agenda for Developing Countries and Economies in Transition* (1998) and *Parental Supervision: The New Paradigm for Foreign Direct Investment and Development* (2001). Daniel H. Rosen looked at investment issues in China in *Behind the Open Door: Foreign Enterprises in the Chinese Marketplace* (1999).

The Center for Global Development has developed an index of investment flows that evaluates developed-country policies to encourage beneficial foreign investment—and discourage harmful foreign investment—in developing countries. The Center sponsors research on FDI and development issues across the developing world.

The Center for Global Development is an independent, nonprofit policy research organization dedicated to reducing global poverty and inequality and to making globalization work for the poor. Through a combination of research and strategic outreach, the Center actively engages policymakers and the public to influence the policies of the United States, other rich countries, and such institutions as the World Bank, the International Monetary Fund, and the World Trade Organization to improve the economic and social development prospects in poor countries. The Center's Board of Directors bears overall responsibility for the Center and includes distinguished leaders of nongovernmental organizations, former officials, business executives, and some of the world's leading scholars of development.

The Center receives advice on its research and policy programs from the Board and from an Advisory Committee that comprises respected development specialists and advocates. The Center's president works with the Board, the Advisory Committee, and the Center's senior staff in setting the research and program priorities and approves all formal publications. The Center is supported by an initial significant financial contribution from Edward W. Scott Jr. and by funding from philanthropic foundations and other organizations.

The Institute for International Economics is a private, nonprofit institution for the study and discussion of international economic policy. Its purpose is to analyze important issues in that area and to develop and communicate practical new approaches for dealing with them. The Institute is completely nonpartisan. The Institute is funded by a highly diversified group of philanthropic foundations, private corporations, and interested individuals. Major institutional grants are now being received from the William M. Keck Jr. Foundation, the New York Community Trust, and the Starr Foundation. About 18 percent of the Institute's resources in our latest fiscal year were provided by contributors outside the United States, including about 8 percent from Japan.

The Board of Directors bears overall responsibilities for the Institute and gives general guidance and approval to its research program, including the identification of topics that are likely to become important over the medium run (one to three years), and which should be addressed by the Institute. The director, working closely with the staff and outside Advisory Committee, is responsible for the development of particular projects and makes the final decision to publish an individual study.

The Center and the Institute would like to thank the Marcus Wallenberg Chair in International Business and Finance at the School of Foreign Service, Georgetown University, for providing the principal funding for the research contained in this volume.

We hope that the studies and other activities of our organizations will contribute to building a stronger foundation for international economic policy around the world. We invite readers of our publications to let us know how they think we can best accomplish this objective.

NANCY BIRDSALL
President
Center for Global Development

C. FRED BERGSTEN
Director
Institute for International Economics

Introduction and Overview

THEODORE H. MORAN, EDWARD M. GRAHAM,
and MAGNUS BLOMSTRÖM

What is the impact of foreign direct investment (FDI) on development? The answer is important for the lives of millions—if not billions—of workers, families, and communities in the developing world. The answer is crucial for policymakers in developing and developed countries and in multilateral agencies. The answer is central to the debate about the costs and benefits of the globalization of industry across borders.

Yet determining exactly how FDI affects development has proven to be remarkably elusive. Investigating how FDI can contribute to, or detract from, the growth and welfare of developing countries is a challenge the Institute for International Economics takes up in the chapters of this conference volume.

Why has the relationship between FDI and development been so difficult to investigate? What quandaries in analysis, or deficiencies in procedure, have impeded the investigation in the past? How can analysis be strengthened, and what do the results show?

This volume gathers together the cutting edge of new research on FDI and host country economic performance, and presents the most sophisticated critiques of current and past inquiries. The volume probes the limits of what can be determined from available evidence and from innovative investigative techniques. It presents new results. This conference volume also concludes with an analysis of the implications for contemporary policy debates, and proposed new avenues for future research.

Theodore H. Moran is Marcus Wallenberg Professor of International Business and Finance at the School of Foreign Service at Georgetown University. Edward M. Graham is senior fellow at the Institute for International Economics. Magnus Blomström is professor at the European Institute of Japanese Studies at the Stockholm School of Economics.

Finding an Empirical Framework
for Policy Analysis

Three bodies of "conventional wisdom" about nonextractive FDI's impact on host countries in the developing world exist:[1]

"Washington Consensus" Enthusiasm. The first source of conventional wisdom can be found in the "Washington consensus," which is still reiterated by multinational investors and business advocacy groups, that asserts FDI is unequivocally "good" for development (as long as the investors do not pollute the environment or blatantly abuse workers), and the more FDI the host country can attract the better.[2]

Academic Skepticism. The second source of conventional wisdom is reflected in academic skepticism that any noteworthy relationship between FDI and development exists. From this perspective, "One dollar of FDI is worth no more (and no less) than a dollar of any other kind of investment."[3]

Dirigisme Resurrected. The third source of conventional wisdom is found in the renewed conviction among (some) developing countries that host country development objectives can be achieved only by imposing performance requirements on multinational investors. The trade-and-investment agenda for the World Trade Organization (WTO), according to some prominent developing countries, must therefore be reshaped to allow host governments to force technology transfer, promote inputs of domestic origin, and ensure that backward linkages to the local economy occur.[4]

The chapters in this volume show that all three of these perspectives are inaccurate and provide misleading—or even harmful—advice about how developing countries might harness FDI to enhance their growth and welfare. To sort through the policy options available, policymakers

---

1. For the special problems of FDI in natural resources and in infrastructure, as well as in manufacturing, see Moran (2005).

2. For a retrospective evaluation of the "Washington consensus," see Williamson (2003).

3. Dani Rodrik, Appel Inaugural Lecture at Columbia University, March 27, 2003. See also Rodrik (1999, 37).

4. Communication by Brazil and India on the need to amend the TRIMs agreement, in *Foreign Direct Investment and Performance Requirements: New Evidence from Selected Countries*, Geneva, UNCTAD, 2003, 38–39. Also, Development Provisions, WTO Secretariat note to the Working Group on the Relationship between Trade and Investment, June 11, 2002.

will want to know whether the evidence supports the view that host countries should

- make a concerted effort (including special incentives and subsidies) to lure foreign investors to choose their economy as a base for operations;

- simply open the economy to foreign firms without any special incentives; or

- advance their own development interests by insisting that foreigners share technology, production, and ownership with indigenous firms.

This conference volume addresses the controversial issues that are central to all three of these options.

New Methodologies and New Results in Measuring FDI's Impact on Development: Searching for Externalities and Spillovers

The studies in this volume start with the first option—which has always been the most severe research challenge—investigating whether it might be in the host country's interest to devote scarce domestic resources to attracting and incorporating FDI into its development strategy.

The answer depends in large part on whether an FDI project generates positive externalities ("spillovers") for the host economy. Positive externalities can be defined as benefits created by the project that are not appropriated by the foreign investor undertaking the project, nor by the factors of production (workers) employed by the project, nor by the suppliers to the project unless possibly the suppliers are able to expand their activity beyond that directly accounted for by the project. A positive externality would be created, for example, if sales to the foreign-controlled enterprise enabled suppliers to increase their efficiency and this resulted in lower prices to clients in the local economy other than the foreign-controlled enterprise.

Such externalities can justify a subsidy to be granted to the undertaking by public authorities, as explained in the study by Blalock and Gertler (chapter 4). The value of the subsidy, of course, should never exceed the value of the positive externalities generated by the project. This poses a challenge, however, because this latter value, as demonstrated in this volume, is extremely hard to calculate, so hard indeed that the extent to which FDI even in net creates positive externalities in developing host nations is subject to some uncertainty. As demonstrated in the studies of this section, past studies have produced highly diverse answers to the questions of whether externalities do exist and how great are their magnitudes.

In principle, it is clear that externalities might be created in a number of ways—via, e.g., movement of workers and managers who have been trained by multinational firms into jobs outside those firms, such that the benefits of the greater "human capital" of these persons are captured by agents in the host economy other than the foreign affiliate; an increase in efficiency of suppliers (see above); leakage of technological and managerial information into the economy as a whole via channels other than suppliers or movement of workers and management; and "demonstration effects" whereby the success of one foreign investor induces other investors to come to the country. But measuring these is fraught with difficulty.

The studies in the first part of this volume provide insights into why externalities are difficult to identify and measure, while showing why past studies have produced such diverse results regarding the existence and magnitude of spillovers. Moreover, these studies suggest how externalities might be more rigorously identified and measured in the future.

Robert E. Lipsey and Fredrik Sjöholm

In chapter 2, Robert E. Lipsey and Fredrik Sjöholm begin their review of previous research by citing their own consternation at an inability to find a "universal relationship" between inward FDI and host country economic performance. Looking first at wage spillovers, they note that foreign firms consistently pay higher wages than domestic firms in both developed and developing countries, after controlling for firm-specific characteristics. Whether the higher foreign-paid wages lead to higher wages in domestically owned firms is more problematic in the studies Lipsey and Sjöholm review, although their own research in Indonesia shows significant spillovers. Investigating the possibility that foreign investors simply move into high-wage geographical locations or high-wage industries, Lipsey and Sjöholm's research suggests that relocation does not cause the correlation. Instead, their findings show that a link between the multinational corporation's presence and the higher domestic wage persists even as the geographical and industry breakdowns become finer.

With respect to productivity spillovers, the authors note that the earlier predominance among researchers who found no beneficial impact from FDI on domestic firms has been giving way to more positive results—a trend that is substantially reinforced from the findings reported in this volume. Reviewing studies on productivity spillovers in Indonesian manufacturing, Lipsey and Sjöholm note that all cross-section studies and three out of four panel data studies find statistically significant intraindustry spillovers (the one that fails to find intraindustry spillovers finds interindustry spillovers instead). Spillovers are highest in sectors with vigorous competition.

In assessing whether any negative effects from FDI exist, Lipsey and Sjöholm note that studies depicting a "harmful" impact by exposing domestic firms to greater competition may miss an important analytical point: If incoming FDI raises average productivity across foreign-owned and domestically owned firms, the outcome for the host country should be considered favorable, even if the least efficient local companies became unprofitable or were forced out of the industry.

Why, they ask, have previous studies come to such varied conclusions? Some analysts have blamed the differences in results on the use of panel data in some studies and cross-section data in others. Lipsey and Sjöholm's investigations, using different economic techniques and data sources, on Indonesian wages and productivity, however, show that this distinction is not crucial. Rather, the diverse results may be attributed, they suggest, to differences in the countries' ability to benefit from FDI, due to varying levels of indigenous human resources, to disparate degrees of private-sector sophistication, to differing levels of competition, and to contrasting host country policies toward trade and investment—all themes that resonate strongly in the other studies included in this volume.

Coming full circle on the impact of FDI on host economies, Lipsey and Sjöholm conclude that—absent consideration of these differences among the settings in which FDI occurs—"the main lesson might be that the search for universal relationships is futile."

Beata Smarzynska Javorcik and Mariana Spatareanu

In chapter 3, Beata Smarzynska Javorcik and Mariana Spatareanu provide a new analytical framework within which researchers can investigate horizontal and vertical spillovers and externalities.

Looking first at horizontal spillovers, Javorcik and Spatareanu point out that researchers face the challenge of disentangling the positive impact of knowledge flows from the potentially negative short-run effect that an increase in competitive pressures from foreign entry may have on some domestic firms. Since it is difficult to capture each effect separately, in a vast majority of cases the research results reflect the combined effect of the two forces.

Javorcik and Spatareanu use surveys commissioned by the World Bank of local firms in Latvia and the Czech Republic in 2003 to assess managers' perception of whether the rising foreign presence in their sector has affected firm performance. For "knowledge spillovers," the survey data identify two principal channels—the movement of labor (managers and workers) from foreign firms to host country companies, and the opportunity for host country companies to observe and imitate best practices and production techniques.

In terms of competitive pressures, 48 percent of Czech firms interviewed and 40 percent of Latvian enterprises believed that the presence of multinationals increased the level of competition in their sector. Almost 30 percent of firms in each country reported losing market share as a result of FDI inflow, and local firms also lost 6 to 10 percent of their employees to multinationals.

The implications for domestic company operations, as reported by the Latvian and Czech firms, were mixed. Firms reporting rising competitive pressures as a result of foreign entry enjoyed a larger increase in employment relative to companies that were not affected by FDI inflows, and experienced faster productivity growth. But firms reporting loss of a market share, which they attributed to foreign presence in their sector, experienced a much larger decline in employment and slower total factor productivity (TFP) growth than other firms.

Turning to vertical spillovers, Javorcik and Spatareanu draw on a survey of 119 majority-owned multinational affiliates operating in the Czech Republic. The results show widespread local sourcing of some kind: 90 percent of 119 multinationals surveyed reported that they purchased product inputs—not just services—from at least one Czech supplier, while the median multinational had a sourcing relationship with 10 Czech firms and a multinational in the top quartile had a sourcing relationship with at least 30 Czech firms. Furthermore, more than a tenth of respondents acquired all of their intermediates from Czech enterprises.

Javorcik and Spatareanu argue that isolating the extent to which vertical spillovers from foreign firms constitute true externalities is complicated, because there are at least three scenarios for the development of supplier relationships between local firms and foreign multinationals. The first possibility is "cherry picking"—that is, multinationals simply award contracts to the best local firms that are already at the required level of sophistication.

The second scenario is that potential suppliers experience what Javorcik and Spatareanu call a "positive productivity shock" after which they reach the performance level sufficient to obtain contracts from a multinational. This shock may include higher requirements demanded by the foreigner (e.g., International Organization for Standardization [ISO] 9000 certification to ensure compliance with internationally recognized standards for quality management) that mesh with the local firm's own motivation to establish a new, superior business relationship (involving advance funding and/or more reliable payment when dealing with foreign affiliates). Supporting this second ("positive productivity shock") scenario, 40 percent of all reporting Czech companies that acquired ISO 9000 certification indicated that they underwent the qualification process in order to become a supplier to the MNC. However, the MNCs did not consider the ISO certification requirement—or technical audits, which they also frequently required as a condition of becoming a supplier—as a form of direct assistance even though both served the Czech firms as a guide to correcting operational deficiencies.

The third scenario is that local suppliers improve their performance while supplying a multinational thanks to explicit assistance extended by the foreign investor. Supporting the third ("externality") scenario, one-fifth of the 119 multinationals surveyed reported providing some type of direct support to the Czech companies they source from. Advance payment and financing were the most frequent form of assistance; employee training and help with quality control ranked second and third. Other types of assistance included supplying inputs, lending/leasing machinery, providing production technology, organizing production lines, providing assistance with financial planning and business strategy, and facilitating introduction to export markets.

All three scenarios support the finding that the presence of foreign firms in downstream industries is positively correlated with higher productivity of domestic firms in the supplier industries. However, the "cherry picking" scenario would not necessarily involve externalities.

Garrick Blalock and Paul J. Gertler

In chapter 4, Garrick Blalock and Paul J. Gertler, like Javorcik and Spatareanu, use interviews with firm managers in Indonesia to illuminate the processes of technology transfer to suppliers, but they go considerably farther in demonstrating—rigorously—the presence of externalities that diffuse throughout the Indonesian economy and generate welfare benefits to both firms and consumers.

The authors' interviews with Indonesian managers provide a detailed description of the assistance foreign investors offer to local firms. For example, before an Indonesian firm could qualify as a supplier an American investor would inspect the local factories, suggest modifications, and then ship their subsequent products for testing in the United States. Once design standards were met, the US firm would send Indonesian firm managers to the parent headquarters to master the multinational's quality control, inventory control, and cost control systems, with future purchases dependent upon reliable performance. Japanese managers depicted a similar sequence, adding that they would introduce qualifying suppliers to related companies in their industrial group, in Indonesia and abroad. Their goal was to enable suppliers to maximize economies of scale and even out capacity utilization. In a reciprocal process, the Japanese affiliates would bring Malaysian and Thai—as well as Indonesian—suppliers into each other's markets to increase competition and reduce dependence on a single supply source.

Moving from descriptive material to econometric analysis, using Indonesian data on manufacturing establishments that have been extensively and conscientiously collected by region since 1988, Blalock and Gertler show that FDI's effect in augmenting suppliers' productivity is large and significant. Their tests then find that this technology transfer to suppliers results in lower prices, increased output, higher profitability, and increased entry in the supplier market. Furthermore, lower supply prices lead to lower prices, increased output, higher profitability, and increased entry throughout the Indonesia economy. The economic returns to the host country exceed the private returns to the multinational investors and their direct suppliers.

As Gordon Hanson points out in his commentary, a rigorous test of FDI's impact requires isolating the relationship between changes in FDI and changes in domestic firm behavior without marring the investigation with other factors that might affect both simultaneously. Hanson notes Blalock and Gertler's exceptional achievement in isolating FDI's impact per se without the disturbing effects of other factors, finding an explicit control group in running regressions and checking for endogeneity. As Hanson notes, "this sort of external validation of FDI spillovers is all too rare in the literature."

In addition, Blalock and Gertler test whether FDI insures against market imperfections that limit credit availability during times of financial stress. They perform a "natural experiment" comparing the response of firms with foreign equity ownership to firms without foreign equity ownership during the 1997–98 Indonesian financial crisis. The results show that foreign investment is less vulnerable than domestic investment during an externally inflicted credit crunch.

Whereas liquidity constraints denied domestic exporters the opportunity to take advantage of the massive Indonesian devaluation, exporters with foreign ownership could access credit through their parent company and use the Indonesian economy as a base for expanded production and exports. Exporters with foreign ownership increased capital investment by 8 percent, domestic employment by 15 percent, and value added by 30 percent more than exporters without. Blalock and Gertler conclude that the ability of foreign firms to sustain investment during times of crisis provides a form of liquidity insurance and hastens economic recovery.

Asim Erdilek

In chapter 5, Asim Erdilek compares the research and development (R&D) activities of foreign investors with domestic firms, and investigates whether domestic firms are more likely to engage in R&D as the foreign investor presence in their sector grows. He uses highly disaggregated data and formulates new R&D indicators beyond those usually found in FDI and R&D literature.

Erdilek finds that MNCs undertake more R&D within the host country than domestic firms, which generates new production techniques that would otherwise not exist. Perhaps more notably, he shows that national firms increase their own R&D activities as multinationals expand in their sector.

Erdelik's data show that foreign establishments with the highest external ownership (81 to 100 percent foreign owned) have a lower propensity to engage in R&D internally than foreign establishments with lower external ownership. But this result must be interpreted carefully in light of the discovery reported later in this volume that MNCs are much more likely to share their most advanced technology, quality control, and marketing procedures with their wholly owned or majority-owned foreign affiliates than with less closely controlled companies, which obviates the need for local R&D except for relatively minor customizing purposes.

Holger Görg and Eric Strobl

In chapter 6, Holger Görg and Eric Strobl argue that the traditional way of measuring technological externalities—productivity spillovers or improvements in domestic establishments' productivity—is too narrow. Quite apart from technological externalities, multinationals can affect indigenous performance through "pecuniary externalities," which may affect entry, growth, and survival of plants in the host economy.

Unlike technological externalities, pecuniary externalities do not affect the production function of the benefiting firm, but rather improve the profitability of the firm via cost reductions or increases in revenues. When multinationals increase output, the demand for intermediate products also increases, which allows local suppliers to produce at a more efficient scale, reduces average costs, and lowers prices to all buyers, foreign and domestic.

Görg and Strobl's empirical estimations use plant-level data from the Republic of Ireland. Using a simple entry model, Görg and Strobl find that the influx of FDI has stimulated the entry of domestic plants in the same industry. Their simulations suggest that without MNCs the actual number of plants would have been considerably less: depending on the counterfactual, as much as 30 percent less. While admitting that their results are quite tentative, Görg and Strobl point out that this exploration of pecuniary externalities has not received much attention in the literature to date.

Ping Lin and Kamal Saggi

In an old joke, an economist is defined as someone who—discovering that something works in practice—wonders whether it will work in theory. Chapter 7, authored by Ping Lin and Kamal Saggi, actually tests the reality of the jest.

Lin and Saggi construct a model that captures two conflicting effects of FDI on local industry. On the one hand, they want to show that an MNC's entry decreases the market share of firms that directly compete with it in the final good market, thereby leading to a decreased demand for the required intermediate good. On the other hand, they also want to show that the MNC's entry expands the number of backward linkages as it locally sources the intermediate good.

Their model captures the complexity of the outcome when multinationals may have a negative impact on their local competitors but a positive impact on local suppliers. Lin and Saggi's model demonstrates that the multi-national's entry enlarges the extent of backward linkages if and only if its technological advantage over local competitors is not too large—in fact, under such circumstances, the effect of increased demand dominates the effect of increased competition.

Thus, rather impressive discoveries of spillovers and externalities pervade the studies in section I of the conference volume. Nevertheless, the authors have a decidedly skeptical view toward the justification for providing, as Gordon Hanson states, "the kinds of subsidies that many countries have begun to offer multinationals."

To anticipate a discussion that will reappear in the concluding section of this volume—on the implications for policymakers—it is important to note that the provision of host country resources to attract and/or provide special treatment to foreign investors can take many forms. For example, host country support for foreign investment can be informational: a country can provide current economic and legal information in a "proactive" fashion to reduce a foreign investor's travel and research costs for comparing production sites. A host country can also entice foreign investors by providing skill-training programs and vocational institutions, modernizing infrastructure, creating industrial parks, and streamlining regulatory agencies, all of which will almost certainly benefit indigenous firms and workers as well. Finally, a host country can shower foreign investors with tax breaks and direct subsidies.

The concluding part of this volume will argue that policymakers should evaluate the wisdom of providing these types of FDI support separately, even when they suspect that there are likely to be positive externalities for the host economy of the kind shown here.

Aggregate Assessment of FDI's Impact on Host Country Growth

What is FDI's impact on host country growth? A large and growing body of literature uses aggregate FDI flows to test whether FDI accelerates economic growth, frequently showing evidence of a positive relationship between FDI and growth. Following Borensztein, De Gregorio, and Lee (1998), much of the research emphasizes that FDI is particularly growth enhancing after the host country acquires a minimum stock of human capital.

Maria Carkovic and Ross Levine

In chapter 8, Maria Carkovic and Ross Levine reassess earlier findings regarding FDI and economic growth, using two new databases that add to the comprehensiveness and accuracy about FDI flows in addition to new techniques not used in previous studies. In particular, they utilize an estimator designed by Arellano and Bover (1995) and Blundell and Bond (1997) (ABBB) to correct deficiencies they identify in existing cross-country studies of FDI and growth. Carkovic and Levine argue that this (ABBB) estimator, which is a modified Generalized Method of Moments (GMM) estimator, is more appropriate to available panel data than one based on ordinary least squares (OLS). But, for comparison, they also run the same regressions using an OLS estimator.

The authors suggest that the ABBB estimator and their specification

- exploit the time-series dimension of the data to produce more precise estimates than do earlier studies;

- eliminate biases associated with traditional cross-country FDI-growth studies by controlling for any country-specific fixed effects;[5]

- control for the potential endogeneity of the explanatory variables to reduce estimation biases; and

- eliminate biases in the estimated coefficients and standard errors in current FDI-growth analyses by explicitly accounting for the inclusion of lagged dependent variables as regressors.

By providing both OLS and the ABBB estimation results, Carkovic and Levine seek to provide a more accurate assessment of the FDI-growth relationship than past aggregate studies, demonstrating—in particular—that the latter estimator fails to demonstrate a robust exogenous effect of FDI on growth under specifications where the former does show such an effect.

Thus, in marked contrast to earlier work, Carkovic and Levine conclude that FDI does not exert a robust, independent impact on economic growth when other factors are taken into account. Even if host countries raise their average years of schooling, they find that FDI flows do not appear to boost growth. Carkovic and Levine argue that while sound host country economic policies may spur both growth and FDI, their results are inconsistent with the view that FDI accelerates growth as a general proposition.

Bruce Blonigen and Miao Grace Wang

In chapter 9, Bruce Blonigen and Miao Grace Wang disagree with Carkovic and Levine. They focus on an issue that often goes unnoticed in empirical

---

5. They accomplish this by introducing a country-specific variable that is assumed to be time-invariant, and then eliminating it by first-differencing independent variables in the time dimension. This is appropriate if country-specific effects are fixed (time-invariant). For more discussion of this approach, see the concluding section of this volume that identifies areas for further research.

cross-country studies of FDI—the use of databases that combine evidence from developed and developing countries. Pooling data this way inherently assumes, Blonigen and Wang point out, that the determinants and effects of FDI are identical for developed and developing countries even though theory often suggests that they may fundamentally differ. As a result, inferences derived from studies with pooled data may be incorrect or misleading for one or both types of countries.

Blonigen and Wang investigate the sensitivity of results when rich and poor country data are pooled for three different types of empirical FDI research: research on the determinants of cross-country FDI activity; research on the effects of FDI on country-level growth; and research on the issue of whether FDI crowds out (or crowds in) domestic investment in the host country. In all three areas, they find evidence that commingling wealthy and poor country data is a faulty method of investigation and leads to mistaken conclusions.

When data are kept segmented, the authors find that vertical motivations for FDI, for example, are more likely to predominate in investment flows to low-wage countries than to high-wage countries, and that FDI is much less likely to crowd out domestic investment in less developed countries than in developed countries. Indeed, in related work, Miao Grace Wang (2004) shows that FDI crowds in domestic investment in non-OECD countries—by stimulating backward or forward production linkages—whereas no such effect is evident in OECD countries.

Looking specifically at the debate about the FDI—host country growth relationship, Blonigen and Wang find that inappropriate pooling of data from developed and developing countries is responsible for estimating insignificant effects of FDI on per capita GDP growth. When mixing of the different bodies of evidence is avoided, they find that FDI does have a significant impact on per capita growth in less developed countries, in a pattern similar to the one found by Borensztein, De Gregorio, and Lee (1998), once a threshold in educational levels has been exceeded. Their estimation techniques employ an OLS estimator with panel data.

Can the apparently contradictory findings about the relationship between FDI and growth from authors Carkovic and Levine and Blonigen and Wang be reconciled? In his commentary, Marc Melitz argues that the answer is yes.

When Carkovic and Levine examine the impact of FDI on host country growth, with controls for initial per capita GDP, skill abundance, inflation, and government size, Melitz points out, their baseline results actually confirm the finding of Blonigen and Wang that above (historical) average levels of FDI are significantly correlated with above (historical) average growth rates. Even in the version of their analysis using the ABBB estimator, Carkovic and Levine's dismissal of the link between FDI and growth comes only after they introduce controls for trade openness and domestic financial credit. This leads Carkovic and Levine to the conclusion that FDI has no independent effect on host country growth.

Melitz notes, however, that the increasing presence of MNCs among developing countries—as Blonigen and Wang point out in their criticism of faulty pooling of data sources—is likely driven more by vertical production relationships than the horizontal FDI relationships that are more prominent among developed countries. Vertical FDI in turn strongly depends upon low trade barriers. Expanded channels of trade are a necessary complement to FDI in which intermediate inputs are imported by the foreign affiliate and exported as a processed product.

Thus, Melitz argues, the results reported by both Carkovic and Levine and Blonigen and Wang seem to point in the same direction. Joint changes in FDI and trade are significantly correlated with growth—increases in FDI that come along with increases in trade lead to higher rates of increase in host country GDP. Indeed, in this light, Melitz concludes it could actually be argued that Carkovic and Levine provide a new underpinning to the FDI-trade-growth relationship by showing that this correlation is not driven by unobserved country characteristics.[6]

Why do changes in FDI that are not accompanied by changes in trade fail to contribute independently to economic growth in economic countries?

Melitz notes that one answer (drawing on the next set of studies in this volume, particularly Moran) might derive from restrictive policies toward FDI on the part of some countries—forbidding majority ownership, imposing joint venture partners, dictating domestic content requirements, protecting local markets—that impose substantial performance penalties on the affiliates and prevent the integration of host country production into the MNCs' international sourcing networks. Increases in FDI in countries with such restrictive policies are not likely to be linked with increases in trade, and could well be associated with declines in trade as affiliate production substitutes for imports. Increases in FDI in countries with more liberal investment policies, in contrast, are likely to lead to joint increases in trade and FDI as affiliates import intermediates and reexport finished products back into the parent's supplier chain, with a positive impact on host country growth.

Susan E. Feinberg and Michael P. Keane

The potent interaction between trade and investment, as mediated within multinational corporate networks, is highlighted in the discoveries of Susan E. Feinberg and Michael P. Keane in their study of the special characteristics of firms that are organized to trade internally. In chapter 10, they ask whether MNCs that are organized to trade intrafirm in developing countries operate differently from MNCs with little or no intrafirm trade.

---

6. For the continuing controversy among Carkovic and Levine, Blonigen and Wang, and Melitz, see the concluding section of this volume, on implications for further research.

In their previous research on MNCs in the United States and Canada, Feinberg and Keane discovered that MNCs that were organized to trade intrafirm were more dynamic technologically than MNCs with no intrafirm trade. In the context of US-Canada trade liberalization, as MNCs expanded their intrafirm trade they transformed the nature of the parent-affiliate relationship, by substantially increasing the production share of bilateral intrafirm shipments of intermediates.

Canadian manufacturing affiliates became more intimately integrated into the MNC's global strategy. Knowledge flows, production coordination, reporting links, and other communication channels expanded both with the US parent and with other foreign divisions of the MNC. This phenomenon that Feinberg and Keane call "deep integration" was supported by both quantitative data and qualitative interviews with managers of MNC affiliates in Canada.

Their results refute the popular conviction in Canada that reduction in tariffs vis-à-vis the United States would "hollow out" Canadian manufacturing. Overall, bilateral trade liberalization was trade creating, as production integration within US MNCs led Canadian affiliates to increase their sales to the United States while the US parents expanded sales in the Canadian market. The result was a win-win process for workers and communities on both sides of the US-Canadian border and elsewhere where the MNC had operations.

Feinberg and Keane extend their analysis to affiliate activity in 48 other developing countries from 1983 to 1996 and discover that MNC affiliates that are organized to trade intrafirm tend to be part of much larger and more active MNC networks (measured either in terms of total foreign sales or number of affiliates) than affiliates that are not. These affiliates generally grow faster and pay higher real wages than affiliates that do not trade intrafirm. They also differ systematically in terms of technology and organization. These affiliates are significantly more likely to have intrafirm trade with the MNC parents, in both directions.

If the US-Canadian experience is a guide, Feinberg and Keane predict that this integration of operations among developed and developing economies could potentially generate dynamic benefits, such as transferring best practices in production and quality control as well as exchanging knowledge about advances in logistics and transportation across developing-country borders.

Feinberg and Keane's observations about the internal integration of production among home and host country affiliates reinforces the findings of both Carkovic and Levine and Blonigen and Wang—as synthesized by Melitz—that rising levels of trade and foreign investment must go together to ensure a positive impact on host country growth. These findings carry a clear policy implication: There is likely to be an important synergy between liberalization of trade and liberalization of investment, leading developing countries to more productive use of local resources and (ceteris paribus) higher domestic growth rates when both occur simultaneously. This is a central theme in the chapters that are collected in the third section of this volume.

Designing Policies to Capture Beneficial (and Avoid Harmful) Economic Impacts of FDI

The studies in this section go well beyond the findings of "diverse" impacts of FDI on a host country economy. The authors identify the conditions under which FDI can be most beneficial and least beneficial—or most harmful—to host country development.

Theodore H. Moran

Expanding on earlier investigations of the relationship between FDI and development undertaken at the Institute for International Economics, in chapter 11 Theodore H. Moran finds a substantial difference in operating characteristics between subsidiaries that are integrated into the international sourcing networks of the parent multinationals, and subsidiaries that serve protected domestic markets and are prevented by mandatory joint venture and domestic content requirements from being so integrated. These different operating characteristics include size of plant, proximity of technology and quality control procedures to the international frontier, speed with which production processes are updated, efficiency of operations, and cost of output. The former subsidiaries have a more positive impact on the host country, often accompanied by vertical backward linkages and externalities of the kind noted by Javorcik and Spatareanu as well as Blalock and Gertler. The latter subsidiaries have a much less positive—and sometimes demonstrably negative—impact on the local economy.

Using detailed case studies of FDI, sector by sector, Moran demonstrates this contrast in performance first in Mexico, Brazil, Malaysia, and Thailand, and then extending across different countries, industries, and time periods. Far from being "anecdotal" in the sense that any random new observation may overturn a previous conclusion, he shows that case study analysis, carefully structured to avoid selection bias and to yield generalizable results, can be an important supplement to statistical analysis.

This difference in affiliates' performance takes the contention of Lipsey and Sjöholm—that perhaps the search for a single universal impact from FDI on the host economy is futile—one step further. Moran's evidence in chapter 11 shows clearly that FDI in manufacturing and assembly does not have one distinct impact on host country development, but rather two clearly divergent effects—the first beneficial, the second harmful.

On the positive side, Moran shows that when parents use affiliates as part of their strategy to remain competitive in international markets they maintain those affiliates at the cutting edge of best technology, management, and quality control. They coordinate production through whole or majority ownership, with freedom to source without reference to domestic content requirements. This model of "parental supervision" meshes closely with the "deep integration" of Feinberg and Keane that provides such powerful benefits through intrafirm trade. It reinforces the earlier finding of Blomström, Kokko, and Zejan (1992) that host countries are likely to receive greater amounts of technology and more advanced production and quality control processes in their domestic economies by not imposing ownership limits or technology sharing mandates on foreign investors than by enacting regulations to force technology sharing.

On the negative side, Moran reproduces cost-benefit analyses showing that a sizable fraction of FDI projects designed for import substitution and protected by trade restrictions actually subtract from host country welfare and—as suspected by Melitz—hinder host country growth. Mandatory joint venture requirements lead foreign investors to use older technologies. Domestic content requirements raise foreign affiliate production costs and hinder exports. The resulting performance penalties effectively preclude the emergence of protected infant industries as world-class competitors.

Moran argues that failure to differentiate between export-oriented FDI and import-substitution FDI, between foreign investors free to source from wherever they wish and foreign investors operating with domestic content requirements, or between foreign investors obliged to operate as minority shareholders and foreign investors with whole or majority ownership, accounts for the inability of earlier studies—such as the oft-cited works of Aitken and Harrison (1999) and Haddad and Harrison (1993)—to make sense of how FDI impacts a host economy.

Guoqiang Long

China is now the largest recipient of FDI in the world. New data on foreign investor behavior in the Chinese market, collected by Guoqiang Long in chapter 12, confirm both the disadvantages of using joint venture and other performance requirements on foreign investors to try to build an advanced industrial base in the host economy, and the benefits of liberalizing investment regulations and exposing foreign as well as domestic firms to international competition.

In a survey of 442 multinational firms operating in China, Long found that foreign wholly owned and majority-owned firms were much more likely to deploy technology as advanced as that used by the parent corporation than firms that had 50-50 shared ownership or firms with majority indigenous ownership. Approximately 32 percent of the foreign wholly owned firms and approximately 40 percent of the majority foreign-owned firms used technology in the Chinese market as advanced as in the parent corporation, whereas only approximately 23 percent of the 50-50 shared ownership firms and approximately 6 percent of the majority indigenous Chinese-owned firms used technology as advanced as in the parent company.

Looking specifically at the automobile industry, China's "swap market for technology" strategy provided trade protection to foreign automobile companies that were willing to operate with Chinese joint venture partners who owned 50 percent of the shares. But the lack of competition in the protected domestic market led to what Long labels a "contradiction" in the swap market for technology approach, with foreign investors turning out models that were increasingly outdated.[7] As China lowers its import barriers to conform to WTO standards, Long observes, market competition has led the foreign automobile firms to introduce newer and more technologically advanced models. He notes that the automobile industry remains one of 75 industries in which foreign companies are required to operate in 50-50 joint venture partnerships. This shows that China's liberalization of foreign investment, like its liberalization of trade, is still far from complete.

Todd J. Moss, Vijaya Ramachandran, and Manju Kedia Shah

In contrast to China's increasingly enthusiastic reception of FDI, African leaders and their general population have remained much more skeptical about the benefits of allowing MNCs to enter their economy. In chapter 13, Todd J. Moss, Vijaya Ramachandran, and Manju Kedia Shah investigate whether Africa's ongoing wariness about FDI is justified.

Moss, Ramachandran, and Shah use new firm-level survey data from the World Bank's Regional Program on Enterprise Development for Kenya, Tanzania, and Uganda to examine some of the common criticisms of FDI in Africa. They investigate the differences between domestic and foreign-owned firms, including firm size, productivity, management, training, trade, investment, and health benefits.

The authors' data suggest that FDI makes positive contributions to workers in the foreign-owned firms and to the host economy more generally. The three-country sample shows that foreign firms are more productive, bring new management skills, invest more heavily in infrastructure and in the training and health of their workers, and are more connected to global markets. Furthermore, foreign firms create value added per worker

---

7. For complementary evidence about the deleterious impact of performance requirements on the auto industry in China, see X. Wang (2004).

approximately twice as high as domestic firms, and their export to output ratio is more than three times as high. They are nearly twice as likely to have a formal training program for workers. Foreign firms provide on-site medical care more frequently as well as accident compensation and insurance. MNCs also invest a greater share of profits back into the firm and report a higher percentage of revenue for tax purposes. Foreign firms invest in infrastructure: 80 percent have their own generators and 28 percent have their own well (versus 26 percent and 9 percent for domestic firms, respectively). These investments in infrastructure suggest three implications. First, this could be viewed as a positive sign that companies are investing for the long term and are contributing to the country's infrastructure development. Second, this confirms that foreign firms find the general business environment a significant barrier to operation. Last, the greater relative investment also suggests that foreign firms are better capitalized to overcome these deficiencies than local firms.

Econometric tests performed by Moss, Ramachandran, and Shah show that the success of foreign firms does not derive by exercising market power or crowding out local industry. In terms of backward linkages, foreign investors rely on local suppliers for 44 percent of their inputs. Based on these results, Moss, Ramachandran, and Shah conclude that many of Africa's lingering objections to FDI are exaggerated or false.

In his commentary, Robert Lawrence exhibits more sympathy for the legacy of suspicion about the benefits of FDI in Africa, noting that much of the nonextractive investment in Africa has been associated with efforts at import-substituting industrialization. Applying the Moran distinction between FDI in protected versus open policy settings, Lawrence notes that the foreign firms' superior performance may not always have enhanced host country growth and welfare. African leaders may have viewed foreign investor behavior for much of history as a successful chase after locally generated rents, with highly protected infant industries repeatedly failing to grow up.

African leaders have not had the experience, notes Lawrence, that Long records for China, where foreign investors have increasingly become a channel to integrate the Chinese economy into world markets. Along the way, China used both sticks and carrots to affect foreign firm behavior. Applying Moran's framework to China, according to Lawrence, would be to conclude that China has succeeded despite the sticks rather than because of them. Applying it to Africa would be to conclude that superior foreign firm performance would be certain to provide greater benefits to countries like Kenya, Tanzania, and Uganda if the FDI occurred in economies that had fewer protections and distortions.

Thus, the studies in this part combine with those in parts I and II to help authorities in developing and developed countries address policy issues associated with FDI and to help future researchers build upon and improve the kinds of investigations provided in this volume.

References

Aitken, Brian J., and Ann E. Harrison. 1999. Do Domestic Firms Benefit from Foreign Direct Investment? Evidence from Venezuela. *American Economic Review* 89, no. 3 (June): 605–18.

Arellano, M., and O. Bover. 1995. Another Look at the Instrumental-Variable Estimation of Error-Components Models. *Journal of Econometrics* 68, no. 1: 29–52.

Blomström, Magnus, Ari Kokko, and Mario Zejan. 1992. *Host Country Competition and Technology Transfer by Multinationals*. NBER Working Paper 4131. Cambridge, MA: National Bureau of Economic Research.

Blundell, R., and S. Bond. 1997. *Initial Conditions and Moment Restrictions in Dynamic Panel Data Models*. University College of London Discussion Paper 97-07. London: University College.

Borensztein, E., J. De Gregorio, and J. W. Lee. 1998. How Does Foreign Direct Investment Affect Economic Growth? *Journal of International Economics* 45, no. 1 (June): 115–35.

Haddad, Mona, and Ann Harrison. 1993. Are There Positive Spillovers from Foreign Direct Investment? Evidence from Panel Data for Morocco. *Journal of Development Economics* 42, no. 1 (October): 51–74.

Moran, Theodore H. 2005. *Foreign Direct Investment and the Development of Low-Income Poorly Performing States*. Washington: Center for Global Development. Forthcoming.

Rodrik, Dani. 1999. *The New Global Economy and Developing Countries: Making Openness Work*. Washington: Johns Hopkins University Press for the Overseas Development Council.

Wang, Miao Grace. 2004. FDI and Domestic Investment: Crowding In or Crowding Out? Photocopy.

Wang, Xiaolu. 2004. People's Republic of China. In *Managing FDI in a Globalizing Economy: Asian Experiences*, ed., Douglas H. Brooks and Hal Hill. New York: Palgrave Macmillan for the Asian Development Bank.

Williamson, John. 2003. The Washington Consensus as Policy Prescription for Development. Washington: Institute for International Economics. Photocopy (December 19).

SEARCHING FOR EXTERNALITIES AND SPILLOVERS

2

The Impact of Inward FDI on Host Countries: Why Such Different Answers?

ROBERT E. LIPSEY and FREDRIK SJÖHOLM

A substantial body of literature has grown around the question of how inward foreign direct investment (FDI) affects host countries. On almost every aspect of this question there is a wide range of empirical results in academic literature with little sign of convergence. At the same time, policy-makers seem to have made their own judgments that inward FDI is valuable to their countries. The United Nations Conference on Trade and Development (UNCTAD) publishes annual data on "changes in national regulations of FDI" and reports that from 1991 through 2002, over 1,500 changes making regulations more favorable and fewer than 100 making regulations less favorable to FDI were made (UNCTAD 2003, 21, table 1.8). The same document reports that "the use of locational incentives to attract FDI has considerably expanded in frequency and value" (UNCTAD 2003, 124). Given the amount of academic literature on the issue, why has it made so little impression on policymaking? Are all these countries foolishly pursuing an ephemeral fad? Are the questions asked in academic literature irrelevant to policy? Are the relevant questions answerable? For that matter, what are the relevant questions?

Robert E. Lipsey is emeritus professor at the City University of New York and a research associate and director of the New York office of the National Bureau of Economic Research. Fredrik Sjöholm is associate professor and researcher at the European Institute of Japanese Studies at the Stockholm School of Economics.

There are many possible effects of FDI inflow on a host country. Since it is generally taken for granted that investing firms possess some technology superior to that of host country firms, higher-quality goods and services could be produced at either lower prices or in greater volume than previously available, resulting in higher consumer welfare. Another possible effect would be that inward investment adds to the host country capital stock, thereby raising output levels. Although this issue has been explored, especially in earlier literature determining whether inward investment or aid supplements or displaces local investment, it is not specific to direct investment. Specific attention to direct investment has been devoted to the question of whether inward investments do involve superior technology and, if they do, whether it "spills over" to domestically owned firms rather than being retained entirely by the foreign-owned firms. A related set of questions is whether the foreign-owned firms pay higher wages for domestic labor, whether those higher wages raise the average wage level in the host country, and whether these higher wages spill over to domestically owned firms. For both wages and productivity, the spillovers to domestically owned firms or establishments could be either positive or negative. Wage spillovers could be negative if, for example, the foreign-owned firms hired the best workers, at their going—or higher—wages, leaving only lower-quality workers at the domestically owned firms. Productivity spillovers could be negative if foreign-owned firms took market shares from domestically owned firms, leaving the latter to produce at lower, less economical production levels.

Survey articles have found inconclusive evidence in the literature regarding the most important effects of inward FDI, especially with respect to spillovers. For example, on wage spillovers, Görg and Greenaway (2001) reported that panel data showed negative spillovers, while cross-sectional data reported positive spillovers. The same research paper found, with respect to productivity spillovers from foreign-owned to domestically owned firms," only limited evidence in support of positive spillovers. . . . Most work fails to find positive spillovers, with some even reporting negative spillovers . . ." (Görg and Greenaway 2001, 23). Görg and Strobl (2001) concluded that the crucial determinant of the findings in 21 studies was whether cross-section or time-series data had been used, with the former typically finding positive spillovers and the latter often negative ones. Lipsey stated that "the evidence for positive spillovers is not strong" (2003, 304) and concluded a review of the literature by saying that "the evidence on spillovers is mixed. No universal relationships are evident" (2004, 365). With respect to effects on host country economic growth, Carkovic and Levine (2002) found no significant effect of FDI inflows over the entire 1960–95 period and only irregularly significant effects in five-year intervals. None of the variables found in other studies *consistently* determine the effect of FDI on growth, although some are significant in some combination of conditioning variables. For instance, Lipsey found it "safe to conclude that there is no universal relationship between the ratio of inward FDI flows to GDP and the rate of growth of a country" (2003, 297).

A crucial feature of these surveys is that the summarized studies do not individually find that wage or productivity spillovers do not exist. Mostly, they find evidence for either positive or negative spillovers. In this chapter, we try to understand why different investigators find contradictory results. Is it that the statistical techniques are different? Are the countries they examine different? Are they asking different questions under the same labels of wages, productivity, or spillovers? We try to answer these questions in two ways. One is to review the individual studies themselves to clarify the questions asked and the data used. The other is to survey studies on data for Indonesia, which cover a long period and are both detailed and accessible, in order to test the implications of different definitions and methods. The studies we review in this chapter examine the effects of FDI on firms and their workers. They are all producer oriented. However, future statistical studies could look at consumption effects. For example, has FDI growth in retailing reduced the price of food and other consumer goods? Has FDI growth in utilities reduced the price of telephone service or home heating and lighting? These possible effects of FDI are almost totally absent from the literature but should be studied.

Wage Spillovers

We begin with the studies of wage spillovers, which are not as numerous as those on productivity. There are several general issues that run through almost all the wage studies. One issue is that wage levels are calculated as total wages or total compensation per worker, but the only measure of skill is a division between production and nonproduction or blue-collar and white-collar workers. Within those categories, almost no studies can distinguish between differences in skill or education level or between employees of foreign-owned and domestically owned plants from differences in wages for identical workers. Similarly, they cannot distinguish between differential changes in skills between the two ownership groups and differential changes in wages for identical and unchanging workers in plants owned by the two ownership groups. A second issue is whether wage comparisons should take account of characteristics that are correlated with foreign ownership but not intrinsically related to it. For example, foreign-owned firms or establishments are typically much larger on average than domestically owned ones, even in developed countries. Especially in developing countries, foreign-owned firms or establishments are more capital intensive and use more purchased materials or components for their production than domestically owned firms. The question is whether these characteristics should be treated as controls—and their influence eliminated—or are they so bound up with foreign ownership that they should not be controlled for? As Aitken, Harrison, and Lipsey (1996, 368) point out, a host country may not care whether higher employee wages in foreign-owned plants result from the fact that they are foreign owned or from the fact that they are large and use capital-intensive technology and/or import-intensive technology. Size, capital intensity, and import intensity may all be elements of the foreign-owned firm's technology.

Empirical studies provide strong evidence of a wage premium in foreign-owned firms (Lipsey 2004). Foreign firms pay higher employee wages in both developed and developing countries, after controlling for firm-specific characteristics. It is of course possible that high employee wages in foreign-owned firms are caused, or at least biased, by foreign takeovers of high-wage domestic firms. In a recent study (Lipsey and Sjöholm 2002)—using a 25-year panel of Indonesian manufacturing establishment data and lacking la-bor force education data, but including most of the typical independent variables—we were able to lay this issue to rest, at least for this one country. Foreign-owned firms did tend to acquire domestic plants with higher than average blue-collar wages for their industries, but the margins over the averages were far too small to account for the wage differential between domestically owned and foreign-owned plants. Thus, selectivity in take-overs could not account for the wage gap. Further evidence included the discovery that after a foreign takeover of a domestically owned plant, both blue-collar and white-collar wages rose strongly, in absolute terms and relative to their industries. Takeovers of foreign-owned plants by domestic firms had the opposite effect on wages, illustrating that foreign takeovers, rather than takeovers in general, produced wage increases. Econometric analyses using the whole panel of establishments found large wage differences in favor of foreign firms at every level of industry and geographical detail, and the differentials remained large even when plant characteristics, such as size and the use of purchased inputs, were introduced into the wage equations. The finding that employee wages were higher in foreign-owned plants and became higher when domestically owned plants became foreign owned was not dependent on the use of cross-section rather than panel data.

Although the literature on wage comparisons between foreign- and domestically owned firms is large, relatively few studies examine the effect of FDI on wages in domestically owned firms. Görg and Greenway (2001) review six studies on wage spillovers and report that of those with conclusions, three panel studies found negative spillovers and two cross-section studies found positive ones. They do not include the information that some of the cross-section estimates for Mexico and Venezuela also give negative coefficients for spillovers, suggesting that the choice of cross-section or panel estimation may not be so crucial.

Other subsequent studies have reported more evidence that wage spillovers occur. Figlio and Blonigen (2000) concluded that the effect of a large new foreign investment in South Carolina on aggregate wage levels was so large that it could not have been solely the result of the high employee wages in the foreign-owned plants but must have involved spillovers to domestically owned plants. Their study differed from most others because it concentrated on geographical effects, rather than the effects within the industry of the investment. Indeed, in the only wage study we know of that uses education as a measurement of the quality of the labor force (Lipsey and Sjöholm 2004b), we made a variety of calculations of spillovers in a cross section of Indonesian manufacturing establishments. Assuming national labor markets within broad industry groups, we found significant wage spillovers to domestically owned plants. Assuming national labor markets within narrower industry groups also revealed significant spillovers, albeit smaller ones. In addition, assuming that an industry within an individual province represented a labor market still revealed that spillovers to domestically owned establishments occur. The combination of higher wages in foreign-owned plants and spillovers to domestically owned plants meant that higher overall wages were associated with foreign ownership. Further evidence that the distinction between cross-section and panel data studies is not the crucial determinant of results on wage spillovers can be found in Driffield and Girma (2002), which uses a panel of establishments in the UK electronics industry from the Annual Respondents Database (ARD) from 1980 to 1992. Driffield and Girma found intraindustry and intraregion wage spillovers from FDI on wages in general, and the effect was larger for skilled than for unskilled workers. A study by Girma, Greenaway, and Wakelin (2001), using firm, rather than establishment, panel data for almost 4,000 firms in the United Kingdom from 1991 to 1996, also found some evidence of wage spillovers. On average, when spillovers were assumed to be identical across industries and firms, Girma, Greenaway, and Wakelin found no significant evidence for them. However, when the effects were permitted to vary across industries, wage spillovers were found and were higher in industries where the productivity gap between foreign and domestic firms was lower. One way this study differs from our earlier research (Lipsey and Sjöholm 2002) is that it excludes firms that changed ownership, thereby eliminating one way in which foreign ownership affects wages. The effects of shifts to foreign ownership had been found in an earlier study to be positive in the United Kingdom, as they were in Indonesia.

The accumulation of studies since the earlier surveys seems to have put to rest the suspicion that the findings of wage spillovers were solely the result of ignoring firm differences in cross-section studies, since the spillovers did appear in panel studies. Something else must account for the negative spillovers or lack of spillovers found in some developing countries. Aside from Indonesia, the positive spillovers have been found most frequently in developed countries. Even in the United Kingdom, large differences in productivity between foreign-owned and domestically owned firms reduced or eliminated spillovers. One possible cause for the negative results in some developing countries is that the gap between foreign-owned and domestically owned firms is too large for one group to influence the other. Another possibility is that the labor markets in some developing countries are too segmented for wages in one group to influence the other. If we compare Mexico and Venezuela, two countries reported to show negative wage spillovers from foreign firms, with Indonesia, the United Kingdom, and the United States, for which positive spillovers were found, labor market conditions do seem different. An "employment laws index" produced by the World Bank (2003), and based upon the work of Botero et al. (2003), had a range in which a high number indicated very restrictive labor laws on hiring, firing, and conditions of employment. On the basis of this index, Mexico and Venezuela were ranked among the most restrictive countries, with index numbers of 77 and 75, respectively. The United Kingdom was rated at 28 and the United States at 22. Indonesia was in between at 57, not flexible by developed-country standards, but relatively flexible for a developing country.

Another topic not always considered is how the relevant labor market is defined. Most studies implicitly define a labor market as an industry—at whatever level of detail industry is reported. Some define the market as an industry within the narrowest geographical area at which industry data are available. That may be appropriate for some countries or industries, but there may also be national labor markets within an industry, or local labor markets that straddle many industries (national labor markets may also straddle many industries). These differences in defining the labor market may affect findings on spillovers. Therefore, consideration of the industry and geographic construction of FDI measures is needed, and the conclusion might be different for wages from what it is for productivity. For wages, the appropriate definition depends on the range of a labor market within which wages tend to be equalized, or at least within which one firm's wages influence those in other firms. The answers might be different in different countries or industries and at different times. In a recent study (Lipsey and Sjöholm 2004b), we tested the effect of different definitions of a labor market by using different industry and geographic classifications to examine the sensitivity of the results. They used FDI measures at two-, three-, and five-digit industry levels and at both the national and province levels to examine the effect of foreign presence on the wages in locally owned Indonesian plants. The results for these various definitions of a labor market are shown in table 2.1. The coefficients vary substantially, but they remain statistically significant in all specifications.[1] The largest coefficients are for

---

1. See Lipsey and Sjöholm (2004b) for the complete empirical specifications and results.

Table 2.1   Wage spillovers in Indonesian manufacturing

FDI variable	Blue-collar wage	White-collar wage
Two-digit national	1.07 (21.83)***	1.04 (16.42)***
Three-digit national	0.28 (6.20)***	0.34 (5.43)***
Five-digit national	0.16 (7.48)***	0.35 (11.46)***
All sectors province	1.05 (32.81)***	1.22 (28.27)***
Two-digit province	0.47 (13.85)***	0.53 (12.26)***
Three-digit province	0.39 (12.93)***	0.44 (12.12)***
Five-digit province	0.24 (11.34)***	0.38 (13.12)***

*** = significance at the 1 percent level

Note: t-statistics are in parentheses.

Source: Lipsey and Sjöholm (2004b).

definitions of the relevant market as either national, at the two-digit industry level, or provincial, for all manufacturing industries combined. However, there is concern that these coefficients may represent the tendency of foreign firms to move into either high-wage geographical locations or high-wage industries. Those possible biases are reduced by further geographical breakdown—by province—and by successively greater industry detail, culminating in breakdowns by five-digit industry and province. The coefficients are greatly reduced in size, but remain strongly significant, showing margins of a quarter for blue-collar and over a third for white-collar workers. The most detailed breakdown does not necessarily give the most accurate estimate of the effect of foreign firms' presence, however. It may miss the effect of higher wages and increased employment in foreign-owned establishments in one industry or province on wages in other industries and provinces—possibly a more important effect than any within the same industry and province. Even the more aggregate measures may understate the wage effect because they are confined to manufacturing, ignoring any impacts on agriculture, services, and trade.

Productivity Spillovers

Many of the same issues that affect studies of wage spillovers occur in the much larger body of literature studying productivity spillovers. In addition, there are broader problems with the productivity measurements. The objective is often described as measuring the spillovers of technology, or knowledge, from foreign-owned to domestically owned firms. In order to simplify measurement, technology is narrowly defined to measure labor productivity, total factor productivity, or differences in production functions. All three are reflections of technology, but they may be both too broad and too narrow. The comparison of production functions, often cited as an ideal method, assumes that there are no differences in technological knowledge involved in choices about factor combinations or plant size. Thus, the operation of a large plant, as opposed to operation of a small plant, requires no different technological mastery. The operation of a capital-intensive plant requires no technological skill beyond that required for a labor-intensive plant. The use of intermediate inputs from abroad or from a parent company involves no technology beyond that of using locally available inputs. These are all assumptions implicit in production function comparisons, but if they are invalid, and locally owned plants do not have the technological skill to operate at the scale and factor combinations of foreign-owned plants, true technological differences between foreign-owned and domestically owned plants are hidden, disguised as differences in scale of production or factor combination choices.

There is another respect in which the definitions of technology are too narrow. For example, if foreign investors' technological superiority consists of knowledge about consumers' tastes in foreign markets, or about marketing a product in local or foreign markets, this knowledge will not be visible in productivity or production function comparisons. Rather, it will be seen in comparisons of export performance, but those are a different set of literature not usually characterized as technology. A very different type of study that takes a broad view of technology is exemplified by Dobson and Chia's (1997) country studies for Asia, Rhee and Belot's (1990) country- and industry-specific case studies of "the critical role of transnational corporations (TNCs) in the transfer of technical, marketing, managerial know-how to developing countries," and Moran's (2001, 2002) many examples of technology transfer. All of these are basically case studies of particular transfers of technology, but not confined to either intra-industry or interindustry transfers and not confined to specific measures of technology. All of them find evidence for transfers of technology, but it is difficult to confront their evidence with the statistical studies described later in this chapter because the questions are so different. The case studies ask whether there are examples in which technology was transferred from foreign-owned to domestically owned firms, and the answer is "yes." In contrast, the statistical studies ask whether *on average* domestically owned firms gain in a particular measure of technology because foreign-owned firms operate in the same industry and the same country or the same region, and the answer is "not universally." Both of these answers could be accurate; neither one contradicts the other, because they are answers to different questions.

Case studies offer great flexibility. The exact nature of the technology transfer can differ from example to example, from industry to industry, and from country to country. The length of time for the transfer to occur and be measured need not be specified in advance and can vary widely. The transfer can be within an industry, to supplying industries, or to consuming industries. This flexibility is an advantage of the case study method, but it comes at a cost: Firms that do not receive foreign technology are often omitted from case studies measuring the effect of transfers. Thus, the universe for measuring effects is not always delineated, and the universe from which the case studies are drawn is not always defined. In contrast, statistical studies tend to be rigid in specifying the length of time over which effects are measured (whether it is a year or a set number of years). They specify some particular definition of a technology transfer (perhaps ignoring other important dimensions), and whether differences among countries or industries are to be studied. Statistical studies assume the relevance of some particular measure of FDI and some functional form for its effects. The studies' greatest advantage is that they tend to examine effects on whole industries, including the unlucky or less competent losers, as well as the successes. With microdata, they can look at the characteristics of firms changing ownership as well as those forced out of an industry, those entering, and those remaining. A goal for case studies might be to assemble a collection of unsuccessful ventures and to compare them with successful ones, not only with respect to their own characteristics but also, even more importantly, with respect to country and industry environments. Baranson's (1967) book on Cummins' experience in India, for example, contains an analysis of the effects of import-substitution policies that can be compared with experiences under more liberal trade regimes.

A general problem with productivity comparisons and spillover studies, compared to wage studies, is their greater need for data. Productivity studies require output measures, usually sales or value added. Sales by foreign-owned firms, particularly exports, are frequently intracompany transactions. The values may not be the same as market values, because there are many incentives to alter them to minimize tax liabilities, and the incentives may be very different for foreign-owned firms from any that domestically owned firms face. Any manipulation of sales values would affect value added even more, and there are incentives to manipulate the profit portion of value added in addition to those affecting sales values. Furthermore, since value added includes profits, it may fluctuate far more over time than any physical measure of production. The use of production functions requires measures of capital input, which are often missing from census data. If measures of capital input are present, their meaning is often questionable, especially in countries that have suffered major inflations, because it is uncertain if and how historical values have been adjusted to current price levels. As with wage spillovers, the Görg and Strobl (2001) and Görg and Greenaway (2001) surveys conclude that the negative results from panel data studies are more reliable than those for cross-sections, and that there is therefore little evidence of positive spillovers from FDI. However, a number of new studies of productivity spillovers based on panel data have appeared. As is true for wage spillovers, these find more evidence for positive spillovers than the earlier ones. For example, Haskel, Pereira, and Slaughter (2002) use a panel of UK manufacturing plants between 1973 and 1992 and find a positive and robust spillover effect of inward FDI on productivity in local plants. Keller and Yeaple (2003) also find positive and robust effects of inward FDI in the United States on productivity in US manufacturing plants between 1987 and 1996. Girma, Greenaway, and Wakelin (2001), using the firm data described above, find that there are spillovers and that they are greater for firms in sectors in which local firms are technologically comparable to the foreign firms. Labor productivity and total factor productivity spillovers are similar in size. As with wage spillovers, the accumulation of studies has eroded the basis for the hypothesis that the distinction between cross-section and panel data studies explains the wide range of findings.

In their panel data study of Venezuela, Aitken and Harrison (1999) show what is probably the strongest evidence for negative productivity spillovers. A rise in the foreign share of ownership in a sector reduced the output of individual domestically owned establishments and reduced their total factor productivity over one- to three-year periods. The first-year negative effect was particularly severe for small domestically owned plants, suggesting that they were the least efficient and most vulnerable to competition from the increasing efficiency associated with rises in foreign ownership. Since Venezuela had been a relatively closed economy to both trade and inward direct investment in manufacturing during this period, it might have accumulated a larger than average stock of small, competitively weak firms.

In another panel study of a relatively closed economy Kathuria (2000) used data for large firms in India from 1975–76 to 1988–89, before the country's period of liberalization. Technical efficiency was measured from a function with value added as the production measure and labor and capital as inputs, and was calculated as the distance between the firm and the most efficient firm in its industry. Spillovers were deemed to have occurred if the dispersion of efficiency levels among domestically owned firms in the industries studied—in which foreign-owned firms were the efficiency leaders—were reduced. The foreign source of the spillovers was measured in two ways: the extent of foreign participation in the industry, which was represented by the foreign-owned firms' share of sales, and the stock of cumulated purchases of foreign technology by local firms. Foreign participation had a negative effect on the dispersion of efficiency among domestically owned firms. This effect was interpreted by the author as indicating negative spillovers. Kathuria points out, however, that a negative spillover in these terms could result if both the foreign firms and the domestically owned firms gained in efficiency but the foreign-owned firms gained more—a result that would have been interpreted as a positive spillover in the Aitken and Harrison framework. The stock of foreign technological capital of the local firms was positively related to their gains in efficiency. When the sample was split between "scientific" and "nonscientific" industries, the spillover effects were confined to the "scientific" group but were offset by a positive coefficient for the cross-product of foreign presence and the local firm's research and development (R&D) effort. The interpretation was that R&D-intensive local firms might have gained, or lost less, from the foreign presence than firms that did less R&D.

Productivity Spillovers in Indonesia

One way of understanding the variety of results would be to apply the same techniques to the identical types of data in different countries. Since we do not have access to data from many countries, we instead review studies of Indonesia and test alternative methods on that country's data. One advantage of using Indonesian data for experimentation is that Indonesia collects consistent microdata on its manufacturing industry and these data have been increasingly used by a number of authors for plant-level studies. A number of studies on Indonesia show that foreign plants have higher productivity than locally owned plants (Takii and Ramstetter 2003; Okamoto and Sjöholm 2005) and that plants that change ownership from local to foreign ownership increase their level of productivity (Anderson 2000). In addition, there are several plant-level studies on productivity spillovers from FDI in Indonesian manufacturing, which are summarized in table 2.2. The first three studies on spillovers from FDI in Indonesia used cross-section analysis (see table 2.2). For instance, Sjöholm (1999a) examined plants in 1980 and 1991 and found both the level and growth of labor productivity to be higher for locally owned plants in sectors with a high foreign share of output. There was no evidence of regional intraindustry spillovers from FDI, but some indications of regional interindustry spillovers.

Sjöholm (1999b) used the same data as his earlier study to examine possible determinants of spillovers. The results suggested that spillovers were positively affected by the technology gap between domestic and foreign plants and by the degree of competition within the sector. Blomström and Sjöholm (1999) examined spillovers from FDI in 1991. Their study differed in design from the previous two mainly in the use of capital stocks rather than investment ratios to control for capital intensity. There were positive spillovers from FDI, and no differences in the spillovers from joint ventures with minority or majority foreign ownership.

Table 2.2 Studies on productivity spillovers from FDI in Indonesian manufacturing

Author(s)	Year(s)	Dependent variable	Measure of foreign presence	Independent variables	t-statistics for foreign share
Blomström and Sjöholm (1999)	1991	Value added per employee	Output (five-digit level)	Capital White/blue Capital utilization Scale Independent dummies	+ ***
Sjöholm (1999a)	1980, 1991	Growth in value added; value added per employee	Output (five-digit level)	Employment Investment Industry and regional characteristics	+ ***
Sjöholm (1999b)	1980, 1991	Growth in value added; value added per employee	Output (five-digit level)	Employment Investment Scale	+ ***
Takii (2001)	1990–95	Value added	Employment (three-digit level)	(translog) Employment Capital Plant-specific effect	+ ***
Todo and Miyamoto (2002)	1995–97	Value added per employee	Absolute amount of FDI output (two-digit level)	Capital Capacity utilization Plant-specific effect	+ ***
Blalock and Gertler (2002)	1988–96	Output	Output (four-digit level; region-industry)	(translog) Employment Capital Raw materials Plant-specific effect	+ ***
Blalock and Gertler (2003)	1988–96	Output	Output (four-digit level; region-industry)	(translog) Employment Capital Raw materials Energy Downstream FDI Plant-specific effect	?

*** = significance at the 1 percent level
+ = positive
? = not statistically significant

Takii (2001) was the first study on spillovers in Indonesia that used panel data, which allowed him to control for plant-specific effects. He examined spillovers during 1990–95 using a translog production function and found positive effects on value added in local firms from the share of foreign employment in the same three-digit International Standard Industrial Classification (ISIC) industry. Moreover, the results suggested that spillovers were relatively large in sectors with relatively new foreign plants and with low gaps in labor productivity between foreign and domestic plants. Takii also found that R&D positively affected spillover in locally owned plants.

The study by Todo and Miyamoto (2002) differs from most of the others by defining the FDI variable as the absolute amount of FDI in a sector. They argued that this measure is more strongly related to the foreign knowledge stock and therefore preferred over the foreign share of a sector. The result showed a positive effect of FDI on local firms' labor productivity after controlling for R&D and training of the workforce.

Blalock and Gertler (2002) also used a translog production function to examine spillovers between 1988 and 1996. Local firms in sectors within regions with a high foreign share of output had high levels of productivity. Moreover, they found a positive effect on spillovers from the technology gap between domestic and foreign plants; spillovers were also positively affected by local firms' R&D and by high levels of education of workers in local firms.

In a second study, Blalock and Gertler (2003), using the same data and a very similar translog production function, found no evidence of positive intraindustry spillovers from FDI. A second measure of FDI in this study is the main difference between the two: Blalock and Gertler (2003) measured FDI in upstream markets to capture spillovers from FDI to local suppliers. They found that downstream FDI was highly significant in the econometric estimations. This variable was constructed by using an input-output table at a sector level, which also includes purchases from its own sector. Therefore, one possibility is that the variable on downstream FDI also captured the effect of horizontal spillovers.

To summarize the results from these seven production spillover studies on Indonesian manufacturing, all cross-section studies and three out of four panel data studies found statistically significant intraindustry spillovers. The one study that failed to find intraindustry spillovers found interindustry spillovers from FDI instead. Judging by these studies of Indonesia, we conclude that the design of econometric studies does not cause the different results found in the literature. Therefore, differences between countries or firms may explain the extent of spillovers. The studies on Indonesia might shed some further light on what these differences could be. Previous literature suggests that competition, the technology gap, and local firms' absorptive capacity will affect the extent of spillovers. Starting with competition, the studies by Sjöholm (1999b) and by Blalock and Gertler (2003) show that spillovers are highest in sectors with high competition. The former study suggests that it is domestic competition, as captured by a Herfindahl index, rather than the degree of protection from imports that affects spillovers. The second study suggests that competition will benefit upstream local suppliers.

The effects of technology gaps on the extent of spillovers is unclear. Takii (2001) found a negative effect on spillovers from the technology gap between local and foreign-owned plants, which has also been found in other countries (Kokko 1994, 1996). Sjöholm (1999b) and Blalock and Gertler (2002) find a positive relation between the technology gap and the degree of spillovers. One explanation for the different results could be that the measure of technology gap differs between studies. Takii measured the technology gap as the difference in labor productivity between domestically owned and foreign-owned plants.[2] Sjöholm used the difference in labor productivity between domestically owned and foreign-owned plants after controlling for the scale of operation and the investment per worker ratio.[3] Finally, Blalock and Gertler used the plant's fixed effect in comparison to the mean fixed effect in the same industry. Another reason why these, and other studies, produce such varying results could be that the relationship is nonlinear. Some technology gap is presumably required for any useful technology spillover to occur. However, it is also plausible that if the gap is too large, the technology in foreign plants will be of little practical use in locally owned plants pursuing very different types of operations.

Differences in spillovers between countries may also be caused by differences in sectors' and plants' absorptive capacity. The studies on Indonesia confirm that such capacity might be important if a firm is to benefit from spillovers. Takii (2001) and Todo and Miyamoto (2002) as well as Blalock and Gertler (2002) found that a firm's own R&D positively affected its ability to benefit from spillovers. The last study also found that plants with more highly educated employees benefit more from the presence of foreign multinational corporations (MNCs). A related question is whether the type of activities pursued by the foreign subsidiaries affects spillovers to domestically owned firms. This issue has been rather neglected in the spillover literature but Todo and Miyamoto (2002) find a positive effect on spillovers from R&D and human resource development in the foreign subsidiaries.

As evident from the earlier discussion, considerable attention has been devoted to differences between econometric methodologies as one possible explanation for the different effects of spillovers among countries. A related, but so far rather neglected, issue is how one should construct measures of FDI. Most studies use the foreign share of a sector's economic

---

2. Takii also used the difference in capital labor ratios and the difference in size as alternative measures of technology gaps. These measures gave inconclusive results.

3. The difference in investment ratios was used as an alternative measure but provided no clear results.

activity as a measure of FDI.[4] One problem with this measure is that the foreign share of a sector might be endogenously determined if productivity spillovers expand activity in local firms. Moreover, this measure assumes that increases of foreign and aggregate activity in the same proportion have no effect on local firms. Castellani and Zanfei (2002) argue that this assumption might produce a downward bias on the estimate of spillovers from FDI. Finally, it is not clear why we would assume the effect from FDI to be linear in the foreign share of an industry's economic activity: spillovers are not obviously maximized at a 100 percent foreign ownership share (Lipsey 2004).

Although the foreign share is widely used as an FDI measure, productivity spillover studies still differ in how this share is constructed. Some measure it as the foreign share of employment, while others measure it as a share of value added or output. Moreover, the foreign share is calculated at different sector levels, ranging from two-digit to five-digit levels of ISIC. Finally, some studies use the foreign industry share at a national level, while others use it at a regional level.

The more narrow the definition of an industry, the more restrictive is our assumption of how widely applicable knowledge from FDI can be for local firms, and our assumption of which domestically owned plants face increased competition from FDI. If we construct the FDI measure on a two-digit level of ISIC, it implies that productivity spillovers might be present between industries at a three- and five-digit level of ISIC but not from one two-digit industry to another. If we construct our measure of FDI at a five-digit level of ISIC, it implies that productivity spillovers can only be captured if they occur within these industries but not if they cross from one five-digit industry to another. It is unclear what a properly defined industry is for an analysis of productivity spillovers. It seems that most studies favor a disaggregated definition of FDI, possibly to increase the variance in the FDI variable. However, this might come at a cost if we miss out on spillovers across narrowly defined industries. Some technologies, such as computer use in tracking sales and inventories, may be very general and easily transmitted across industries, while others may be specific to particular production processes. Clearly, the industry definition will also have implications for what we attribute to interindustry versus intraindustry spillovers.

The choice to construct the FDI measure at a national level or at a regional level might also be important. Choosing the most appropriate level to use depends on whether the spillover has a spatial dimension—for example, if it primarily benefits plants within the same region. The Jaffe, Trajtenberg, and Henderson (1993) study is often referred to when a regional measure

---

4. There are exceptions, see, for example, the previously discussed study by Todo and Miyamoto (2002). See also Barrell and Pain (1997), who use aggregate FDI in a constant elasticity of substitution (CES) production function and find positive effects from FDI on technical progress in EU countries.

of FDI is used (Sjöholm 1999a, Blalock and Gertler 2002, Lipsey and Sjöholm 2004b). Their study shows that university R&D primarily benefits other inventors within the same geographic area. Hence, their study relates to innovation, and it is possible, but not certain, that the same result also exists for spillovers. Whether or not spillovers are geographically concentrated depends on, for instance, whether imitation, competition, or supply of linkage industries are enhanced by geographic proximity to the foreign firms.

If we believe that technology spillovers are geographically concentrated, the next question will be: What is an appropriate geographic aggregation level? Studies on Indonesia have used both districts (Sjöholm 1999a) and provinces (Sjöholm 1999a; Blalock and Gertler 2002, 2003). One methodological problem is that spillovers are not likely to follow administrative units even if they are localized. For instance, the largest share of Indonesian manufacturing is located in the province of Western Java. This is largely because the industry sector has grown out of its original base in Jakarta. Jakarta and the West Java cities of Bogor, Tanggerang, and Berakasi constitute one industrial cluster, the Jabotabek area (Henderson, Kuncoro, and Nasution 1996). If technology spillovers from FDI exist, and even if such spillovers are only effective with geographic proximity, a foreign firm in Jakarta is likely to have positive effects on local firms within the whole Jabotabek area. However, Jabotabek spreads out over two provinces and about ten districts, which indicates the problem of using administrative geographic units in constructing measures of regional FDI.

Spatial concentration of FDI may be another obstacle to analyzing regional FDI measures. However, such concentration is common in most countries, including Indonesia. For instance, about 80 percent of all FDI in Indonesian manufacturing is located in 3 out of 27 provinces (East Java, West Java, and Jakarta), which is a higher concentration than for manufacturing in general (Sjöholm 2002, Sjöberg and Sjöholm 2004). If, for instance, we construct our FDI measure at a province level and at a five-digit level of ISIC—including about 300 industries—less than 25 percent of the region-industry combinations will have FDI. Thus, it may be desirable to take account of the selection of locations in analyzing the effects of FDI.

An experiment with different industry and geographical definitions of the relevant scope for productivity spillovers is described in table 2.3. Spillovers are estimated at the national level and the province level for all sectors combined and at two-, three-, and five-digit industrial breakdowns. More specifically, we used Indonesian plant level data for 1996 to estimate the following expression:

$$\text{Laborprod}_{ij} = \text{constant} + \text{FDI} + \text{Education}_{ij} + \text{Capital}_{ij} + \text{Size}_{ij} + \text{Public}_{ij}$$

where *Laborprod* is value added per employee, *Capital* is energy consumption per employee, *Size* is the total number of workers, *Public* is a dummy variable

Table 2.3 Productivity spillovers in Indonesian manufacturing (dependent variable: value added per employee)

FDI variable	Coefficient of FDI
Two-digit/national	0.28 (3.94)***
Three-digit/national	0.44 (5.55)***
Five-digit/national	0.19 (5.25)***
All sectors/province	0.94 (19.05)***
Two-digit/province	0.27 (5.44)***
Three-digit/province	0.44 (9.79)***
Five-digit/province	0.23 (6.44)***

*** = significance at the 1 percent level

Note: t-statistics are in parentheses.

Source: Authors' calculations.

for public ownership, and *Education* is the share of employees with primary, junior, senior, and university education for both blue- and white-collar workers. For the sake of clarity, we show only the coefficients of the different FDI variables in table 2.3.

The main impression from the results in table 2.3 is that geographical influences are minor; the spillover coefficients at the national level are almost identical to those at the province level at each level of industry detail. The industry level does make a difference. The coefficient is highest at the all-sector level, indicating a greater influence of foreign presence on domestic establishment productivity for manufacturing as a whole than within two-, three-, or five-digit industries. The coefficient is higher at the three-digit level than at the two-digit level, as one would expect if spillovers tended to be largest within a narrow industry. However, the effect becomes smaller when we move to the five-digit industries. The behavior of productivity spillovers contrasts with that of wage spillovers (table 2.1), where going from the national to the province level raised the spillover coefficient at the three-digit and five-digit industry levels. The difference between the wage and productivity spillovers is mostly, although not entirely, consistent with the idea that wage spillovers come through competition for labor in geographically narrow labor markets, while productivity spillovers result from competition in countrywide product markets.

Conclusions

Why do studies of spillovers reach such diverse conclusions? With respect to wage spillovers, the use of cross-section or panel data does not seem to determine the result. As far as we can judge from Indonesia, the tendency of foreign-owned firms to gravitate to high-wage industries, while it exists, does not explain the apparent spillovers and neither does any tendency of foreign firms to take over high-wage local firms within industries. Aside from Indonesia, most of the evidence for wage spillovers comes from developed countries, particularly the United States and the United Kingdom. One hint that differences in labor market institutions might be important for the degree of wage spillovers is that two countries found to have negative spillovers were countries with very restrictive labor laws, while the United States and the United Kingdom were among the least restrictive. With respect to productivity spillovers, an accumulation of panel data studies has erased the previous unanimity of panel data results in showing negative or no spillovers. As with wages, firm-specific characteristics do not explain all the higher productivity found for domestic firms in industries where foreign-owned firms were important. The econometric method does not seem to be the crucial determinant of the result.

An explanation that seems plausible at this point is that countries and firms within countries might differ in their ability to benefit from the presence of foreign-owned firms and their superior technology. There might be countries or industries in which the domestically owned sector is too small or unable to learn from foreign-owned firms. In those cases, the domestic sector may be crowded out by competition from the more efficient foreign-owned firms. The state of the domestically owned sector might depend not only on the stage of development of the economy, but also on the type of trade regime. A heavily protected domestically owned sector might be inefficient and lacking in entrepreneurship. It makes sense that the arrival of foreign firms with technology greatly superior to that of domestically owned firms should inflict damage on at least some domestic firms. The least efficient, perhaps often the smallest, might become unprofitable or be forced out of the industry. One might view that outcome as favorable for the host country as a whole if the average productivity of foreign-owned and domestically owned firms together increased. Few studies take account of both the exit and the entrance of new firms, both of which are important for assessing the overall impact of inward FDI.

If country and industry differences are important to the impact of inward FDI on host countries, the main lesson might be that the search for universal relationships is futile. In that case, the question shifts from how inward FDI affects every host country and industry to which types of industries and host countries are affected, and what the impact is on each. It is in identifying the characteristics of firms, industries, and countries that promote the transfer of technology that case studies can be most valuable. Their flexibility with respect to assumptions regarding timing and types of technology transfer suggests what statistical studies should look for and how the variables should be defined, especially if they encompass a wide range of both successful and unsuccessful ventures.

Why has academic skepticism about the impact of FDI not influenced policy more strongly? One reason is probably the diversity of findings. Another is the narrow scope of technology in the statistical tests. It relies on the assumption that the scale of operations and the import of components from abroad, and particularly from other related firms, do not constitute part of affiliate technology, but are simple inputs, accessible to local as well as foreign firms. Policymakers may have found these assumptions implausible.

References

Aitken, Brian J., and Ann E. Harrison. 1999. Do Domestic Firms Benefit from Direct Foreign Investment? Evidence from Venezuela. *American Economic Review* 89, no. 3 (June): 605–18.

Aitken, Brian J., Ann E. Harrison, and Robert E. Lipsey. 1996. Wages and Foreign Ownership: A Comparative Study of Mexico, Venezuela, and the United States. *Journal of International Economics* 40, no. 3-4 (May): 345–71.

Anderson, Gary W. Jr. 2000. Multinational Corporations and Tacit Knowledge: Determination of Entry Mode and Impact of Entry. Paper presented at the 7th Convention of the East Asian Economic Association, Singapore, November 17–18.

Baranson, Jack. 1967. *Manufacturing Problems in India: The Cummins Diesel Experience.* Syracuse, NY: Syracuse University Press.

Barrell, R., and N. Pain. 1997. Foreign Direct Investment, Technological Change, and Economic Growth within Europe. *Economic Journal* 107, no. 445 (November): 1770–86.

Blalock, Garrick, and Paul J. Gertler. 2002. *Firm Capabilities and Technology Adoption: Evidence from Foreign Direct Investment in Indonesia.* Working Paper, Department of Applied Economics and Management, Cornell University. Ithaca, NY: Cornell University. www.aem.cornell.edu/faculty_sites/gb78/ (accessed January 3, 2004).

Blalock, Garrick, and Paul J. Gertler. 2003. *Technology from Foreign Direct Investment and Welfare Gains through the Supply Chain.* Working Paper, Department of Applied Economics and Management, Cornell University. Ithaca, NY: Cornell University. www.aem.cornell.edu/faculty_sites/gb78/ (accessed January 3, 2004).

Blomström, Magnus, and Fredrik Sjöholm. 1999. Technology Transfer and Spillovers: Does Local Participation with Multinationals Matter? *European Economic Review* 43, no. 4–6 (April): 915–23.

Botero, Juan, Simeon Djankov, Rafael La Porta, Florencio Lopez-de-Silanes, and Andrei Shleifer. 2003. *The Regulation of Labor.* NBER Working Paper 9756. Cambridge, MA: National Bureau of Economic Research.

Carkovic, Maria, and Ross Levine. 2002. *Does Foreign Direct Investment Accelerate Economic Growth?* Department of Finance Working Paper (June). Minneapolis: University of Minnesota.

Castellani, Davide, and Antonello Zanfei. 2002. Multinational Companies and Productivity Spillovers: Is There a Specification Error? ISI Università di Urbino. Photocopy.

Dobson, Wendy, and Chia Siow Yue, eds. 1997. *Multinationals and East Asian Integration.* Ottawa, Canada: International Development Research Centre.

Driffield, N., and Sourafel Girma. 2002. *Regional Foreign Direct Investment and Wage Spillovers: Plant-Level Evidence from the Electronics Industry.* Research Paper 2002/04. Nottingham, UK: Leverhulme Centre for Research on Globalisation and Economic Policy.

Figlio, David N., and Bruce A. Blonigen. 2000. The Effects of Foreign Direct Investment on Local Communities. *Journal of Urban Economics* 48, no. 2 (September): 338–63.

Girma, Sourafel, David Greenaway, and Katherine Wakelin. 2001. Who Benefits from Foreign Direct Investment in the UK? *Scottish Journal of Political Economy* 48, no. 2 (May):119–33.

Görg, Holger, and David Greenaway. 2001. *Foreign Direct Investment and Intra-industry Spillovers: A Review of the Literature.* Globalisation and Labor Markets Programme Research Paper No. 2001/37. Nottingham, UK: Leverhulme Centre for Research on Globalisation and Economic Policy.

Görg, Holger, and Eric Strobl. 2001. Multinational Companies and Productivity Spillovers: A Meta-analysis. *Economic Journal* 111, no. 475 (November): F723–39.

Haskel, Jonathan E., Sonia C. Pereira, and Matthew J. Slaughter. 2002. *Does Inward Foreign Direct Investment Boost the Productivity of Domestic Firms?* NBER Working Paper 8724. Cambridge, MA: National Bureau of Economic Research.

Henderson, Vernon J., Ari Kuncoro, and Damhuri Nasution. 1996. The Dynamics of Jabotabek Development. *Bulletin of Indonesian Economic Studies* 32, no. 1 (April): 71–95.

Jaffe, Adam B., Manuel Trajtenberg, and Rebecca Henderson. 1993. Geographic Localization of Knowledge Spillovers as Evidenced by Patent Citations. *Quarterly Journal of Economics* 108, no. 3 (August): 577–98.

Kathuria, Vinish. 2000. Productivity Spillovers from Technology Transfer to Indian Manufacturing Firms. *Journal of International Development* 12, no. 3: 343–69.

Keller, Wolfgang, and Stephen R. Yeaple. 2003. *Multinational Enterprises, International Trade, and Productivity Growth: Firm Level Evidence from the United States.* NBER Working Paper 9504. Cambridge, MA: National Bureau of Economic Research

Kokko, Ari. 1994. Technology, Market Characteristics, and Spillovers. *Journal of Development Economics* 43, no. 2 (April): 279–93.

Kokko, Ari. 1996. Productivity Spillovers from Competition Between Local Firms and Foreign Affiliates. *Journal of International Development* 8, no. 4 (April): 517–30.

Lipsey, Robert E. 2003. Foreign Direct Investment, Growth, and Competitiveness in Developing Countries. In *The Global Competitiveness Report, 2002–2003,* ed., Peter K. Cornelius. New York: Oxford University Press.

Lipsey, Robert E. 2004. Home- and Host-Country Effects of Foreign Direct Investment. In *Challenges to Globalization,* ed., Robert E. Baldwin and L. Alan Winters. Chicago: University of Chicago Press.

Lipsey, Robert E., and Fredrik Sjöholm. 2002. *Foreign Firms and Indonesian Manufacturing Wages: An Analysis with Panel Data.* NBER Working Paper 9417 (December). Cambridge, MA: National Bureau of Economic Research.

Lipsey, Robert E., and Fredrik Sjöholm. 2004a. Foreign Direct Investment, Education, and Wages in Indonesian Manufacturing. *Journal of Development Economics* 73, no. 1 (February): 415–22.

Lipsey, Robert E., and Fredrik Sjöholm. 2004b. FDI and Wage Spillovers in Indonesian Manufacturing. *Review of World Economics* 140, no. 2: 287–310.

Moran, Theodore H. 2001. *Parental Supervision: The New Paradigm for Foreign Direct Investment.* Washington: Institute for International Economics.

Moran, Theodore H. 2002. *Beyond Sweatshops: Foreign Direct Investment and Globalization in Developing Countries.* Washington: Brookings Institution Press.

Okamoto, Yumiko, and Fredrik Sjöholm. 2005. FDI and the Dynamics of Productivity in Indonesian Manufacturing. *Journal of Development Studies* 41, no. 1 (January): 160–82.

Rhee, Yung Whee, and Therese Belot. 1990. *Export Catalysts in Low-Income Countries.* Word Bank Discussion Paper 72. Washington: World Bank.

Sjöberg, Örjan, and Fredrik Sjöholm. 2004. Trade Liberalization and the Geography of Production: Agglomeration, Concentration and Dispersal in Indonesia's Manufacturing Industry. *Economic Geography* 80, no. 3 (July): 287–310.

Sjöholm, Fredrik. 1999a. Productivity Growth in Indonesia: The Role of Regional Characteristics and Direct Foreign Investment. *Economic Development and Cultural Change* 47, no. 3 (April): 559–84.

Sjöholm, Fredrik. 1999b. Technology Gap, Competition and Spillovers from Direct Foreign Investment: Evidence from Establishment Data. *Journal of Development Studies* 36, no. 1 (October): 53–73.

Sjöholm, Fredrik. 2002. The Challenge of FDI and Regional Development in Indonesia. *Journal of Contemporary Asia* 32, no. 3: 381–93.

Takii, Sadayukii. 2001. *Productivity Spillovers and Characteristics of Foreign Multinational Plants in Indonesian Manufacturing 1990–95.* ICSEAD Working Paper 2001-14. Kitakyushu, Japan: ICSEAD.

Takii, Sadayukii, and Eric D. Ramstetter. 2003. *Employment, Production, Labor Productivity, and Foreign Multinationals in Indonesian Manufacturing, 1975–2000.* ICSEAD Working Paper 2003-25. Kitakyushu, Japan: ICSEAD.

Todo, Yasuyuki, and Koji Miyamoto. 2002. *Knowledge Diffusion from Multinational Enterprises: The Role of Domestic and Foreign Knowledge-Enhancing Activities.* OECD Technical Paper 196. Paris: OECD Development Centre.

UNCTAD. 2003. *World Investment Report 2003.* UNCTAD: New York and Geneva.

World Bank. 2003. *Doing Business.* Washington: World Bank.

3

Disentangling FDI Spillover Effects: What Do Firm Perceptions Tell Us?

BEATA SMARZYNSKA JAVORCIK and MARIANA SPATAREANU

Policymakers in developing countries place attracting foreign direct investment (FDI) high on their agenda, expecting FDI inflows to bring new technologies and know-how to their economy, which will help increase the productivity and competitiveness of domestic industries. Many governments go beyond national treatment of multinationals by offering foreign companies, through subsidies and tax holidays, more favorable conditions than those granted to domestic firms. As economic rationale for this special treatment, policymakers often cite positive externalities generated by FDI through productivity spillovers to domestic firms.

Despite its importance to public policy choices, there is little conclusive evidence on whether domestic firms benefit from foreign presence in their country. Research based on firm-level panel data, which examines whether the productivity of domestic firms is correlated with the extent of foreign presence in their sector, tends to produce mixed results and often fails to find a significant effect in developing countries. However, the picture is more optimistic for vertical spillovers, namely those occurring through contact between multinationals and their local suppliers of intermediate inputs. New research (e.g., Javorcik 2004b) demonstrates that the productivity of domestic firms is positively correlated with the presence of multinationals in downstream industries.

Beata Smarzynska Javorcik is senior economist at the Development Economics Research Group at the World Bank and research affiliate at the Centre for Economic Policy Research. Mariana Spatareanu is researcher at the Development Economics Research Group at the World Bank. The views expressed in the chapter are those of the authors and should not be attributed to the World Bank or its executive directors.

This chapter's purpose is to shed some light on the difficulties facing researchers tackling the issue of FDI spillovers. We examine horizontal and vertical spillovers in the context of Romania and the Czech Republic and demonstrate how starkly the conclusions may differ depending on the country analyzed, despite using the same methodology and comparable data. Then we discuss potential explanations for these differences by arguing that a plethora of issues may have prevented researchers from reaching clear-cut conclusions on the subject.

In the context of intraindustry (or horizontal) spillovers researchers face the challenge of disentangling the positive impact of knowledge flows from the potentially negative short-run effect that an increase in competitive pressures from foreign entry may have on some domestic firms.[1] Since it is difficult to capture each phenomenon separately, most of the empirical results reflect the combined effect of the two forces. To demonstrate that the two effects actually occur, we choose a somewhat unconventional approach and focus on local firms' perceptions of how foreign presence in the same sector has affected their performance. The perceptions, collected in surveys commissioned by the World Bank in Latvia and the Czech Republic in 2003, confirm the existence of knowledge transfer through the demonstration effect and the movement of labor. The perceptions also confirm the presence of the competition effect, which in the short run may have an adverse effect on some firms. Moreover, they illustrate that the relative prevalence of the two effects differs across countries and thus provide a plausible explanation for the differences in the results for different economies.

The situation is no less complex in the case of vertical spillovers from multinationals to their local suppliers, since several scenarios are also possible. The first possibility is "cherry picking." In this scenario multinationals simply award contracts to the best local firms that already possess the required level of sophistication and thus spillovers do not occur. The second scenario is that potential suppliers experience a positive productivity shock and subsequently reach a sufficient level of productivity to work with a multinational. This shock may come from either the multinational's assistance before starting a sourcing relationship or a local firm's own efforts motivated by the prospect of a new business relationship. It may also be completely unrelated to either cause. The third possibility is that local suppliers improve their performance *while* doing business with a multinational due to more stringent requirements or knowledge transfer from the multinational. Finally, a combination of these mechanisms may occur. All, except the first scenario, would lead researchers to conclude that

---

1. Keep in mind that spillovers are only one way in which FDI inflows affect the host economy. Thus, even if spillovers result in a negative distributional effect on a particular group (e.g., shareholders in local businesses in this case), the host economy as a whole may benefit from the presence of foreign investors.

the productivity of domestic firms in the supplying sector is positively correlated with the presence of foreign firms in downstream industries. Again, all, apart from the "cherry picking" scenario, can be viewed as broadly defined spillovers. However, the analysis, which relies on industry-level proxies for vertical spillovers, does not pinpoint which of the above-mentioned mechanisms is at play. Doing so would be interesting and useful as each scenario may have a different policy implication. To learn about the plausibility of each scenario we again turn to the survey data.

Finally, we review several recent studies that suggest that the existence and extent of FDI spillovers may be driven by the composition of FDI inflows, adding to the difficulties facing researchers examining this question. For instance, spillovers may be affected by the incidence of wholly owned subsidiaries relative to projects with shared domestic and foreign ownership as well as by the nationality of foreign investors.

In the face of difficulties associated with capturing spillover effects and the multitude of factors that can influence the extent of spillovers in each economy, we caution researchers about drawing generalized conclusions about the existence of externalities associated with FDI in developing countries.

A Tale of Two Countries and Two Spillover Patterns

A Brief Look at the Relevant Literature

Spillovers from FDI occur when the entry or presence of multinational corporations increases the productivity of domestic firms in a host country and the multinationals do not fully internalize the value of these benefits. Spillovers may occur when local firms improve their efficiency by copying technologies or marketing techniques of foreign affiliates either through observation or by hiring workers trained by the affiliates. Another kind of spillover occurs if multinational entry leads to more severe competition in the host country market and forces local firms to use their existing resources more efficiently or to search for new technologies (Blomström and Kokko 1998).

If domestic firms and multinationals compete in the same sector, the latter have an incentive to prevent technology leakage and spillovers from occurring. This can be achieved through formal protection of their intellectual property, trade secrecy, paying higher wages to prevent labor turnover, or operating only in countries or industries where domestic firms have limited imitative capacities to begin with. Several studies (for example, Aitken, Harrison, and Lipsey 1996, Girma, Greenaway, and Wakelin 2001) document that foreign firms pay higher wages than domestic enterprises. Multinationals are also sensitive to the strength of intellectual property rights protection in host countries (Javorcik 2004b).

However, multinationals have no incentive to prevent technology diffusion to upstream sectors, since they may benefit from the improved performance of intermediate input suppliers. Thus, contacts between multinational firms and their local suppliers are the most likely channel through which spillovers would manifest themselves. Such spillovers may occur through: (1) direct knowledge transfer from foreign customers to local suppliers; (2) imposing higher requirements for product quality and on-time delivery, which provide incentives to domestic suppliers to upgrade their management or technology; and (3) multinational entry increasing the demand for intermediate products, which allows local suppliers to reap the benefits of scale economies.

Indeed, existing literature has found more evidence in favor of vertical rather than horizontal spillovers in developing countries. For instance, studies by Aitken and Harrison (1999) on Venezuela, Djankov and Hoekman (2000) on the Czech Republic, and Konings (2001) on Bulgaria, Romania, and Poland cast doubt on the existence of horizontal spillovers from FDI in these countries. These researchers either fail to find a significant positive effect or produce evidence of negative spillovers. In other words, the presence of multinational corporations is found either to have no impact or to negatively affect domestic firms in the same sector. This result, however, cannot be generalized to include all developing countries. For example, Damijan et al. (2003) detect the presence of positive intraindustry spillovers in Romania but not in six other transition economies, including the Czech Republic. At the same time, Kinoshita (2001) reports that research and development (R&D)-intensive sectors in the Czech Republic benefit from horizontal spillovers.[2]

The evidence that vertical spillovers occur through contact between multinationals and their local suppliers appears to be stronger. The results, which are consistent with the existence of such spillovers in developing countries, have been provided by Blalock and Gertler (2004) for Indonesia, Javorcik (2004a) for Lithuania, and Schoors and van der Tol (2001) for Hungary. However, as we discuss later in this chapter, not all types of FDI appear to be associated with vertical spillovers.

Searching for Spillovers in Romania and the Czech Republic

We use case studies of Romania and the Czech Republic to examine the differences in horizontal and vertical spillovers. To make the results as comparable as possible, we use the same data source (*Amadeus* database), the same time period (1998–2000), use and the same methodology. Both

---

2. For a survey of the literature on horizontal spillovers, see Görg and Strobl (2001).

countries share the common heritage of more than 40 years of central planning, both started transformation to a free-market economy in the early 1990s, and both enjoy relatively large pools of skilled labor. However, their transition paths have been different: Although the Czech Republic made large strides in reform at the beginning of the last decade, reforms in Romania have lagged behind. As a result, the Czech Republic has been receiving large FDI inflows for over 10 years while foreign investors have been more cautious with Romania and started entering the country on a larger scale only in the second half of the 1990s.

For each country we estimate a production function regression in which we allow foreign firms to affect the productivity of domestic enterprises through horizontal and backward linkages. We estimate the model in first differences and employ the semiparametric estimation procedure suggested by Olley and Pakes (1996) to calculate the total factor productivity (TFP). Since we are interested in the effect foreign presence has on the local economy, we estimate the model on the sample of domestic firms. In addition, we include time, industry and region dummies, and correct standard errors to take into account the fact that the measures of potential spillovers are industry specific while the observations in the dataset are at the firm level.[3]

The results for Romania, presented in the first two columns of table 3.1, provide evidence consistent with the existence of intraindustry spillovers from FDI. The magnitude of the effect is economically meaningful as a one-standard-deviation increase in the presence of multinationals in the same sector results in a 3.3 percent increase in the value added of each domestic firm. The presence of a positive effect confirms the results of Damijan et al. (2003), who examined this question using the Romanian data from the same source but concentrated on the earlier period (1994–98) and employed a different methodology. As for vertical spillovers, we do not find a significant effect in our preferred specification with the Olley-Pakes correction and thus conclude that FDI in downstream sectors has no effect on the productivity of domestic firms in the supplying industries.

The results for the Czech Republic (presented in columns three and four) contrast with the findings for Romania. The proxy for intraindustry effects is not statistically significant, which is again consistent with the results of Damijan et al. (2003). Furthermore, there appears to be no evidence of vertical spillovers.

How can we explain the differences between the findings for Romania and the Czech Republic? While it is possible that they can be attributed to differences in the host country characteristics, the short period covered by the analysis, or the shortcomings of the dataset, in the remainder of the chapter we focus on other potential explanations.

---

3. More details about the dataset, variable definitions, and other methodological issues can be found in Javorcik and Spatareanu (2003).

Table 3.1 Production function regression: Results for Romania versus Czech Republic, 1998–2000

| | Romania | | Czech Republic | |
	Δ ln VA	Δ ln TFP	Δ ln VA	Δ ln TFP
Δ ln K	0.127*** (0.004)		0.116*** (0.022)	
Δ ln L	0.573*** (0.010)		0.313*** (0.077)	
Δ ln horizontal	0.0031* (0.0016)	0.0028* (0.0016)	0.0047 (0.0041)	-0.0003 (0.0043)
Δ ln vertical	20.0043** (0.0021)	-0.0034 (0.0022)	0.0095 (0.0167)	0.0095 (0.0168)
Observations	71,517	71,517	7,400	7,303
Adjusted R^2	0.13	0.02	0.04	0.02
F-stat	53.15	10.87	3.57	2.54
Prob > F-stat	0.00	0.00	0.00	0.00

***, **, * denotes significance at the 1, 5, and 10 percent level, respectively.
Δ = change in
F-stat = F-statistic
K = capital
L = labor
ln = national logarithm
TFP = total factor productivity
VA = value added

Notes: Logarithm of TFP has been calculated using the Olley-Pakes methodology. All models include year, industry, and region-fixed effects. Standard errors corrected for clustering on industry year are listed in parentheses.

Source: Authors' calculations.

Dissecting Horizontal Spillovers

Aitken and Harrison (1999) postulated that the presence of multinationals may have two opposing effects on domestic firms operating in the same industry. On the one hand, foreign presence may enhance the productivity of domestic firms through knowledge transfer. Such transfer may occur as local producers observe technologies and marketing techniques used by multinationals or hire workers trained by foreign companies. On the other hand, foreign firms entering the same industry may take market share away from local companies forcing them to spread the fixed costs over a smaller production scale, increasing the average cost and resulting in a lower observed productivity. While this effect may disappear in the long run as less competitive local producers exit, it may be observable in the period immediately following the foreign entry.

It is challenging to disentangle the two effects in an econometric analysis, and, thus, depending on the relative strength of the knowledge transfer versus the competition effect, various studies have produced very different results depending on the country and the time period in question or even the methodology applied. Moreover, very few studies have made a serious attempt to control for the competition effect. A notable exception is a study by Haskel, Pereira, and Slaughter (2002) that included proxies for industry concentration, import penetration, and a firm's market share in the estimation. However, the study focused on the United Kingdom and not on a developing country.

Even though the explanation focusing on the two opposing effects appears to be plausible, does any evidence confirm its validity? Rather than adding the above-mentioned controls to our econometric analysis, which would be associated with high data requirements as we would want to work with all the firms in the Czech Republic rather than a sample, we use a somewhat unconventional approach and simply ask firms about the effects the entry of multinationals into their sector has had on their operation.

This approach may be subject to several criticisms. First, survey respondents may not answer the questions truthfully. We believe that this is unlikely to be a serious concern, since both surveys were conducted by highly reputable companies that guaranteed full anonymity to respondents. Moreover, respondents were free to decline in participating in the survey or answering a particular question. The second, more serious, concern is that the perceptions of firms may be influenced by their performance. For instance, firms in a difficult financial situation may be likely to blame their poor performance on the "unfair competition" from foreign affiliates operating in their industry. While this concern is valid, the correlations between firms' perceptions and performance, presented below, do not always follow the expected direction, which provides some indication that the extent of bias may be limited. Nevertheless keeping this concern in mind, we only consider correlations without trying to infer the direction of causality. In sum, while we are aware of the potential pitfalls of our approach, we believe that the survey results can inform the discussion of FDI spillovers.

The enterprise surveys, presented in this chapter, were commissioned by the Foreign Investment Advisory Services (FIAS), a joint facility of the World Bank and the International Finance Corporation, in Latvia and the Czech Republic during 2003. Both surveys were conducted by professional polling companies through face-to-face interviews at respondents' offices. All respondents were guaranteed full anonymity. In Latvia, 407 firms were interviewed and 52 percent of respondents were located in the capital city of Riga while the rest were located around the country. Of the 407 firms, 67 percent of respondents were private domestic firms, 19 percent privatized state-owned companies, 2 percent were firms remaining in public hands, and

Figure 3.1   Perceived effects of FDI in the Czech Republic and Latvia

percent of respondents

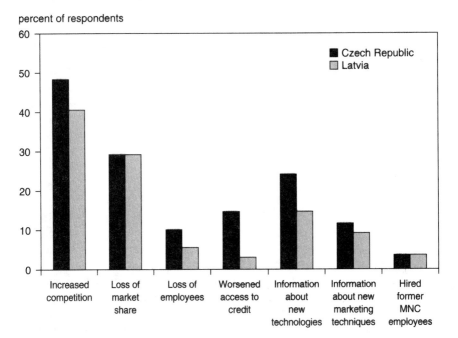

MNC = multinational corporation

Source: Authors' calculations.

11 percent were firms with foreign capital participation. In the Czech Republic, 391 local companies and 119 multinationals were interviewed. About 21 percent of the respondents were located in the capital city of Prague while the rest were located across all regions of the country. All of the companies included in the survey were private. In both countries, the surveys focused on the manufacturing sectors. The results of the Czech survey are supplemented with financial information on interviewed firms from the *Amadeus* database. Such information is available for about 114 local firms in the sample. The additional information mainly covers the 1995–2000 time period.

The perceptions of local firms collected in the surveys suggest that indeed there may exist two opposing effects associated with foreign entry. As illustrated in figure 3.1, 48 percent of the interviewed Czech firms believed that the presence of multinationals increased the level of competition in their sector. The same was true of 41 percent of Latvian enterprises. About 29 percent of firms in each country reported losing market share as a result of FDI inflow. Six to ten percent of firms lost employees to multinationals. Finally, 15 percent of Czech firms and 3 percent of Latvian enterprises believed that foreign presence worsened their access to credit. There is also some evidence in favor of knowledge spillovers. Almost 25 percent of respondents in the Czech Republic and 15 percent in Latvia learned about new technologies from multinationals. Similarly, 12 percent and 9 percent, respectively, of the respondents in the Czech Republic and Latvia benefited from learning about new marketing techniques by observing multinationals. Thus, the survey results indicate the presence of the demonstration effect. The movement of labor, however, seems to have been less prevalent as only 4 percent of firms in both countries reported hiring workers previously employed by multinationals.

The relative importance of the positive and negative impacts differs between the two countries. For instance, while 29 percent of firms in both countries believed they lost market share to multinationals, only 15 percent of Latvian firms seemed to benefit from the demonstration of new technologies compared to 24 percent of Czech companies.

How do these perceptions translate into actual firm performance? We use the Czech data to examine correlations between perceptions and firm performance in terms of employment changes and total factor productivity (TFP) growth between 1997 and 2000.[4] While correlations do not tell us anything about the direction of causality, we still find them instructive. As illustrated in figure 3.2, firms reporting rising competitive pressures as a result of foreign entry experienced a larger increase in employment relative to companies that were not affected by FDI inflows. Moreover, they also had a faster productivity growth.[5] On the other hand, firms reporting loss of market share, which they attributed to foreign presence in their sector, experienced a much larger decline in employment and a slower TFP growth than other firms (see figure 3.3). Companies that lost employees to multinationals saw a larger drop in employment and a higher increase in productivity (figure 3.4).

Turning to the firms' perceptions about knowledge flows, those that reported learning about new technologies from multinationals outperformed others in terms of employment and productivity growth (figure 3.5). The same was true of Czech enterprises that hired workers previously employed by multinationals (figure 3.6).[6] Czech firms claiming to benefit from information about new marketing strategies used by multinationals did worse with respect to productivity (figure 3.7). We stress again that we

---

4. TFP levels are calculated based on the figures from the *Amadeus* database using the Olley-Pakes (1996) procedure applied to the pooled sample, since the small number of observations does not allow for estimation for each industry separately. The change in TFP is defined as ln TFP_{i2000} − ln TFP_{i1997}, and the change in employment is calculated analogously.

5. It is possible that foreign entry led to the exit of least productive firms and resulted in the survival of the firms with the greatest potential for productivity improvements. Unfortunately, we are unable to capture this in our sample.

6. The seemingly missing bar for the "yes" group in figure 3.7 is because the average change in employment was close to zero.

Figure 3.2 Entry of MNCs increased competition in the Czech Republic, 1997–2002 (average change)

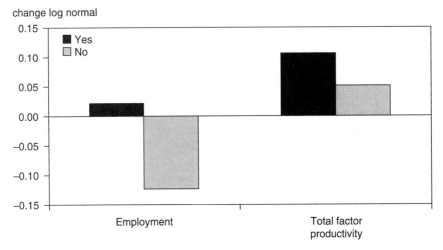

MNC = multinational corporation
Source: Authors' calculations.

are unable to infer causality from these correlations since, for instance, firms that are in general better positioned to improve their productivity may also be able to take advantage of knowledge spillovers. Similarly, firms may improve their performance thanks to the knowledge brought by workers trained by multinationals or better-performing firms may attract employees previously working for multinationals.

In summary, the survey results are consistent with the existence of both positive and negative effects associated with foreign entry into an industry. Thus, they suggest that the econometric studies, which rely on estimating production functions and do not have good controls for the level of competition and the movement of labor between foreign and domestic firms, are most likely capturing the combined effect of the increased competition and knowledge transfer. Since the relative magnitude of the effects will likely vary by country, different results from various studies are not surprising.

How Do Vertical Spillovers Work?

While the existing literature is quite upbeat about the existence of vertical spillovers from FDI, the studies tell us little about the mechanism behind the observed correlation attributed to vertical spillovers. As mentioned in the introduction, several possibilities exist.

Figure 3.3   Czech firms lost market share due to entry of MNCs, 1997–2000 (average change)

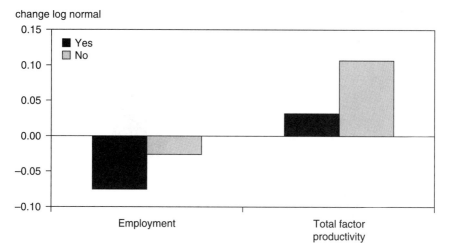

MNC = multinational corporation

Source: Authors' calculations.

First, it is possible (though less likely) that vertical spillovers do not occur. Multinationals "cherry pick" by simply awarding contracts to the best local firms that are already advanced enough to fulfill the necessary requirements. Multinationals may also choose to operate in countries and sectors where local sourcing is possible, or, if the host country's level of development does not allow for local sourcing, multinationals may choose to import intermediate inputs. However, to the extent that the existing studies control for the latter phenomenon, their results suggest a limited plausibility of this scenario.

The second scenario is that potential suppliers experience a positive productivity shock and subsequently reach a sufficient level of productivity to work with a multinational. This shock may come from either the multinational's assistance before starting a sourcing relationship or a local firm's own efforts motivated by the prospect of a new business relationship. It may also be completely unrelated to either cause. The difference between this scenario and the one outlined above is that by offering the prospect of more lucrative contracts (thanks either to higher prices or greater reliability of payments) multinationals create incentives for local firms to improve themselves and in this way their presence becomes associated with spillovers. The self-selection of firms to supply multinationals would be analogous to the findings of the literature on exporting. For instance, Bernard and Jensen (1999) and Clerides, Lach, and Tybout (1998) show that more productive firms become exporters but no improvements in produc-

Figure 3.4 Czech firms lost employees to MNCs, 1997–2000
(average change)

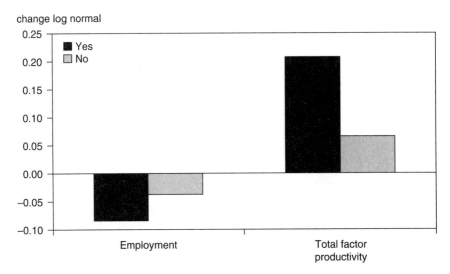

MNC = multinational corporation
Source: Authors' calculations.

tivity are registered due to learning from selling in foreign markets. The plausibility of this mechanism has also been demonstrated in the theoretical literature. In a general equilibrium model with productivity heterogeneity across firms, Melitz (2003) shows that if there are sunk costs associated with export market entry, firms with higher ex ante productivity self-select into exporting, while those with lower productivity choose to supply only the domestic market. Given the fact that multinational corporations tend to have higher requirements in terms of quality, technological sophistication, and on-time delivery, especially when compared to domestic buyers in developing and transition economies, becoming a supplier to a multinational is likely to be associated with some fixed cost on the part of local firms.

The third possibility is that local suppliers improve their performance *while* doing business with a multinational due to more stringent requirements or knowledge transfer from the multinational. There are several reasons why we would expect this to happen. By interacting with multinationals, local firms expose themselves to greater competition, since they compete not only with other local firms but also with potential suppliers from abroad. Local firms are also under pressure to improve their performance in order to retain their supplier status. Further, as suggested by anecdotal evidence (Moran 2001), they may also benefit from direct assis-

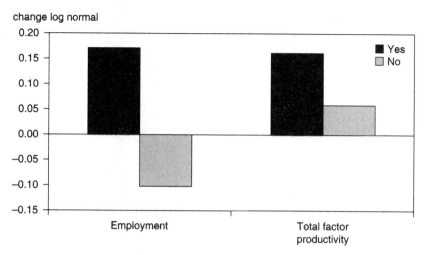

MNC = multinational corporation

Source: Authors' calculations.

tance and knowledge transfer from their multinational customers. Finally, a combination of these mechanisms may occur.

All except the first scenario would lead researchers to conclude that the presence of foreign firms in downstream industries is positively correlated with the productivity of domestic producers in the supplying sector. Again, all, apart from "cherry picking," can be viewed as broadly defined spillovers. However, the analysis, which relies on industry-level proxies for vertical spillovers, does not pinpoint which of the above-mentioned mechanisms is at play. Doing so would be interesting and useful as each scenario may have a different policy implication. For instance, if indeed local suppliers learn from their interactions with multinationals, then using policy instruments to attract FDI or establishing supplier development programs may be justified. If, however, the improvements in productivity result from the prospect of receiving more lucrative contracts from foreign buyers, then a similar outcome could be achieved by securing better access to foreign markets through multilateral or preferential trade agreements and/or facilitating the flow of information about foreign markets and business opportunities available there. In the next section we return to the Czech survey to shed some light on this complex issue. First, however, we set the context by demonstrating that local sourcing is indeed widespread among multinationals operating in the Czech Republic.

Figure 3.6 Czech firms hired employees trained by MNCs, 1997–2000 (average change)

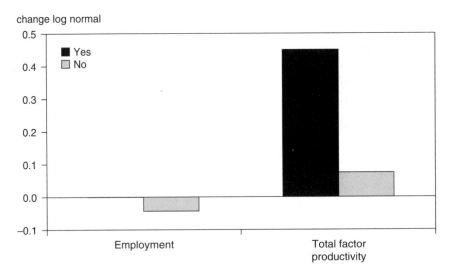

change log normal

MNC = multinational corporation
Source: Authors' calculations.

Determinants of Multinationals' Sourcing Patterns

In order to gain some understanding of the factors driving the sourcing pattern and the decision making process of multinationals, 119 multinatioals operating in the Czech Republic were included in the survey. The interviewed firms were majority-owned foreign subsidiaries representing almost all manufacturing industries: fabricated metals (19 firms); publishing and printing (14); rubber (11); machinery (10); apparel (9); electrical machinery (9); food products (8); textiles (7); nonmetallic mineral products (7); furniture (6); pulp and paper (4); wood products (3); chemicals (3); radio, TV, and communications equipment (3); leather (2); basic metals (1); medical equipment (1); motor vehicles (1); and other transport equipment (1).

The survey results suggest that multinationals are actively engaged in local sourcing in the Czech Republic. Of the multinational respondents, 90 percent reported purchasing inputs from at least one Czech company.[7] The median multinational in the sample had a sourcing relationship with 10 Czech suppliers while a multinational in the top quartile had at least 30. As illustrated in table 3.2, Czech companies were the most important supplier group, followed by other European suppliers (located in the European

---

7. Note that the question specifically asked respondents not to include suppliers of services, such as catering or cleaning.

Figure 3.7 Czech firms learned about new marketing strategies from MNCs, 1997–2000 (average change)

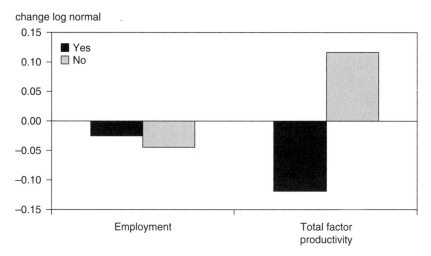

MNC = multinational corporation
Source: Authors' calculations.

Union or Eastern Europe) and then other multinationals operating in the Czech Republic. There was also a limited amount of sourcing from North America, Russia, and the Commonwealth of Independent States (CIS).

When asked about the current share of inputs purchased from each type of supplier (in terms of value), multinationals indicated sourcing *on average* 48.3 percent of inputs from Czech enterprises, as compared to 33.3 and 12.6 percent from firms in the European Union/Eastern Europe and multinationals located in the Czech Republic, respectively (see figure 3.8).[8] The share of inputs coming from the other regions appeared to be negligible. Since the average figures do not always give an accurate impression, it is worthwhile to report some more statistics. Fifty-five out of the 114 multinationals that answered this question reported buying at least 50 percent of their inputs from Czech suppliers. More than 10 percent of respondents acquired all of their intermediates from Czech enterprises. Approximately 40 percent of multinationals expected to purchase more inputs from Czech suppliers in the future. However, the anticipated increase is unlikely to be large (see figure 3.8).

The sourcing patterns of multinationals appear to be quite persistent. There is a large correlation (.9) between the share of local inputs sourced at present and that expected in the next 2 to 3 years. Having said that, the

---

8. Note that multinationals with no sourcing from a particular group of suppliers are included in that group's average.

Table 3.2 Distribution of MNC suppliers in the Czech Republic, 1997–2000

	Czech firms	MNCs operating in the Czech Republic	European Union or Eastern Europe	North America	Russia/ Common-wealth of Independent States
Number of multinationals reporting each type of suppliers	107	56	85	18	9
Multinational (25th percentile)	5	2	2	1	1
Median multinational (50th percentile)	10	4	5	1	2
Multinational (75th percentile)	30	10	10	4	2

MNC = multinational corporation

Source: Authors' calculations.

future increase in local sourcing is likely to come from multinationals that either do not purchase their intermediates locally or those with limited local sourcing. Multinationals buying the majority of intermediates from Czech suppliers expect a slight decline in the coming years (see table 3.3 for more details).

The multinational's decision to choose one type of supplier over another is driven by several factors. The top reasons reported for cooperating with Czech suppliers included: low prices (71 percent); geographic proximity, which allowed for a better relationship with a supplier (64 percent); savings on transport costs (56 percent); and savings on import duties (44 percent). Sourcing from foreign firms located in the Czech Republic was primarily driven by the fact that these firms were global suppliers of the multinationals (45 percent) and offered more competitive prices (45 percent), higher-quality products (29 percent), or products not available from Czech firms (29 percent). As before, savings on transport costs (34 percent) and benefits of proximity (30 percent) mattered as well. Finally, importing inputs from abroad was primarily driven by using a parent company's global suppliers (46 percent), implementing the decision of the parent company (37 percent), unavailability of particular products from Czech firms (36 percent), or desire to purchase higher-quality inputs (30 percent). In 80 percent of cases, management at the multinational plant in the Czech Republic rather than foreign owners based abroad made the sourcing decisions.

When asked about the reasons for not sourcing more from Czech firms, multinationals pointed to the lack of suitable products (38 percent), the inability of Czech firms to make timely deliveries (19 percent), and local

Figure 3.8   Share of intermediate inputs sourced by supplier type in the Czech Republic, 1997–2000

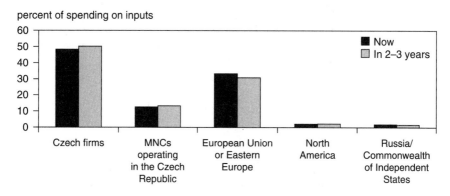

MNC = multinational corporation

Source: Authors' calculations.

firms' lack of resources required to become a supplier (16 percent). The fact that the decision to source from suppliers other than Czech firms is in many cases due to lower quality of goods sold by domestic firms. This suggests that for many local firms upgrading their products is a precondition to supplying multinationals.

The composition of inputs sourced by foreign customers again highlights the importance of having a high-quality product and the necessity of frequent upgrading, both of which are essential to a supplier's success with a multinational. Almost half of all inputs purchased by multinationals consisted of parts and components or final products (on average 32.4 and 15.6 percent, respectively). Raw materials constituted 36 percent and packaging 14 percent of purchased inputs.

While multinationals have high requirements vis-à-vis their suppliers, 20 percent of them also offered some type of support to the Czech companies they source from. Advance payment and financing were the most popular form of assistance, which is consistent with the finding (indicated earlier) that financial constraints are an obstacle to increasing sourcing from Czech firms. Employee training and help with quality control ranked second and third, respectively, which again reflect the importance of input quality in multinational sourcing decisions. Other types of assistance included: supplying inputs, lending/leasing machinery, providing production technology, financial planning, organization of production lines, business strategy, and finding export markets (see figure 3.9).

While the incidence of direct assistance to suppliers is not very high, its impact should not be underestimated. The benefits of support provided by multinationals to their local suppliers have been documented in numerous case studies from around the world (see Moran 2001). The following

Table 3.3 Expected changes to local sourcing patterns of MNCs in the Czech Republic

Share of intermediates currently sourced from Czech firms (percent)	Expected increase in 2–3 years (percent)	Number of respondents
0	6.4	14
1–25	3.1	27
26–50	2.0	20
51–75	−2.1	17
76–100	−0.1	35
Total	1.5	113

Source: Authors' calculations.

example from the Czech Republic may also serve as an illustration. After a Czech company, which makes castings of aluminum alloys for the automotive industry, signed its first contract with a multinational customer, the staff from the multinational visited the Czech firm's premises for two days each month to assist with the quality control system. Subsequently, the Czech firm applied these improvements to its other production lines (not serving this particular customer), thus reducing the number of defective items produced and improving overall productivity (Javorcik 2004a). Without doubt, such assistance contributes to the improved performance of the suppliers observed in the Czech Republic and other countries.

Mechanisms Behind Vertical Spillovers: What Do Survey Results Tell Us?

The responses to the survey provide some support to all three scenarios outlined earlier. They suggest that better-performing firms tend to get contracts from multinationals. They also indicate that local firms make improvements to their operations in anticipation of supplying multinationals, and, in some cases, local firms are assisted in this process by their prospective customers. Finally, the results show that multinationals offer assistance to their suppliers but its extent is limited.

We begin our discussion with arguments demonstrating that suppliers to multinationals tend to exhibit superior performance and that firms make improvements in order to become suppliers. The key factor that allows Czech companies to make sales to multinationals is having a product of suitable quality. This view is consistent with the fact that 80 percent of survey respondents sell the same product to both multinationals and local customers and only 5 percent of respondents sell an improved version of the product to multinationals and its basic version to local customers. Only 21 percent of firms reported developing the product specifically for the multinational customer and in only 5.5 percent of cases the multinational helped in the development process. In 26 percent of firms the product was

Figure 3.9 Assistance extended to domestic suppliers by MNCs operating in the Czech Republic

number of multinationals

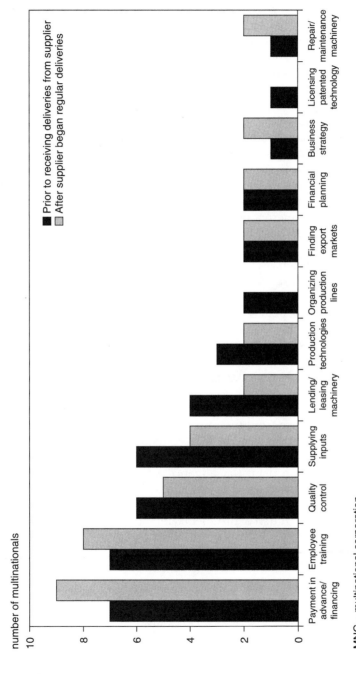

MNC = multinational corporation
Source: Authors' calculations.

developed in-house, and only 4 percent of companies developed products based on technology licensed from abroad.

While Czech suppliers appear to be engaged in product upgrading, a vast majority of such activities is based on their own efforts. More than a quarter of multinationals reported that the complexity and/or quality of products bought from the Czech suppliers increased during the two years before the study. In more than half of the cases, the supplier made improvements independently of the multinational. In the remaining cases, the improvement was a result of the multinational imposing higher requirements on their suppliers. Only in a handful of responses (15 percent) did multinationals indicate that the change was a direct result of the assistance provided to the supplier.

Having a suitable product is a necessary but not a sufficient condition for becoming a supplier. Many multinationals perform technical audits of their prospective suppliers and/or require quality certification, such as ISO 9000 awarded by the International Organization for Standardization (ISO).[9] The technical audits, while not considered by multinationals as a form of assistance, may be invaluable to prospective suppliers since they may point out operational deficiencies they were previously unaware of. The same may be true of the ISO certification process. The pressure from multinationals is often the driving force behind obtaining the quality certifications, as 17 percent of Czech companies surveyed reported getting an ISO certification *in order to become suppliers to multinationals*. These firms constituted 40 percent of all companies reporting having such a certification.

The survey results also suggest that multinationals make a deliberate effort to transfer knowledge to their local suppliers, although its extent and form vary by country. For instance, 33 percent of the suppliers in Latvia and 14.6 percent in the Czech Republic reported receiving various forms of assistance from their multinational customers.[10] Given the fact that credit constraints faced by local companies were mentioned by multinationals as one of the factors preventing them from sourcing more inputs locally, it is not surprising that advance payment and financing topped the list in both countries (see tables 3.4 and 3.5). It was followed by leasing of machinery and employee training in the Czech Republic and supplying inputs and organization of production lines in Latvia. Other forms of assistance were related to quality control, obtaining licenses for new technology, and production technology.

---

9. ISO 9000 is a quality standard that has become an international reference for quality requirements in business-to-business dealings. It refers to what the organization does to enhance customer satisfaction by meeting customer and applicable regulatory requirements as well as to continually improve its performance in this regard. For more details, see www.iso.org.

10. To make the results comparable between the two countries, in this case suppliers were defined as local firms selling to multinationals operating in their country or abroad.

**Table 3.4 Assistance received by Czech suppliers[a]
from multinational customers**

Assistance	Number of firms	Number providing assistance for a fee
Advance payment and financing	14	2
Leasing/lending machinery	7	2
Employee training	7	1
Quality control	5	1
Business strategy	5	0
Supplying inputs	2	1
Production technology	3	1
Organization of production lines	3	1
Finding export markets	3	1
Obtaining licenses for new technology	2	1
Financial planning	2	0
Maintenance of machinery	2	1
Inventory management	1	0

a. 25 companies reported receiving assistance.

Source: Authors' calculations.

While there is some evidence of technology transfer taking place (through leasing of machinery, assistance with production technology, or new technology licensing), the picture is consistent with the earlier observation that most companies in the Czech Republic acquire production technology on their own. Thus, the knowledge transfer is more likely to pertain to general business practices rather than specific technologies. Knowledge transfer takes the form of employee training, help with quality control, organization of production lines, or inventory management. While fees are charged for some forms of support, the majority of it is free.

The complexity of the issues outlined above suggests that further research is needed in order to better understand the mechanisms involved in vertical spillovers and their policy implications.

Further Complications—Do Characteristics of FDI Projects Affect Spillovers?

Our discussion so far has ignored a further complication in studying FDI spillovers, namely, the effect of the composition of FDI inflows. In this section, we focus on three examples of how the degree of foreign ownership, investor nationality, and market orientation of investors affect spillovers.

Why should the degree of foreign ownership influence the extent of horizontal spillovers? First, it is generally believed that the participation of local capital in an FDI project reveals the multinational's proprietary technology

Table 3.5   Assistance received by Latvian suppliers[a] from multinational customers

Assistance	Number of firms	Number providing assistance for a fee
Advance payment and financing	15	8
Supplying inputs	12	10
Organization of production lines	9	5
Leasing/lending machinery	8	8
Employee training	7	4
Finding export markets	7	2
Production technology	4	0
Quality control	1	0
Obtaining licenses for new technology	1	1
Maintenance of machinery	1	1

a. 36 companies reported receiving assistance.

Source: Authors' calculations.

and thus facilitates spillovers. This belief has led many governments in developing countries to introduce restrictions on the extent of foreign ownership allowed in firms operating in their country.[11] The fear of technology leakage, especially in countries with a limited rule of law, may induce multinationals with the most sophisticated technologies to shy away from shared ownership and instead choose to invest only in wholly owned subsidiaries (for evidence see Smarzynska and Wei 2000; Javorcik and Saggi 2004). Moreover, Ramachandran (1993) demonstrates that foreign investors tend to devote more resources to technology transfer to their wholly owned subsidiaries than to partially owned affiliates. In the same manner, Mansfield and Romero (1980) point out that the transfer of technology is more rapid within wholly owned networks of multinationals' subsidiaries than to joint ventures or licensees. Hence, the overall relationship between the share of foreign ownership and spillovers is a result of two forces—local participation as a mechanism facilitating knowledge transfers versus a higher technological content and, thus, greater potential for spillovers of wholly owned projects.

Turning to determinants of vertical (or interindustry) spillovers, it has been argued that affiliates established through either joint ventures or mergers and acquisitions are more likely to source their inputs locally than those taking the form of newly created (or greenfield) plants (UNCTAD 2001). While the latter need to put significant efforts into developing linkages with local suppliers, the former can take advantage of the supplier relationships of the acquired firm or the local partner. Empirical evidence

---

11. For instance, in the 1980s restrictions on foreign ownership were present in China, India, Indonesia, Malaysia, Mexico, Nigeria, Pakistan, the Republic of Korea, and Sri Lanka (UNCTAD 1987).

to support this view has been found for Japanese investors (Belderbos, Capannelli, and Fukao 2001) and for Swedish affiliates in Eastern and Central Europe (UNCTAD 2001). Anecdotal evidence also suggests that foreign investors acquiring local firms in transition countries tend to dramatically reduce the number of local suppliers.

Several studies explore this issue. Two studies postulate that having a minority versus a majority stake in an investment project should translate into different levels of horizontal spillovers. While Blomström and Sjöholm (1999), employing cross-section data on Indonesian firms, find that there is no statistically significant difference between positive intraindustry spillovers associated with minority- and majority-owned foreign projects, Dimelis and Louri (2001), using cross-sectional data on Greek manufacturing firms, demonstrate that spillovers stemming from minority-owned foreign establishments are larger than those from majority-owned ones.

In contrast, in a recent study (Javorcik and Spatareanu 2003), we focused on differences in spillovers associated with wholly owned foreign affiliates and projects with joint domestic and foreign ownership. That analysis, based on an unbalanced panel of Romanian firms during 1998–2000, produced evidence consistent with positive intrasectoral spillovers resulting from the former but not the latter type of FDI. This finding is consistent with the argument that foreign investors tend to put more resources into technology transfer to their wholly owned subsidiaries than to partially owned projects. As for vertical spillovers, our results indicate that the presence of partially foreign-owned projects is correlated with higher productivity of domestic firms in upstream industries, which suggests that domestic suppliers benefit from contacts with multinational customers. The opposite is true, however, in the case of wholly owned foreign affiliates, which appear to have a negative effect on domestic firms in upstream industries. These results are consistent with the observation that foreign investors entering a host country through greenfield projects are less likely to source locally than those engaged in joint ventures or partial acquisitions. They are also in line with the evidence suggesting that wholly owned foreign subsidiaries use newer or more sophisticated technologies than jointly owned investment projects, and thus it may be more difficult for them to find suitable suppliers locally.

Similarly, Javorcik's (2004a) study on Lithuania shows that positive vertical spillovers are associated with projects with shared domestic and foreign ownership but not with wholly owned foreign investments.

Another characteristic of FDI inflows that may affect spillovers is the nationality of foreign investors. Javorcik, Saggi, and Spatareanu (2004), who examine this question in the context of Romania, argue that such differences are likely to exist for two reasons. First, as the theoretical models of vertical linkages predict, the share of intermediate inputs sourced by multinationals in a host country is positively correlated with the distance between the multinational's headquarters and the production plant in the host country (Rodriguez-Clare 1996).[12] A larger share of local sourcing implies more contacts between multinationals and local firms in upstream sectors and a greater potential for knowledge transfer. Therefore, they expect a higher degree of vertical spillovers to be associated with American and Asian investors than with European multinationals, since home countries of the former are located much farther away from Romania.

Second, preferential trade agreements, which cover some but not all investors' home countries, are likely to affect the sourcing patterns of multinationals. For example, since Romania signed the Association Agreement with the European Union, its tariffs on imports from the European Union on the one hand, and United States and Japan on the other hand, are sharply different. During 1999, the average tariff applied by Romania on manufacturing imports from the United States and Japan was 15.78 percent, whereas the corresponding tariff on imports from the European Union was only 4.88 percent. Obviously, such a tariff structure creates a disincentive for American investors to source intermediates from their home country. Further, multinationals using Romania as an export platform can enjoy preferential (or even duty-free) access to the European Union provided a sufficient share of their product's value was added within the area covered by the agreement. This implies that while European investors' intermediate inputs purchased from their home country suppliers comply with the rules of origin, this is not the case for home country suppliers of American or Asian multinationals. Therefore, if multinationals cater primarily to export markets, American and Asian investors may have a greater incentive than European multinationals to source from Romania, and thus their presence may be associated with greater knowledge spillovers to Romanian firms in the supplying sectors.[13]

Further, the low propensity of European investors to source intermediate inputs from Romania may actually hurt domestic firms in upstream sectors. Entry of foreign investors is likely to increase the level of competition in downstream industries and drive weaker firms out of business. As they exit, part of their market share may be acquired by European multinationals, resulting in lower demand for domestically produced interme-

---

12. This prediction is confirmed by empirical evidence. Hanson, Mataloni, and Slaughter (2003) demonstrate that sales of intermediate inputs by US multinationals to their overseas affiliates decline with the trade costs.

13. Of course, this will not be true of all American or Asian investors, since many of them may still choose to import their inputs from the European Union. Nevertheless, a broad trend following this pattern could be expected. Similarly, a certain number of European investors could engage in local sourcing. Overall, however, one would expect that importing intermediate inputs would be more advantageous to European than to other multinationals, since they can combine sourcing for their headquarters, the Romanian plants, and possibly sister companies in Europe in order to enjoy volume discounts. It has been pointed out that centralized or pooled group sourcing arrangements may encourage affiliates to use foreign sources even when local suppliers are available (see UNCTAD 2001, 136).

diate inputs. Moreover, European investors entering Romania by acquiring local firms are likely to sever existing linkages with local suppliers, which again lowers the demand for domestically produced intermediates. A drop in demand for intermediates will force producers in the supplying sectors to spread their fixed cost over a smaller market share and thus will lower their productivity.

Several case studies from the automotive industry suggest that investor nationality may affect the extent of local sourcing. For instance, UNCTAD (2001, 166) reports that in the case of Suzuki's investment in Hungary, the rules of origin under the Association Agreement with the European Union were a factor in the firm's decision to operate in the country, create local linkages, and increase local value added, in order to enjoy duty-free access for car exports to the European Union. Similarly, Daewoo, which invested in Romania, stated that it intended to reach a 60 percent localization level of production. In 1997, 16.9 percent of the components of Daewoo's Cielo model were produced in Romania, and the 300 Romanian components were supplied by 43 Romanian companies. In 1997, about 40 percent of Cielos produced in Romania were exported, mainly to other Eastern European countries that signed the Association Agreement with the European Union. On the other hand, when the French multinational Renault purchased an equity stake in Dacia, the Romanian car maker, in 1999, it promised to continue sourcing inputs from local suppliers provided they lived up to its expectations. This, however, does not seem to have been the case. In 2002, 11 foreign suppliers of the French group were expected to start operating in Romania, thus replacing the Romanian producers from whom Dacia used to source (*Ziarul Financiar* [Financial Newspaper], April 19, 2001).

Javorcik, Saggi, and Spatareanu (2004) test their hypothesis using Romanian data from the *Amadeus* database for the period 1998–2000. They find a statistically significant and positive association between the presence of American and Asian companies in downstream sectors and the productivity of Romanian firms in the supplying industries. At the same time, the productivity of Romanian firms in the supplying sectors is negatively correlated with the operations of European investors in downstream industries. The differences between the effects associated with investors of different origin are statistically significant. The findings are robust to controlling for firm-specific fixed effects. Moreover, the results do not change after implementing the Olley and Pakes (1996) correction for endogeneity of input selection. Javorcik, Saggi, and Spatareanu (2004) conclude that the observed pattern is consistent with the hypothesis that FDI inflows from distant source countries and from countries that are not part of preferential trade agreements are more likely to be associated with local sourcing and vertical productivity spillovers.

Finally, there is yet another factor that may influence the degree of vertical spillovers—the market orientation of foreign investors. Case studies and the evidence from specific sectors suggest that domestic market-oriented affiliates tend to source more locally than foreign affiliates focused on export-ing. Export-oriented affiliates may source higher-quality inputs, thus lead-ing to greater learning on the part of suppliers. Javorcik (2004a) looked at this question in the context of Lithuania and found that there is some indi-cation that domestic market-oriented FDI projects are correlated with greater productivity spillovers to local suppliers in upstream sectors, but the evidence is not very robust.

Conclusions

Despite its importance to public policy, there is little conclusive evidence on the existence of spillovers in developing countries. It is a complex issue with no easy answers. As discussed above, in the face of difficulties associated with capturing the spillover effects and the multitude of factors that can influence the extent of spillovers in each country, we caution researchers about using limited evidence to draw generalized conclusions about the existence of externalities associated with FDI in developing countries.

References

Aitken, Brian J., and Ann E. Harrison. 1999. Do Domestic Firms Benefit from Direct Foreign Investment? Evidence from Venezuela. *American Economic Review* 89, no. 3: 605–18.

Aitken, Brian, Ann E. Harrison, and Robert E. Lipsey. 1996. Wages and Foreign Ownership: A Comparative Study of Mexico, Venezuela and the United States. *Journal of International Economics* 40, no. 3–4: 345–71.

Belderbos, Rene, Giovanni Capannelli, and Kyoji Fukao. 2001. Backward Vertical Linkages of Foreign Manufacturing Affiliates: Evidence from Japanese Multinationals. *World Development* 29, no. 1: 189–208.

Bernard, Andrew B., and J. Bradford Jensen. 1999. Exceptional Exporter Performance: Cause, Effect, or Both? *Journal of International Economics* 47: 1–25.

Blalock, Garrick, and Paul J. Gertler. 2004. Welfare Gains from Foreign Direct Investment through Technology Transfer to Local Suppliers. Cornell University. Photocopy.

Blomström, Magnus, and Ari Kokko. 1998. Multinational Corporations and Spillovers. *Journal of Economic Surveys* 12, no. 2: 1–31.

Blomström, Magnus, and Fredrik Sjöholm. 1999. Technology Transfer and Spillovers: Does Local Participation with Multinationals Matter? *European Economic Review* 43, no. 4–6: 915–23.

Clerides, Sofronis K., Saul Lach, and James R. Tybout. 1998. Is Learning by Exporting Important? Micro-Dynamic Evidence from Colombia, Mexico, and Morocco. *Quarterly Journal of Economics* 113, no. 3: 903–47.

Damijan, Joze P., Mark Knell, Boris Majcen, and Matija Rojec. 2003. The Role of FDI, R&D Accumulation and Trade in Transferring Technology to Transition Countries: Evidence from Firm Panel Data for Eight Transition Countries. *Economic Systems* 27: 189–204.

Dimelis, Sophia, and Helen Louri. 2001. *Foreign Direct Investment and Efficiency Benefits: A Conditional Quantile Analysis.* CEPR Working Paper 2868. London: Center for Economic Policy Research.

Djankov, Simeon, and Bernard Hoekman. 2000. Foreign Investment and Productivity Growth in Czech Enterprises. *World Bank Economic Review* 14, no. 1: 49–64.

Girma, Sourafel, David Greenaway, and Katharine Wakelin. 2001. Who Benefits from Foreign Direct Investment in the UK? *Scottish Journal of Political Economy* 48, no. 2: 119–33.

Görg, Holger, and Eric Strobl. 2001. Multinational Companies and Productivity Spillovers: A Meta-Analysis. *The Economic Journal* 111: 723–39.

Hanson, Gordon, Raymond Mataloni, and Matthew Slaughter. 2003. *Vertical Production Networks.* NBER Working Paper 9723. Cambridge, MA: National Bureau of Economic Research.

Haskel, Jonathan E., Sonia C. Pereira, and Matthew J. Slaughter. 2002. *Does Inward Foreign Direct Investment Boost the Productivity of Domestic Firms?* NBER Working Paper 8724. Cambridge, MA: National Bureau of Economic Research.

Javorcik, Beata Smarzynska. 2004a. Does Foreign Direct Investment Increase the Productivity of Domestic Firms? In Search of Spillovers through Backward Linkages. *American Economic Review* 94, no. 3: 605–27.

Javorcik, Beata Smarzynska. 2004b. The Composition of Foreign Direct Investment and Protection of Intellectual Property Rights: Evidence from Transition Economies. *European Economic Review* 48, no. 1: 39–62.

Javorcik, Beata Smarzynska, and Kamal Saggi. 2004. *Technological Asymmetry and the Mode of Foreign Investment.* World Bank Policy Research Working Paper 3196. Washington: World Bank.

Javorcik, Beata Smarzynska, and Mariana Spatareanu. 2003. *To Share or Not to Share: Does Local Participation Matter for FDI Spillovers?* World Bank Policy Research Working Paper 3118. Washington: World Bank.

Javorcik, Beata Smarzynska, Kamal Saggi, and Mariana Spatareanu. 2004. *Does It Matter Where You Come From? Vertical Spillovers from FDI and Investor Nationality.* World Bank Policy Research Working Paper 3449. Washington: World Bank.

Kinoshita, Y. 2001. *R&D and Technology Spillovers via FDI: Innovation and Absorptive Capacity.* CEPR Discussion Paper 2775. London: Centre for Economic Policy Research.

Konings, Jozef. 2001. The Effects of Foreign Direct Investment on Domestic Firms. *Economics of Transition* 9, no. 3: 619–33.

Mansfield, Edwin, and Anthony Romero. 1980. Technology Transfer to Overseas Subsidiaries by US-Based Firms. *Quarterly Journal of Economics* 95, no. 4: 737–50.

Melitz, Marc. 2003. The Impact of Trade on Intra-Industry Reallocations and Aggregate Industry Productivity. *Econometrica* 71, no. 6: 1695–725.

Moran, Theodore H. 2001. *Parental Supervision: The New Paradigm for Foreign Direct Investment and Development.* Washington: Institute for International Economics.

Olley, Steven G., and Ariel Pakes. 1996. The Dynamics of Productivity in the Telecommunications Equipment Industry. *Econometrica* 64, no. 6: 1263–97.

Ramachandran, Vijaya. 1993. Technology Transfer, Firm Ownership, and Investment in Human Capital. *Review of Economics and Statistics* 75, no. 4: 664–70.

Rodriguez-Clare, Andres. 1996. Multinationals, Linkages, and Economic Development. *American Economic Review* 85: 852–73.

Schoors, Koen, and Bartoldus van der Tol. 2001. The Productivity Effect of Foreign Ownership on Domestic Firms in Hungary. Paper presented at the International Atlantic Economic Conference in Philadelphia, PA.

Smarzynska, Beata, and Shang-Jin Wei. 2000. *Corruption and Composition of Foreign Direct Investment: Firm Level Evidence from Transition Economies.* NBER Working Paper 7969. Cambridge, MA: National Bureau of Economic Research.

United Nations Conference on Trade and Development (UNCTAD). 1987. *Arrangements between Joint Venture Partners in Developing Countries.* Advisory Study 2. New York: United Nations.

United Nations Conference on Trade and Development (UNCTAD). 2001. *World Investment Report. Promoting Linkages.* New York and Geneva: United Nations.

4

Foreign Direct Investment and Externalities: The Case for Public Intervention

GARRICK BLALOCK and PAUL J. GERTLER

Policymakers often argue that developing countries should encourage foreign direct investment (FDI) as a means of promoting economic growth. Central to the argument in support of FDI is the proposition of externalities—the total social benefits of FDI must exceed that internalized by the foreign entrant and its host economy partners. Using a rich dataset of Indonesian manufacturing firms, we investigate two rationales for policies encouraging FDI. First, we show that technology transferred from foreign entrants to local suppliers diffuses throughout the host country and generates welfare benefits to both firms and consumers. Second, we show that foreign investment is less vulnerable than domestic investment to liquidity constraints during times of financial crisis. Hence, FDI insures against market imperfections that limit credit availability in crisis. We discuss each of these externalities in turn.

Garrick Blalock is assistant professor, Department of Applied Economics and Management, Cornell University. Paul J. Gertler is professor at the Haas School of Business at the University of California, Berkeley, and research fellow at the National Bureau of Economic Research. We are indebted to Indra Surbakti, Fitria Fitrani, Kai Kaiser, and Jack Molyneaux for their assistance in compiling the data. We received helpful advice from David I. Levine, David Mowery, Pranab Bardhan, Ann Harrison, Mary Amati, James E. Blalock, Haryo Aswicahyono, and Thee Kian Wei. We thank the Institute of Business and Economic Research (IBER) and Management of Technology (MOT) program, both at the University of California, Berkeley, for their generous financial support. Finally, we are grateful to the factory managers in Indonesia who kindly participated in interviews.

Technology Spillover from FDI

The literature on technology spillover from FDI largely refers to the effect of foreign entrants on local incumbents. Proponents of FDI have argued that local firms can observe and adopt the technology brought from abroad and hence improve productivity. This "spillover" of technology thus creates an externality justifying policies encouraging FDI.

In contrast, we argue that technology diffusion from FDI is more likely directed to local suppliers than to local competitors, as a strategy to build efficient supply chains for multinationals' overseas operations. By transferring technology to local suppliers, multinationals may be able to improve quality and lower the price of nonlabor inputs. Indeed, while multinational enterprises may invest overseas to obtain low-wage labor or to avoid costly barriers to foreign markets, they realize the full benefit of expansion only if the efficiency of supply markets abroad matches or exceeds that of their home manufacturing base. To lower the prices and raise the quality of inputs abroad, multinationals might deliberately transfer technology to local vendors.

Such a strategy would cause foreign technology to diffuse along supply chains, rather than through spillovers to competitors. Indeed, anecdotal evidence from interviews we conducted with multinational and local firm managers in Indonesia suggests close cooperation through vertical linkages. Such cooperation, described below, exemplifies the mechanisms through which learning from FDI can occur vertically.

A cost-reduction motive implies that multinationals transfer technology along the supply chain to suppliers because such a transfer confers a private benefit to them. Therefore, unless an additional social benefit occurs, there is no case for public subsidies to stimulate technology transfers from multinationals. However, we argue that market imperfections cause multinationals to transfer technology widely, inducing heightened competition that benefits the whole economy. Since the multinational does not take this benefit into account, the social benefits from the technology transfer are greater than the private benefits. Without public subsidy, the multinational may transfer less technology than would be socially optimal.

How might the social benefits develop? The primary motivation for multinationals to transfer technology to suppliers is to enable higher-quality inputs at lower prices. One problem with this strategy is that if the enabling technology is transferred only to one upstream vendor, then the multinational is vulnerable to holdup. To mitigate holdup risk, the multinational could diffuse the technology widely—either by direct transfer to additional firms or by encouraging spillover from the original recipient. The technology's wide diffusion would then encourage entry in the supplier market, thereby increasing competition and lowering prices. However, the multinational cannot prevent the upstream suppliers from also selling to the multinational's competitors in the downstream market. The lower input prices may induce entry and more competition in the downstream market, thereby lowering prices and increasing output.

If prices fall enough, the multinational might be worse off by transferring technology to its upstream suppliers. In this case, the multinational would not have an incentive to transfer the technology. Pack and Saggi (2001), however, demonstrate that this concern is not justified under reasonable assumptions. As long as there is not too much entry, profits will rise in both the downstream and upstream markets, which suggests that the new surplus generated from increased productivity and reduced deadweight loss from increased competition might be split between consumers and producers in a Pareto improving distribution.

In this chapter we test the hypotheses that transfers of technology along the supply chain from FDI occur and that they lead to Pareto welfare improvements in terms of lower prices, higher production, and higher profits. The analysis is in two parts.

The first part measures the effect of FDI on local supplier productivity by estimating a production function using a rich panel dataset on local and foreign-owned Indonesian manufacturing establishments. Specifically, we test whether the productivity of firms increased when the share of their sector's output sold to foreign-owned firms increased. The results indicate that local firm productivity rises as the share of output sold to foreign-owned firms rises, which is consistent with the hypothesis that local suppliers acquire technology from the multinationals that buy the local suppliers' products.

The second part of the analysis examines the market and welfare effects of FDI technology diffusion, as hypothesized in Pack and Saggi (2001). We first estimate the effect of downstream FDI on upstream market concentration, prices, output, and value added. Further, we estimate the same metrics on firms in sectors downstream of sectors that supply multinational customers. We find that downstream FDI increases the output and value added of upstream firms and decreases prices and market concentration in upstream markets. We also find higher output and value added amongst downstream firms and lower prices and market concentration in markets downstream of markets supplying multinationals. This finding suggests that FDI leads to Pareto improving welfare effects— for example, benefits for consumers in terms of lower prices and for firms in the form of greater value added—transmitted both up and down the supply chain from FDI's technology spillovers.

Liquidity Insurance from FDI

A dramatic currency devaluation and a crippling decline of the banking sector are consequences of financial crises, as seen in East Asia, Latin America, and Russia. The combination of these two events can devastate new investment. Whereas net exporting firms should benefit from better terms of trade and increase investment, the collapse of the banking sector may prevent access to needed credit. Although changing terms of trade affect firms equally, ceteris paribus, the degree to which liquidity constraints bind may vary by firms' ownership. In particular, firms with foreign ownership may overcome liquidity constraints if they can access overseas credit through their parent companies. The possibility that foreign firms could continue to invest when local firms could not suggests a second externality of FDI: some insurance against liquidity constraints.

The unprecedented scale of Indonesia's currency devaluation and the severity of its banking sector's troubles provide a unique setting for our study. The East Asian financial crisis had a devastating effect on the Indonesian economy. The official measure of GDP dropped 13 percent in 1998, and investment fell 45 percent in 1998 alone, followed by a smaller decline in 1999. Some of this devastation is surprising since the financial crisis was associated with the largest real devaluation in recorded history. A US dollar could buy four to six times as much volume of Indonesian exports in early 1998 as in mid-1997. Although rapid Indonesian inflation eliminated roughly half the nominal devaluation, a 2:1 real devaluation remains almost unprecedented. With this large a change in trade terms, conventional trade theory suggests that Indonesian firms should have enjoyed an export boom.

At the same time, this event is not known as a currency crisis but as a financial crisis (*krismon*, or monetary crisis, in Indonesian). Most banks in Indonesia were insolvent by 1998. Press reports indicated that many firms, even those that wanted to export, were unable to access capital. Lenders had difficulty distinguishing between insolvent borrowers—for whom new loans would go toward old loan repayment rather than productive investments—and firms that legitimately needed funds for ongoing operations or attractive investments. Moreover, even if a lender could identify solvent firms, International Monetary Fund (IMF) banking reforms may have reduced many banks' willingness to make *any* loans. Under threat of closure if they could not meet raised reserve requirements, in the short run banks may have preferred holding cash to granting even highly profitable loans.

It is plausible that these problems were less severe at plants with foreign owners, who presumably had access to the accounts and could confirm the desirability of new investment and monitor spending. Foreign owners, particularly large multinationals, could finance their Indonesian factories internally or through lines of credit available to the parent company.

We proceed as follows. The next three sections review the extant literature on technology transfer and introduce the conceptual framework and underlying theory for our study. The fifth section provides some background on manufacturing and FDI in Indonesia, and the sixth section describes the data. The seventh section details the identification strategy and results for the productivity effects of FDI. The eighth section reviews the results for the market and welfare effects of FDI, the ninth section discusses liquidity insurance from FDI, and the final section provides a conclusion.

Conceptual Framework of Technology Transfer from FDI

Most of the literature recognizes two major channels for technology transfer from FDI: horizontal flows to local competitors (sometimes called "spillover" because it is largely an externality), and vertical flows to backwardly linked suppliers. We define technology broadly to mean the managerial practices, production methods, and other tacit and codified know-how by which a firm transforms capital, labor, and materials into a product. Below we describe the mechanisms by which local firms could learn through each channel and summarize the empirical evidence.[1] We first discuss horizontal transfer, which has been the focus of most empirical work, and suggest why recent studies have found mixed evidence of transfer through this channel. We next discuss vertical transfer, the emphasis of this chapter, and argue that the incentives of multinational investors could promote technology transfer through this channel. Finally, we describe why vertical transfers would induce competition and the circumstance under which the technology transfer induces a Pareto improvement in welfare.

Horizontal Technology Transfer

Multinational entry may provide positive technological externalities to local competitors through a number of mechanisms. First, the local firms may be able to learn simply by observing and imitating the multinationals. Second, employees may leave multinationals to create or join local firms. Third, multinational investment may encourage the entry of international trade brokers, accounting firms, consultant companies, and other professional services, which then may become available to local firms as well.

Multinational entry may also hurt local firms. First, foreign firms may hire talent away from local firms, thereby creating a "brain drain." Second, foreign firms, which often pay higher wages, may raise wages for all firms in competitive labor markets (Aitken, Harrison, and Lipsey 1996). If the higher wages do not reflect an improvement of employee capabilities, which may be the case if the multinational faces public pressure in its home market to improve overseas workers' conditions, then firms may substitute capital for labor in an otherwise (prior to the wage increase) inefficient manner.

---

1. Kumar (1996), Blomström and Kokko (1997), Keller (2001), and Moran (2001) provide extensive literature reviews.

Empirical studies of technology spillover have found mixed results. The studies, which regress local firm productivity on within-sector FDI, fall into two categories: those that use cross-sectional data (e.g., Caves 1974, Globerman 1979, and Blomström and Wolff 1994) and those that use panel data (e.g., Haddad and Harrison 1993, Kokko 1994, Aitken and Harrison 1999, and Haskel, Pereira, and Slaughter 2002). The former typically find a positive correlation between local firm productivity and FDI. However, cross-sectional analysis cannot distinguish whether FDI actually increases local firm productivity or whether multinational investors simply invest in inherently more productive sectors. Studies using panel data, which can control for investor selection bias, reach differing conclusions. On one hand, Aitken and Harrison's (1999) examination of Venezuelan factories finds net negative benefits to local firms, a result they attribute to the effect of foreign competition. On the other hand, Haskel, Pereira, and Slaughter (2002) employ similar methods with a panel dataset of factories in the United Kingdom and draw the opposite conclusion.

Host economy heterogeneity and limitations of production function estimation likely explain the contrary results. First, the technology gap between foreign and domestic firms likely varies by country and industry. In cases in which the gap is wide, local firms may lack the absorptive capacity needed to recognize and adopt the new technology. Similarly, the degree to which foreign and domestic firms actually compete in the same market will also vary. Domestic firms may produce for the local market, while multinationals produce for export. Because of differences in quality and other attributes, exported and domestically consumed goods may entail different production methods that reduce the potential for technology transfer. Second, multinationals may enact measures to minimize technology leakage to local competitors. In particular, multinationals with nonprotectable technology may not enter the market at all if they rely on a technological advantage to sustain rents. Again, the level of technology multinationals bring to the host economy and the degree to which it can be protected will vary widely. Last, production function estimation may confound the productivity gains from technology transfer with the efficiency losses from increased competition. If multinationals capture market share, then local firms may underutilize existing capacity in the short run. Although local firms will eventually redeploy slack resources, production function estimation will interpret nonutilized resources as a productivity loss in the short run.

Vertical Technology Transfer

Vertical technology transfer could occur through both *backward* (from buyer to supplier) and *forward* (from supplier to buyer) linkages. Because most multinationals in Indonesia are export oriented and generally do not supply Indonesian customers, we focus on technology transfer through backward linkages. That is, we examine the effect of *downstream* FDI on the performance of local suppliers.

Two arguments suggest that supply chains may be conduits for technology transfer. First, whereas multinationals seek to minimize technology leakage to competitors, they have incentives to improve the productivity of their suppliers—for example, through training, quality control, and inventory management. To reduce dependency on a single supplier, the multinational may establish such relationships with multiple vendors, which benefits all firms that purchase these vendors' output. Second, while the technology gap between foreign and domestic producers may limit within-sector technology transfer, multinationals likely procure inputs requiring less sophisticated production techniques for which the gap is narrower.

Evidence of technology transfer through vertical supply chains is well documented in case studies. For example, Kenney and Florida (1993) and MacDuffie and Helper (1997) provide a rich description of technology transfer to US parts suppliers following the entry of Japanese automobile makers. Until recently, empirical analysis, however, has generally been limited to small samples, such as the study by Lall (1980), which documents technology transfer from foreign firms through backward linkages in the Indian trucking industry. Kugler (2000) is the first large-sample empirical study and shows that FDI in one sector of Colombian manufacturing can precede productivity gains in another. Kugler, however, does not identify backward linkages or any particular causal mechanisms for the intersector spillover. Blalock (2002) and Javorcik (2004) find causal evidence of technology transfer through backward linkages in the manufacturing sectors of Indonesia and Lithuania respectively.

Anecdotal evidence from interviews with multinational and Indonesian firms points to the specific mechanisms through which vertical technology may occur.[2] An American firm reported that its process of qualifying domestic suppliers involved several stages over a few years. First, the American firm's engineers would visit the local factory to inspect its facilities and suggest needed modifications. Next, a sample product was sent to a testing facility in the United States. If the product was approved, the suppliers were sent to overseas training classes to learn the multinational's systems for inventory control, quality control, and cost accounting. Thereafter, the supplier would be asked to produce a small amount of the total production demand. Only after the supplier had successfully established a record of delivering on time and within specification would the multinational qualify it as a large-scale supplier.

Managers from a Japanese multinational reported a similar process. They added that it was common for them to introduce good suppliers to affiliate

---

2. We interviewed managers from two American, two Japanese, and two Indonesian firms in Jakarta during July 2000.

companies in their industrial group, both in Indonesia and in other countries. By doing so, they could increase their suppliers' economies of scale and smooth their capacity utilization. Likewise, the same Japanese firm reported that it often used suppliers in Malaysia and Thailand that were referred to it by affiliate companies. This reduced the dependence on local suppliers and ensured that Indonesian vendors were competitive within the region. The goal, noted by the manager, was to guarantee a reliable supply of parts from a handful of the best local firms in Southeast Asia.

Not all of the foreign firms reported success in local procurement. Another Japanese firm noted that it bought very little from local suppliers, other than cardboard boxes and paper packaging. The manager noted that although he would like to buy more locally and faced some pressure to do so, it was just not practical. Most local firms could not meet his requirements for quality, price, and delivery performance. Instead, he preferred to buy from the firm's established vendors in Japan. He added, however, that many of those vendors were themselves producing in Indonesia and surrounding countries.

Indonesian suppliers cited some benefits from selling to foreign customers. One vendor reported that his relationship with a large Japanese firm was valuable because the customer sent engineers from Japan annually to review his production methods and suggest improvements for cost reduction. He added that the Japanese firm's desire for extremely consistent product attributes had prompted him to invest in new machinery imported from Switzerland. In contrast, however, he stated that his relationship with an American buyer had been less successful. The Americans, he complained, had unobtainable goals for cost reduction, did not provide him with sufficient lead time for orders (necessitating that he pay expensive overtime wages), and offered no technical support to meet their requirements. In the end, the American firm rejected much of his supply on quality grounds (which he disputed), and he voluntarily severed the relationship.

Many of the reported mechanisms for technology transfer through supply chains would apply equally to exports. One Indonesian firm reported that it exported 100 percent of its output to Germany. Its main customer, a large German consumer goods company, reportedly sent efficiency experts to advise on how best to expand production capacity. In fact, during the day of the interview, four product designers from the German customer were at the plant advising how to adapt the product appearance to suit new consumer trends. The Indonesian manager observed that the increased sales, which were largely driven by lower labor costs following the massive devaluation of the rupiah in 1997, had strained his accounting resources. He complained that the higher volume made it difficult for his planners to know if production was on schedule. Consequently, he could not respond quickly to customer requests for time-critical orders. To solve the problem, the Indonesian manager had just ordered inventory control software from

Europe. When financing the purchase, one of the largest capital investments since building the factory, he had borrowed from the Jakarta branch of an American bank using the German customer's letter of intent to order as evidence of his creditworthiness.[3]

Market Competition and Welfare Effects of Technology Transfer

We hypothesize that multinationals transfer technology to suppliers to reduce input costs and increase quality. However, if the multinational aids only a single supplier, the supplier can play holdup and capture all of the rents from its increased productivity. In this case, the multinational would not benefit from the technology transfer. The multinational could overcome this vulnerability, however, by distributing the technology widely to multiple suppliers and potential entrants. This would create multiple sources of superior supply and would encourage entry (competition) that would lower prices. Total surplus rises because the new technology increases productivity and because the deadweight from imperfect competition falls. The downstream multinational captures some of the rent, because the prices it pays for supplies have fallen. However, if there is not too much entry, the suppliers may also capture some of the rent in terms of profits resulting from increased productivity and sales (Pack and Saggi 2001).

We would thus expect to see direct technology transfer to several suppliers, or a program that makes the technology broadly available to the supply sector. Moreover, technology leaks between the original local technology recipient and its rivals is possible. In fact, if any horizontal technology transfer is to occur, it seems more likely to happen among local supply firms than between foreign and local firms in the end-product market.

Although the multinational has an incentive to aid many suppliers, doing so may inadvertently aid competitors if the more productive supply base is a nonexcludable benefit. In other words, the multinational cannot prevent its now more productive suppliers from selling to the multinationals' rivals at lower prices in the downstream market. The lower supply prices may induce entry and increase competition so that prices fall in the downstream markets. This increases surplus by lowering costs of production and by reducing deadweight loss from imperfect competition. In addition, the lower supply prices increase surplus not only in the multinational's market but in all of the markets to which the suppliers sell.

---

3. A number of interviewed managers mentioned the role of foreign firms in helping Indonesian suppliers obtain credit during the Asian financial crisis. Because 1996 is the last year of empirical analysis for this study, this role does not affect the results in our study.

Generally, in a developing country, export-oriented foreign firms are more productive than domestic firms and seldom compete with domestic makers, so aiding local buyers may not concern multinationals. However, foreign firms may be concerned that their investment in the local supply chain will eventually benefit later foreign entrants. Given this possibility, foreign firms might be reluctant to transfer technology to suppliers.

Pack and Saggi (2001) show that, provided new competition is not too great, the benefits of a competitive supply base to the multinational buyer outweigh the rents lost to freeloading rivals. Perhaps surprisingly, technology diffusion and leakage to other local suppliers can also benefit the initial local recipient. In the case of a single supplier and single buyer with some market power, both parties set prices above marginal cost—the "double marginalization problem." If technology diffusion to other upstream firms allows more capable suppliers to enter, then one would expect market concentration and input prices to fall. Further, given the benefit of lower-priced inputs, firms downstream of that upstream sector will lower prices and increase output, and new firm entry may occur. The stronger demand downstream would, in turn, prompt higher output upstream that would help the initial technology recipient (Rodriguez-Clare 1996). Lower prices and greater volume clearly generate a surplus for consumers. Pack and Saggi (2001) note that in some cases, firms may also be able to capture some of the surplus because the benefits of lower input prices and higher volume outweigh the costs of greater competition. Hence, we would expect to see firm value added—a proxy for profitability—rise.[4] Figure 4.1 illustrates the total effect of FDI.

If this is true, then technology transfer to suppliers is in multinationals' interest, but the benefits accrue widely to all sectors and consumers not only through improved productivity but also through increased competition resulting in lower deadweight loss. Hence, technology transfer induces a Pareto improvement in welfare. However, a multinational might not take into account the social benefits of increased competition and, therefore, may transfer too little technology. In this case, it would be socially optimal to facilitate the transfer of technology from multinationals to local suppliers.

Testable Implications of Technology Transfer Through Supply Chains

Although the specific mechanisms for technology transfer described above are typically unobservable in the data, one can identify technology trans-

---

4. We define value added as revenue minus wages and the cost of materials and energy. This is similar to EBITDA—earnings before interest, taxes, depreciation, and amortization—a common proxy for profitability.

Figure 4.1   Flow of technology and welfare effects from FDI

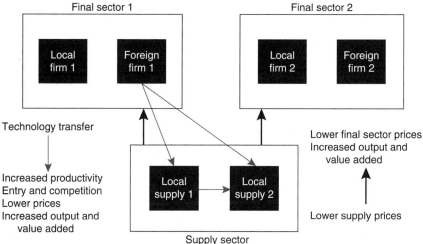

fer indirectly by otherwise unexplained productivity gains. If vertical supply chains are conduits for technology transfer, then one would expect, ceteris paribus, that local firms in industries and regions with growing levels of downstream FDI would show greater productivity growth than other local firms. Furthermore, one would expect to see lower concentration, lower prices, higher output, and more value added in these beneficiary sectors, as well as in sectors downstream of them. The methodology for testing the productivity effects is described in the seventh section, and the methodology for testing the market and welfare effects is described in the eighth section. Both are preceded by some background on Indonesian manufacturing and a description of the data in the following two sections.

Conceptual Framework for FDI and Liquidity Insurance[5]

The imperfection of capital markets and liquidity constraints are well documented (Fazzari, Hubbard, and Petersen 1988; Hoshi, Kashyap, and Scharfstein 1991; and Minton and Schrand 1999; see also surveys by Hubbard 1998 and Caballero and Krishnamurthy 1999). The key insight of these papers is that some firms are likely to have access to capital and thus their invest-

---

5. Our discussion here summarizes material from Blalock, Gertler, and Levine (2004), to which interested readers are referred for a more in-depth discussion.

ment responds to future profit opportunities. Other firms are likely to have limited access to capital and thus investment responds to current cash flow more than to future profit opportunities. The referenced studies have used a number of strategies to identify firms at high versus low risk of liquidity constraints. The current analysis extends this literature by using foreign ownership as an indicator of high probability of liquidity constraints—an assumption we discuss at length below.

A second set of literature examines financial crises, with an emphasis on how they reduce banks' willingness to lend to borrowers with weak balance sheets (for example, Bernanke and Gertler 1989). Recent work has examined how currency and financial crises affect investment (see Aguiar 2002, Forbes 2002, Agenor and Montiel 1996, Reinhart and Calvo 2000). Many of these analyses have differentiated how the crisis affects the tradable sector (where a devaluation is likely to expand opportunities for profitable investment) from nontradable sectors. Like Desai, Foley, and Forbes (2003), which reviews US multinational investment during a variety of currency crises, we differentiate foreign-owned from locally owned firms within the tradable sector. We find that foreign-owned firms respond very differently from local firms to financial shocks.

A third set of literature examines how financial crises affect FDI (see, for example, Lipsey 2001). We extend this literature by explicitly comparing the response of foreign-owned and comparable locally owned firms. Thus we see whether the differences previous analyses have discovered are largely due to size and industry, or due to ownership itself. As such, we are part of the tradition of researchers examining how FDI affects the host economy differently from locally owned investment (see, for example, Aitken and Harrison 1999; Blalock and Gertler 2004).

Theories

First, we review what outcomes conventional trade theory predicts should follow a massive real devaluation. Then, we discuss theories of investment subject to financial constraints as well as a set of theories that are clearly relevant during a financial crisis. We close this section with a discussion of how foreign ownership might mitigate financial constraints and increase the relevance of standard trade theory predictions.

Trade Theory

Conventional trade theory assumes that relative prices are important, and no price is more important than the relative price of currency—the real exchange rate. When a currency undergoes a real devaluation, exports become more competitive. In addition, firms that compete against imported goods become more competitive. These increases in competitiveness should have several testable implications: higher profits, more employment, and increased investment. A number of studies, such as Aguiar (2002), demonstrated such findings using firm data.

Working in the other direction, firms that import most of their raw and intermediate goods, in contrast, become less competitive. For firms that both import and export, trade theory predicts that net exports (exports minus imports) are what should predict shifts in competitiveness.

Trade theory predicts that the expansionary effect of devaluation will be muted if competitors also have devaluations. In Indonesia's case, Thailand and Malaysia, for example, also devalued around 1997 and China had also undergone a large devaluation shortly before. Because these countries' real devaluation was much smaller than Indonesia's, one would still predict higher net exports for Indonesia.

Trade theory also suggests that the expansionary effect of a nominal devaluation will be muted if inflation reduces the improvement in competitiveness. Such inflation is a common occurrence after nominal devaluations and often implies that the real exchange rate remains fairly stable. Indonesia, as expected, had a massive spike in inflation with the price level (as measured by the wholesale price index) roughly doubling from December 1997 to December 1998. Inflation fell to low levels by the start of 1999, and the cumulative inflation from 1997 to 2000 left the majority of the initial real devaluation intact.

In fact, US dollar exports of manufactured goods rose from 50 billion in 1996–97 to 53 billion in 1999 (IMF 2000, table 42). Thus, while exports were roughly flat in dollar terms and (presumably) in quantity terms, their value roughly doubled in inflation-adjusted rupiah terms assuming the relative price of exports remained unchanged.

Financial Constraints

Why did the dollar volume of manufacturing exports not increase? One reason may be the poor state of Indonesia's banking industry. Any downturn increases banks' lending risk because more of their customers are near bankruptcy. Indonesia's notorious lack of financial transparency and weak bankruptcy laws amplified this effect, since banks were unable to verify which customers were already bankrupt. Loans to bankrupt customers were unlikely to ever be repaid.

In addition, after the financial crisis banks stated that they preferred to lend to customers with whom they had an ongoing relationship (Agung et al. 2001). As numerous banks closed during and after the financial crisis, relationship-specific ties were broken, and some viable firms may have lost access to credit.

As the crisis continued, Indonesia established new regulatory mechanisms that forced most banks to recognize their underperforming loans (Enoch et al. 2001). The result was extremely low capital in banks, which further discouraged lending.

The outcome of the slower demand for and supply of credit was dramatic. Between 1996 and 2000 the real value of credit from commercial banks to the manufacturing sector fell by roughly half (comparing IMF 2000, table 35, on credit with the earlier tables on Wholesale Price Indexes (WPI) and Consumer Price Indexes (CPI)). Presumably credit from foreign sources fell even faster as foreign capital poured out of Indonesia during the crisis.

Lower demand for credit caused most of this decline in total credit. Nevertheless, if constraints on credit supply by potentially credit-worthy borrowers caused even a portion of the decline, it is unsurprising that investment fell. Analyzing surveys of banks and of manufacturing plants, Agung et al. (2001) concluded that lack of bank capital (as opposed to high borrower risk) caused much of the slowdown in lending.

Foreign Ownership and Financial Constraints

Above we argued that domestic banks may have refused loans to firms that could export profitably since the banks could not determine which firms were already bankrupt and unlikely to repay their loans. An Indonesian plant with substantial foreign ownership should not have this problem, as the foreign owner can document that the plant is, in fact, making money. Indeed, evidence suggests that foreign affiliates often substitute internal borrowing for external borrowing when operating in environments with poorly developed financial markets (Desai, Foley, and Hines 2003).

For firms that primarily sell to the domestic market, the benefits of foreign ownership may be slight; such firms frequently should contract output regardless of liquidity constraints. Thus, the hypothesis of foreign ownership as an antidote to financial crisis should be most visible for firms that export or compete with imports.

Three forces mitigate this hypothesis. First, some assembly plants import materials whose value constitutes a large proportion of final sales. Even so, the devaluation greatly reduced the cost of labor—the main cost as a share of value added. Nevertheless, to the extent that the percentage of imports and exports is exogenous, standard trade theory suggests that net exports (that is, exports minus imports) should matter more than the export share in predicting desired expansion after the devaluation and financial crisis.

Second, the financial crisis was accompanied by an increase in political risk. Foreign firms might consider the weaker currency insufficient to counteract the risks of large capital losses. Particularly if managers are risk averse, they might be loath to invest in Indonesia if the economy were likely to implode so badly that basic infrastructure eroded, a civil war broke out, or some other catastrophic event that would depreciate assets occurred. For example, rioters opposed to IMF programs presumably led all foreigners to fear for their personal safety and that of their assets.

Although plausible, it is not clear why rising political risk affected foreign owners more than many domestic investors. That is, a substantial majority of Indonesia's large companies are owned by those closely associated with Suharto (Fisman 2001), by the ethnic Chinese minority in Indonesia, or by businessmen who are both. These groups had strong reasons to fear that either a new government might take over their businesses or a mob might destroy them. These risks may have been larger than those faced by foreign investors.

Third, firms with foreign equity ownership, as well as those that export, may disproportionately have been those with foreign debt. The devaluation vastly increased the rupiah cost-of-servicing debt denominated in dollars, yen, or other hard currencies.

Indonesian Manufacturing and Foreign Investment Policy

Indonesia's manufacturing sector is an attractive setting for research on FDI and technology transfer for several reasons. First, with the fourth largest population in the world and thousands of islands stretching over three time zones, the country has abundant labor and natural resources to support a large sample of manufacturing facilities in a wide variety of industries. Furthermore, the country's size and resources support a full supply chain, from raw materials to intermediate and final goods, and both export and domestic markets. Second, rapid and localized industrialization provides variance in manufacturing activity in both time and geography. Third, the country's widespread island archipelago geography and generally poor transportation infrastructure create a number of local markets, each of which can support independent supply chains. Fourth, a number of institutional reforms of investment law have dramatically increased the amount of FDI and export activity in recent years. In particular, the nature and timing of these reforms provide exogenous variation in FDI by region, industry, and time that will be exploited in the econometric identification. Last, Indonesian government agencies employ a number of well-trained statisticians who have collected exceptionally rich manufacturing data for a developing country. The remainder of this section provides some background on Indonesian manufacturing and foreign investment policy with the intent of highlighting institutional changes that contribute to the longitudinal variation we exploit in the econometric identification. Readers not interested in this background may skip ahead without loss of continuity.

Growth in Manufacturing

The Indonesian economy and the manufacturing sector grew dramatically from the late 1970s until the recent financial crisis.[6] Indonesia enjoyed an average annual GDP growth rate of 6–7 percent, and manufacturing, which drove most of this growth, expanded from 11 percent of GDP in 1980 to 25 percent in 1996 (Nasution 1995). Government initiatives to reduce dependency on oil and gas revenue in the mid-1980s—principally liberalization of financial markets and foreign exchange, a shift from an import-substitution regime to export promotion, currency devaluation, and relaxation of foreign investment laws—facilitated the large increase in manufacturing output (Goeltom 1995).

Foreign Investment Policy

Over the past 40 years, government regulation has shifted dramatically from a policy antagonistic to FDI to a policy actively encouraging it (Wie 1994a, 137–66; Hill 1988; Pangestu 1996). Following independence from the Netherlands in 1945, the Sukarno government nationalized many of the former Dutch manufacturing enterprises. Weak property rights and socialist rhetoric kept foreign investment at a trickle throughout the 1950s and 1960s.

The first reforms came in 1967 as part of the "New Order" economic regime of Suharto, who had purged the government of left-wing elements during his rise to power. Many of the assets nationalized after independence were returned and the 1967 Foreign Investment Law No. 1 established a licensing procedure for foreign operations that remains the basis of current policy. Although, in principle, Foreign Investment Law No. 1 allowed FDI with few restrictions, in practice obtaining an operating license was onerous. Nevertheless, FDI, primarily from Japan, did begin to flow into labor-intensive sectors, such as textiles.

Negative nationalistic reaction to foreign investment and complaints from local firms prompted the Indonesian government to impose restrictions, particularly on entrants that produced for the local market. Opposition to FDI culminated in violent protests during the 1974 Jakarta visit of Japanese Prime Minister Kakuei Tanaka. Suharto responded with a presidential decree restricting the sectors open for new foreign investment and

---

6. Hill (1988) and Pangestu and Sato (1997) provide detailed histories of Indonesian manufacturing from the colonial period to the present.

limiting the maximum allowable foreign equity in manufacturing operations. Most notably, all new investment had to be through joint ventures with Indonesian partners, who were required to own at least 20 percent of equity initially and 51 percent within 10 years of operation.

Because of the restrictions on equity holdings, foreign firms adopted other mechanisms for controlling their operations. Japanese investors, for example, would maintain effective control of joint ventures in which they had minority equity stakes by increasing the debt-to-equity ratio and licensing or leasing production technology and equipment (Wie 1994b). Embedded in such arrangements was the option to withhold the financing, equipment, and know-how needed for the plant's viability if the foreign investor considered that it did not have effective control.

Following the collapse of oil prices in the mid-1980s, the Indonesian government began to seek outside investment more actively. From 1986 to 1994, it introduced a number of exemptions to the 1974 regulations. The exemptions were targeted to multinationals investing in particular locations, notably a bonded zone on the island of Batam (only 20 kilometers from Singapore), government-sponsored industrial parks, and undeveloped provinces of east Indonesia. The new policy also granted exemptions to investment in capital-intensive, technology-intensive, and export-oriented sectors. The exemptions typically allowed a lower minimum initial Indonesian equity stake, a lower long-term Indonesian equity target, and a longer period to achieve that target (often as long as 20 years). Moreover, the reforms reduced or eliminated import tariffs for certain capital goods and for materials that would be assembled and exported.

Finally, in 1994 the government lifted nearly all equity restrictions on foreign investment. Multinationals in most sectors were allowed to establish and maintain operations in perpetuity with 100 percent equity. In a handful of sectors deemed strategically important, a nominal 5 percent Indonesian holding was required with no further requirement to divest. These reforms have been accompanied by large increases in both the absolute and the relative value of foreign production in Indonesian manufacturing.

The Indonesian Financial Crisis

Beginning in August 1997, Indonesia, like other nations severely affected by the Asian financial crisis, experienced a sudden and widespread financial panic. By January 1998, the Indonesian rupiah (Rp) was worth 15 percent of its value six months earlier, and GDP growth fell from +8 percent in 1996 to −13 percent in 1998. Austerity measures, inflation, very high interest rates, and a massive credit crunch brought the crisis from the financial sector to manufacturing plants. Box 4.1 lays out a timeline of the crisis.

Box 4.1 Timeline of the Indonesian financial crisis

1997

July 2	Thai baht is floated and depreciates by 15–20 percent
July 11	Widening of rupiah band
July 24	Currency meltdown with severe pressure on baht, ringgit, peso, and rupiah
August 14	Ending of rupiah band and immediate plunge
November 1	Sixteen banks closed, with promise of more to follow. Deposits were not guaranteed
November 5	Three-year standby agreement with IMF approved
Mid-December	Almost half of Indonesian bank deposits exit the system

1998

Mid-January	Further downward pressure on the rupiah
January 27	Bank deposits formally guaranteed by the new superagency, the Indonesia Bank Reconstruction Agency
March 11	President Suharto reelected
Mid-May	Widespread rioting
May 21	Vice President Habibe succeeds Suharto as president

Source: Enoch et al. (2001).

Data

The analysis is based on data from the Republic of Indonesia's *Budan Pusat Statistik* (BPS), the Central Bureau of Statistics.[7] The primary data are taken from an unpublished annual survey of manufacturing establishments with more than 20 employees conducted by *Biro Statistik Industri,* the Industrial Statistics Division of BPS. Additional data include the input-output (IO) table and several input and output price deflators.

The principal dataset is the *Survei Tahunan Perusahaan Industri Pengolahan* (SI), the Annual Manufacturing Survey conducted by the Industrial Statistics Division of BPS. The SI dataset is designed to be a complete annual enumeration of all manufacturing establishments with 20 or more employees from 1975 onward. Depending on the year, the SI includes up to 160 variables covering industrial classification (five-digit International Standard of Industrial Classification (ISIC) code), ownership (public, private, or foreign), status of incorporation, assets, asset changes, electricity, fuels, income, output, expenses, investment, labor (head count, education, wages), raw material use, machinery, and other specialized questions.

---

7. We identify names in Bahasa Indonesian, the language of most government publications, with italics. Subsequently, we use the English equivalent or the acronym.

**Table 4.1 Key variables affecting technology spillover,
1988 and 1996**

	Number domestic firms	Number foreign firms	Horizontal FDI	Downstream FDI	Suppliers' downstream FDI
1988	8,888	276	.131	.060	.074
1996	14,912	888	.232	.094	.118

BPS submits a questionnaire annually to all registered manufacturing establishments, and field agents attempt to visit each nonrespondent to either encourage compliance or confirm that the establishment has ceased operation.[8] Because field office budgets are partly determined by the number of reporting establishments, agents have some incentive to identify and register new plants. In recent years, over 20,000 factories have been surveyed annually. Government laws guarantee that the collected information will be used only for statistical purposes. However, several BPS officials commented that some establishments intentionally misreport financial information out of concern that tax authorities or competitors may gain access to the data. Because the fixed-effect analysis admits only within-factory variation on a logarithmic scale, errors of under- or overreporting will not bias the results provided that each factory consistently misreports over time. Further, even if the degree of misreporting for a factory varies over time, the results are unbiased provided the misreporting is not correlated with other factory attributes used in the analysis.

Our analysis starts from 1988, the first year data on fixed assets are available. To avoid measurement error in price and other uncertainties introduced by the 1997–98 Asian financial crisis, 1996 is the last year for our analysis of technology spillover. The key variables are described in and summarized for 1988 and 1996 in table 4.1. The table indicates a large increase in the number of foreign factories, which increased from 276 in 1988 to 888 in 1996. On average, foreign factories are bigger (as measured by value added, employees, and capital), more capital intensive (as measured by capital per employee), more productive (as measured by value added per employee), and more export oriented (as measured by percentage of production exported). (See table 4.2.)

---

8. Because some firms may have more than one factory, we henceforth refer to each observation as an establishment, plant, or factory. BPS also submits a different questionnaire to the head office of every firm with more than one factory. Although the data from the head office were not available for this study, early analysis by BPS suggests that fewer than 5 percent of factories belong to multifactory firms. Thus, we generalize our results and discuss them in terms of firms.

Table 4.2   Descriptive statistics of foreign and domestic firms, 1988 and 1996

	Domestic	Foreign
1988		
log(capital)	11.257	14.086
Employees	124	364
log(materials)	11.171	14.421
log(energy)	7.388	8.881
log(value added)	10.438	14.068
log(value added per worker)	6.447	8.765
1996		
log(capital)	11.691	14.659
Employees	147	584
log(materials)	11.588	14.893
log(energy)	7.347	8.618
log(value added)	11.039	14.580
log(value added per worker)	6.973	8.967

Note: Capital, materials, energy, and value added are reported in thousands of 1988 rupiah.

We derived interindustry supply chains using IO tables published by BPS in 1990 and 1995. The tables show the value added of goods and services produced by the economic sector and how this value is distributed to other economic sectors. The IO tables divide manufacturing activity into 89 sectors, and BPS provides concordance tables linking the 1990 and 1995 IO codes to five-digit ISIC codes as described in Blalock (2002). We deflated output, materials, energy, and capital to express values in real terms. Blalock (2002) describes the deflator calculation in detail.

Not surprisingly, particularly in a developing-country environment, a high level of nonreporting and obvious erroneous responses to many of the survey questions occur, particularly to questions that require some accounting expertise (for example, for answers to questions regarding the replacement and book value of fixed assets). We removed establishments with especially numerous nonresponses to fundamental questions such as number of employees. In other cases, we imputed some variables to correct for nonreporting in just one or two years or to fix obvious clerical mistakes in data keypunching. We cleaned each variable independently and only removed establishments from the analysis for which the needed variables could not be constructed. For example, establishments with missing wage data could be used for output regression but not for value added regression. Thus, readers will notice slight differences in the sample count across different regressions. We also note that analysis on completely raw data yields very similar results to what we report, although standard errors are slightly higher. Blalock (2002) describes the process by which we prepared the data in more detail.

Productivity Effects of FDI

Our strategy to identify the effect of downstream FDI on productivity is to examine whether domestic establishments that sell more to foreign-owned firms produce more, ceteris paribus. We estimate this effect using a translog production function with establishment fixed effect, year-region dummies, and measures of FDI. The translog production function controls for input levels and scale effects. The establishment fixed effects control for time-invariant differences across sectors and firms, and the year-region dummies control for local market changes over time common to all firms in that region. Specifically, we define the establishment-level translog production function as:

$$\ln Y_{it} = \beta_0 Downstream\_FDI_{jrt} + \beta_1 \ln K_{it} + \beta_2 \ln L_{it} + \beta_3 \ln M_{it} + \beta_4 \ln E_{it}$$
$$+ \beta_5 \ln^2 K_{it} + \beta_6 \ln^2 L_{it} + \beta_7 \ln^2 M_{it} + \beta_8 \ln^2 E_{it}$$
$$+ \beta_9 \ln K_{it} \ln L_{it} + \beta_{10} \ln K_{it} \ln M_{it} + \beta_{11} \ln K_{it} \ln E_{it}$$
$$+ \beta_{12} \ln L_{it} \ln M_{it} + \beta_{13} \ln L_{it} \ln E_{it} + \beta_{14} \ln M_{it} \ln E_{it}$$
$$+ \lambda_{gt} + \alpha_i + \gamma_t + \varepsilon_{it} \tag{4.1}$$

where Y_{it}, K_{it}, L_{it}, M_{it}, and E_{it} are, respectively, the amounts of production output, capital, labor, raw materials, and energy (fuel and electricity) for establishment i at time t, and λ_{gt} is an indicator for the interaction of each of the four island groupings g and year t, α_i is a fixed effect for establishment i, and γ_t is a dummy variable for year t. A positive coefficient on downstream FDI indicates that it is associated with higher productivity. Output, capital, materials, and energy are nominal rupiah values deflated to 1983 rupiah. Labor is the total number of production and nonproduction workers. We assume that ε_{it} is independent and identically distributed.[9] We estimate equation (4.1) on a sample of locally owned factories.

Measuring Horizontal and Downstream FDI

We use a long-standing measure of horizontal FDI in the literature: the share of a sector's output in a particular market that is produced by foreign-owned firms. Specifically,

$$Horizontal\_FDI_{jrt} = \sum_{i \in jrt} \frac{Foreign\_OUTPUT_{it}}{\sum_{i \in jrt} OUTPUT_{it}} \tag{4.2}$$

where $i \in jrt$ indicates a factory in a given sector, region, and time, $OUTPUT_{it}$ is the output of factory i, and $Foreign\_OUTPUT_{it}$ is the output of factory i if the factory is foreign, and zero otherwise.

---

9. See Blalock and Gertler (2004) for more extensive empirical work that relaxes the constraint of i.i.d. error terms.

The measure of horizontal FDI varies by industrial sector, region, and time. The approach appeals to Indonesia's vast island geography and poor interregion transportation infrastructure in assuming local markets, so that any technology spillover from foreign firms to local rivals most likely occurs only between firms that are geographically close. We consider each of Indonesia's 23 provinces on the four main island groups of Sumatra, Java and Bali, Kalimantan, and Sulawesi, to be a separate region. Because there is little industrialization in the rural outer islands of the nation, we have not included them in the sample.

While horizontal FDI is straightforward to measure, downstream FDI is somewhat more complicated. In principle, we would like to measure the share of a firm's output that is sold to foreign-owned firms. However, we would then worry about the endogeneity of a particular factory's decision to sell to multinational customers. Moreover, and more importantly, this information is not available in our dataset. Instead, we proxy the share of an establishment's output sold to foreign firms with the share of a sector's output in a market that is sold to foreign firms.

How do we measure the share of sector j's output, in market k, that is sold to foreign firms in year t? From the IO tables we know the amount firms in one sector purchase from each of the other sectors. We also know the share of output in sector j that is produced by foreign-owned firms— for example, horizontal FDI. If we assume that a firm's share of a sector's use of a particular input is equal to its output share, then a measure of the share of a sector's output sold to foreign firms is the sum of the output shares purchased by other sectors multiplied by the share of foreign output in each purchasing sector.

For example, consider three sectors: wheat flour milling, pasta production, and baking. Suppose that half of the wheat flour sector output is purchased by the bakery sector and the other half is purchased by the pasta sector. Furthermore, suppose that the bakery sector has no foreign factories but that foreign factories produce half of the pasta sector output. The calculation of downstream FDI for the flour sector would yield $0.25 = 0.5(0.0) + 0.5(0.5)$. Formally, equation 4.3 expresses the calculation for sector j, region r, at time t.

$$Downstream\_FDI_{jrt} = \sum_k \alpha_{jkt} Horizontal\_FDI_{krt} \qquad (4.3)$$

where α_{jkt} is the proportion of sector j output consumed by sector k. Horizontal FDI is our measure of the share of a sector's output in a local market that is produced by foreign-owned firms. Values of α_{jkt} before and including 1990 follow from the 1990 IO table, values of α_{jkt} from 1991 through 1994 are linear interpolations of the 1990 and 1995 IO tables, and values of α_{jkt} from 1995 on are from the 1995 IO table. Recall that α_{jkt} does not have a region r subscript because the IO table is compiled for the entire national economy.

Table 4.3 Descriptive statistics for measures of FDI

Variable	Mean	Standard deviation
Downstream FDI	.042	.097
Horizontal FDI	.112	.250
Suppliers' downstream FDI	.036	.062

The measure of downstream FDI varies by industrial sector, region, and time. Again, the approach appeals to Indonesia's vast island geography and poor interregion transportation infrastructure in assuming local markets—for example, the intermediate goods output is consumed by firms in the same region. Table 4.3 shows the mean and standard deviation for these two measures of FDI and a third one described in the next section. Table 4.4 displays the correlation between them. We note that sectors often buy from themselves. That is, the value of sector index j and index k may be the same. In sectors that sell heavily to themselves, some overlap between the three measures of FDI exists. To limit the estimation to the nonoverlapping variation in the three measures, we include both downstream FDI and horizontal FDI in our examination of productivity.

Productivity Results

Table 4.5 reports the results of estimating equation 4.1 using an establishment-level fixed-effect estimator on a sample of domestic firms.[10] Column (1) shows downstream FDI, column (2) shows horizontal FDI, and column (3) shows the effect of both. The coefficient on horizontal FDI is close to zero, suggesting that there is little learning from direct foreign competitors. In contrast, the effect of downstream FDI is large and significant, indicating that firms with growing FDI downstream acquire technology through the supply chain.

Because the estimation is a log linear production function, the coefficients approximate elasticities and have intuitive interpretations. The 0.087 coefficient on downstream FDI suggests that firm output increases over 8 percent as the share of foreign ownership downstream rises from 0 to 1. In practice, increases in share of downstream FDI of approximately 20 percent are common, suggesting that the actual realized productivity gain might be close to 2 percent (.2 times .087).

---

10. A Hausman test showed significant correlation between individual establishment effects and the other regressors, thereby rejecting a random-effects model.

Table 4.4　Correlation between measures of FDI

Variable	Downstream FDI	Horizontal FDI	Suppliers' downstream FDI
Downstream FDI	1.00		
Horizontal FDI	0.34	1.00	
Suppliers' downstream FDI	0.55	0.44	1.00

Note: Capital, materials, energy, and value added are reported in thousands of 1988 rupiah.

Market and Welfare Effects

The previous section, we believe, provides convincing evidence that productivity increases when the share of output purchased by foreign firms rises. This is consistent with downstream foreign-owned firms transferring technology to upstream suppliers. In this section, we examine the market and welfare consequences of transferring this technology and test whether it results in Pareto improvements in welfare as hypothesized in Pack and Saggi (2001). In particular, we test the hypotheses that (1) technology transfer upstream to suppliers results in entry, lower prices, increased output, and higher profitability in the upstream market; and (2) lower supply prices lead to entry, lower prices, increased output, and increased profitability in the downstream market.

Methods and Identification

Again, we are not able to directly measure the transfer of technology. Rather, we measure the sectors and location where and when foreign companies entered downstream of local companies. We examine the effect of changes in the share of output purchased by foreign firms on prices, concentration, and profitability in the supply sector. Specifically, we estimate several reduced-form models. Equation 4.4 measures the effect of FDI on concentration.

$$HI_{srt} = \beta_0 Downstream\_FDI_{jrt} + \alpha_{sr} + \lambda_{gt} + \gamma_t + \varepsilon_{srt} \qquad (4.4)$$

where HI_{srt} is the Herfindahl concentration index for five-digit ISIC sector s in region r in time t. Note that we use the 89 IO table codes, indicated by subscript j, to define sectors for supply chains. However, for calculating concentration indexes, which do not require the IO table, one can more narrowly define industries by the 329 ISIC codes, indicated by subscript s. α_{sr} is a fixed effect for the interaction of sector s and region r, λ_{gt} is intended to capture time-variant conditions affecting particular island groupings of the country, and ε_{srt} is an error term. We use similar reduced-form equations to explore the effect of downstream FDI on prices, output, and value added.

Table 4.5   Production function estimation on domestic establishments

	(1)	(2)	(3)
Downstream FDI	0.087		0.090
	(4.33)		(4.40)
Horizontal FDI		−0.004	−0.009
		(0.34)	(0.88)
FDI in log(labor)	0.590	0.590	0.590
	(29.98)	(29.94)	(29.98)
log(capital)	0.109	0.109	0.109
	(12.67)	(12.66)	(12.66)
log(materials)	0.200	0.200	0.200
	(21.76)	(21.71)	(21.76)
log(energy)	0.123	0.124	0.123
	(17.98)	(18.17)	(17.99)
log(K)*log(K)	0.005	0.005	0.005
	(9.57)	(9.57)	(9.58)
log(L)*log(L)	0.026	0.026	0.026
	(10.53)	(10.52)	(10.53)
log(M)*log(M)	0.050	0.050	0.050
	(89.47)	(89.53)	(89.45)
log(E)*log(E)	−0.010	−0.010	−0.010
	(24.24)	(24.24)	(24.25)
log(K)*log(L)	0.028	0.028	0.028
	(16.35)	(16.41)	(16.35)
log(K)*log(M)	−0.028	−0.028	−0.028
	(32.50)	(32.51)	(32.50)
log(K)*log(E)	0.006	0.006	0.006
	(8.57)	(8.55)	(8.57)
log(L)*log(M)	−0.089	−0.089	−0.089
	(49.64)	(49.61)	(49.64)
log(L)*log(E)	0.023	0.023	0.023
	(15.88)	(15.80)	(15.87)
log(M)*log(E)	−0.005	−0.005	−0.005
	(6.52)	(6.60)	(6.51)
Constant	3.882	3.885	3.883
	(56.04)	(56.09)	(56.05)
Observations	108,100	108,100	108,100
Number of establishments	23,815	23,815	23,815
R-squared	0.81	0.81	0.81

Notes: Establishment fixed effects, island-year, and year dummy variables are included but not reported.
Absolute value of t-statistics is in parentheses.
Capital, materials, energy, and value added are reported in thousands of 1988 rupiah.

We then consider the hypotheses regarding feedback to the downstream market, in particular, that the lower supply prices induce entry, lower prices, and higher profits. We test this hypothesis by examining the effects of changes in foreign ownership in sectors purchasing from a particular supply sector on the performance of other sectors supplied by that sector. In other words, we question the effect of buying from sectors that supply multinationals and call this the suppliers' downstream FDI. We measure suppliers' downstream FDI as the value of downstream FDI in each of the sectors upstream of the focal sector weighted by the share of focal sector inputs provided by that sector.

$$Suppliers'\_Downstream\_FDI_{jrt} = \sum_k \alpha_{jkt} Downstream\_FDI_{krt} \qquad (4.5)$$

where α_{jkt} is the share of sector j inputs obtained from sector k.

We then reestimate our reduced-form equations for concentration, prices, output, and value added replacing downstream FDI with suppliers' downstream FDI to gauge the welfare effects in sectors downstream of those sectors supplying multinationals. We calculate the effect of horizontal FDI on the same metrics to capture the effect of direct competition with foreign firms on domestic industry.

Market and Welfare Results

We estimate the effect of FDI on concentration and prices at the market level—province markets in the case of concentration and national markets in the case of prices, for which we do not have regional variation. The effect of FDI on output and value added is calculated at the firm level.[11]

Concentration and Price

Both downstream FDI and suppliers' downstream FDI are significantly associated with a decrease in market concentration, measured by a Herfindahl index. This association suggests that foreign entry downstream will lead to more competition in upstream supply markets. Likewise, other sectors downstream of those upstream markets also show increases in competition.

In sector horizontal FDI, downstream FDI, and suppliers' downstream FDI are all associated with a decline in prices. In other words, FDI competition lowers prices in the entry market, the supply markets, and other markets downstream of the supply markets.

---

11. We report only general results here. Details of the estimation and regression tables are available in Blalock and Gertler (2004).

Output and Value Added

We next consider output and value added. Because these outcomes are measured at the firm level, we can estimate the effect of FDI separately on domestic and foreign firms. We first look at domestic firms. Given that FDI lowers prices, one expects to see an increase in output. Both downstream FDI and suppliers' downstream FDI increase output, likely through the effect of FDI on prices and the demand added by the new entry. In isolation, in-sector horizontal FDI has no effect on volume. However, when horizontal FDI is considered together with downstream FDI and suppliers' downstream FDI, it lowers output. This is likely due to some correlation among the three measures of FDI. Whereas downstream FDI and suppliers' downstream FDI reflect the benefits of technology transfer, horizontal FDI also has a competitive effect if foreign firms take away market share from domestic rivals. We next estimate value added to determine whether domestic firms capture any of the surplus generated from lower prices and higher output. Again, both downstream FDI and suppliers' downstream FDI lead to greater value added, suggesting that firms are capturing some of the welfare benefits of vertical technology transfer. Domestic firms, however, fare far worse when they compete directly with foreign entrants as evidenced by the lower value added associated with horizontal FDI.

We now turn to output and value added outcomes for foreign firms. To avoid the obvious endogeneity that an establishment's own foreign ownership adds to horizontal FDI, we have only included *other* firms' foreign equity in the calculation. As was the case with domestic firms, an increase in downstream FDI and suppliers' downstream FDI is associated with increases in both volume and value added. As with domestic firms, there is no direct effect of horizontal FDI in isolation. However, when horizontal FDI is included together with downstream FDI and suppliers' downstream FDI (thereby removing any part of horizontal FDI that might overlap with the downstream FDI measures), it significantly reduces both output and value added. We interpret this to mean that foreign firms benefit from the entry of other multinationals *provided* that the new entrants do not directly compete in the same sector.

Liquidity Insurance from FDI

Data and Methodology

We measure the effect of the crisis on three firm-level outcomes: value added, labor, and capital. Each of the three outcome measures captures different responses to the crisis. Value added should mirror profitability and reflect the overall effect of the devaluation. That is, exporting firms with domestic materials should see value added rise even with no other changes in production. We expect labor to also reflect the overall effect of the devaluation, but subject to access to short-term working capital. Lastly, capital should reflect the expected persistent effect of the devaluation subject to access to long-term capital.

Experience with the data suggests that labor is one of the more reliable variables reported. Value added is also well measured because both the total value of output and wages are well reported. There were higher rates of nonreporting or obvious erroneous reporting for materials, but we have used interpolation and imputation to make corrections or remove data as needed. Our third measure, capital, represents the biggest challenge with data, because of the high levels of nonreporting firms and the inaccuracy of reported values. We used a number of methods to construct capital measures, as described in Blalock (2002). More generally, however, we avoid problems of capital estimation by not relying on either absolute capital levels or first differences in capital. As shown below, our identification comes from second differencing—the change in capital over time for one group of firms *relative* to another group.

Our methodology is twofold.[12] First, we compare the effect of the crisis on wholly Indonesian-owned firms, both exporters and nonexporters. Our aim is to establish exporters as beneficiaries of the rupiah devaluation. Second, we compare the postcrisis outcomes of Indonesian-owned exporters with those of foreign-owned exporters. The identifying assumption is that the rupiah devaluation should have affected foreign and domestic exporters in the same manner, all else being equal. We argue that changes in the investment patterns between foreign and domestic exporters, relative to their precrisis trends, could result from their different financing sources. Whereas domestic firms would either have to borrow from domestic banks struggling from insolvency or convince foreign banks of their creditworthiness, foreign firms could obtain internal credit through their parent companies.

As discussed above, exporters and foreign firms were more likely to have had debts denominated in US dollars, Japanese yen, and other hard currencies. In fact, because the Bank of Indonesia has historically supported a gradual depreciation of the rupiah against the dollar, many firms had borrowed abroad to take advantage of lower rates. With the implicit understanding that the exchange rate would not change dramatically in the short run, few firms had hedged their positions (Blustein 2001). In many cases, the change in the value of outstanding loans left many companies insolvent following the devaluation. In contrast, those with loans in rupiah enjoyed a large discount in the cost of repaying their debt.

---

12. Please see Blalock, Gertler, and Levine (2004) for a more detailed description of the methods and identification issues.

To control for the effect of debt on postcrisis outcomes, we constructed leverage measures—the ratio of debt to assets—for each firm. Unfortunately, the data do not reveal whether the debt was denominated in rupiah or hard currency. However, the data do reveal if a firm has received a loan from a foreign bank. To approximate foreign currency–denominated debt, we labeled the leverage of firms that had ever received any foreign loans as foreign leverage. Firms that had never reported receiving foreign loans were designated as having domestic leverage, which is mutually exclusive of foreign leverage.

Equation 4.6 estimates the effect of the crisis on firm outcomes.

$$\ln Outcome_{it} = \beta_0(Exporter * Post)_{it} + \beta_1(Foreign\_Leverage * Post)_{it}$$
$$+ \beta_2(Domestic\_Leverage * Post)_{it} + \alpha_i + \gamma_t + \varepsilon_{it} \qquad (4.6)$$

where $Outcome_{it}$ is the log of labor, the log of value added, and the log of capital in the respective specifications, $(Exporter * Post)_{it}$ is the interaction of indicators for a precrisis (anytime during 1994–96) exporting establishment i and postcrisis years (1999–2000), $(Foreign\_Leverage * Post)_{it}$ and $(Domestic\_Leverage * Post)_{it}$ are the interactions of foreign and domestic leverage, respectively, and postcrisis years, α_i is a fixed effect for factory i, and γ_t is a dummy variable for year t. We intentionally do not use data from 1997 and 1998. The rapid inflation and devaluation of the rupiah during this period made any interpolation of pecuniary terms difficult, if not impossible. By 1999, the currency had stabilized, and we believe that variance in monetary values reflects true firm heterogeneity rather than spurious noise resulting from widely volatile exchange rates.

We next estimate equation 4.6 for the population of just exporting firms and substituting $(Foreign * Post)_{it}$ for $(Exporter * Post)_{it}$.

$$\ln Outcome_{it} = \beta_0(Exporter * Post)_{it} + \beta_1(Foreign\_Leverage * Post)_{it}$$
$$+ \beta_2(Domestic\_Leverage * Post)_{it} + \alpha_i + \gamma_t + \varepsilon_{it} \qquad (4.7)$$

where $Foreign$ is an indicator for firms with foreign equity.

It is important to note that the estimation uses only within-firm estimation. Time-invariant attributes of the firm, such as its management, industry, and location are all removed by the fixed effect. Equation 4.6 thus asks how the difference between domestic exporters and nonexporters changed after the crisis, *conditional on all the unobserved static characteristics of the firms.* Likewise, equation 4.7 asks how the difference between foreign and domestic exporters changed following the crisis, again, controlling for firm unobservables.

Liquidity Insurance Results

Table 4.6 shows the estimation of equation 4.6. Because of the rapid rupiah devaluation during 1997 and 1998, a difference of just a few weeks in the reporting date could dramatically affect values. To avoid this bias, the estimation includes only the pre- and postcrisis years and drops 1997 and 1998. The odd columns (1), (3), and (5) show the effect of exporting on value added, labor, and capital for the population of domestic firms. The even columns (2), (4), and (6) show the effect of foreign ownership on value added, labor, and capital for the population of all exporting firms.

Consider first the effect of exporting on postcrisis outcome. Among domestic firms, those that were exporters prior to the crisis saw their value added grow 20 percent relative to those that did not export. Further, the same exporting firms saw labor grow about 12 percent more that that of non-exporting firms. However, the pattern does not repeat for investment—there is no significant difference in capital postcrisis for domestic exporters versus domestic nonexporters.

Next consider the same analysis for the population of domestic and foreign firms exporting before the crisis. Those with foreign ownership saw value added grow 30 percent over domestic exporters. Foreign exporters likewise saw labor grow about 15 percent over domestic firms. Finally, exporters with foreign equity saw an increase in capital 8 percent greater than that of domestic exporters. The key observation here is that *all* exporters increased their value added and employment after the crisis, but *only* exporters with foreign ownership increased investment.

We next turn to the leverage measures, which are most telling for the population of domestic firms—see columns (1), (3), and (5). Whereas foreign multinationals are likely hedged against exchange rate fluctuations and largely insulated from the rupiah's value since they export mostly output, Indonesian firms are more likely to get caught with a burgeoning foreign debt. Indeed, the interaction of foreign leverage and the postcrisis indicator in the capital estimation (column 5) suggests that firms with large foreign debts invested less postcrisis than others.

Summary and Implications

Our findings have two key implications. First, FDI is a source of technology in emerging markets, and this technology generates welfare benefits that may warrant public policy intervention. Second, FDI can provide credit liquidity in times of financial crisis, a benefit that also warrants public intervention.

Both the econometric analysis and the manager interviews suggest that vertical supply chains are conduits for technology transfer from FDI. Indonesian factories in industries with growing downstream FDI experience

Table 4.6 Fixed-effect estimation on domestic establishments (models 1, 3, 5) and exporting establishments (models 2, 4, 6)

	(1) log (value added)	(2) log (value added)	(3) log (labor)	(4) log (labor)	(5) log (capital)	(6) log (capital)
Exporter*Postcrisis	0.203 (9.87)		0.123 (16.03)		-0.019 (1.12)	
Foreign*Postcrisis		0.339 (8.17)		0.154 (8.56)		0.088 (2.26)
Foreign Leverage*Postcrisis	-0.000 (0.93)	0.022 (2.11)	-0.000 (0.21)	0.008 (1.76)	-0.001 (3.04)	0.023 (1.83)
Domestic Leverage*Postcrisis	0.001 (1.65)	0.003 (2.02)	0.000 (0.23)	0.000 (0.32)	-0.001 (1.30)	-0.001 (1.05)
1990	-0.571 (31.77)	-0.662 (20.46)	-0.203 (30.18)	-0.313 (22.23)	-0.490 (35.90)	-0.672 (24.11)
1991	-0.452 (26.46)	-0.545 (18.03)	-0.164 (25.66)	-0.263 (20.08)	-0.448 (34.80)	-0.573 (22.26)
1992	-0.339 (20.60)	-0.424 (14.82)	-0.122 (19.90)	-0.187 (15.07)	-0.347 (28.20)	-0.412 (17.11)
1993	-0.228 (14.36)	-0.272 (9.86)	-0.061 (10.15)	-0.098 (8.11)	-0.267 (22.41)	-0.313 (13.51)
1994	-0.093 (5.97)	-0.151 (5.66)	-0.016 (2.78)	-0.035 (3.02)	-0.172 (14.95)	-0.187 (8.43)
1995	-0.091 (6.07)	-0.151 (5.89)	-0.003 (0.52)	-0.018 (1.59)	-0.142 (12.81)	-0.135 (6.35)
1999	-0.293 (17.73)	-0.120 (4.39)	-0.112 (18.38)	-0.026 (2.23)	-0.428 (33.97)	-0.482 (20.14)
2000	-0.372 (22.25)	-0.262 (9.48)	-0.110 (17.85)	-0.028 (2.33)	-0.426 (31.87)	-0.497 (19.22)
Constant	11.854 (1145.67)	13.524 (755.84)	4.637 (1197.81)	5.476 (704.54)	12.403 (1608.81)	13.827 (923.53)
Observations	62,817	22,515	65,110	23,037	46,819	16,179
Number of establishments	9,444	3,324	9,477	3,327	7,350	2,571
R-squared	0.03	0.04	0.03	0.06	0.07	0.08

Notes: Absolute value of t-statistics is in parentheses.

103

greater productivity growth, ceteris paribus, than other factories. This finding is consistent with the incentives of multinational enterprises, which only realize the full benefit of investment abroad if they can procure high-quality inputs at low cost. To build efficient supply chains overseas, many multinationals will strategically transfer technology to local vendors.

The observation of technology transfer alone is insufficient to inform public policy. If the full benefit of FDI is internalized between two private parties, then there is no need for government intervention. Our results show that FDI does indeed generate an externality—lower prices and greater output—that benefits suppliers, final goods makers, and consumers. Because the benefits of FDI in the economy exceed the private returns to both the multinational and its direct suppliers, the total amount of FDI will be less than the socially optimal amount without intervention.

Our analysis of investment during the financial crisis suggests another benefit of FDI. Trade theory suggests that exporting firms should increase profits, expand employment, and invest in new capital following a real devaluation. For domestic exporters, we observe the first two effects but do not see evidence of increased investment even though conditions warrant it. Liquidity constraints are a likely explanation. Whereas increases in employment could be financed through cash flow, capital investment required obtaining credit from a struggling financial sector. In contrast, exporters with foreign ownership did expand investment. A priori, we see no reason why investment would depend on ownership other than financing availability. While domestic exporters may have faced a credit crunch, exporters with foreign ownership could access credit through their parent company and, thus, insure themselves against liquidity constraints. The ability of foreign firms to sustain investment during times of crisis provides a form of liquidity insurance and hastens economic recovery.

References

Aguiar, Mark. 2002. *Investment, Devaluation, and Foreign Currency Exposure.* Working Paper. Chicago: University of Chicago, Graduate School of Business.

Agung, Juda, Bambang Kusmiarso, Bamgang Pramono, Erwin G. Hutapea, Andry Prasmuko, and Nugroho Joko Prastowo. 2001. *Credit Crunch in Indonesia in the Aftermath of the Crisis: Facts, Causes and Policy Implications.* Discussion Paper. Jakarta: Bank Indonesia.

Aitken, Brian, Ann E. Harrison, and Robert E. Lipsey. 1996. Wages and Foreign Ownership: A Comparative Study of Mexico, Venezuela, and the United States. *Journal of International Economics* 40, no. 3-4: 345–71.

Aitken, Brian J., and Ann E. Harrison. 1999. Do Domestic Firms Benefit from Direct Foreign Investment? Evidence from Venezuela. *American Economic Review* 89, no. 3: 605–18.

Bernanke, Ben, and Mark Gertler. 1989. Agency Costs, Net Worth, and Business Fluctuations. *American Economic Review* 79, no. 1: 14–31.

Blalock, Garrick. 2002. Technology Adoption from Foreign Direct Investment and Exporting: Evidence from Indonesian Manufacturing. Ph.D. thesis, University of California, Berkeley, Haas School of Business.

Blalock, Garrick, and Paul J. Gertler. 2004. *Welfare Gains from Foreign Direct Investment through Technology Transfer to Local Suppliers.* Working Paper. Ithaca, NY: Cornell University, Department of Applied Economics and Management. aem.cornell.edu/faculty_sites/gb78.

Blalock, Garrick, Paul J. Gertler, and David I. Levine. 2004. *Investment Following a Financial Crisis: Does Foreign Ownership Matter?* Working Paper. Ithaca, NY: Cornell University, Department of Applied Economics and Management. aem.cornell.edu/faculty_sites/gb78.

Blomström, Magnus, and Ari Kokko. 1997. *How Foreign Investment Affects Host Countries.* Washington: World Bank International Economics Department, International Trade Division.

Blomström, Magnus, and Edward N. Wolff. 1994. Multinational Corporations and Productivity Convergence in Mexico. In *Convergence of Productivity: Cross-National Studies and Historical Evidence,* ed., W. J. Baumol, R. R. Nelson, and E. N. Wolff. New York: Oxford University Press.

Blustein, Paul. 2001. The Chastening: Inside the Crisis that Rocked the Global Financial System and Humbled the IMF. *Public Affairs,* 1st ed.: 431. New York.

Caballero, Ricardo J., and Arvind Krishnamurthy. 1999. *Emerging Market Crises: An Asset Markets Perspective.* Working Paper. Cambridge, MA: Massachusetts Institute of Technology.

Caves, Richard E. 1974. Multinational Firms, Competition and Productivity in Host-Country Markets. *Economica* 41, no. 162: 176–93.

Desai, Mihir, C. Fritz Foley, and Kristen J. Forbes. 2003. *Shelters from the Storm: Multinational Linkages During Currency Crises.* Working Paper. Ann Arbor, MI: University of Michigan Business School.

Desai, Mihir, C. Fritz Foley, and James R. Hines, Jr. 2003. *A Multinational Perspective on Capital Structure Choice and Internal Capital Markets.* NBER Working Paper 9715. Cambridge, MA: National Bureau of Economic Research.

Enoch, Charles, Barbara Baldwin, Olivier Frecaut, and Arto Kovanen. 2001. *Indonesia—Anatomy of a Banking Crisis: Two Years of Living Dangerously—1997–99.* IMF Working Paper 01/52 (May 1). Washington: International Monetary Fund.

Fazzari, Steven M., Glenn R. Hubbard, and Bruce C. Petersen. 1988. Financing Constraints and Corporate Investment. *Brookings Papers on Economic Activity:* 141–95.

Fisman, Raymond. 2001. Estimating the Value of Political Connections. *American Economic Review* 91, no. 4: 1095–102.

Forbes, Kristin J. 2002. *How Do Large Depreciations Affect Firm Performance?* NBER Discussion Paper 9095. Cambridge, MA: National Bureau of Economic Research.

Globerman, Steven. 1979. Foreign Direct Investment and Spillover Efficiency Benefits in Canadian Manufacturing Industries. *Canadian Journal of Economics* 12, no. 1: 42–56.

Goeltom, Miranda S. 1995. *Indonesia's Financial Liberalization: An Empirical Analysis of 1981–88 Panel Data.* ISEAS Current Economic Affairs Series. Singapore: ASEAN Economic Research Unit, Institute of Southeast Asian Studies.

Haddad, Mona, and Ann Harrison. 1993. Are There Positive Spillovers from Direct Foreign Investment? Evidence from Panel Data for Morocco. *Journal of Development Economics* 42, no. 1: 51–74.

Haskel, Jonathan E., Sonia C. Pereira, and Matthew J. Slaughter. 2002. *Does Inward Foreign Direct Investment Boost the Productivity of Domestic Firms?* NBER Discussion Paper 8433. Cambridge, MA: National Bureau of Economic Research.

Hill, Hal. 1988. *Foreign Investment and Industrialization in Indonesia.* East Asian Social Science Monographs. Singapore and New York: Oxford University Press.

Hoshi, Takeo, Anil Kashyap, and David Scharfstein. 1991. Corporate Structure, Liquidity, and Investment: Evidence from Japanese Industrial Groups. *Quarterly Journal of Economics* 106, no. 1: 33–60.

Hubbard, Glenn R. 1998. Capital-Market Imperfections and Investment. *Journal of Economic Literature* 36, no. 1: 193–225.

International Monetary Fund (IMF). 2000. *Indonesia: Statistical Appendix.* IMF Staff Country Report 00/133. Washington: International Monetary Fund.

Javorcik, Beata Smarzynska. 2004. Does Foreign Direct Investment Increase the Productivity of Domestic Firms? In Search of Spillovers through Backward Linkages. *American Economic Review* 94, no. 3: 605–27.

Keller, Wolfgang. 2001. *International Technology Diffusion.* NBER Working Paper 8573. Cambridge, MA: National Bureau of Economic Research.

Kenney, Martin, and Richard L. Florida. 1993. *Beyond Mass Production: The Japanese System and Its Transfer to the US.* New York: Oxford University Press.

Kokko, Ari. 1994. Technology, Market Characteristics, and Spillovers. *Journal of Development Economics* 43, no. 2: 279–93.

Kugler, Maurice. 2000. The Diffusion of Externalities from Foreign Direct Investment: Theory Ahead of Measurement. Discussion Papers in Economics and Econometrics. Southampton, England: Department of Economics, University of Southampton.

Kumar, Nagesh. 1996. *Foreign Direct Investments and Technology Transfers in Development: A Perspective on Recent Literature.* Discussion Paper Series. Tokyo: The United Nations University, Institute for New Technologies.

Lall, Sanjaya. 1980. Vertical Inter-Firm Linkages in LDCs: An Empirical Study. *Oxford Bulletin of Economics and Statistics* 42: 203–26.

Lipsey, Robert. 2001. *Foreign Direct Investors in Three Financial Crises.* Discussion Paper 8084. Cambridge, MA: National Bureau of Economic Research.

MacDuffie, John Paul, and Susan Helper. 1997. Creating Lean Suppliers: Diffusing Lean Production through the Supply Chain. *California Management Review* 39, no. 4: 118–51.

Minton, Bernadette A., and Catherine Schrand. 1999. The Impact of Cash Flow Volatility on Discretionary Investment and the Costs of Debt and Equity Financing. *Journal of Financial Economics* 54, no. 3: 423–60.

Moran, Theodore H. 2001. *Parental Supervision: The New Paradigm for Foreign Direct Investment and Development.* Washington: Institute for International Economics.

Nasution, Anwar. 1995. The Opening-Up of the Indonesian Economy. In *Indonesian Economy in the Changing World,* vol. 32, ed., D. Kuntjoro-Jakti and K. Omura. Tokyo: Institute of Developing Economies.

Pack, Howard, and Kamal Saggi. 2001. Vertical Technology Transfer Via International Outsourcing. *Journal of Development Economics* 65, no. 2: 389–415.

Pangestu, Mari. 1996. *Economic Reform, Deregulation, and Privatization: The Indonesian Experience.* Jakarta: Centre for Strategic and International Studies.

Pangestu, Mari, and Yuri Sato. 1997. *Waves of Change in Indonesia's Manufacturing Industry.* Tokyo: Institute of Developing Economies.

Reinhart, Carmen, and Guillermo Calvo. 2000. When Capital Inflows Come to a Sudden Stop: Consequences and Policy Options. In *Key Issues in Reform of the International Monetary and Financial System,* ed., Peter B. Kenen and Alexander K. Swoboda. Washington: International Monetary Fund.

Rodríguez-Clare, Andrés. 1996. Multinationals, Linkages, and Economic Development. *American Economic Review* 86, no. 4: 852–73.

Wie, Thee Kian. 1994a. Intra-Regional Investment and Technology Transfer in Indonesia. In *Symposium on Intra-Regional Investment and Technology Transfer,* ed., Kenichi Yanagi. Tokyo: Asian Productivity Organization.

Wie, Thee Kian. 1994b. *Technology Transfer from Japan to Indonesia.* Kyoto: International Research Center for Japanese Studies.

5

R&D Activities of Foreign and National Establishments in Turkish Manufacturing

ASIM ERDILEK

Technical progress is the major source of productivity growth in the long run. Research and development (R&D), resulting in new knowledge, new processes, and new goods, is a major source of technical progress according to the R&D-based endogenous growth theory (Romer 1990). Multinational corporations (MNCs), most of them based in developed countries, play a major role in global R&D and in the international transfer of technology. Foreign direct investment (FDI), most of it undertaken by MNCs, is a major vehicle of technology transfer to developing countries (Moran 1998, 2001, chapter 11 of this volume). FDI can be a major vehicle of technology transfer to and diffusion in developing countries via positive externalities through four channels (Organization for Economic Cooperation and Development, or OECD, 2002a, 98; Blomström and Kokko 1998, 11–15):

■ Horizontal linkages: National firms may adopt foreign technologies or upgrade their own technologies under greater competition from foreign firms in the same industry.

■ Vertical (backward and forward) linkages: Foreign firms may transfer technology to national firms that are their suppliers or customers in different industries.

■ Labor mobility: Employees of foreign firms may transfer their knowledge to national firms when changing employers or starting their own firms.

Asim Erdilek is professor of economics at the Weatherhead School of Management, Case Western Reserve University. I thank Gordon Hanson, Theodore H. Moran, and the other conference participants for their comments on an earlier and longer version of this chapter.

- R&D internationalization: R&D activities of foreign firms may help strengthen host country capability for R&D directly or indirectly by stimulating the R&D activities of national firms.

I concentrate on the fourth channel in terms of a panel data–based investigation of the R&D activities of foreign-owned ("foreign") and nationally owned ("national") establishments in Turkish manufacturing. I focus not only on whether foreign and national establishments differ in the levels and compositions of their R&D activities but also whether sectoral FDI concentration has a spillover effect on the R&D activities of national establishments.

Background and Literature Review

MNCs play a critical role in global R&D and in the international transfer of technology. They own, produce, and control most of the world's advanced technology, since they are responsible for a significant part of global R&D. In fact, the desire to acquire modern technology may have become the most important reason why most countries try to attract FDI as the flows of technology to MNC affiliates dominate all types of formal technology transactions between countries (Blomström, Kokko, and Zejan 1992; Blomström and Kokko 1998, 2003; Kokko and Blomström 1995). Moreover, these inflows of new technology to MNC affiliates create the potential for technology spillovers to the host country (Blomström and Kokko 1993, 1998, 2003; Kokko and Blomström 1995).

In its recent *World Investment Reports* the United Nations Conference on Trade and Development (UNCTAD 2002, 18) has emphasized the importance of R&D by foreign affiliates in host countries:

> Another important aspect of international production is innovative activity by foreign affiliates. The presence of research and development (R&D) can signify that affiliates are engaging in complex and high value functions. R&D can contribute to capacity-building in host countries and provide spillover benefits to local researchers.

Also,

> The specific advantages of R&D by foreign affiliates must also be remembered. Affiliates can gain from the access they have to R&D in the parent firm's networks. Local firms can capture spillover benefits from R&D in foreign affiliates by learning from their research methods, hiring their trained employees and collaborating with them on specific projects or as suppliers (UNCTAD 2003a, 106).

Foreign affiliates of MNCs undertake R&D primarily to adapt their parents' processes or products to local markets' requirements (Kumar 2001; Fors and Zejan 1996).

Most MNCs concentrate their R&D in their home countries or other developed countries (UNCTAD 2002, 18–20). US MNCs conducted 87 percent of their R&D at home in 1998 (although foreign affiliates accounted for about one-third of their global sales). Japanese MNCs conducted 97 percent of their R&D at home in 1995 (although foreign affiliates accounted for about one-quarter of their global sales). MNCs' concentration of R&D in their home country may be due to three reasons: (1) effective control and economies of scale in the R&D activity; (2) agglomeration economies from clustering of R&D personnel and activities; and (3) stronger intellectual property protection in developed countries than in developing countries (OECD 2002a, 103).

According to UNCTAD (UNCTAD 2002, 19, table I.10), foreign affiliates' share of R&D in total R&D of host countries is lower than their share in production but with wide variations. Innovative corporate activity as measured by patents is still predominantly located close to the firm's headquarters (OECD 1999). In 1994, the R&D carried out by foreign subsidiaries represented only 11 percent of the total R&D of 12 major OECD countries. In general, the R&D intensity of domestic firms was higher than that of foreign subsidiaries. According to the OECD (OECD 2002b, 307, annex table 18), in 1995, R&D expenditures by foreign affiliates in Turkey accounted for 32.8 percent of total business R&D, the second highest percentage among the OECD countries after Ireland, which accounted for 64.6 percent (see also UNCTAD 2002, 19, table I.10). During 1986–99, R&D expenditures by foreign affiliates increased both in real terms and as a share of business in many of the OECD countries, including Canada, France, Ireland, Japan, Sweden, the United Kingdom, and the United States. In Ireland and Hungary, foreign affiliates accounted for more than two-thirds of business R&D in 2000. In 2001, R&D conducted abroad and by foreign affiliates accounted, on average, for about 12 percent of the total industrial R&D expenditures in the OECD countries (OECD 2003).

Compared with the substantial research on the globalization of R&D by MNCs among developed countries (Zander 1998; Branstetter 2000, 2001; Serapio and Dalton 1999; Florida 1997; Kumar 2001; Cantwell and Janne 1999; Zander 1997, 1999; Meyer-Krahmer and Reger 1999; Gerybadze and Reger 1999; Niosi and Godin 1999; Asakawa 2001; Granstrand 1999; Fisch 2003; Zedtwitz and Gassman 2002; Cantwell and Iammarino 2003), there is relatively little empirical research on the R&D activities of MNCs in developing countries (Blomström and Kokko 1998, 14–15). Chuang and Lin (1999) find that in Taiwanese manufacturing, R&D and FDI are substitutes, after they correct for selection bias. They conclude that since foreign firms can receive technological support from their parent company, they have little incentive to conduct R&D themselves. Kearns and Ruane (2001) show, on the basis of a plant-level analysis of different R&D activity measures and after controlling for plant and sector characteristics, that R&D-active MNC plants (with majority foreign ownership) in Ireland had a higher probability of survival and created higher-quantity and better-quality jobs during 1986–96 than non-R&D active MNC plants.

Amsden et al. (2001) conclude, on the basis of firm-level interviews, that the type of R&D undertaken by MNCs in Singapore cannot be categorized as even applied research and that most R&D is tightly coupled with solving production problems. Their conclusion is not supported, however, by Sigurdson and Palonka, who show that Singapore has become, thanks to generous government grants and public R&D institutions, a major R&D center for many MNCs, especially in the information technology and pharmaceutical industries (Sigurdson and Palonka 2002, 21–24). On the other hand, Sigurdson and Palonka (2002, 11–14) conclude that FDI in Indonesia has been less effective in transferring technology, with almost all R&D conducted by government research institutes with little relevance for the needs of the industrial sector. They attribute the failure of FDI to contribute to Indonesia's technological development to the local firms' lack of absorptive capacity and ineffective government policies. Todo and Miyamoto, however, find that in Indonesian manufacturing the R&D activities of foreign firms improved the productivity of national firms, especially of those national firms that also carried out R&D. Their conclusion is that "in order to benefit more from diffusion of advanced knowledge from MNEs [multinational enterprises], governments of less developed countries are advised to encourage FDI associated with R&D activities and human resource development" (Todo and Miyamoto 2002, 27).

Costa and de Queiroz find that foreign industrial affiliates in Brazil had more complex and deeper technological capabilities than their national firms, reflecting their more effective R&D activities. They conclude that "even larger domestic firms are lagging behind their local foreign rivals in further technology development" (Costa and de Queiroz 2002, 1441). Liu and Chen, using industry-level panel data, find that R&D intensity of foreign firms in Taiwan is positively associated with export orientation, local sourcing of materials and capital goods, and sectoral availability of R&D personnel (Liu and Chen 2003). According to an unpublished study cited in UNCTAD (2003b, 106), in India "foreign affiliates reveal a lower R&D intensity than their local counterparts after taking account of extraneous factors." According to UNCTAD (2003c, 141–76), in the South African automotive industry, R&D intensity (R&D expenditures as percentage of sales) of exporting firms tended to be significantly higher (2.55 percent) than that of nonexporting firms (0.95 percent) and that "transfer of technology and other spillovers have been significant features associated with the investment in local subsidiaries by parent companies" (UNCTAD 2003c, 150). Javorcik and Saggi, on the basis of a partial equilibrium duopoly model of mode choice, predict that direct foreign investors with more advanced technologies would prefer full ownership to joint ventures relative to those with less advanced technologies (Javorcik and Saggi 2004). They test their prediction successfully with survey data from Eastern European transition economies and the former Soviet republics (Javorcik and Saggi 2004). The implication is that joint ventures are likely to carry out more R&D than wholly owned ones in order to close the technology gap.

To summarize the literature review, the limited empirical evidence on the R&D activities of foreign firms in developing countries, although mixed, suggests that on the whole inward FDI stimulates host country R&D. Furthermore, in order for national firms to benefit from technology spillovers, including those from the R&D activities of foreign firms, they must also be R&D active.

As for host country intervention to promote foreign firms' R&D activities, among developed countries, Australia has applied an R&D requirement in terms of R&D expenditures (UNCTAD 2003b, 28). Among developing countries, India seems to be the only one to impose a mandatory R&D requirement in some circumstances (UNCTAD 2003b, 105–06). A few other developing countries such as Chile, Malaysia, and South Africa have imposed voluntary R&D requirements in return for FDI incentives (UNCTAD 2003b, 28). The tangible results have been, unsurprisingly, meager. In Malaysia, for example, although foreign affiliates have contributed significantly to the country's R&D activities, the R&D requirements have not played an important role (UNCTAD 2003b, 152–59). According to UNCTAD (2003b, 28):

> The main problem is that a firm is unlikely to set up R&D activities in the absence of local capabilities and technical skills to absorb, adapt and develop technology and know-how. Thus, in comparison with the availability and quality of appropriately skilled labour, the provision of fiscal or financial incentives is of limited relevance for R&D investments.

Turkey's R&D Trends and Policies

As a developing country Turkey lags behind developed countries in its R&D intensity (OECD 2002b, 32, figure 1.8). Gross domestic expenditure on R&D (GERD) as a proportion of gross domestic product (GDP) was 0.32 percent in 1990. It rose to 0.53 percent in 1991 but then dropped to 0.49 percent in 1992, 0.44 percent in 1993, and 0.36 percent in 1994. In 1995, it was up slightly to 0.38 percent. Between 1996 and 2000, the GERD-to-GDP ratio increased from 0.45 percent to 0.64 percent (Elci 2003, 19). These ratios are very small compared to other OECD countries. Moreover, universities conduct more than two-thirds of the R&D in Turkey, while the private business sector accounts for about only one-fifth of the total national R&D. In 1995, about two-thirds of all R&D was financed by the government, while the business enterprises accounted for the rest. Manufacturing industry constitutes the largest portion of the total business enterprise R&D expenditures. Its share declined, however, from 95 percent in 1990 to 92 percent in 1995.

The Technology Development Foundation of Turkey (TTGV), founded in 1991 and funded by the World Bank, is a member of the Association for

Technology Implementation in Europe (TAFTIE). The TTGV provides R&D support to Turkish industry through soft loans—up to 50 percent of the proposed project budgets—with long repayment periods. All firms, regardless of size or years in existence, that submit R&D project proposals are eligible for R&D support. In fact, 73 percent of the firms supported by the TTGV to date have been small or medium-size enterprises (SMEs) (with fewer than 250 employees), and 51 percent have been less than 10 years old. Since 1995 the Scientific and Research Council of Turkey (TUBITAK), founded in 1963, has provided R&D grants through its Technology Monitoring and Evaluation Board (TIDEB), with SMEs accounting for 70 percent of the companies supported to date. Close to 80 percent of the companies applying for R&D support from either of these two sources have received it (Elci 2003, 28). There are also various other incentives, in the form of different state subsidies, for R&D besides those provided by the TTGV (Elci 2003, 29–31). A country's protection of intellectual property rights (IPR) affects both its appeal as a host country, especially for FDI in R&D facilities, and the transfer of state-of-the-art technology to MNCs' foreign subsidiaries (Mansfield 1994). IPR protection is important for R&D and for innovation through international trade, FDI, and licensing in major industrializing countries (Maskus 2000). Thus, unsurprisingly, inadequate IPR protection has often been mentioned as a major reason for Turkey's relative lack of appeal as a host country (Foreign Investment Advisory Service, or FIAS 2001a, 2001b; Erdilek 2003). For example, the US government has repeatedly complained about this, placing Turkey on the Special 301 Watch, or the Priority Watch List, and suspending its Generalized System of Preferences (GSP) trade privileges in the 1990s. Since the 1994 establishment of the Turkish Patent Institute, the 1995 Trade-Related Aspects of Intellectual Property Rights (TRIPS) Agreement of the World Trade Organization (WTO), and especially the country's 1996 Customs Union Agreement with the European Union (EU), which was aimed at achieving full EU membership, Turkey's IPR protection has increased significantly (Elci 2003).

Data

Establishment-level panel data used in this study come from two separate sources of the Turkish State Institute of Statistics (SIS) for 1993 to 1995, which I bridged by using common establishment codes. The first source of data is the Annual Manufacturing Industry Survey ("Manufacturing Survey"), and the second source of data is the Survey of Research and Development in Turkish Industry ("R&D Survey"). The Industrial Statistics Section of the SIS carries out the Annual Surveys of the Manufacturing Industry that cover all establishments regardless of size. The Science-Technology, Information Indicators and Analysis Division of the SIS carries out the Annual Surveys of Research and Development in Turkish Industry in compliance with the standard OECD methodology (OECD 1994), referred to as the Frascati Manual. OECD annually publishes the aggregated Frascati Manual–based R&D statistics of Turkey and its other members in the *OECD Science, Technology and Industry Scoreboard* (OECD 2003).

Although the Manufacturing Survey also contains data on R&D expenditures, they are not as reliable as those in the R&D Survey. I use establishment and sectoral explanatory variables based on data from the Manufacturing Survey to analyze the establishment R&D activities from the R&D Survey. All the Turkish lira values for 1994 and 1995 are deflated by the four-digit sector-specific annual producer price deflators in the absence of deflators for the input-supplying sectors. The rather short three-year duration of the panel is because readily available and reliable foreign ownership data did not exist for the earlier years, and data for later years were not yet accessible.

The OECD methodology defines R&D[1] as "creative work undertaken on a systematic basis in order to increase the stock of knowledge, including knowledge of man, culture and society, and the use of this stock of knowledge to devise new applications" (OECD 1994, 13). The OECD methodology involves the measurement of two inputs: R&D expenditures (current and capital) and R&D personnel (in terms of full-time equivalence). The Frascati Manual divides R&D into three activities: basic research, applied research, and experimental development (OECD 1994, 50–51). The manual also distinguishes among three types of R&D personnel: researchers, technicians, and other supporting staff (OECD 1994, 67–68).

Two basic issues—censoring and selection bias—need to be addressed concerning the data (Baltagi 2001, chapter 11; Greene 2003, chapter 22). The censoring issue arises in the case of censored observations in R&D in the Manufacturing Survey. The Manufacturing Survey includes all establishments, most of which conduct no R&D according to the survey's single R&D question (which does not define R&D) about their R&D expenditures. So, the R&D-related dependent variables are censored from below at zero, requiring censored regression (tobit) estimations. The second issue, addressed below, arises in the form of possible sample selection bias in the R&D Survey, which includes only a handful of primarily large establishments that conduct R&D according to the precise and restrictive OECD definition.

During 1993–95, 14.40 percent of all establishments indicated having R&D in the Manufacturing Survey but only 1.39 percent indicated having R&D in the R&D Survey.[2] The lower percentage in the R&D Survey can be attributed to either the precise and restrictive OECD definition of R&D in that survey

---

1. OECD uses R&D as the acronym for research and experimental development whereas it typically stands for research and development.

2. The relevant statistical tables of this section, omitted due to space restrictions, are available from the author upon request.

or the possible sample selection bias in favor of larger establishments. For the three individual years, the data are quite similar, except that the percentages of establishments indicating R&D have increased slightly but steadily during 1993–95 according to both surveys. Although we do not see much difference in the responses to the two surveys across time, we do see a sharp difference across national and foreign establishments. In both surveys, the percentage of foreign establishments with R&D is significantly higher than that for national establishments. The difference is relatively much greater in the R&D Survey, with only 1.03 percent of the national but 13.24 percent of the foreign establishments indicating R&D programs.

The major difference in the responses to the two surveys is due to establishment size, which is measured by total revenue. According to the Manufacturing Survey, establishments in all five total revenue quintiles have R&D, but the R&D propensity increases significantly with total revenue. According to the R&D Survey, however, almost all the establishments with R&D programs are in the largest total revenue quintile, which raises the issue of possible sample selection bias. According to the SIS, the R&D Survey is administered to all establishments with R&D departments and to all R&D centers in the country.[3] It covers all state economic enterprises, which are all large, and all large private companies ranked in terms of their sales and value added. It also covers, however, SMEs that either conduct R&D under the aegis of technology centers and/or have applied to various government agencies such as TTGV and TUBITAK for R&D support (SIS 1997, VIII). Therefore, it appears that no clear-cut sample selection bias exists in the R&D Survey, and that it reflects largely the strong association between R&D propensity and establishment size. Nevertheless, I estimated the Heckman selection model (heckit) by the full information maximum-likelihood estimator, which is preferable to the two-step efficient estimator, for all the random-effects tobit regressions to show that, on the whole, no conclusive econometric evidence exists for sample selectivity.[4] The Marmara region, which is Turkey's most industrialized region, accounted for slightly more than half of all the establishments in the Manufacturing Survey.[5] Its dominance among the seven regions was even greater in terms of foreign establishments; it accounted for two-thirds of all foreign establishments. The dominance of the Marmara

---

3. Unfortunately, the SIS did not provide information on the response rates to its surveys.

4. Using the Heckman selection model, developed for cross-section data, to test and correct for sample selection bias in panel data is problematic, since there are two selectivity bias correction terms in panel data instead of one as in cross-section data (Baltagi 2001, 220). The Heckman selection model estimation results are available from the author upon request.

5. The seven regions of Turkey are Marmara, Aegean, Mediterranean, central Anatolia, Black Sea, eastern Anatolia, and southeastern Anatolia.

region was even greater in the R&D Survey. The R&D Survey contains no observations from the least developed Eastern Anatolia and Southeastern Anatolia regions.

Foreign establishments accounted for 28.54 percent of the observations in the R&D Survey, as opposed to 3.00 percent of the observations in the Manufacturing Survey. Although foreign establishments accounted for 22.18 percent of the total revenue in the Manufacturing Survey, their share of the total R&D expenditure was 55.43 percent in the R&D Survey. Although they accounted for 10.99 percent of the total employment in the Manufacturing Survey, their share of the total R&D employment was 47.02 percent in the R&D Survey. The average R&D expenditure/total revenue ratio of foreign establishments, 0.8670 percent, was much greater than that of national establishments, 0.1987 percent.[6] The overall average R&D expenditure/total revenue ratio of 0.3470 percent in manufacturing is quite close to the economywide ratios mentioned earlier.

When we examine the distribution of foreign establishments by total revenue quintiles and ownership percentage groups, we observe that foreign establishments, regardless of percentage of ownership, tend to be of larger size than national establishments. Their share in the total revenue quintiles increases from the smallest to the largest across all five ownership percentage groups. The largest total revenue quintile contains the majority of foreign establishments across each of the five ownership percentage groups and accounts for more than two-thirds of all the foreign establishments. Although the highest foreign ownership percentage group has the largest share (more than one-third) of foreign establishments, the distribution of foreign establishments across the five ownership percentage groups does not follow a definite pattern.

Research Questions

I tried to answer the following research questions on the basis of the data from the Manufacturing and R&D Surveys:

- Do the compositions of R&D activities in terms of three types of R&D expenditure and three types of R&D personnel differ between national and foreign establishments?

- How significant are foreign ownership by establishment and foreign ownership concentration by sector for the probability that an establishment will have R&D activity?

---

6. In an earlier study, my estimate of this ratio for foreign firms was 0.7 percent (Erdilek 1982, 80).

■ How significant are foreign ownership by establishment and foreign ownership concentration by sector in explaining 13 different R&D activity indicators?[7]

Methodology, Model, and Hypotheses

First, I used two-sample t-tests with unequal variances as well as Hotelling's T-squared generalized means test to find out whether foreign and national establishments differ statistically in their R&D propensities as well as their compositions of R&D expenditures and personnel. Then, I estimated random-effects logit regression, random-effects tobit regression, and ordered logit regression models in which I controlled for establishment characteristics such as private versus public ownership, size, vertical (backward) integration, and regional location, as well as for sector characteristics in terms of international competitiveness and industrial concentration. I was limited by the data in my choice of explanatory variables. I could not control for some important establishment characteristics such as years of existence, entry and exit, capital intensity, exports, and imports since I had no data.[8]

In the random-effects logit regressions, the dependent variable is a dummy variable, indicating the absence (= 0) or presence (= 1) of (either aggregate or one of three specific types of) R&D activity. In the random-effects tobit regressions, which have the same explanatory variables as the random-effects logit regressions, the continuous dependent variable is one of the 13 different R&D activity measures. In the ordered logit regressions,

---

7. The 13 R&D activity indicators are: (1) total R&D expenditure to total revenue ratio; (2) total R&D full-time equivalent (FTE) employment to the total employment ratio; (3) total R&D FTE personnel salary to total employee compensation ratio; (4) average R&D FTE salary; (5) percentage of basic research in total R&D expenditure; (6) percentage of applied research in total R&D expenditure; (7) percentage of experimental development in total R&D expenditure; (8) percentage of researchers in total R&D FTE employment; (9) percentage of technicians in total R&D FTE employment; (10) percentage of other supporting staff in total R&D FTE employment; (11) percentage of researchers' FTE salary in total R&D FTE personnel salary; (12) percentage of technicians' FTE salary in total R&D FTE personnel salary; and (13) percentage of other supporting staff's FTE salary in total R&D FTE salary.

8. As Gordon Hanson commented, the basic assumption in using the random-effects logit and random-effects tobit estimations is that the unobserved establishment-level heterogeneity is uncorrelated with the observed establishment characteristics (Greene 2003, 689–94; Baltagi 2001, 206–14). If this assumption is violated, the random-effects coefficient estimates will be inconsistent. Unfortunately, the Hausman-Taylor instrumental variable estimation method for error components that deals with this potential problem in continuous dependent variable models is not applicable to the binary choice or limited dependent variable models I used.

which have the same explanatory variables as the random-effects tobit regressions, the dependent variable is one of the 13 different R&D activity measures each grouped into 6 categories. I estimate the following regression equation:

$$
\begin{aligned}
\text{R\&DActivity}_{ijt} = \; & \text{Constant} + \beta_1 \text{EstablishmentFDIShareGroup}_{ijt} \\
& + \beta_2 \text{SectorFDIShare}_{jt} + \beta_3 \text{RevenueGroup}_{ilt}(\text{Revenue}_{ijt}) \\
& + \beta_4 \text{EstablishmentPrivateOwnership}_{ijt} \\
& + \beta_5 \text{VerticalIntegration}_{ijt} + \beta_6 \text{ComparativeAdvantage}_{jt} \\
& + \beta_7 \text{HerfindahlIndex}_{jt} + \beta_8 \text{Year}_t + \beta_9 \text{Region}_{kt} + \mu_{ijt}
\end{aligned}
$$

where i = establishment, j = sector, k = region, l = revenue group, t = time, and

$$
\text{SectorFDIShare}_{jt} = \frac{\Sigma_j \text{EstablishmentFDIShare}_{ijt} * \text{Employment}_{ijt}}{\Sigma_i \text{Employment}_{ijt}}
$$

EstablishmentFDIShareGroup represents six dummy variables indicating the percentage of foreign ownership: 1 (= 0 percent foreign ownership), 2 (= 1–20 percent), 3 (= 21–40 percent), 4 (= 41–60 percent), 5 (= 61–80 percent), and 6 (= 81–100 percent). In the regressions run with only national establishments these variables are omitted, and in the regressions run with foreign establishments only the last five are used. Establishments with 0 percent foreign ownership are identified as national establishments. SectorFDIShare, the sectoral employment-weighted FDI concentration, is computed as foreign ownership percentage, averaged across all establishments in a sector, weighted by each establishment's share in that sector's employment. This variable is used as a proxy for spillover effects. RevenueGroup represents the dummy variables for the five establishment revenue groups, with equal number of observations, according to rising revenue levels. EstablishmentPrivateOwnership is a dummy variable indicating the absence (= 0) or presence (= 1) of private ownership. Establishments with 0 percent private ownership are identified as public (state-owned) establishments. VerticalIntegration is the establishment value added to output ratio, measuring backward (upstream) integration, i.e., the extent of intermediate manufacturing in the value chain. ComparativeAdvantage in each sector is measured by net exports divided by the sum of exports and imports in that sector. HerfindahlIndex represents Herfindahl sectoral concentration in terms of establishment revenues. Year and Region are dummy variables for the three years and the seven regions, respectively.

From the regression results, I expect, as my ad hoc hypotheses:

- Foreign establishments have a higher R&D propensity based on the analysis of my data from the SIS surveys.

- Establishments with higher percentage of foreign ownership have higher R&D propensity based on the empirical FDI literature.[9]

- National establishments in sectors with higher FDI concentration have higher R&D propensity—a positive spillover effect—because of either labor mobility or competitive pressures from foreign establishments.

- Establishments with larger revenues have higher R&D propensity based on the empirical industrial organization literature.[10]

- Public establishments have higher R&D propensity since they are, on the average, larger than private establishments and benefit more directly from state R&D incentives.

- Establishments with greater (backward) vertical integration have higher R&D propensity, since a longer value chain, extended to intermediate manufacturing, as opposed to mere assembly, increases either the need or the scope for R&D.

- Establishments in sectors with higher relative net exports have lower R&D propensity, since Turkish manufacturing's comparative advantage lies in labor-intensive sectors with lower skills and technologies.[11]

- Establishments in sectors with higher Herfindahl indices have higher R&D propensity, since higher concentration reflects less domestic competition and higher profitability, which can result in higher net revenues to finance R&D.[12]

---

9. Moran (1998, 126) concludes, on the basis of empirical evidence, that "the greater the activity of wholly owned subsidiaries in a given economy the more likely the prospects for spillovers and externalities to domestic firms," although he does not refer to R&D activities specifically. Moran (2001, and chapter 11 of this volume) reiterates the importance of full foreign ownership for the subsidiary's use of the state-of-the-art technologies. Javorcik and Spatareanu, too, conclude, based on empirical results for Romania, that wholly owned foreign firms receive more technology transfer than partially owned ones (Javorcik and Spatareanu 2003). Blomström and Sjöholm (1999) hypothesize that the greater the parent control, based on increasing percentage of ownership, the greater the incentive to transfer more sophisticated technologies to foreign affiliates. According to their empirical results for Indonesia, based on cross-section data for 1991, however, the degree of foreign ownership does not affect either the level of labor productivity in foreign establishments or the spillovers to national establishments, only foreign ownership matters (Blomström and Sjöholm 1999).

10. The empirical literature consensus is that the elasticity of R&D with respect to firm size is close to unity (Gustavsson and Poldahl 2003).

11. Among developed countries, comparative advantage and R&D are usually positively correlated, but for developing countries such as Turkey the correlation could be negative, especially in cases of import-substitution industrialization.

12. The effect of industrial concentration on R&D, both theoretically and empirically, has been controversial, however, since Schumpeter postulated a negative relationship between competition and innovation 70 years ago (Gustavsson and Poldahl 2003).

■ Establishments located in the more developed regions, such as Marmara, Aegean, and Mediterranean, have a higher R&D propensity, reflecting their better infrastructure and the greater availability of highly skilled labor.

Empirical Results

Before investigating the significance of foreign ownership by establishment and foreign ownership concentration by sector for the probability that an establishment will have R&D activity in the Manufacturing and the R&D Survey through random-effects logit, I ran Hotelling's T-squared generalized means test as well as a two-sample t-test with unequal variances to show that foreign establishments had indeed statistically significant higher R&D propensity according to both surveys.[13]

Moreover, before investigating the significance of foreign ownership by establishment and foreign ownership concentration by sector for the various R&D expenditure- and R&D employment-based variables through random-effects tobit, I ran Hotelling's T-squared generalized means test as well as a two-sample t-test with unequal variances to show foreign ownership indeed mattered. Foreign establishments had statistically significant higher average percentages in all three types of R&D activity, although the rankings were the same for both groups. As expected, basic research accounted for the lowest and experimental development accounted for the highest average percentage. However, foreign establishments had statistically significant lower average percentages of basic research and applied research R&D expenditure and higher average percentages of experimental development R&D expenditure. On the average, foreign and national establishments differed in the composition of their R&D personnel, but the difference was not highly significant. The rankings of the three types of R&D personnel were the same for both groups. As expected, researchers accounted for the highest and other supporting staff accounted for the lowest average percentage. On the average, foreign and national establishments also differed in the composition of their R&D personnel total compensation—the difference was statistically more significant than their R&D personnel composition. The rankings of the three types of R&D personnel total compensation were the same for both groups. As expected, researchers accounted for the highest and the other supporting staff accounted for the lowest average percentage.

In summary, although foreign establishments devoted a lower percentage of their R&D expenditure to basic research and applied research, they had higher average percentages of researchers and technicians in their R&D

---

13. The relevant statistical tables, omitted due to space restrictions, are available from the author upon request.

personnel and paid higher proportions of their total R&D compensation to researchers and technicians than national establishments. Therefore, it is unsurprising that foreign establishments had statistically significant higher average R&D salary than national establishments.

Finally, foreign establishments had statistically significant higher R&D performance indices, in terms of R&D intensity (ratio of R&D expenditure to total revenue), R&D employment intensity (ratio of R&D employment to total employment), and R&D salary intensity (ratio of R&D employee compensation to total employee compensation) than national establishments.

I conclude, therefore, that foreign establishments in Turkish manufacturing during 1993–95 were on the average more active in R&D activities than national establishments. The question that remains is whether this difference was a result of their foreign status per se or some other explanatory variables such as their average larger size. The regression results presented below will attempt to answer that question.

In all the regressions, I specify three models. The first model includes both national and foreign establishments, the second model includes only national establishments, and the third model includes only foreign establishments. Although the panel has 30,948 observations, all the regressions are based on 30,573 observations for which data exist for all the explanatory variables.[14]

Random-Effects Logit Regression Results

Random-Effects Logit Regression Results for R&D Activity in the Manufacturing Survey

Table 5.1 presents the random-effects logit regression results for the Manufacturing Survey–based R&D activity indicator. Foreign ownership is positively and significantly associated with the presence of R&D activity when all establishments are included, but this association does not get stronger with increasing percentage of foreign ownership. The minority foreign ownership group 3, with 21–40 percent, has the strongest association in terms of the odds ratio. Increasing percentage of foreign ownership is not, however, significantly associated with the presence of R&D activity when only foreign establishments are included. Sectoral FDI concentration is positively and significantly associated with the presence of R&D activity— i.e., there is a spillover effect from foreign establishments to national establishments. There is no spillover effect when only foreign establishments are

---

14. The tables containing the summary statistics for the regression variables as well as the tables containing the pairwise correlation coefficients for the explanatory variables, omitted due to space restrictions, are available from the author upon request.

Table 5.1 Random-effects logit results for R&D activity in the Manufacturing Survey

Variable	Model (1): All establishments	Model (2): National establishments	Model (3): Foreign establishments
Constant	−5.5639841 (22.63)**	−5.5414014 (22.67)**	−1.5728112 (0.79)
Foreign ownership group 2 (1–20 percent)	0.8740066 2.3964935 (2.48)*	n.a.	n.a.
Foreign ownership group 3 (21–40 percent)	1.6089281 4.9974518 (4.03)**	n.a.	n.a.
Foreign ownership group 4 (41–60 percent)	1.3060664 3.6916238 (4.52)**	n.a.	n.a.
Foreign ownership group 5 (61–80 percent)	1.3857398 3.9977822 (2.85)**	n.a.	n.a.
Foreign ownership group 6 (81–100 percent)	0.8814141 2.4143113 (3.34)**	n.a.	n.a.
Foreign ownership share group 2 (21–40 percent)	n.a.	n.a.	0.2188673 1.2446661 (0.28)
Foreign ownership share group 3 (41–60 percent)	n.a.	n.a.	−0.2261132 0.7976278 (0.28)
Foreign ownership share group 4 (61–80 percent)	n.a.	n.a.	−0.4606459 0.6308760 (0.44)
Foreign ownership share group 5 (81–100 percent)	n.a.	n.a.	−0.8185475 0.4410719 (1.01)
Employment-weighted sector FDI share	0.0175988 1.0177545 (4.10)**	0.0169249 1.0170690 (3.79)**	0.0352433 1.0358717 (1.88)
Total revenue group 2	0.4638451 1.5901766 (4.52)**	0.4661498 1.5938458 (4.57)**	−0.6777123 0.5077773 (0.33)
Total revenue group 3	1.0268003 2.7921176 (9.89)**	1.0302789 2.8018471 (9.98)**	−0.1032099 0.9019376 (0.06)
Total revenue group 4	1.4869114 4.4234121 (14.13)**	1.4893397 4.4341666 (14.19)**	0.2148765 1.2397088 (0.12)

(table continues next page)

Table 5.1   Random-effects logit results for R&D activity in the Manufacturing Survey *(continued)*

Variable	Model (1): All establishments	Model (2): National establishments	Model (3): Foreign establishments
Total revenue group 5	2.4534530	2.4213921	1.4429452
	11.6284303	11.2615257	4.2331449
	(22.49)**	(22.26)**	(0.81)
Observations	30,573	29,654	919
Groups	12,871	12,568	376
Wald chi^2	975.23	793.56	45.00
Prob > chi^2	0.0000	0.0000	0.0004
Log likelihood	−10,589.074	−10,109.273	−471.51463
Rho	.5938589	.5843096	.7613425
Likelihood-ratio test of rho = 0:			
chibar^2 (01)	2,007.52	1,811.50	170.54
Prob ≥ chibar^2	0.000	0.000	0.000

chibar^2 = The likelihood ratio test statistic of rho.
Wald chi^2 = The Wald hypothesis test statistic for the model.

Notes: Each cell lists the coefficient (b), the coefficient transformed to the odds ratio (i.e., e^b instead of b), and the absolute value of z statistics in parentheses (* = significance at 5 percent; ** = significance at 1 percent). The cells for the other explanatory variables are omitted due to space restrictions. Rho is the proportion of the total variance contributed by the panel-level variance component. If rho equals zero, then the panel estimator and the pooled estimator are not different. The likelihood-ratio test compares the panel estimator with the pooled estimator through the null hypothesis that they are not different.

included. Establishment size, measured by total revenue, is positively and significantly associated with the presence of R&D activity, when either all or only national establishments are included. Moreover, this association gets stronger with increasing total revenue. Private ownership is positively and significantly associated with the presence of R&D activity in the first two models.[15] It is dropped from the third model since all foreign establishments are private. Vertical integration is positively and significantly associated with the presence of R&D activity when either all or only national establishments are included. Comparative advantage is negatively and significantly associated with the presence of R&D activity in all three models. Herfindahl index is positively and significantly associated with the presence of R&D activity in only the first two models. The region dummy variables (relative to the Marmara region) are mostly negative but not all significant. The year dummy variables (relative to 1993) are positive in all three models but significant in only the first two. All three regressions

---

15. The regression coefficients for the rest of the explanatory variables, omitted from tables 5.1–5.6 due to space restrictions, are available from the author upon request.

are statistically significant in terms of the Wald chi-square statistic. This holds for all the other estimations reported below. In all three regressions, the proportion of the variance contributed by the panel-level variance is important according to the likelihood-ratio test, which compares the pooled estimator (logit) with the panel estimator. This holds for the second random-effects logit estimations as well as for most of the random-effects tobit estimations reported below.

Random-Effects Logit Regression Results for R&D Activity in the R&D Survey

Table 5.2 presents the random-effects logit regression results for the R&D Survey–based overall R&D activity (combined basic, applied, and experimental development activities) indicator. Foreign ownership is positively and significantly associated with the presence of R&D activity when all establishments are included, but this association does not automatically get stronger with increasing percentage of foreign ownership. Foreign ownership group 4, with 41 to 60 percent, has the strongest association in terms of the odds ratio (in contrast to the minority foreign ownership group 2, with 21 to 40 percent, according to the Manufacturing Survey–based results). Increasing percentage of foreign ownership, relative to the foreign establishments in the 1 to 20 percent foreign ownership group 2, is negative but for only two of the four foreign ownership share groups significantly associated with the presence of R&D activity when only foreign establishments are included. Sectoral FDI concentration is positively and significantly associated with the presence of R&D activity but does not indicate a spillover effect from foreign establishments to national establishments since it is insignificant when only national establishments are included. Establishment size, measured by total revenue, is positively and significantly associated with the presence of R&D activity in all three models. This confirms the result from the previous regression that large establishment size has a very strong association with the propensity to conduct R&D. Private ownership is negatively and significantly associated with the presence of R&D activity, contrary to the result obtained from the Manufacturing Survey–based regressions. Vertical integration is positively and significantly associated with the presence of R&D activity in the first two models. For only foreign establishments, however, vertical integration is negatively associated with R&D activity. Comparative advantage is negatively and significantly associated with the presence of R&D activity in the first two models. Herfindahl index is positively but not significantly associated with the presence of R&D activity in all three models. The year dummy variables are mostly positive but not significant in contrast to the results based on the Manufacturing Survey.

To sum up these two sets of random-effects logit regression results, although obtained from two different R&D databases, they are on the

Table 5.2   Random-effects logit results for R&D activity in the R&D Survey

Variable	Model (1): All establishments	Model (2): National establishments	Model (3): Foreign establishments
Constant	−26.7572766 (12.08)**	−56.3301782 (10.87)**	−8.1077674 (4.66)**
Foreign ownership group 2 (1–20 percent)	15.4792238 5.27888e+06 (7.90)**	n.a.	n.a.
Foreign ownership group 3 (21–40 percent)	13.7973853 9.82038e+05 (8.15)**	n.a.	n.a.
Foreign ownership group 4 (41–60 percent)	16.6917325 1.77471e+07 (10.67)**	n.a.	n.a.
Foreign ownership group 5 (61–80 percent)	14.2997731 1.62298e+06 (8.18)**	n.a.	n.a.
Foreign ownership group 6 (81–100 percent)	14.4534434 1.89256e+06 (9.49)**	n.a.	n.a.
Foreign ownership share group 2 (21–40 percent)	n.a.	n.a.	−0.8246977 0.4383675 (0.74)
Foreign ownership share group 3 (41–60 percent)	n.a.	n.a.	−5.0553583 0.0063751 (3.49)**
Foreign ownership share group 4 (61–80 percent)	n.a.	n.a.	−0.5208829 0.5939959 (0.37)
Foreign ownership share group 5 (81–100 percent)	n.a.	n.a.	−7.1678178 0.0007710 (4.31)**
Employment-weighted sector FDI share	0.0509063 1.0522243 (3.03)**	0.0254935 1.0258212 (1.27)	0.0883789 1.0924020 (2.46)*
Total revenue	0.0000031 1.0000031 (10.95)**	0.0000064 1.0000064 (11.96)**	0.0000015 1.0000015 (5.02)**
Observations	30,573	29,654	919
Groups	12,871	12,568	376
Wald chi^2	205.58	186.58	43.99
Prob > chi^2	0.0000	0.0000	0.0001
Log likelihood	−1,008.1027	−760.34778	−176.74422
Rho	.9887685	.997746	.9663656

(table continues next page)

Table 5.2 Random-effects logit results for R&D activity in the R&D Survey (continued)

Variables	Model (1): All establishments	Model (2): National establishments	Model (3): Foreign establishments
Likelihood-ratio test of rho = 0:			
chibar² (01)	1,529.12	1,354.02	224.99
Prob ≥ chibar²	0.000	0.000	0.000

chibar² = The likelihood ratio test statistic of rho.
Wald chi² = The Wald hypothesis test statistic for the model.

Notes: Each cell lists the coefficient (b), the coefficient transformed to the odds ratio (i.e., e^b instead of b), and the absolute value of z statistics in parentheses (* = significance at 5 percent; ** = significance at 1 percent). The cells for the other explanatory variables are omitted due to space restrictions. Rho is the proportion of the total variance contributed by the panel-level variance component. If rho equals zero, then the panel estimator and the pooled estimator are not different. The likelihood-ratio test compares the panel estimator with the pooled estimator through the null hypothesis that they are not different.

whole quite similar. Foreign ownership has a positive and significant association with the presence of R&D activity among all establishments. The strength of this association, however, does not increase linearly with the percentage of foreign ownership. Among foreign establishments, on the other hand, no significant positive association exists between percentage of foreign ownership and R&D activity. In fact, the association is mostly negative, relative to the foreign establishments in the 1 to 20 percent foreign ownership group, although not always significant. As for sectoral FDI concentration, it is positively and significantly associated with the presence of R&D activity when all establishments are included. There is a strong spillover effect from foreign establishments to national establishments in the Manufacturing Survey but not in the R&D Survey. The only consistent difference between the two sets of results pertains to the role of private versus public ownership.

Random-Effects Tobit Regression Results[16]

Random-Effects Tobit Regression Results for R&D Intensity

According to table 5.3, foreign ownership is positively and significantly associated with an establishment's R&D intensity (the establishment ratio of total R&D expenditures to total revenue) only in the first model. This

16. Due to space restrictions, the detailed results for only 3 of the 13 R&D activity indicators are reported here. The detailed results for the other 10 R&D activity indicators are available from the author upon request.

Table 5.3 Random-effects tobit results for R&D intensity (total R&D expenditure to total revenue)

Variable	Model (1): All establishments	Model (2): National establishments	Model (3): Foreign establishments
Constant	−1.09843e−01 (16.02)**	−1.47246e−01 (13.78)**	−3.18070e−02 (7.72)**
Foreign ownership group 2 (1–20 percent)	3.93983e−02 (6.74)**	n.a.	n.a.
Foreign ownership group 3 (21–40 percent)	3.74816e−02 (4.21)**	n.a.	n.a.
Foreign ownership group 4 (41–60 percent)	4.59615e−02 (9.08)**	n.a.	n.a.
Foreign ownership group 5 (61–80 percent)	4.31465e−02 (3.86)**	n.a.	n.a.
Foreign ownership group 6 (81–100 percent)	3.36599e−02 (5.28)**	n.a.	n.a.
Foreign ownership share group 2 (21–40 percent)	n.a.	n.a.	−1.20165e−03 (0.37)
Foreign ownership share group 3 (41–60 percent)	n.a.	n.a.	−4.58608e−03 (1.46)
Foreign ownership share group 4 (61–80 percent)	n.a.	n.a.	−9.99723e−04 (0.23)
Foreign ownership share group 5 (81–100 percent)	n.a.	n.a.	−7.92196e−03 (2.56)*
Employment-weighted sector FDI share	5.17936e−04 (4.31)**	3.01457e−04 (1.76)	4.83735e−04 (4.89)**
Total output	6.81756e−09 (13.31)**	8.55314e−09 (12.69)**	3.22311e−09 (8.67)**
Observations	30,573	29,654	919
Groups	12,871	12,568	376
Wald χ^2	407.28	315.61	156.62
Prob > χ^2	0.0000	0.0000	0.0000
Log likelihood	180.20566	3.4251852	230.80861
Rho	.8144392	.8461469	.843226
Likelihood-ratio test of rho = 0: chibar^2(01)	1,062.98	891.26	218.75
Prob ≥ chibar^2	0.000	0.000	0.000

chibar^2 = The likelihood ratio test statistic of rho.
n.a. = not applicable
Wald χ^2 = The Wald hypothesis test statistic for the model.

Notes: The absolute value of z statistics is in parentheses (* = significance at 5 percent; ** = significance at 1 percent). The cells for the other explanatory variables are omitted due to space restrictions. Rho is the proportion of the total variance contributed by the panel-level variance component. If rho equals zero, then the panel estimator and the pooled estimator are not different. The likelihood-ratio test compares the panel estimator with the pooled estimator through the null hypothesis that they are not different.

association is strongest for the foreign ownership group 4, with 41 to 60 percent, confirming the result obtained from the logit regression based on the R&D Survey. In the third model, however, the association among all foreign establishments turns negative, and the highest foreign ownership percentage (81 to 100 percent) dummy variable becomes significantly negative. In other words, foreign establishments close to or with wholly foreign ownership seem to have markedly lower R&D intensity relative to other foreign establishments. This is robust across all the tobit regressions. Sectoral FDI concentration is positively and significantly associated with the presence of R&D activity but does not indicate a spillover effect from foreign establishments to national establishments since it is insignificant when only national establishments are included. This outcome confirms the result obtained from the logit regression based on the R&D Survey. Establishment size, measured in this regression by total output instead of total revenue to avoid endogeneity, is positively and significantly associated with R&D intensity in all three models. This result is robust across all of the tobit regressions. Private ownership is negatively and significantly associated with R&D intensity, confirming the result obtained from the logit regression based on the R&D Survey. This result is robust across most of the tobit regressions. Vertical integration is positively and significantly associated with R&D intensity in the first two models. In the third model, the association turns negative but is insignificant. This result is robust across most of the tobit regressions. Comparative advantage is negative and significantly associated with R&D intensity in all the models. This result, too, is robust across most of the tobit regressions. Herfindahl index is positively and significantly associated with R&D intensity in only the second model. In the other tobit regressions, both the sign and the significance of this variable change without a definite pattern. The year dummy variables are mostly negative but not all significant.

Random-Effects Tobit Results for R&D Employment Intensity

According to table 5.4, foreign ownership is positively and significantly associated with an establishment's R&D employment intensity (the establishment ratio of total R&D FTE employment to total employment) in the first model. This association is strongest, however, for the first foreign ownership group 2, with 1 to 20 percent. In the third model, on the other hand, the association is significantly negative across all share groups—i.e., relative to the foreign establishments in the 1 to 20 percent foreign ownership group 2, foreign establishments with higher foreign ownership percentage have markedly lower R&D employment intensity. Sectoral FDI concentration is positively and significantly associated with the R&D employment intensity in all three models. There is a positive and significant spillover effect from foreign establishments to national establishments.

Table 5.4 Random-effects tobit results for R&D employment intensity (total R&D FTE personal to total employment)

Variable	Model (1): All establishments	Model (2): National establishments	Model (3): Foreign establishments
Constant	−1.18435e−01 (14.23)**	−1.36673e−01 (19.09)**	−1.59042e−02 (2.21)*
Foreign ownership group 2 (1–20 percent)	5.27645e−02 (11.13)**	n.a.	n.a.
Foreign ownership group 3 (21–40 percent)	4.41409e−02 (8.17)**	n.a.	n.a.
Foreign ownership group 4 (41–60 percent)	3.10452e−02 (6.84)**	n.a.	n.a.
Foreign ownership group 5 (61–80 percent)	4.85842e−02 (7.10)**	n.a.	n.a.
Foreign ownership group 6 (81–100 percent)	3.40671e−02 (7.35)**	n.a.	n.a.
Foreign ownership share group 2 (21–40 percent)	n.a.	n.a.	−3.38735e−02 (5.57)**
Foreign ownership share group 3 (41–60 percent)	n.a.	n.a.	−3.42875e−02 (5.59)**
Foreign ownership share group 4 (61–80 percent)	n.a.	n.a.	−2.53224e−02 (3.37)**
Foreign ownership share group 5 (81–100 percent)	n.a.	n.a.	−3.30750e−02 (5.71)**
Employment-weighted sector FDI share	6.37011e−04 (5.33)**	4.46969e−04 (3.20)**	1.07963e−03 (5.41)**
Total revenue	6.50696e−09 (11.99)**	1.12227e−08 (18.51)**	6.13397e−09 (8.71)**
Observations	30,573	29,654	919
Groups	12,871	12,568	376
Wald chi^2	670.90	506.12	285.91
Prob > chi^2	0.0000	0.0000	0.0000
Log likelihood	118.83522	−.31301305	111.07835
Rho	.8697904	.9028705	.9222484
Likelihood-ratio test of rho = 0: chibar^2(01)	1,448.25	1,179.05	221.98
Prob ≥ chibar	0.000	0.000	0.000

chibar^2 = The likelihood ratio test statistic of rho.
FTE = full-time equivalent
n.a. = not applicable
Wald chi^2 = The Wald hypothesis test statistic for the model.

Notes: The absolute value of z statistics is in parentheses (* = significance at 5 percent; ** = significance at 1 percent). The cells for the other explanatory variables are omitted due to space restrictions. Rho is the proportion of the total variance contributed by the panel-level variance component. If rho equals zero, then the panel estimator and the pooled estimator are not different. The likelihood-ratio test compares the panel estimator with the pooled estimator through the null hypothesis that they are not different.

Random-Effects Tobit Results for R&D Salary Intensity

According to table 5.5, foreign ownership is positively and significantly associated with an establishment's R&D salary intensity (the establishment ratio of total R&D full FTE total salary to total employment compensation) in the first model. In the third model, however, the foreign ownership percentage is significantly negative across two of the four share groups. Sectoral FDI concentration is positively and significantly associated with the R&D salary intensity in all three models. There is a positive and significant spillover effect from foreign establishments to national establishments.

To sum up the random-effects tobit results, foreign ownership has a positive and significant association with the 13 different R&D activity measures among all establishments. The strength of this association, however, does not increase linearly with the percentage of foreign ownership. On the contrary, the association is relatively stronger for establishments with minority foreign ownership (1 to 20 percent and 21 to 40 percent). Among only foreign establishments, however, the association is mostly negative relative to the foreign establishments in the 1 to 20 percent foreign ownership group, although not always significant. As for sectoral FDI concentration, it is positively and significantly associated with the R&D activity measures in all but a very few of the regressions.

Ordered Logit Results

The regression coefficients from the random-effects tobit results are hard to interpret to understand how the increasing percentage of foreign ownership, relative to national ownership, affects R&D activities. In order to deal with this issue, I ran ordered logit (proportional odds) estimations with the same explanatory variables but on the ordered grouping of the dependent variables into six groups.[17] The first group of each dependent variable contains those establishments for which the dependent variable is zero; the next five groups are the quintiles ranging from the smallest to the largest. Table 5.6 contains the results for only the first model, which includes all establishments, and for only the first 3 of the 13 R&D activity measures.[18] According to the comparison of the odds ratios, although foreign ownership is positively and significantly associated with the R&D activity variables, this association becomes progressively weaker in terms

---

17. Since ordered logit, which is not yet available as a panel-data estimator, is normally applied to cross-section data, its application to my study is open to question. However, I can defend the use of ordered logit with panel data by accounting for the clustering of the observations on establishments—i.e., specifying that observations are independent across establishments but not necessarily within clusters of establishments.

18. The complete ordered logit results, omitted due to space restrictions, are available from the author upon request.

Table 5.5 Random-effects tobit results for R&D salary intensity (total R&D FTE compensation to total employment compensation)

Variable	Model (1): All establishments	Model (2): National establishments	Model (3): Foreign establishments
Constant	−2.58662e−01 (22.21)**	−2.86576e−01 (17.41)**	−7.6635e−02 (7.49)**
Foreign ownership group 2 (1–20 percent)	9.67897e−02 (7.52)**	n.a.	n.a.
Foreign ownership group 3 (21–40 percent)	1.00096e−01 (6.27)**	n.a.	n.a.
Foreign ownership group 4 (41–60 percent)	9.25064e−02 (8.87)**	n.a.	n.a.
Foreign ownership group 5 (61–80 percent)	1.05639e−01 (5.96)**	n.a.	n.a.
Foreign ownership group 6 (81–100 percent)	4.75605e−02 (4.14)**	n.a.	n.a.
Foreign ownership share group 2 (21–40 percent)	n.a.	n.a.	−5.66511e−03 (0.70)
Foreign ownership share group 3 (41–60 percent)	n.a.	n.a.	−2.26059e−02 (2.63)**
Foreign ownership share group 4 (61–80 percent)	n.a.	n.a.	−1.90467e−02 (1.86)
Foreign ownership share group 5 (81–100 percent)	n.a.	n.a.	−6.03924e−02 (6.55)**
Employment-weighted sector FDI share	1.03392e−03 (4.24)**	8.66017e−04 (2.32)*	9.44466e−04 (3.24)**
Total revenue	1.51032e−08 (11.42)**	1.75203e−08 (11.23)**	1.03965e−08 (10.58)**
Observations	30,573	29,654	919
Groups	12,871	12,568	376
Wald chi^2	465.28	285.45	226.08
Prob > chi^2	0.0000	0.0000	0.0000
Log likelihood	−159.89006	−225.37648	95.780304
Rho	.8287291	.8441411	.8778222
Likelihood-ratio test of rho = 0:			
chibar^2 (01)	1238.27	1016.07	244.69
Prob ≥ chibar^2	0.000	0.000	0.000

chibar^2 = The likelihood ratio test statistic of rho.
FTE = full-time equivalent
n.a. = not applicable
Wald chi^2 = The Wald hypothesis test statistic for the model.

Notes: The absolute value of z statistics is in parentheses (* = significance at 5 percent; ** = significance at 1 percent). The cells for the other explanatory variables are omitted due to space restrictions. Rho is the proportion of the total variance contributed by the panel-level variance component. If rho equals zero, then the panel estimator and the pooled estimator are not different. The likelihood-ratio test compares the panel estimator with the pooled estimator through the null hypothesis that they are not different.

Table 5.6 Ordered logit results

Variable	Total R&D expenditure to total revenue ratio	R&D employment to total employment ratio	R&D total salary to total employment compensation ratio
Foreign ownership group 2 (1–20 percent)	12.25886 (5.99)**	11.93809 (5.74)**	12.12679 (5.79)**
Foreign ownership group 3 (21–40 percent)	10.77301 (3.97)**	11.25853 (4.38)**	11.07071 (4.29)**
Foreign ownership group 4 (41–60 percent)	7.90234 (4.58)**	7.421534 (4.16)**	7.305323 (4.26)**
Foreign ownership group 5 (61–80 percent)	6.339716 (2.91)**	5.952683 (2.69)**	5.433879 (2.50)*
Foreign ownership group 6 (81–100 percent)	3.971396 (2.98)**	4.093725 (3.11)**	4.040593 (3.12)**
Employment-weighted sector FDI share	1.033751 (3.76)**	1.03197 (3.56)**	1.031915 (3.58)**
Observations	30,573	30,573	30,573
Wald chi^2	349.42	364.50	374.39
Prob > chi^2	0.0000	0.0000	0.0000
Log pseudo-likelihood	−2,495.9931	−2,501.8354	−2,500.5778
Pseudo R^2	0.1546	0.1527	0.1531

chibar^2 = The likelihood ratio test statistic of rho.
Wald chi^2 = The Wald hypothesis test statistic for the model.

Notes: In each cell, the first entry is the odds ratio, and the second entry, in parentheses, is the absolute value of the z statistics (* = significance at 5 percent; ** = significance at 1 percent). The cells for the other explanatory variables are omitted due to space restrictions. The robust (Huber/White/sandwich variance estimator–based) standard errors are adjusted for clustering on establishment, specifying that the observations are independent across clusters (establishments) but not necessarily within clusters.

of decreasing odds ratios as the percentage of foreign ownership increases. Sectoral FDI concentration is positively and significantly associated with all the R&D activity variables, but this association is weaker than the association for foreign ownership. In other words, the direct effect of foreign ownership is relatively much more important than its indirect effect. In summary, the ordered logit results regarding the direct and indirect association between foreign ownership and R&D activities confirm those from the random-effects tobit regressions.

Summary and Conclusions

The FDI literature suggests that R&D activities of foreign firms may help strengthen host country capability for R&D directly or indirectly by stimulating the R&D activities of national firms. In this study, I investigated the R&D activities of Turkish manufacturing establishments, using panel data for 1993–95 from two different sources of the Turkish State Institute of Statistics. I bridged these two sources of data through common establishment codes to shed light on the presence, types, and levels of R&D activities, focusing on the differences between nationally owned and foreign-owned establishments and on spillover effects from foreign to national establishments. In doing so, I controlled for establishment characteristics such as private versus public ownership, size, vertical (backward) integration, and regional location as well as for sector characteristics such as international competitiveness and industrial concentration.

My three basic conclusions about the association between foreign ownership and R&D activities (the presence of aggregate R&D activity and the 13 R&D activity measures):

- Among all (national and foreign) establishments, foreign ownership is, on the whole, positively and significantly associated with R&D activities. This association does not become stronger, however, with increasing percentage of foreign ownership. On the contrary, it becomes weaker. The association is relatively strongest for the two lowest foreign ownership percentage groups (1 to 20 percent and 21 to 40 percent)— i.e., for minority foreign ownership.

- Among only foreign establishments, however, the rising percentage of foreign ownership is, on the whole, negatively although not often significantly associated with R&D activities. This negative association is most often significant for establishments with the highest foreign ownership percentage (81 to 100 percent). In other words, foreign establishments close to or with wholly foreign ownership seem to have markedly lower R&D propensity relative to other foreign establishments.

- Sectoral FDI concentration is positively and significantly associated with R&D activities among all or only national establishments. Among all establishments, this indirect effect of foreign ownership is relatively weaker, however, than its direct effect, measured in terms of an establishment's foreign ownership percentage. Among only national establishments, this indirect effect, although not always statistically significant, represents a spillover effect from foreign establishments to national establishments. Among only foreign establishments, this indirect effect is also positive but not always statistically significant.

In summary, my empirical results strongly support the positive role of FDI in the Turkish manufacturing-sector R&D activities but indicate that this positive role is stronger in establishments with minority foreign ownership than those with majority or full foreign ownership. My results also support the indirect role of FDI in terms of the positive spillover effect of foreign ownership on R&D activities of national establishments. In future research, these results should be extended with additional Turkish data, covering more years and more establishment characteristics. They should also be extended to other developing countries with the use of comparable data and techniques to discover whether the Turkish case is generalizable.

My results suggest that just as the internationalization of R&D has become increasingly important among developed countries, developing countries, too, can benefit from R&D internationalization through inward FDI. R&D activities of foreign firms can serve as a crucial channel for not only the transfer of technology but also the ability to absorb and even create technology. These specific empirical results need to be carefully interpreted and their policy implications properly considered. Even if a foreign establishment, especially a majority- or wholly owned one, does not conduct much R&D, it could have access to its parent's R&D and could use the parent's best technology.[19] Therefore, we cannot conclude that the lower R&D propensity of majority- or wholly owned foreign establishments necessarily implies their technological laggardness. The inverse association between percentage of foreign ownership and R&D propensity could indicate the reluctance of foreign parents to share their R&D activities and best technologies with national partners, in the absence of effective control and especially in the absence of effective intellectual property protection. This could induce minority-owned foreign establishments to perform more R&D to compensate for that reluctance. Accordingly, the proper policy implication for host country governments is not to insist on minority foreign ownership by imposing performance requirements in order to promote local R&D, but to provide the environment and the infrastructure, including the protection of intellectual property rights, that are most conducive to R&D activities of both foreign and national firms.

References

Amsden, Alice H., Ted Tschang, and Akira Goto. 2001. *Do Foreign Companies Conduct R&D in Developing Countries? A New Approach to Analyzing the Level of R&D, with an Analysis of Singapore.* Working Paper 14. Tokyo: Asian Development Bank Institute.

Asakawa, Kazuhiro. 2001. Organizational Tension in International R&D Management: The Case of Japanese Firms. *Research Policy* 30: 735–57.

Baltagi, Badi H. 2001. *Econometric Analysis of Panel Data,* 2d ed. Chichester, UK: John Wiley and Sons, Ltd.

Blomström, Magnus, and Ari Kokko. 1993. *Policies to Encourage Inflows of Technology through Foreign Multinationals.* NBER Working Paper 4289. Cambridge, MA: National Bureau of Economic Research.

---

19. As Theodore H. Moran commented, export-oriented versus domestic market–oriented foreign establishments can differ in their R&D activities. Export-oriented establishments can utilize their foreign parents' best technology without requiring much R&D, whereas domestic market–oriented establishments might need extensive R&D to customize their parents' products and processes to local market conditions. Unfortunately, I could not investigate this possibility due to lack of establishment-specific international trade data.

Blomström, Magnus, and Ari Kokko. 1998. Multinational Corporations and Spillovers. *Journal of Economic Surveys* 12, no. 3: 247–77.

Blomström, Magnus, and Ari Kokko. 2003. *Human Capital and Inward FDI.* Working Paper 167. Stockholm: Industrial Institute for Economic and Social Research.

Blomström, Magnus, Ari Kokko, and Mario Zejan. 1992. *Host Country Competition and Technology Transfer by Multinationals.* NBER Working Paper 4131. Cambridge, MA: National Bureau of Economic Research.

Blomström, Magnus, and Fredrik Sjöholm. 1999. Technology Transfer and Spillovers: Does Local Participation with Multinationals Matter? *European Economic Review* 43: 915–23.

Branstetter, Lee G. 2000. *Is Foreign Direct Investment a Channel of Knowledge Spillovers? Evidence from Japan's FDI in the United States.* NBER Working Paper 8015. Cambridge, MA: National Bureau of Economic Research.

Branstetter, Lee G. 2001. Are Knowledge Spillovers International or Intranational in Scope? Microeconometric Evidence from the U.S. and Japan. *Journal of International Economics* 53, no. 1 (February): 53–79.

Cantwell, John, and Simona Iammarino. 2003. Multinational Corporations and European Regional Systems of Innovation. In *Studies in Global Competition Series*, ed., John Cantwell and David Mowery. New York: Routledge.

Cantwell, John, and Odile Janne. 1999. Technological Globalization and Innovative Centres: The Role of Corporate Technological Leadership and Locational Hierarchy. *Research Policy* 28, no. 2–3 (March): 119–44.

Chuang, Yih-Chyi, and Chi-Mei Lin. 1999. Foreign Direct Investment, R&D, and Spillover Efficiency: Evidence from Taiwan's Manufacturing Firms. *The Journal of Development Studies* 35, no. 4 (April): 117–37.

Costa, Ionara, and Sergio Robles Reis de Queiroz. 2002. Foreign Direct Investment and Technological Capabilities in Brazilian Industry. Research Policy 31, no. 8–9 (December): 1431–43.

Elci, Sirin. 2003. Innovation Policy in Seven Candidate Countries: The Challenges— Innovation Policy Profile: Turkey. *Final Report Volume 2.7*, ed. CORDIS. Brussels: Enterprise Directorate-General of the European Union Commission.

Erdilek, Asim. 1982. *Direct Foreign Investment in Turkish Manufacturing: An Analysis of the Conflicting Objectives and Frustrated Expectations of a Host Country, Kieler Studien 169.* Tüebingen: J. C. B. Mohr.

Erdilek, Asim. 2003. A Comparative Analysis of Inward and Outward FDI in Turkey. *Transnational Corporations* 12, no. 3: 79–106.

FIAS (Foreign Investment Advisory Service). 2001a. Turkey: A Diagnostic Study of the Foreign Direct Investment Environment. Washington: FIAS.

FIAS (Foreign Investment Advisory Service). 2001b. Turkey: Administrative Barriers to Investment. Washington: FIAS.

Fisch, Jan Hendrik. 2003. Optimal Dispersion of R&D Activities in Multinational Corporations with a Genetic Algorithm. *Research Policy* 32, no. 8 (September): 1381–96.

Florida, Richard. 1997. The Globalization of R&D: Results of a Survey of Foreign-Affiliated R&D Laboratories in the United States. *Research Policy* 26, no. 1 (March): 85–103.

Fors, Gunnar, and Mario Zejan. 1996. *Overseas R&D by Multinationals in Foreign Centers of Excellence.* Working Paper 458. Stockholm: Industrial Institute for Economic and Social Research.

Gerybadze, Alexander, and Guido Reger. 1999. Globalization of R&D: Recent Changes in the Management of Innovation in Transnational Corporations. *Research Policy* 28, no. 2–3 (March): 251–74.

Granstrand, Ove. 1999. Internationalization of Corporate R&D: A Study of Japanese and Swedish Corporations. *Research Policy* 28, no. 2–3 (March): 275–302.

Greene, William H. 2003. *Econometric Analysis*, 5th ed. Upper Saddle River, NJ: Prentice Hall.

Gustavsson, Patrik, and Andreas Poldahl. 2003. *Determinants of Firm R&D: Evidence from Swedish Firm Level Data.* Working Paper 178. Stockholm: Stockholm School of Economics and European Institute of Japanese Studies.

Javorcik, Beata Smarzynska, and Kamal Saggi. 2004. *Technological Asymmetry among Foreign Investors and Mode of Entry. Trade and Development Research Group.* Washington: World Bank.

Javorcik, Beata Smarzynska, and Mariana Spatareanu. 2003. *To Share or Not to Share: Does Local Participation Matter for Spillovers from Foreign Direct Investment?* Policy Research Working Paper 3118. Washington: World Bank.

Kearns, Allan, and Frances Ruane. 2001. The Tangible Contribution of R&D-Spending Foreign-Owned Plants to a Host Region: A Plant Level Study of the Irish Manufacturing Sector (1980–1996). *Research Policy* 30, no. 2 (February): 227–44.

Kokko, Ari, and Magnus Blomström. 1995. Policies to Encourage Inflows of Technology through Foreign Multinationals. *World Development* 23, no. 3 (March): 459–68.

Kumar, Nagesh. 2001. Determinants of Location of Overseas R&D Activity of Multinational Enterprises: The Case of US and Japanese Corporations. *Research Policy* 30, no. 1 (January): 159–74.

Liu, Meng-chun, and Shin-Horng Chen. 2003. *International R&D Deployment and Locational Advantage: A Case Study of Taiwan.* Working Paper 10169. Cambridge, MA: National Bureau of Economic Research.

Mansfield, Edwin. 1994. *Intellectual Property Protection, Foreign Direct Investment and Technology Transfer.* IFC Discussion Paper 19. Washington: World Bank.

Maskus, Keith E. 2000. *Intellectual Property Rights in the Global Economy.* Washington: Institute for International Economics.

Meyer-Krahmer, Frieder, and Guido Reger. 1999. New Perspectives on the Innovation Strategies of Multinational Enterprises: Lessons for Technology Policy in Europe. *Research Policy* 28, no. 7 (September): 751–76.

Moran, Theodore H. 1998. *Foreign Direct Investment and Development: The New Policy Agenda for Developing Countries and Economies in Transition.* Washington: Institute for International Economics,

Moran, Theodore H. 2001. *Parental Supervision: The New Paradigm for Foreign Direct Investment and Development.* Washington: Institute for International Economics.

Niosi, Jorge, and Benoit Godin. 1999. Canadian R&D Abroad Management Practices. *Research Policy* 28, no. 2–3 (March): 215–30.

OECD (Organization for Economic Cooperation and Development). 1994. *The Measurement of Scientific and Technical Activities: Proposed Standard Practice for Surveys of Research and Experimental Development* (Frascati Manual). Paris.

OECD (Organization for Economic Cooperation and Development). 1999. *Managing National Innovation Systems.* Paris.

OECD (Organization for Economic Cooperation and Development). 2002a. *Foreign Direct Investment for Development: Maximizing Benefits and Minimizing Costs.* Paris.

OECD (Organization for Economic Cooperation and Development). 2002b. *OECD Science, Technology and Industry Outlook 2002.* Paris.

OECD (Organization for Economic Cooperation and Development). 2003. *OECD Science, Technology and Industry Scoreboard.* Paris.

Romer, P. M. 1990. Endogenous Technological Change. *Journal of Political Economy* 98, no. 5 (October): 71–102.

Serapio, Manuel G., and Donald H. Dalton. 1999. Globalization of Industrial R&D: An Examination of Foreign Direct Investments in R&D in the United States. *Research Policy* 28, no. 2–3 (March): 303–16.

Sigurdson, Jon, and Krystyna Palonka. 2002. *Technological Governance in ASEAN—Failings in Technology Transfer and Domestic Research.* Working Paper 162. Stockholm: Stockholm School of Economics and European Institute of Japanese Studies.

SIS (State Institute of Statistics). 1997. *Research and Development Statistics 1990–1995*. Ankara, Turkey: SIS.

Todo, Yasuyuki, and Koji Miyamoto. 2002. *Knowledge Diffusion from Multinational Enterprises: The Role of Domestic and Foreign Knowledge-Enhancing Activities*. OECD Development Center Technical Papers 196. Paris: OECD.

UNCTAD (United Nations Conference on Trade and Development). 2002. *World Investment Report 2002: Transnational Corporations and Export Competitiveness*. New York and Geneva: United Nations.

UNCTAD (United Nations Conference on Trade and Development). 2003a. *World Investment Report 2003: FDI Policies for Development: National and International Perspectives*. New York and Geneva: United Nations.

UNCTAD (United Nations Conference on Trade and Development). 2003b. *Foreign Direct Investment and Performance Requirements: New Evidence from Selected Countries*. New York and Geneva: United Nations.

UNCTAD (United Nations Conference on Trade and Development). 2003c. *Transfer of Technology for Successful Integration into the Global Economy. UNCTAD/Ite/Ipc/2003/6*. New York and Geneva: United Nations.

Zander, Ivo. 1997. Technological Diversification in the Multinational Corporation—Historical Evolution and Future Prospects. *Research Policy* 26, no. 2 (May): 209–27.

Zander, Ivo. 1998. The Evolution of Technological Capabilities in the Multinational Corporation—Dispersion, Duplication and Potential Advantages from Multinationality. *Research Policy* 27, no. 1 (May): 17–35.

Zander, Ivo. 1999. How Do You Mean 'Global'? An Empirical Investigation of Innovation Networks in the Multinational Corporation. *Research Policy* 28, no. 2–3 (March): 195–213.

Zedtwitz, Maximilian von, and Oliver Gassman. 2002. Market Versus Technology Drive in R&D Internationalization: Four Different Patterns of Managing Research and Development. *Research Policy* 31, no. 4 (May): 569–88.

6

Foreign Direct Investment and Local Economic Development: Beyond Productivity Spillovers

HOLGER GÖRG and ERIC STROBL

The increasing importance of multinational corporations (MNCs) and associated foreign direct investment (FDI) for international production has prompted considerable interest in the effects of MNCs on host countries. Specifically, it has long been recognized not only that FDI leads to an inflow of capital into a country, but that foreign affiliates located in the host country can benefit indigenous firms through technological spillovers. These spillovers arise because MNCs generally bring some sort of firm-specific assets (Markusen 2002) that allow them to compete successfully abroad.[1] These firm-specific assets, which can manifest themselves in various forms—for example, as superior marketing, management, or production techniques—can be conveniently described as "technological advantages" (foreign affiliates often use more advanced technology than indigenous firms). Since this technology has, at least to some extent, the characteristics of a public good, technological spillovers that benefit indigenous firms are possible.

Holger Görg is lecturer in economics and research fellow in the Leverhulme Centre for Research on Globalisation and Economic Policy at the University of Nottingham. He is also affiliated with DIW Berlin. Eric Strobl is associate professor at the University of Paris X. The authors are grateful to Forfás for the provision of data and to Marcus Breathnach for helpful advice. Holger Görg gratefully acknowledges financial support from the Leverhulme Trust under Programme Grant F114/BF and the European Commission under Grant No. SERD-2002-00077. Eric Strobl is grateful for his Marie Curie Research Fellowship.

1. There is, however, recent literature that argues that firm-specific assets are not necessary for multinationals to emerge. See, for instance, Fosfuri and Motta (1999).

Only recently has the theoretical literature pointed out that in the presence of imperfect competition and increasing returns to scale, linkages between MNCs and indigenous firms can also lead to pecuniary externalities benefiting firms in the host country (see Markusen and Venables 1999). In contrast to technological externalities, pecuniary externalities do not affect the production function of the benefiting firm, rather they affect the profit function via cost reductions or increased revenues. In a nutshell, increases in output by multinationals lead to an expansion of demand for intermediate products supplied by indigenous suppliers. This increase allows domestic suppliers to produce at a more efficient scale, thereby reducing average costs, which will ultimately reduce the price that multinationals and other domestically based final good producers pay for intermediates.

The empirical literature on technological externalities and the measurement of spillovers to date have largely focused on measuring productivity spillovers from MNCs to domestic firms in the host country.[2] This literature has its origins in studies by Caves (1974) and Globerman (1979), who analyzed productivity spillovers in Australia and Canada, respectively. Their initial approach has been refined and extended subsequently by, for example, Blomström and Persson (1983) and, most recently, Girma, Greenaway, and Wakelin (2001) and Keller and Yeaple (2003). However, to the best of our knowledge, only a scant number of attempts at measuring other channels of technological spillovers or indeed pecuniary spillovers have occurred.

Our purpose in this chapter is to discuss alternative means of assessing the impact of multinationals on industrial development. We examine the effects of MNCs on the development of domestic firms using the example of the Republic of Ireland, which appears to be a model case study given the importance of MNCs for its economy. For example, data from the Irish Central Statistics Office show that foreign multinationals in Ireland accounted for roughly 47 percent of manufacturing employment and 77 percent of net output in manufacturing in 1996. The corresponding figures in 1983 (the first year for which these data are available) were 38 and 58 percent respectively, which illustrates the increasing importance of multinationals for Irish manufacturing. While indigenous manufacturing tended to be concentrated on traditional and food-sector manufacturing activities, MNCs have invested primarily in modern high-tech sectors. This has led to a rapid increase in the significance of the high-tech sectors for the Irish economy (Barry and Bradley 1997). Furthermore, many observers have argued that the influx of FDI into the Irish economy has had significant

---

2. Görg and Strobl (2001) review empirical studies of productivity spillovers, using meta-analysis techniques. Görg and Greenaway (2004) provide a review of the issues from a more policy oriented viewpoint.

effects on the growth of the economy (see, for example, Sachs 1997; de la Fuente and Vives 1997).

This chapter looks at some of the microeconomic mechanisms through which such growth effects may work. In particular, we examine the effect on the entry and post-entry performance, in terms of survival and growth, of new plants. To this end, we not only discuss our previous work on these issues but also extend it in new directions.

The remainder of our chapter is organized as follows. In the second section we emphasize the importance of linkages for allowing technological and pecuniary externalities from FDI to occur. We also provide evidence of the incidence of linkages between foreign and indigenous firms in Irish manufacturing. The third section reviews the evidence of a "conventional" study of productivity spillovers by Ruane and Uğur (2005) for Ireland. The fourth section discusses our study of the effect of multinationals on domestic plant entry (Görg and Strobl 2002a). We also extend our previous work by looking at simulations that attempt to calculate what would have happened to the population of domestic plants in the absence of multinationals. By reviewing our study in Görg and Strobl (2003), the fifth section examines whether multinationals can assist new domestic plants to survive via technology spillovers. In the sixth section we extend the discussion of postentry effects of multinationals by looking at the effect on plant growth. In the final section, we offer concluding remarks and an assessment of the evidence to date.

Linkages

MNCs can be expected to have minimal effect on the domestic economy if they operate in so-called enclave sectors with no contacts with the domestic economy. Hence, it is unsurprising that the importance of backward or forward linkages between MNCs and domestic suppliers and/or customers has also been emphasized in the literature on externalities. In their review of the literature on productivity spillovers, Blomström and Kokko (1998, 248) point out that "local firms may be able to improve their productivity as a result of forward or backward linkages with MNC affiliates." Linkages are also important components in the models by Rodriguez-Clare (1996) and Markusen and Venables (1999), where multinationals can foster the development of domestic firms by creating linkages and expanding demand for local supplies.

An analysis of linkages between MNCs and domestic firms in Irish manufacturing industries can, therefore, provide information as to whether the conduit of external effects from multinationals exists. Data on linkages are available from the *Annual Survey of Irish Economy Expenditures*, which is undertaken annually by Forfás, the policy and advisory board for industrial development in Ireland.[3] The summary statistics, which are published by Forfás (1999), calculate backward linkages as the share of raw materials and components purchased in Ireland relative to total raw materials and components used.[4] Unfortunately, the survey does not include data to analyze forward linkages.

Table 6.1 presents the data for the value of backward linkages by foreign-owned firms in manufacturing industries. These figures exclude firms in the food and beverage sectors, which seems reasonable since one would expect firms in these sectors to have higher linkages than firms in other sectors due to the availability of perishable inputs. The tobacco sector is also excluded because of the sectoral aggregation of the data. As illustrated, the overall extent of backward linkages in foreign firms was about 18 percent in 1996.

Table 6.1 also shows that foreign manufacturing firms increased their linkages between 1987 and 1996 by roughly 3 percentage points. Although the aggregate data may suggest that the development of linkages has stagnated since the mid-1990s, Görg and Ruane (2001) present econometric evidence to suggest that individual firms increase their linkages over time. They undertake a firm-level econometric study of linkages between multinationals and indigenous firms in the Irish electronics sector between 1982 and 1995. On the basis of these results, Görg and Ruane argue that the apparent stagnation in the aggregate level of linkages can be attributed to the increase in the number of new foreign firms in Ireland and does not represent stagnation at the firm level. New foreign firms start off with an initially low level of linkage, but increase their linkages over time as they become accustomed to the supplier environment.[5]

Based on the arguments presented above, we suggest that the greater the extent of backward linkages between indigenous and foreign-owned firms, the greater the possibility of externalities from foreign firms benefiting domestic firms. An important caveat to this argument is that the potential for externalities through backward linkages is also associated with the goods being purchased. For example, the potential externalities from an electronics multinational buying electronic components might be greater than they are for the same firm buying packaging material. However, data

---

3. The survey is sent out to firms with more than 30 employees in manufacturing and internationally traded services industries. Although it is not compulsory for firms to take part in the survey, response rates are normally such that firms responding to the survey account for around 60–80 percent of employment of the target population each year (O'Malley 1995). The survey includes information on output and employment as well as on each firm's input purchases.

4. Note that Rodriguez-Clare (1996) and Alfaro and Rodriguez-Clare (2004) suggest calculating linkage coefficients as the ratio of the value of inputs bought domestically to total employment in the firm. This takes into account different input intensities for domestic and foreign firms. However, such data are not published by Forfás.

5. See also Kennedy (1991, 82–105) for similar arguments.

Table 6.1   Backward linkages by foreign-owned firms in manufacturing industries, 1987–96 (purchase of raw materials and components in millions of euro, constant 1997 prices)

Year	Total purchases	Irish purchases	Irish percent of total
1987	3,286	516	15.7
1988	3,828	611	16.0
1989	4,238	702	16.6
1990	4,226	792	18.7
1991	4,313	823	19.1
1992	4,819	921	19.1
1993	5,379	1,063	19.8
1994	6,403	1,243	19.4
1995	8,434	1,666	19.8
1996	9,548	1,756	18.4

Note: Manufacturing excludes food, drink, and tobacco.

Source: Forfás (1999).

to answer such a question are not available to us at present. Acknowledging this limitation, the level and growth of linkages in foreign firms may still suggest that there is further scope for positive effects through externalities between foreign and indigenous firms. Next, we discuss the channels for such externalities.

Productivity Spillovers

MNCs can affect indigenous firms through productivity. Because MNCs use a higher level of technology, and technology, or knowledge, has certain characteristics of public goods, indigenous firms may benefit from spillovers. If there are technological externalities, the presence of MNCs leads to productivity increases in domestic firms, allowing them to become more efficient. Productivity spillovers are difficult to measure since, as Krugman (1991, 53) observes, "knowledge flows . . . leave no paper trail by which they may be measured and tracked." The approach adopted in the empirical literature therefore largely avoids the (arguably difficult to answer) question as to how productivity spillovers actually occur, and focuses instead on the simpler issue of whether or not the presence of multinationals affects productivity in domestic firms.

However, the presence of multinationals can also have negative effects on the productivity of host country firms. As Aitken and Harrison (1999) argue, multinationals producing at lower marginal costs than host country firms have an incentive to increase output and attract demand away from these firms. This will cause host country rivals to cut production that, if they face fixed costs of production, will raise their average cost. Also, to the extent that the presence of multinationals leads to higher wage demands in the economy, this will increase a firm's average costs. Whether the effect of MNCs on productivity of host country firms is, on average, positive or negative is, therefore, ambiguous and needs to be decided empirically.

An empirical analysis of productivity spillovers usually comprises an econometric analysis in which labor productivity or total factor productivity in domestic firms is regressed on a number of independent variables assumed to have an effect on productivity. One variable is a measure of the presence of foreign firms in either the same industry (horizontal spillovers) or in vertically linked industries (vertical spillovers), usually defined as the share of employment, sales, or capital by foreign-owned firms. If the regression analysis yields a positive and statistically significant estimate of the coefficient on the foreign presence variable, this is taken as evidence that spillovers from MNCs to domestic firms occurred. This approach dates back to the studies by Caves (1974), Globerman (1979), and Blomström and Persson (1983), which focus on horizontal spillovers using cross-section industry-level data. The initial approach has been refined and extended to use firm-level panel data (e.g., Girma, Greenaway, and Wakelin 2001; Keller and Yeaple 2003) and to investigate vertical spillovers (Javorcik 2004; Girma, Görg, and Pisu 2004).

Ruane and Uğur (2005) implement this "conventional" approach using firm-level panel data available from the Irish Central Statistics Office from 1991 to 1998. They regress labor productivity (defined as net output per worker) on the employment share of foreign-owned firms in the same industry (defined alternatively at the two-, three-, and four-digit level) and control for capital intensity, skill intensity, and firm-specific time-invariant effects. Ruane and Uğur do not find any statistically significant evidence for productivity spillovers from these regressions. In alternative estimations, they use a similar setup but include total employment in foreign-owned firms in the industry as the "spillover variable," also controlling additionally for total employment in domestic firms. From these estimations they find robust evidence for horizontal spillovers based on the four-digit definition of the industry, but not for the two- or three-digit definitions. One possible explanation for Ruane and Uğur's lack of significant spillovers is that they do not allow for heterogeneity among domestic firms in terms of absorptive capacity.

Rather than spending more time discussing the "conventional" approach of measuring productivity spillovers, we suggest that it may also be possible to explore other ways of measuring technological externalities. While, as discussed above, the production function approach to measuring productivity spillovers has been dominant in the literature, it takes account of only one dimension of benefits from multinationals by measuring the effect of foreign presence on the productivity of existing domestic firms. This neglects a number of other potentially positive effects of multinationals. Pecuniary spillovers—for example, multinationals increasing market size for domestic suppliers—can benefit entry, survival, and growth of domestic establishments. Also, increases in productivity through technological externalities will, all other things being equal, reduce a host country firm's average cost of production, which has obvious benefits for the firm in terms of its survival and growth performance.[6] Therefore, we will now discuss the effects that multinationals, by creating pecuniary as well as technological externalities, have on the entry and post-entry performance of indigenous firms.

Multinational Effect on Domestic Plant Entry

Multinationals benefit indigenous firms through both technological and pecuniary externalities, given that MNCs may increase demand for domestically produced supplies. Markusen and Venables (1999) show formally that multinationals can change the structure of imperfectly competitive industries in the host country by fostering the development of domestic industry through pecuniary externalities. The model features two types of industries, intermediate and final consumer good producing, and both industries are assumed to be imperfectly competitive with increasing returns to scale of production. The model also features three types of firms: domestic firms producing intermediate goods, domestic firms producing final consumer goods, and multinational firms producing final consumer goods.

According to the model the presence of multinationals has three effects on the host economy. First, a competition effect occurs as multinationals compete with domestic final good producers. The increase in total output due to output produced by multinationals decreases the market price, which leads to the exit of some domestic firms. Thus, multinationals crowd out domestic firms. Second, multinationals create additional demand for domestically produced intermediate goods through linkages with indigenous suppliers. In an imperfectly competitive domestic supplier industry, this leads to decreasing average costs and to increases in profits for intermediate good producers, which, in turn, may induce entry into the intermediate good–producing sector. This entry causes the third effect, namely a fall in the price of intermediates that favors customer firms through lower input prices. Customer firms can be both domestic and multinational final good–producing firms. Through these effects multinationals may induce

---

6. Technological externalities can also benefit indigenous firms' export performance (see Aitken, Hanson, and Harrison 1997; Barrios, Görg, and Strobl 2003), which Blomström and Kokko (1998) refer to as "market access spillovers." Another way of assessing whether technological externalities lead to spillovers from foreign firms is by examining research and development (R&D) spillovers (see, for example, Wakelin 2001 for the United Kingdom) and their effects on indigenous firms. As far as we are aware, there has not yet been any analysis of R&D spillovers or export spillovers from MNCs for the Irish economy.

the entry of domestic intermediate good producers as well as domestic final good–producing firms.[7]

Whether the latter two positive effects outweigh the potential negative competition effect remains an empirical question. In Görg and Strobl (2002a) we tackle this issue using plant-level data for manufacturing industries in Ireland from 1972 to 1995.[8] We argue that the competition effect was probably negligible in Ireland over that period. Most of the multinationals in Ireland since the 1970s operated in high-tech sectors, which were largely underdeveloped. Both an explicit industrial strategy by Irish policymakers and the country's relatively cheap pool of skilled and educated workers contributed to this underdevelopment. This argument is supported by the fact that a simple shift-and-share analysis of sectoral employment share dynamics shows that most of the employment losses of the indigenous sector from 1972 to 1995 were due to a decline in importance of indigenous employment-intensive sectors.

In order to test whether the data support the contention that multinationals on net acted to encourage the entry of indigenous plants, we run a simple entry-rate model in Görg and Strobl (2002a):

$$E_{jt} = f(FOR_{jt}, X_{jt})$$ (6.1)

where E is the entry rate, defined alternatively as the total gross and net number of indigenous entrants over t to $t + 1$ relative to total plant population in industry j at time t, and X is a vector of plant and industry characteristics assumed to affect a plant's entry rate. In accordance with authors such as Mata and Machado (1996) X includes measures of a plant's employment size at time t, minimum efficient scale defined as the log of median employment size in sector j, the sectoral Herfindahl index of sector j measured in terms of plants' employment shares, and the net sectoral

---

7. The latter two effects resemble the backward and forward linkage effects Hirschman (1958) found in his earlier study. Rodríguez-Clare (1996) examines a similar mechanism in a more aggregate two-country model with countries specializing in the production of different goods. Multinationals can help develop domestic supplier industries that in turn lead to the development of indigenous final good producers. See also Barrios, Görg, and Strobl (2005) for a related theoretical approach and empirical evidence on the effect of multinationals on the development of the domestic industry.

8. The primary data source for all of our empirical work reported subsequently is the annual employment panel survey carried out since 1972 by Forfás. The survey covers all known active manufacturing plants, with the response rate being generally over 99 percent. The unit of observation is the individual plant, for which the number of permanent full-time and part-time employees is reported. Each plant is, among other things, identified by a unique plant number, the year of startup, nationality of ownership, and its four- to five-digit NACE (nomenclature générale des activités économiques dans les communautés européennes— General Industrial Classification of Economic Activities within the European Communities) code sector. These identifiers are changed only if there is an actual change of ownership. A plant is classified as foreign owned if 50 percent or more of its shares are held by foreign owners.

(employment) growth rate. Most importantly, the model includes a measure of multinational presence within a sector, FOR, defined as the share of employment by MNCs in sector j at time t.

The main estimation results, taken from our work in Görg and Strobl (2002a), are given in table 6.2. As illustrated in the first column, the presence of MNCs acts to significantly increase the gross entry rate of domestic plants. The actual size of the coefficient suggests that a 1 percent increase in MNCs increases the gross entry rate by 0.06 percentage points. One could argue that what one is interested in when evaluating the effects of multinationals on indigenous development is the net entry rate rather than the gross entry rate, since the latter is more likely to include any competition effect (i.e., plant exit due to competition). We therefore also report the results of using the net entry rate as the dependent variable in the second column of table 6.2. As illustrated in the second column, the coefficient on FOR remains statistically significant. Notable, however, is that the size is virtually unchanged to that of the gross entry rate regression, suggesting that there is little additional negative or positive effect on startups controlling for exits.[9]

As an extension to our earlier work in Görg and Strobl (2002a) we can use the coefficient estimate from the net entry rate in table 6.2 to run a simple simulation of how multinationals have affected the evolution of the domestic plant population size. More precisely, consider that the actual size of the plant population at any time t is given by

$$P_t = P_0 + \sum_{t=1}^{t=T} (NE_t)(P_{t-1}) \qquad (6.2)$$

where P_t is the actual size of plant population at time t, P_0 is the actual plant population at time 0 (the beginning of the sample period), P_{t-1} is the actual size of plant population at time $t - 1$, and NE_t is the actual indigenous net entry rate from $t - 1$ to t. One should note that the product $(NE_t)(P_{t-1})$ is simply the observed number of entrants between $t - 1$ and t.

Using this identity we can construct hypothetical values by considering alternative values of the degree of multinational presence by

$$P_t^h = P_0 + \sum_{t=1}^{t=T} [(NE_t) + \beta(FOR_t^h - FOR_t)](P_{t-1}) \qquad (6.3)$$

where P_t^h is the estimated hypothetical plant population at time t, FOR_t is the actual foreign share of employment at time t, FOR_t^h is some choice of

---

9. The results of a positive entry effect are robust to a number of specifications. In particular, to defining the FOR variable in terms of plant share instead of employment share, to including of up to three lags of the FOR variable, and to the inclusion of vertical measure of FOR (which turns out to be not statistically significant in most cases). Also, note that in a companion study, we find in Görg and Strobl (2002b) that the presence of MNCs reduces the startup size of domestic new entrants.

Table 6.2 Effect of MNCs on domestic entry rate, 1973–95

	Gross entry rate	Net entry rate
FOR	0.061* (0.024)	0.060* (0.027)
SIZE	−0.602* (0.194)	−0.522* (0.275)
Observations	1,496	1,496
R^2	0.15	0.14

* signifies 5 percent significance level.
FOR = measure of MNCs' share of employment within a sector
MNC = multinational corporation
SIZE = plant's employment size

Notes: Heteroskedasticity-consistent standard errors are in parentheses. Estimation conducted using a fixed-effects estimator and including measure of minimum efficient scale, average plant age, industry growth, and full set of time dummies. Manufacturing is broken into a total of 68 sectors.

Source: Results from Görg and Strobl (2002a).

hypothetical foreign share of employment that may vary over t or be time invariant, and β is a (estimated) parameter that relates *FOR* to the plant population size.

One should note that in equation 6.3 we are implicitly assuming that multinational presence, *FOR*, is a significant determinant of the indigenous net entry rate and thus of the plant population size at any time t. Equation 6.3 thus allows one to calculate what the plant population size would have been if the degree of multinational presence had been different from that observed in reality. A natural candidate of β is of course the estimated coefficient on *FOR* reported in table 6.2, so one only needs to choose a hypothetical value for *FOR*. We experiment with two such values.

First, we keep *FOR* fixed at its 1972 level, the start of our sample period, which allows us to calculate the indigenous plant population size in Ireland if no new multinationals entered the market. However, this may be an unrealistic scenario. Many of the multinationals that existed at the beginning of the 1970s may have either changed their size or left Ireland entirely. Thus, alternatively, we followed these multinationals over time and calculated their share relative to total employment in 1972 for each and every subsequent period.

The actual, the 1972 level, and the evolution of the share of the 1972 incumbent multinational plants are illustrated in figure 6.1. Accordingly, the share of multinationals in total employment rose from about a third to nearly a half by the end of the 20th century. However, if one only consid-

Figure 6.1 Evolution of actual and incumbent multinational employment share, 1972–2000

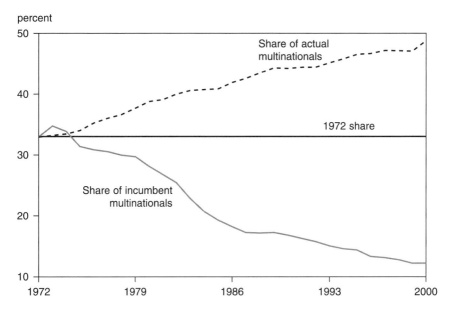

percent

Share of actual multinationals

1972 share

Share of incumbent multinationals

Source: Authors' calculations.

ers those multinationals incumbent in 1972 one discovers that this rise was due to new multinational entrants, as the importance of incumbents fell both because of exits and downsizing.

We calculated the hypothetical indigenous plant population series by inserting actual values for initial indigenous plant population size and the net entry rates in equation 6.3. We used two alternatives to proxy the hypothetical foreign share, first, the initial degree of foreign presence and, second, the share of employment in multinationals incumbent in 1972. These alongside the actual evolution of the indigenous plant population size are illustrated in figure 6.2. As evident from the dotted line, the indigenous plant population stood at around 3,700 plants in 1972. It rose considerably until about the mid-1980s, from which point this trend reversed. Our simulations show that holding the share of multinationals fixed at the level in 1972 would have resulted in considerably lower plant population size—by the year 2000 the total number of indigenous plants would have been nearly 800 less (*hypothetical1*). If one further considers the fact that the multinationals that existed in 1972 both exited Ireland and downsized, the difference relative to the actual observed is even more drastic. Specifically, we find that the absence of the total cumulative effect that multinational presence had in each year on the domestic plant startup rate would have reduced the plant population size by about 30 percent or by nearly 1,700 plants (*hypothetical2*).

Figure 6.2 Simulations of domestic plant population size, 1972–2000

number of domestic plants

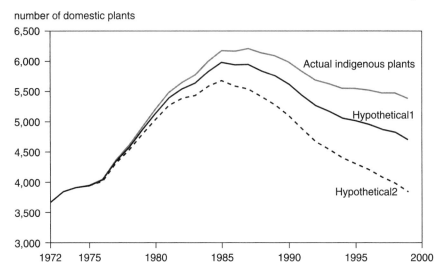

Legend:
- Actual indigenous plants
- Hypothetical1
- Hypothetical2

Source: Authors' calculations.

It is important to point out that the actual figures presented here are somewhat tentative and must be viewed with some caution. This arises in part from the very simplicity of the simulations that make them tractable. However, there are also a number of underlying assumptions that should, at the very least, be taken into consideration. First, we assume that the effect of multinational presence is of a relatively short-term nature, which is in part supported by our results in Görg and Strobl (2002a). The methodology used also assumes that the exit and downsizing of incumbent multinationals is independent of both new domestic and foreign entrants over the period. If this is not the case, our simulations may be either over or underestimating the impact of MNCs, depending on whether such entries tend to reinforce or counteract the share loss of the incumbents. Finally, it must be pointed out that we assume that the other control variables are not affected by changes in the foreign share variable.

Plant Survival

Once a plant has entered the market, the presence of multinationals in the host country may affect the postentry performance of the plant in a number of ways. First, an increase in productivity through technology spillovers (as argued in the third section) will, all other things being equal, reduce a host country plant's average cost of production. This may have implications for the survival of domestic plants, as we discuss in Görg and Strobl (2003).

Audretsch (1991, 1995) argues that the probability of plant i remaining in industry j at time t is determined by a plant's price-cost margin—for example, the degree to which price exceeds average cost. According to this argument a plant's ability to increase price and/or reduce average cost will have a positive effect on plant survival, ceteris paribus. In this framework, technology spillovers from MNCs and the associated increase in productivity enable host country plants to produce at lower average cost for a given level of production, which increases their price-cost margins. All other things equal, this leads to a higher probability of survival for host country establishments. Of course, if negative competition effects are important, the presence of multinationals may actually reduce the survival of domestic establishments. Whether the effect of MNCs on the survival of indigenous plants is, on average, positive or negative is, therefore, ambiguous and needs to be decided empirically.

In Görg and Strobl (2003) we investigate whether the presence of multinational companies in sector j has any effect on the survival of indigenous plants in the same sector, ceteris paribus. With regard to indigenous establishments, we would expect a potential technology gap to exist between these firms and MNCs (due to MNCs' firm-specific assets), which creates the opportunity for technology spillovers between the two groups. In order to properly disentangle the role of plant- and industry-specific factors from that of the presence of MNCs on the survival of plants, we postulate a Cox proportional hazard model,

$$h(t) = h_0(t)e^{(\beta_1 FOR_t + \beta_2 Z_t)} \tag{6.4}$$

where $h(t)$ is the rate at which plants exit at time t given that they have survived in $t - 1$ and h_0 is the baseline hazard function when all of the covariates are set to zero. FOR is a proxy for the presence of foreign multinationals in a sector and is defined as the share of employment by MNCs in sector j at time t. Z is a vector of covariates that are identified in the industrial organization literature as having an effect on plant survival, including plant size, industry minimum efficient scale, industry concentration, and industry growth. Z also includes a dummy variable equal to 1 if a plant was set up before Ireland's accession to the European Union in 1973 since one may expect such establishments to adjust only slowly to the new policy regime (see Walsh and Whelan 2000) and therefore to have lower survival rates. We focus on the survival of indigenous establishments, and separate these plants further into high- and low-tech sectors to allow for differences in absorptive capacity and, hence, obtain more homogenous comparison groups.

Estimation of the Cox proportional hazard model, the results of which are summarized in table 6.3, shows that, within the high-tech sectors, the presence of MNCs reduces indigenous plants' hazard of exiting (i.e., increases

Table 6.3 Survival analysis of indigenous plants using a Cox proportional hazard model, 1973–95

	High tech	Low tech
FOR	−1.794* (0.831)	−0.076 (0.228)
SIZE	−0.014* (0.004)	−0.008* (0.001)
Number of observations	14,641	116,340
Number of subjects	1,495	11,217
Log likelihood	−3,025	28,870
Wald test ($\beta_i = 0$)	235*	1,519*

* signifies 5 percent significance level.
FOR = measure of MNC's share of employment within a sector
SIZE = plant's employment size

Notes: Heteroskedasticity-consistent standard errors are in parentheses. Hazard model includes measure of minimum efficient scale, Herfindahl index, industry growth, dummy for plants established before 1973, and a full set of time dummies. Manufacturing is broken into a total of 68 sectors.

Source: Results from Görg and Strobl (2003).

their chances of survival). We take this as evidence that technological spillovers have benefited indigenous establishments. In the low-tech group we find that the presence of MNCs does not appear to affect plant survival in either direction. This could indicate that, even though there is a technology gap between these firms, which creates a potential for technology spillovers, these do not occur—perhaps because indigenous low-tech firms are unable to absorb the potential spillovers (see, for example, Girma and Görg 2002). In other words, the technology gap between these two groups is too wide, indigenous firms operating in low-tech sectors do not have the absorptive capacity to learn from foreign firms.

Multinational Effect on Plant Growth

Multinationals can also affect the post-entry growth of indigenous establishments. First, as described in Markusen and Venables' (1999) model, increases in demand for intermediate products and changes in prices create pecuniary externalities that benefit indigenous plants. The expanded market size may allow indigenous plants to grow faster than in the previously smaller market. Second, technological externalities may improve the performance of domestic plants and, hence, their growth performance. Third, the pecuniary externalities that increase entry of domestic plants (as discussed in the third section) may also increase competition in the industry, however, and may reduce the growth performance of incumbent plants.

To investigate the effect of MNCs' presence on the post-entry growth of indigenous plants, we postulate the following empirical model for the growth, GRO, of plant i (measured in terms of employment growth) between $t + 1$ and t:[10]

$$GRO_{it+1} = \beta_1 + \beta_2 FOR_{jt} + \beta_3 SIZE_{it} + \beta_4 SIZE_{it}^2 + \beta_5 AGE_{it}$$

$$+ \beta_6 AGE_{it}^2 + \beta_7 NETS_{jt} + \lambda_t + \eta_i + \varepsilon_{it} \tag{6.5}$$

where FOR is the percentage of employment in the sector due to MNCs, SIZE is given as the ranking of the plant's size, measured as employment, within its sector every year,[11] AGE is measured as years since its startup date, and NETS is the net sectoral growth rate defined for 68 subsectors. Furthermore, λ are year-specific effects modeled as time dummies, η is a time-invariant establishment-specific effect, and ε is an error term assumed to be independent across plants and time.

There has been much debate on the growth rates of small relative to large firms (see, for instance, Hart and Oulton 1996). Although this discussion is far from conclusive, it does cast considerable doubt on whether small firms can be considered identical in behavior to large firms. Thus, to truly disentangle the effect of ownership one should control for plant size. We have also included plant size squared to allow for a nonlinear relationship between employment growth and its size.

Plant age is included in order to take into account that rate of growth may also change as plants move through their life cycle. Age itself, regardless of start-up period, may influence the growth rate (see, for instance, Dunne and Hughes 1994; Dunne, Roberts, and Samuelson 1989). On the one hand, plants may take some time before they reach their optimal size; on the other hand, long-established incumbents may have absolute cost advantages vis-à-vis newer entrants. Similarly as for size we have included age squared to allow for the possibility of nonlinear relationships.

Most importantly for this purpose, we have included the share of employment by foreign firms in the plant's sector, FOR, as a proxy for the presence

---

10. This model is in line with similar empirical work in the empirical industrial organization literature (see, for instance, Dunne and Hughes 1994; Dunne, Roberts, and Samuelson 1989).

11. An alternative measure of size would have been the actual level of employment, although this would clearly be endogenous given the definition of the dependent variable.

of foreign multinationals. Finally, equation 6.5 includes the net sectoral growth rate and time dummies to control for sectoral and aggregate economic conditions.

In estimating equation 6.5 we used a fixed-effects estimator that purges the plant-specific, time-invariant effects, both observed and unobserved, from the equation, which circumvents possible measurement problems due to potential correlation between unobserved factors and our explanatory variables. Furthermore, we reduce our sample to observations from continuing plants, as in Hart and Oulton (1996). Thus, our results should be interpreted as effects on growth conditional on remaining in the industry.

Our results for estimating equation 6.5 are provided in the first column of table 6.4. In terms of our explanatory variables we first find that the net sectoral growth rate, as would be expected, is positively related to a plant's net employment growth rate. Thus, if an establishment is located in a sector that is experiencing economic growth it is also likely to grow. We also discover that larger plants experience lower rates of net employment growth. This relationship, however, takes a convex form, indicating that this effect occurs at a diminishing rate. While age in levels appears not to be a significant factor in determining an indigenous plant's employment growth, age squared is negative and significant, indicating that the relationship between age and employment growth is not of a simple linear or concave/convex form.[12]

Finally, and most importantly from our point of view, we find that the presence of MNCs decreases the growth of indigenous plants significantly after controlling for other factors. This suggests that indigenous establishments located in sectors with high foreign presence grow more slowly than other plants. To interpret this result, it may be helpful to recall our finding from the fourth section: the presence of MNCs fosters plant entry. Hence, if there is a large foreign presence, more indigenous plants are in the market, leading to increased competition. This may imply that individual plants grow more slowly because of the higher degree of competition in the sector.

Similar to our analysis of plant survival, we also divided our sample into indigenous plants operating in low- and high-tech sectors and estimated equation 6.5 for these two subsamples; the results are given in the second and third columns of table 6.4. As you can see, the results of the overall sample hold for all covariates for these two subsamples, except for the age terms. In the case of the high-tech sectors older indigenous plants experience higher employment growth, whereas the result for the low-tech sam-

---

12. If age squared was excluded, then age turned out to be negative and significant. Also, including higher-order terms did not change the original result. Given that these other specifications showed no noticeable changes in our other explanatory variables, and our main focus is on the impact of FDI presence, we did not pursue this matter further.

Table 6.4   Results of the growth regression

	All	High tech	Low tech
FOR	−0.147*	−0.414*	−0.142*
	(0.017)	(0.068)	(0.000)
SIZE	−0.004*	−0.007*	−0.004*
	(0.000)	(0.000)	(0.000)
SIZE²	4.65e–06*	1.11e–05*	4.40e–04*
	(8.69e–08)	(5.18e–07)	(8.84e–08)
AGE	9.48e–05	0.008*	−0.001
	(3.60e–04)	(0.001)	(0.000)
AGE²	−9.54e–06*	7.89e–07	−7.51e–06
	(3.83e–06)	(1.67e–05)	(3.92e–06)
NETS	0.138*	0.157*	0.135*
	(0.013)	(0.048)	(0.014)
CON	0.337*	0.522*	0.336*
	(0.009)	(0.042)	(0.009)
Number of observations	121,776	13,436	108,340
$F(\beta_i = 0)$	437.05*	73.12*	377.93*
$F(\beta_{TIME} = 0)$	58.87*	12.73*	52.78*
R^2	0.007	0.003	0.007

* signifies 5 percent significance level.
AGE = plant age
CON = constant
FOR = measure of MNC's share of employment within a sector
NETS = net sectoral growth rate
SIZE = plant's employment size

Note: Heteroskedasticity-consistent standard errors are in parentheses.

Source: Authors' calculations.

ple is statistically insignificant. More importantly, however, we find that the negative effect of FDI presence on indigenous plant employment growth holds for both the high- and low-tech sector, although the coefficient appears to be larger for the former. We could interpret this result as an indication of the relative importance of technological and pecuniary externalities in driving these effects. While technological externalities can be expected to benefit high- and low-tech establishments differently (due to higher levels of absorptive capacity in high-tech sectors), there is no obvious reason why pecuniary externalities should have different effects on these two groups.

Conclusions

In this chapter we discussed how the presence of MNCs and their potential externalities can benefit domestic firms and also assist in the development of local establishments in the host country. We presented empirical results on the effect of MNCs on entry, productivity, survival, and employment growth in indigenous plants in the Republic of Ireland. To date, the literature has focused primarily on measuring productivity spillovers from foreign to indigenous firms, which result from technological externalities. We argue that this focus neglects other important sources and channels for spillovers from multinationals. Multinationals benefit indigenous firms through not only technological externalities but pecuniary externalities as well. MNCs increase demand for intermediate goods supplied domestically, which, in the presence of imperfect competition and increasing returns to scale, affects indigenous firms through market expansions for domestic supplies as well as price changes. We demonstrate that technological and pecuniary externalities can affect indigenous plants' entry and post-entry performance in terms of productivity, survival, and growth.

Our analysis points to a number of important issues for further research in this area. First, one may argue that the "traditional" way of measuring technological externalities—for example, productivity spillovers—as improvements in domestic establishments' productivity is a very narrow concept. It makes sense to look at the effects of technological externalities on plant or firm performance (such as survival or growth) and to assess the effects of technological externalities more thoroughly. Second, apart from technological externalities, multinationals can affect indigenous performance through pecuniary externalities, which may affect entry, growth, and survival of plants. To date, however, this possibility has not received much attention in the literature.

A drawback of most of the empirical studies to date is the way they treat the specific mechanisms by which the spillovers are supposed to occur as a "black box." "Conventional" spillover studies usually regress total factor or labor productivity of domestic firms on a number of covariates, including a measure of the extent of multinational presence in an industry. A similar criticism, of course, also applies to our empirical work herein. While this can give an indication as to the overall effect of foreign presence on productivity, entry, survival, or growth, it does not allow one to discern the channels through which these effects operate. While this is arguably difficult to achieve with the data available, it should be a priority for further research. Not only would it be important from an academic point of view, it is also necessary for guiding policymakers toward the channels through which spillovers occur. Theoretical work has recently stressed the importance of worker movements for technology spillovers (Fosfuri, Motta, and Rønde 2001; Glass and Saggi 2002). Our work in Görg and Strobl (2005) looks at productivity premia in firms owned by individuals who gained experience in foreign multinationals, which is a step in the right direction. Also, the case studies reported by Moran (2001) as well as the survey evidence in Javorcik and Spatareanu (see chapter 3) provide vital insights into the "black box."

One should also note that recent evidence for Ireland and other countries seem to indicate that spillovers may occur primarily at the local rather than at the national level (see, for instance, Barrios, Bertinelli, and Strobl 2005; Girma and Wakelin 2001; and Driffield 2001). This may not be surprising given the fair amount of evidence that linkages, either horizontal or vertical, between production units are mostly local in nature. It may be even more unsurprising when one considers the effects of FDI as multinationals are considered to be more R&D intensive than local firms (see Markusen 2002); there is also plenty of support regarding which knowledge flows measured through R&D are subject to distance decay effects (see Bottazzi and Peri 2003).

Finally, an important issue is whether the experiences of the Irish case, where FDI has been widely accepted as a conduit for economic development, can be applied to other countries. In this respect, we need to point out that there are certain aspects of Irish industrial development that suggest that Ireland's experience may not be easily replicable by other potential host countries trying to attract MNCs. For example, Ireland's proactive industrial policy, particularly creating linkages between MNCs and indigenous suppliers (Görg and Ruane 2001) as well as the possible benefits from agglomeration economies (Barry, Görg, and Strobl 2003), could affect the contribution of MNCs to indigenous development.[13] Thus, our empirical results, while they may be encouraging for other countries attempting to embark on industrial development with the help of attracting MNCs, may not be as encouraging for other countries. A full discussion of this issue, however, is beyond the scope of the present chapter.

References

Aitken, Brian J., and Ann E. Harrison. 1999. Do Domestic Firms Benefit from Direct Foreign Investment? Evidence from Venezuela. *American Economic Review* 89, no. 3 (June): 605–18.

Aitken, Brian J., Gordon H. Hanson, and Ann E. Harrison. 1997. Spillovers, Foreign Investment, and Export Behavior. *Journal of International Economics* 43, no. 1–2 (August): 103–32.

Alfaro, Laura, and Andres Rodríguez-Clare. 2004. Multinationals and Linkages: An Empirical Investigation. *Economica* 4, no. 2 (Spring): 113–69.

Audretsch, David B. 1991. New-Firm Survival and the Technological Regime. *Review of Economics and Statistics* 60: 441–50.

Audretsch, David B. 1995. *Innovation and Industry Evolution.* Cambridge, MA: MIT Press.

Barrios, Salvador, Louisito Bertinelli, and Eric Strobl. 2005. Multinationals and Regional Indigenous Development. *Annals of Regional Science.* Forthcoming.

---

13. Lipsey (2002) also makes the point that the Irish experience may be quite unique and difficult to replicate by other countries.

Barrios, Salvador, Holger Görg, and Eric Strobl. 2003. Explaining Firms' Export Behaviour: R&D, Spillovers and the Destination Market. *Oxford Bulletin of Economics and Statistics* 65, no. 4 (September): 475–96.

Barrios, Salvador, Holger Görg, and Eric Strobl. 2005. Foreign Direct Investment, Competition and Industrial Development in the Host Country. *European Economic Review*. Forthcoming.

Barry, Frank, and John Bradley. 1997. FDI and Trade: The Irish Host-Country Experience. *Economic Journal* 107, no. 445 (November): 1798–811.

Barry, Frank, Holger Görg, and Eric Strobl. 2003. Foreign Direct Investment, Agglomerations and Demonstration Effects: An Empirical Investigation. *Review of World Economics/ Weltwirtschaftliches Archiv* 139, no. 4: 583–600.

Blomström, Magnus, and Ari Kokko. 1998. Multinational Corporations and Spillovers. *Journal of Economic Surveys* 12, no. 3 (August): 247–77.

Blomström, Magnus, and Håkan Persson. 1983. Foreign Investment and Spillover Efficiency in an Underdeveloped Economy: Evidence from the Mexican Manufacturing Industry. *World Development* 11, no. 6 (June): 493–501.

Bottazzi, Laura, and Giovanni Peri. 2003. Innovation and Spillovers in Regions: Evidence from European Patent Data. *European Economic Review* 47, no. 4 (August): 687–710.

Caves, Richard E. 1974. Multinational Firms, Competition, and Productivity in Host-Country Markets. *Economica* 41, no. 162 (May): 176–93.

Central Statistics Office. 1997. *Census of Industrial Production 1995*. Dublin: Stationary Office.

de la Fuente, A., and X. Vives. 1997. The Sources of Irish Growth. In *International Perspectives on the Irish Economy*, ed., Alan W. Gray. Dublin: Indecon.

Driffield, Nigel, 2001. Regional Policy and the Impact of FDI in the UK. In *Inward Investment, Technological Change and Growth*, ed., Nigel Pain. Basingstoke: Palgrave.

Dunne, Paul, and Alan Hughes. 1994. Age, Size, Growth and Survival: UK Companies in the 1980s. *Journal of Industrial Economics* 42, no. 2 (June): 115–40.

Dunne, Timothy, Mark J. Roberts, and Larry Samuelson. 1989. The Growth and Failure of U.S. Manufacturing Plants. *Quarterly Journal of Economics* 103, no. 4 (November): 671–98.

Forfás. 1999. *Annual Survey of Irish Economy Expenditures: Results for 1997*. Dublin.

Fosfuri, Andrea, and Massimo Motta. 1999. Multinationals without Advantages. *Scandinavian Journal of Economics* 101, no. 4 (December): 617–30.

Fosfuri, Andrea, Massimo Motta, and Thomas Rønde. 2001. Foreign Direct Invesment and Spillovers Through Workers' Mobility. *Journal of International Economics* 53, no. 1 (February): 205–22.

Girma, Sourafel, and Holger Görg. 2002. *Foreign Direct Investment, Spillovers and Absorptive Capacity: Evidence from Quantile Regressions*. GEP Research Paper 02/14. Nottingham: University of Nottingham.

Girma, Sourafel, Holger Görg, and Mauro Pisu. 2004. *The Role of Exports and Linkages for Productivity Spillovers from FDI*. GEP Research Paper 04/30. Nottingham: University of Nottingham.

Girma, Sourafel, David Greenaway, and Katharine Wakelin. 2001. Who Benefits from Foreign Direct Investment in the UK? *Scottish Journal of Political Economy* 48, no. 2 (May): 119–33.

Girma, Sourafel, and Katharine Wakelin. 2001. *Regional Underemployment: Is FDI the Solution?* GEP Research Paper 01/11. Nottingham: University of Nottingham.

Glass, Amy, and Kamal Saggi. 2002. Multinational Firms and Technology Transfer. *Scandinavian Journal of Economics* 104, no. 4 (December): 495–514.

Globerman, Steven. 1979. Foreign Direct Investment and "Spillover" Efficiency Benefits in Canadian Manufacturing Industries. *Canadian Journal of Economics* 12, no. 1 (February): 42–56.

Görg, Holger, and David Greenaway. 2004. Much Ado About Nothing? Do Domestic Firms Really Benefit from Foreign Direct Investment? *World Bank Research Observer* 19, no. 2 (Fall): 171–97.

Görg, Holger, and Frances Ruane. 2001. Multinational Companies and Linkages: Panel-Data Evidence for the Irish Electronics Sector. *International Journal of the Economics of Business* 8, no. 1 (February): 1–18.

Görg, Holger, and Eric Strobl. 2001. Multinational Companies and Productivity Spillovers: A Meta-Analysis. *Economic Journal* 111, no. 475 (November): F723–39.

Görg, Holger, and Eric Strobl. 2002a. Multinational Companies and Indigenous Development: An Empirical Analysis. *European Economic Review* 46, no. 7 (July): 1305–22.

Görg, Holger, and Eric Strobl. 2002b. Multinational Companies and Entrant Start-up Size: Evidence from Quantile Regressions. *Review of Industrial Organization* 20, no. 1 (February): 15–31.

Görg, Holger, and Eric Strobl. 2005. Spillovers from Foreign Firms Through Worker Mobility: An Empirical Investigation. *Scandinavian Journal of Economics*. Forthcoming.

Görg, Holger, and Eric Strobl. 2003. Multinational Companies, Technology Spillovers, and Plant Survival. *Scandinavian Journal of Economics* 105, no. 4 (December): 581–95.

Hart, Peter E., and Nicholas Oulton. 1996. Growth and Size of Firms. *Economic Journal* 106, no. 127 (September): 1242–52.

Hirschman, Albert O. 1958. *The Strategy of Economic Development.* New Haven: Yale University Press.

Javorcik, Beata Smarzynska. 2004. Does Foreign Direct Investment Increase the Productivity of Domestic Firms? In Search of Spillovers through Backward Linkages. *American Economic Review* 94, no. 3 (July): 605–27.

Keller, Wolfgang, and Stephen Yeaple. 2003. *Multinational Enterprises, International Trade, and Productivity Growth: Firm-Level Evidence from the United States.* NBER Working Paper 9504. Cambridge, MA: National Bureau of Economic Research.

Kennedy, Kieran A. 1991. Linkages and Overseas Industry. In *Overseas Industry in Ireland,* ed., Anthony Foley and Dermot McAleese. Dublin: Gill and Macmillan.

Krugman, Paul R. 1991. *Geography and Trade.* Cambridge, MA: MIT Press.

Lipsey, Robert E. 2002. Discussion of EU Accession and Prospective FDI Flows to CEE Countries: A View from Ireland. In *Foreign Direct Investment in the Real and Financial Sector of Industrialised Countries,* ed., H. Herrmann and Robert E. Lipsey. Berlin: Springer.

Markusen, James R. 2002. *Multinational Firms and the Theory of International Trade.* Cambridge, MA: MIT Press.

Markusen, James R., and Anthony J. Venables. 1999. Foreign Direct Investment as a Catalyst for Industrial Development. *European Economic Review* 43, no. 2 (February): 335–56.

Mata, José, and José A. E. Machado. 1996. Firm Start-up Size: A Conditional Quantile Approach. *European Economic Review* 40, no. 6 (June): 1305–23.

Moran, Theodore H. 2001. *Parental Supervision: The New Paradigm for Foreign Direct Investment and Development.* POLICY ANALYSIS IN INTERNATIONAL ECONOMICS 64. Washington: Institute for International Economics.

O'Malley, Eoin. 1995. *An Analysis of Secondary Employment Associated with Manufacturing Industry.* General Research Series Paper 167. Dublin: Economic and Social Research Institute.

Rodríguez-Clare, Andres. 1996. Multinationals, Linkages, and Economic Development. *American Economic Review* 86, no. 4 (September): 852–73.

Ruane, Frances, and Ali Uğur. 2005. Foreign Direct Investment and Productivity Spillovers in Irish Manufacturing Industry: Evidence from Plant Level Panel Data. *International Journal of the Economics of Business* 12, no. 1 (February): 53–65.

Sachs, Jeffrey D. 1997. Ireland's Growth Strategy: Lessons for Economic Development. In *International Perspectives on the Irish Economy,* ed., A. W. Gray. Dublin: Indecon.

Wakelin, Katharine. 2001. Productivity Growth and R&D Expenditure in UK Manufacturing Firms. *Research Policy* 30, no. 7 (August): 1079–90.

Walsh, Patrick Paul, and Ciara Whelan. 2000. The Importance of Structural Change in Industry for Growth. *Journal of the Statistical and Social Inquiry Society of Ireland* 29: 1–32.

7

Multinational Firms and Backward Linkages: A Critical Survey and a Simple Model

PING LIN and KAMAL SAGGI

There exist two opposing views in development economics regarding the effect of foreign direct investment (FDI) on a host country's industrial development. According to one view, multinationals are seen as agents that increase competition in the host economy, transfer modern technology, and help achieve a more efficient allocation of resources. Furthermore, this optimistic view argues that inward FDI pushes the process of industrial development forward by creating linkages with the rest of the economy.[1] This view is challenged by those that are concerned about the substantial market power enjoyed by multinationals and the negative effects that can arise from such market power.

In this chapter, we develop a simple model that explores FDI's effect on backward linkages and that accommodates both of these preceding views. The model considers the effects of a multinational's entry that enjoys market power and also transfers technology to the local economy. We also provide a detailed discussion of the existing analytical work on FDI and backward linkages in order to highlight the contribution made by our model and to indicate avenues for future research.

Basically, we argue that the degree to which FDI creates linkages with the rest of the economy should be a function of the technology transferred

Ping Lin is associate professor of economics at Lingnan University, Hong Kong. Kamal Saggi is professor of economics at Southern Methodist University. We are thankful to the Georgetown SSE-IIE workshop participants, especially Ted Moran, for many useful comments.

1. The concept of linkages is drawn from Hirschmann (1958). See Moran (1998, 2001) for recent comprehensive surveys of FDI's effects on the economic development of host countries.

by multinational firms. We explore the connection between technology transfer and linkages by focusing on a single industry with a two-tier production structure. In the model, production of the final good requires an intermediate input that is produced by m local suppliers ($m \geq 1$).[2] The final good is produced by n local firms ($n \geq 1$) and a single multinational firm. The model contrasts market equilibrium under autarky with that under entry by the multinational firm.

Relative to autarky, the multinational firm's entry has two conflicting effects on the degree of backward linkages in the domestic industry. On the one hand, such entry lowers the degree of backward linkage because the output level of a typical local firm shrinks relative to autarky due to competition from the multinational (competition effect). On the other hand, the multinational also sources the intermediate locally and thereby generates additional demand for the intermediate good (demand effect). The main result is that the net effect that the multinational has on the degree of backward linkages in the local economy (as well as on the profitability of local suppliers of the intermediate good) depends on the technological asymmetry between the multinational and its local competitors. When the multinational has only a moderate technological advantage over local firms, its entry increases both the degree of backward linkage and the profitability of local suppliers. However, when the multinational's advantage over local firms is large, its entry has exactly the opposite effect.

The above results depend upon two crucial underlying assumptions: the multinational (1) sources the intermediate in the local market, and (2) its technology is superior to that of its local competitors. The local sourcing assumption captures the idea that inward FDI in the production of the final good creates demand for local suppliers. The production of most manufactured goods requires multiple intermediate goods and services, all of which are tradable to different degrees. What is important for the logic underlying this model is that the multinational chooses to source some intermediates locally (due to policy measures or constraints imposed by the nature of production technologies such as just-in-time inventory). So long as tradable intermediates are complementary to those that must be sourced locally, the effects captured by the model will remain relevant.

The assumption that the multinational has more advanced technology than its local competitors hardly needs defense. In fact, the theory of the multinational firm is itself built on the premise that multinationals rely on intangible assets such as superior technology to successfully compete with local firms that are better acquainted with the host country environment (Markusen 1995). A wealth of evidence indicates that multinationals usu-

---

2. In a similar model, Roy and Viaene (1998) examine the incentives to undertake FDI in the intermediate goods market when downstream firms import the intermediate from abroad. By contrast, this chapter examines FDI's effects in the final goods market.

ally possess technologies that are superior to those of local firms in developing countries (see Markusen 1995; Moran 1998; and Saggi 2002). For example, in recent years, over 80 percent of global royalty payments for international transfer of technology were made from subsidiaries to their parent firms (UNCTAD 1997). Similarly, during 1985–97 between two-thirds and nine-tenths of technology flows were intrafirm in nature.

The view of backward linkages that is captured in the model is somewhat novel, since the model is one of oligopolistic competition. For example, the price response of the intermediate good to the multinational's entry implies that profits of local firms decline for two separate reasons. First, local firms lose because competition from a more efficient firm reduces their market share. Second, they suffer from the increased price of the intermediate good caused by the demand effect.[3] Thus, the model highlights another channel through which the entry of multinationals can affect their local rivals. It is worth noting that the intermediate good in our model can also be thought of as a specialized/skilled labor that has some market power (for example due to unionization) or is available in short supply because of which the multinational's entry leads to an increase in its price (as illustrated in Glass and Saggi 1999).

Empirical studies indicate that the positive impact of FDI on local suppliers may be even greater in the presence of vertical technology transfer (VTT) from multinationals (see Batra and Tan 2002 for evidence of such vertical transfers in Malaysia; Javorcik 2004 for the case of Lithuania; and Lall 1980 for India). Case study evidence also indicates that such transfers are pervasive. For example, Moran (1998) notes that the performance of the Mexican auto parts industry was improved (as per the admission of the suppliers themselves) due to the readiness of multinationals to invest in high quality vertical relationships. As per Peres Nuñez (1990), multinationals in the Mexican automotive sector conducted production audits, held weekly coordination meetings, and provided technical training in zero-defects and just-in-time procedures to their suppliers. Similarly, in the electronics sector, Moran (2001) notes that in Malaysia, foreign investors helped their local subcontractors keep pace with modern technologies by assigning technicians to the suppliers' plants to help set up and supervise large-volume automated production and testing procedures. Similar evidence exists for other sectors and countries, and such evidence is discussed in great detail in Moran (1998, 2001).

It is clear that local suppliers benefit from vertical technology transfer. However, it is worth noting that the local competitors of the multinational also stand to partially benefit from such technology transfer due to decline in the cost of production of the intermediate good. To fully evaluate the

---

3. In Markusen and Venables' (1999) monopolistic competition model, equilibrium prices of intermediate goods do not respond to the entry of multinationals—see their equation 7.6.

effects of vertical technology transfer, the model is extended to allow for the possibility of such transfer from the multinational for the case of two final good producers and one local supplier. We find that vertical technology transfer necessarily benefits the local firm whereas the multinational gains only when its technological advantage over the local firm is moderate. Furthermore, there exist levels of technology transfer that can make even the local firm better off relative to autarky.

Existing Analytical Work on Linkages

A voluminous informal as well as empirical body of literature exists on backward linkages. For example, the 1996 issue of the *UN World Investment Report* was devoted entirely to the effects of FDI on backward linkages in host countries. However, analytical models that explore the relationship between multinationals and backward linkages in the host country are scarce. To the best of our knowledge, only a few such studies exist: Markusen and Venables (1999) and Rodriguez-Clare (1996) are two prominent examples. Both studies provide important insights regarding the two-way relationship between multinationals and linkages. Markusen and Venables (1999) note that multinationals can have a profound effect on backward linkages, industrial development, and the welfare of the host country if their entry affects the structure of imperfectly competitive industries. In fact, one can make a stronger statement: Since multinationals operate mostly in oligopolistic industries, their entry must have substantial effects on local market structure, especially in small developing countries.

In the models of Rodriguez-Clare (1996) and Markusen and Venables (1999) the intermediate goods sector is monopolistically competitive so that the effects of foreign investment occur by altering the incentives for entry into such markets. In both models, Ethier's (1982) formulation of the so-called love-of-variety production function for final goods lies at the heart of the interaction between multinationals and local suppliers. These models omit strategic considerations that arise in oligopolistic environments and instead emphasize the demand-side effects of multinationals' entry on the host economy. In addition, the Markusen and Venables model also allows for a competition effect wherein the entry of a multinational damages its local rivals.

Alfaro and Rodriguez-Clare (2003) use plant-level data from several Latin American countries to evaluate the linkage effects of multinational firms. Their empirical work is motivated by a modified version of the model presented in Rodriguez-Clare (1996); they make the important point that many empirical studies lack a tight link to existing theoretical models and often use inappropriate measures to evaluate the linkage effects of multinationals. However, with a few exceptions, it appears that empirical researchers have not been provided with theoretical models that provide tight empirical predictions.

While existing models focus mostly on the demand pulling effect of the entry of multinationals, in Lin and Saggi (2004) we consider how such an entry might affect the supply side of the intermediate good sector. In particular, we raise the following questions: First, what is the relationship between VTT from a multinational to its local suppliers and the equilibrium degree of backward linkages? Second, and more importantly, how does the nature of contractual relationships between multinationals and their local suppliers affect the degree of backward linkages in the local industry?

To address these questions, we develop a two-tier model in which the production of a final good requires an intermediate good and market structure at both stages of production is oligopolistic. Upon entry, the multinational sources the intermediate good locally and also engages in VTT to its suppliers guided by a contractual agreement. Two types of contractual relationships are considered: one in which suppliers must abide by an exclusivity condition that precludes them from serving the multinational's local rivals and another in which they face no such restriction.

We note that exclusivity necessarily implies delinking between local firms and their suppliers. Such delinking makes the intermediate good market less competitive due to market separation (or foreclosure of competition) and causes the total output of the intermediate good (as well as the final good) to shrink. The delinking effect is reminiscent of an astute observation made by Rodriguez-Clare (1996): When analyzing the effect of multinationals on backward linkages in a host country, it is important to recognize that multinationals do not just create new linkages—they also displace preexisting linkages between local firms and suppliers. In our model, such displacement occurs contractually whereas in Rodriguez-Clare (1996) it occurs if the multinational finds it optimal to source intermediates from its source country headquarters (which is the case when communication costs are high).

Our model (Lin and Saggi's 2004) permits an investigation of conditions under which the multinational prefers to impose exclusivity on its local suppliers as well as factors that lead the latter to accept such a condition. In general, a multinational faces conflicting incentives regarding the usages of exclusivity. On the one hand, the multinational has a strategic incentive to prevent its local rivals from benefiting from VTT, which can be accomplished via exclusivity. On the other hand, the multinational would also like a large number of suppliers to serve it in order to secure the intermediate at a more competitive price. However, exclusivity tends to discourage local suppliers from serving the multinational since they have to give up the opportunity of serving other local producers. It turns out that, in equilibrium, the multinational is able to implement exclusivity if and only if the extent of VTT exceeds a critical level. By contrast, when the degree of VTT is low, only a small number of local suppliers are willing to accept an exclusivity contract, which leads the multinational to prefer nonexclusivity.

While several insightful analyses of backward linkages exist, the model developed below and the one presented in Lin and Saggi (2004) are among the few that allow for oligopolistic competition in the product market and market power in the intermediate good's production. These models complement the insights provided by existing literature that focuses mostly on models of monopolistic competition in which free entry typically erodes all rents.

A Research Agenda

In our view, there are at least three main areas that deserve further research:

- Existing literature has not adequately addressed the connection between technology transfer and backward linkages. The analytical literature on multinationals and technology transfer is vast and has been surveyed by Blomström and Kokko (1998) and Saggi (2002). However, with the exception of Pack and Saggi (2001) much of this literature has ignored VTT between multinationals and their suppliers. This is unfortunate since empirical evidence on VTT is quite positive—see Lall (1980), Moran (1998), Blalock and Gertler (2002), and Javorick (2004).[4] In the model below, we consider the impact of both horizontal and VTT on the degree of backward linkages.

- In general, the literature on backward linkages has ignored strategic interaction among multinationals despite the evidence that multinationals are quite responsive to each other's choices. For example, one feature of Markusen and Venables' (1999) model is that there is free entry in the intermediate market and suppliers do not behave strategically. While facilitating the discussion of variety-enhancing backward linkage effects, models of monopolistic competition cannot address issues for which strategic interaction between firms is important. For instance, by raising the demand for the intermediate goods, the entry of multinationals may strengthen the research and development (R&D) incentives of local suppliers (to lower production costs and/or to improve quality). Such R&D-type backward linkage effects may be better addressed in an oligopolistic model rather than in a monopolistic competition model.[5]

---

4. Cheung and Lin (2004) allow for both horizontal and vertical spillovers in their recent empirical study of FDI and innovation in China.

5. We plan to pursue such R&D type backward linkage effects in an oligopolistic model in future research.

- Not enough is known about the nature of vertical relationships between multinationals and their local suppliers. In particular, the literature has focused exclusively on market interaction and paid insufficient attention to the nature of contracts between multinationals and their local suppliers. As argued in the introduction, contractual relationships are particularly relevant in the context of technology transfer, as they might help multinationals safeguard their intellectual property. Contractual agreements may cause market separation in the intermediate good sector, thus affecting the degree of backward linkages. Our model (Lin and Saggi 2004) provides some analysis but substantial further work is needed in this area.

Model

Preferences in the domestic economy are quasi-linear over two goods x and y: $U(x,y) = u(x) + y$. Good y serves as a numeraire good, and it is produced under perfect competition with constant returns-to-scale (CRS) technology: one unit of labor produces one unit of y. Labor is the sole factor of production. Because of the CRS technology in the y sector, the wage rate ϖ in the local economy in terms of the numeraire good equals 1.

There are n local firms (also called home firms, or h, and denoted by $j = 1 \ldots n$) and one foreign firm (called multinational and denoted by f) that produce good x. Producers of good x are called firms from hereon. The multinational and its local competitors choose their output levels in a Cournot fashion—i.e., each firm chooses its output taking as given the output levels of its rivals.

For producing one unit of good x the multinational requires λ_f units of labor and μ units of an intermediate good (or service) z. The corresponding technological parameters for local firms are λ_h and μ_h (normalized to 1), where $\lambda_h \geq \lambda_f$ and $1 \geq \mu$. Thus, the multinational's technology can be superior in two different ways: it might either require fewer workers per unit of output or fewer units of the intermediate good z (or both). Note that if $\mu < \lambda_f/\lambda_h$ then the multinational is a less intensive user of the intermediate good z than the local firm (as in Markusen and Venables 1999).

Given these technologies, the marginal cost of production under FDI for firm j is given by

$$c_j^F = \lambda_j.1 + \mu_j\omega^F = \lambda_j + \mu_j\omega^F \tag{7.1}$$

where ω^F denotes the price of the intermediate under FDI and $j = h, f$. The intermediate good z is produced by m local producers (which we call suppliers from hereon). One unit of the intermediate requires θ units of labor.[6]

---

6. Later in the chapter, we allow for cost-lowering technology transfer from the multinational to local suppliers.

By assumption, the multinational must source the intermediate from local suppliers. Of course, the greater the extent to which production of good x requires some nontradable services the greater the relevance of the assumption of local sourcing.[7]

Let $p(Q)$ be the inverse demand function for good x generated by consumer optimization, where Q is total consumption of good x and p denotes its price. Let q_j denote the output produced by firm j, where $j = h, f$. Given the demand function, firm j's profit function under regime k, where $k = A$ (autarky), F is given by

$$\pi_j^k(q_j, q_{-j}) = \left[p(Q) - c_j^k \right] q_j \tag{7.2}$$

where $j = h, m$, and c_j^k denotes a firm's marginal cost of production under regime k. To simplify the analysis, assume that the inverse demand function is linear:

$$p(Q) = \alpha - Q \tag{7.3}$$

where Q denotes the total output of the final good and α denotes home market size. To establish a benchmark for our analysis, we begin by describing the market equilibrium under autarky—a situation where the multinational cannot enter the local market.

Autarky

Under autarky, the multinational cannot supply any output to the local market (so $q_f = 0$) and home firms compete with each other buying the intermediate good z from local suppliers. Taking the price of the intermediate ω as given, a typical home firm, h, chooses its output q_j to maximize its profit

$$\text{Max}(p(Q) - \lambda_h - \omega) q_j \tag{7.4}$$

where Q denotes the aggregate output of all local firms. The first-order condition for this problem is given by

$$p(Q) + p'q_j - \lambda_h - \omega = 0 \tag{7.5}$$

Using the linear demand function specified in equation 7.3, we have

$$q_j = (\alpha - \lambda_h - \omega)/(n + 1), j = 1 \dots n \tag{7.6}$$

---

7. Trade in services has not been liberalized to the same extent as trade in goods. Under the General Agreement on Trade in Services (GATS), countries have made limited commitments to liberalize their services markets. See Hoekman and Saggi (2000).

Summing the above equation yields the derived demand curve for the intermediate good:

$$\omega = \alpha - \lambda_h - Q(n + 1)/n \tag{7.7}$$

where $Q = n\, q_j$. Facing the above derived demand curve, suppliers of the intermediate good compete by choosing their respective quantities in Cournot-Nash fashion. The equilibrium output of a typical supplier equals

$$q_i^A = n(\alpha - \lambda_h - \theta)/[(m + 1)(n + 1)], i = 1 \ldots m \tag{7.8}$$

The price of the intermediate good equals

$$\omega^A = [\alpha - \lambda_h + m\theta]/[m + 1] \tag{7.9}$$

The level of backward linkages (BL) under autarky (A) is defined as the total amount of the intermediate good demanded by local firms:

$$BL^A = mq_i^A \tag{7.10}$$

Remark 1: *The degree of backward linkage under autarky increases in the home market size (α) while it decreases in the supplier's unit labor requirement (θ) and in a local firm's unit labor requirement (λ_h).*

Finally, the profit of each supplier equals

$$\pi_i^A = [n/(n + 1)][(\alpha - \lambda_h - \theta)/(m + 1)]^2, i = 1 \ldots m \tag{7.11}$$

while that of each local firm equals

$$\pi_j^A = [m^2/(n + 1)^2][(\alpha - \lambda_h - \theta)/(m + 1)]^2, j = 1 \ldots n \tag{7.12}$$

In what follows, we next consider market competition under the multinational's entry.

Multinational's Entry into the Market

We are interested in the effect of the multinational's entry on the degree of backward linkages in the economy. In order to determine this effect, the equilibrium in the local market needs to be derived. Given the price of the intermediate good (ω), firms choose their output levels. The multinational firm's output equals

$$q_f = \{\alpha - (n + 1)\,\lambda_f + n\lambda_h - \omega\,[(n + 1)\,\mu - n]\}/(n + 2) \tag{7.13}$$

whereas that of a typical local firm equals

$$q_j = [\alpha - 2\lambda_h + \lambda_f - \omega(2 - \mu)]/(n + 2), j = 1 \ldots n \qquad (7.14)$$

The derived demand for the intermediate good is thus given by

$$Q = nq_j + \mu q_f \qquad (7.15)$$

which, after simplification, can be written as

$$\omega = [\alpha' - (n + 2)/H(n, \mu)]Q \qquad (7.16)$$

where

$$H(n, \mu) \equiv 2n(1 - \mu) + (n + 1)\mu^2 \qquad (7.17)$$

and

$$\alpha' \equiv \{(n + \mu)\alpha - n\lambda_h(2 - \mu) + \lambda_f[n - \mu(n + 1)]\}/H(n, \mu) \qquad (7.18)$$

Given this, Cournot competition among suppliers yields the equilibrium quantity of each supplier:

$$q_i^F = \{(n + \mu)\alpha - n\lambda_h(2 - \mu) + \lambda_f[n - \mu(n + 1)] - \theta H(n, \mu)\}/[(m + 1)(n + 2)],$$

$$i = 1 \ldots m \qquad (7.19)$$

To ease exposition, for the rest of the chapter, assume that $\lambda_h = \lambda_f = \lambda$. Then, the derived demand for the intermediate good can be written as

$$\omega = [(n + \mu)(\alpha - \lambda) - (n + 2)Q]/H(n, \mu) \qquad (7.20)$$

Using the above derived demand curve, we can solve for the equilibrium of the model. In particular, the equilibrium quantity of a supplier equals:

$$q_i^F = [(n + \mu)(\alpha - \lambda) - \theta H(n, \mu)] / [(m + 1)(n + 2)] \qquad (7.21)$$

and its profit equals

$$\pi_i^F = [(n + 2)/H(n, \mu)][q_i^F]^2 \qquad (7.22)$$

The price of the intermediate good is given by

$$\omega^F = [(n + \mu)(\alpha - \lambda) + m\theta H(n, \mu)] / [(m + 1) H(n, \mu)] \qquad (7.23)$$

As before, the level of backward linkages (BL) under FDI (F) is defined by the total output of the intermediate good produced by local suppliers:

$$BL^F = mq_i^F \qquad (7.24)$$

Multinational's Effect on Backward Linkages

Relative to autarky, the multinational's entry has two conflicting effects on the degree of backward linkages in the domestic industry. On the one hand, such entry lowers the degree of backward linkages because the output level of a typical home firm shrinks relative to autarky due to competition from the multinational (competition effect). On the other hand, the multinational also starts sourcing the intermediate locally, thereby generating additional demand for the locally produced intermediate good (demand effect). We explore below the conditions under which FDI generates a net positive linkage effect.

The degree of backward linkages under FDI (BL^F) simplifies to

$$BL^F = [m(n + \mu)(\alpha - \lambda) - \theta H(n, \mu)] / [(m + 1)(n + 2)] \tag{7.25}$$

Comparison with the level of backward linkages in autarky (BL^A) yields the main result of the model, which is:

$$BL^F \geq BL^A \text{ iff } \mu \geq \mu^*(n) \equiv n/(n + 1) \tag{7.26}$$

Proposition 1: *The multinational's entry raises the level of backward linkages in the host industry iff its technological advantage over local firms falls below a critical threshold (i.e., $\mu > \mu^*(n)$).*

If μ (the multinational's technological advantage over its local rivals) is small, then the competition effect of the multinational's entry is strong whereas the demand effect (measured by μq_f) is weak. As a result, the multinational's entry lowers the level of backward linkages. If μ is large, the opposite happens: The competition effect is weak, and the demand effect is strong. As a result, the multinational's entry raises the level of backward linkages. It is worth emphasizing that local suppliers actually suffer from FDI when the multinational's technological superiority over local firms is large. This might seem paradoxical, but it is not so. For example, in the limit where $\mu \to 0$, local suppliers are clearly worse off under FDI, since the multinational generates no demand for the local intermediate so that only the competition effect remains.

The fact that $\mu^*(n)$ increases in n, implies that the more competitive the local market (for the final good) is, the less likely it is that the multinational's entry raises the level of backward linkages. This occurs because when a large number of competing firms are in the market, the derived demand effect created by the multinational's entry is rather weak.

The following corollary is worth noting.

Corollary 1: *If the multinational has the same technology as local firms (i.e. $\mu = 1$), its entry necessarily raises the level of backward linkages:*

$$BL^F\big|_{\mu=1} = m(n + 1)(\alpha - \lambda - \theta) / [(m + 1)(n + 2)] > BL^A \tag{7.27}$$

Consider now how the multinational's entry affects other equilibrium variables and the profitability of local firms and suppliers. Comparing the price of the intermediate (ω) under FDI (F) to that under autarky (A) yields:

$$\omega_i^F \geq \omega_i^A \text{ iff } \mu \geq \mu^* (n) \tag{7.28}$$

Proposition 2: *Compared to autarky, the price of the intermediate (as well as the profit of a typical local supplier) is higher under FDI iff* $\mu > \mu^*(n)$.[8]

How does the multinational's entry affect local firms? The above analysis informs us that local firms stand to lose for two separate reasons. First, they lose because of the competition effect—local firms lose market share to the multinationals. Second, they also lose if the intermediate good becomes more expensive due to the multinational's entry. However, an interesting point to note is the following observation.

Remark 2: *The losses that the local firms suffer from an increase in competition may be partly offset by a reduction in the intermediate price (which happens when* $\mu < \mu^*(n)$).

Local suppliers can benefit from FDI not only because of an increase in derived demand but also via technology transfer. We next consider such a scenario.

Vertical Technology Transfer

To facilitate analytical progress, we set $n = m = 1$ (there is only one supplier and one local competitor of the multinational). Under VTT, the multinational transfers technology to the local supplier that lowers its marginal cost from θ to $(\theta - t)$. The variable t can be thought of as the extent (or the quality) of technology transfer. Our first point is the following:

Remark 3: *Technology transfer to the home supplier creates a trade-off for the multinational. On the one hand, it benefits the multinational by lowering the price of the home intermediate. On the other hand, such technology transfer also lowers the cost of production of the multinational's local competitor.*

An immediate question arises: Do conditions under which technology transfer by the multinational makes all three agents (the local supplier, the multinational, and the local firm) better off under FDI exist? It is trivial

---

8. To see the effect on the profit of a typical supplier, note that

$$\pi_i^F \geq \pi_i^A \Leftrightarrow [(n + \mu)(\alpha - \lambda) - \theta H(n, \mu)]^2 / [(m + 1)^2 (n + 2)H(n, \mu)]$$
$$\geq n/(n + 1)(\alpha - \lambda - \theta)^2 / (m + 1)^2 .$$

At $\mu = \mu^*(n)$, we have $n + \mu = H(n, \mu) = n(2 + n)/(n + 1)$ and the above inequality binds. Since π_i^F increases in μ, Proposition 2 holds.

to note that technology transfer always benefits the supplier. The multinational's profit increases with t if and only if

$$\partial \pi_m^F / \partial t > 0 \Leftrightarrow 2q_m^F (\partial q_m^F / \partial t) > 0 \Leftrightarrow 2\mu > 1 \tag{7.29}$$

Similarly, the local firm's profit increases with technology transfer if and only if

$$\partial \pi_h^F / \partial t > 0 \Leftrightarrow 2q_h^F (\partial q_h^F / \partial t) > 0 \Leftrightarrow 2 > \mu \tag{7.30}$$

which always holds. The above inequalities imply our second main point.

Remark 4: *While the local firm always benefits from VTT to the supplier, the multinational gains only when its technological advantage over the local firm is moderate.*

Thus, what is not clear is whether the multinational gains from VTT although the local firm necessarily benefits. The intuition for this result is that the reduction in the intermediate price matters more for the local firm, since its technology uses the intermediate more intensively. For the multinational to also gain, its usage of the intermediate good must not be too small. Note also that when the technologies of the two firms are almost symmetric (which happens when μ is close to 1) both firms gain from VTT.

A harder question remains unanswered: Can it be the case that the improvement in the supplier's technology is sufficient to offset the loss the local firm suffers (due to the multinational's entry) relative to autarky? Let t_h define the threshold level of VTT that leaves the local firm indifferent between autarky and FDI:

$$\pi_h^F (\omega^F [t_h]) = \pi_h^A \tag{7.31}$$

where

$$\omega^F(t) = (\alpha/4)(1 + \mu)/(1 - \mu + \mu^2) + (\theta - t)/2 \tag{7.32}$$

and

$$t_h = (\alpha/2)[2\mu (\mu - 1) - 1] / \{[\mu (\mu - 1) + 1](\mu - 2)\}$$
$$+ (2\mu - 1)\theta / (2\mu - 4) \tag{7.33}$$

Clearly, the bigger the local market, the larger the extent of technology transfer required for the local firm to be indifferent between FDI and autarky. While the algebra gets complicated, intuition suggests (and numerical examples show) that the bigger the technological advantage of the multinational over its local competitor, the larger the threshold t_h. In other words, the local firm would need to be compensated by a large drop in the price of the intermediate when the technology used by the multinational is much superior to its own.

Suppose that the multinational has enough knowledge capital to actually transfer technologies equal to or better than t_h. Given that, is it willing to do so? The answer depends upon how costly technology transfer is for the multinational. If such costs are low (or near zero), the multinational does so when $2\mu > 1$.

Finally, how does technology transfer to local suppliers alter the degree of backward linkages in the local industry? As expected, technology transfer by the multinational enhances the degree of backward linkages in the local industry.[9]

Conclusion

A classic issue in economic development is the effect multinational firms have on the industrial development of host countries. Within this general theme, those that view FDI to be beneficial to the host country's development have often stressed its role in generating linkages within the economy. Perhaps the further encouragement of backward linkages is one reason why many countries impose domestic content requirements on multinationals: Such policies require multinationals to source a certain amount of their inputs (or a certain proportion of their value added) within the local market.

However, very few analytical studies of backward linkages of FDI exist. We have surveyed the existing literature and based on that survey suggest three areas for future research: the interplay between VTT and backward linkages; strategic interactions among multinational firms; and the nature of contractual relationships between multinationals and their local suppliers.

A simple model incorporating both horizontal and vertical technology transfer in a two-tier oligopolistic structure is also presented. This model captures in a straightforward way both the competition effect and the demand effect of FDI. Entry of a multinational firm raises the demand for locally made intermediate goods, while creating competition for incumbent producers of the final good and thereby lowering their demand for the intermediate good. In our model, the multinational's entry raises the degree of the backward linkages in the local economy if, and only if, its technological advantage in producing the final good is not too large over its local competitors—under such circumstances the demand creation effect dominates the competition effect. The results of the model conform to those of several empirical studies: although multinationals have a negative impact on their local competitors, they have a positive impact on their local suppliers especially when they transfer technology to them.[10]

---

9. Even in the general case, technology transfer lowers the threshold μ^* above which the multinational's entry raises the degree of backward linkages. We have $\partial \mu^* / \partial t = -\partial BL^F / \partial \mu / \partial BL^F / \partial t < 0$.

10. See Saggi (2002, 2004) for discussions of the horizontal and vertical effects of multinational firms on host industries.

While our model provides some interesting insights, it does make some strong assumptions. In particular, the model considers only one multinational firm. Furthermore, we cannot study the development of the intermediate good sector since further entry of suppliers is ruled out. Regarding the first limitation, the model can be extended to allow for multiple multinationals, and we speculate that our main conclusions would remain valid under such a setting. When multiple multinationals may enter the local market, the aggregate effect of such entry would continue to depend on the relative magnitudes of both the competition effect and the demand effect. Of course, the balance between these effects will depend upon the technological advantages of a typical multinational over local producers and the number of such local producers as well as the number of multinationals.

Now consider the issue of further entry of suppliers. Recall that Rodriguez-Clare (1996) has already developed a framework where the increase in demand for intermediate goods generated by multinationals leads to an expansion in the variety of such goods available in the local economy via the entry of new suppliers. Such expansion benefits competitors of the multinational firm by increasing their productivity. However, in Rodriguez-Clare's model, price effects are not crucial because of the setup of monopolistic competition. By contrast, the present model allows for price effects while ruling out further entry of suppliers. Thus, an oligopoly model of linkages with free entry of multinationals and local suppliers seems worthy of future research.

References

Aitken, Brian, and Ann E. Harrison. 1999. Do Domestic Firms Benefit from Direct Foreign Investment? Evidence from Venezuela. *American Economic Review* 89, no. 3: 605–18.

Alfaro, Laura, and Andrés Rodriguez-Clare. 2003. Multinationals and Linkages: An Empirical Investigation. Harvard Business School. Photocopy (November).

Batra, Geeta, and Hong W. Tan. 2002. Inter-Firm Linkages and Productivity Growth in Malaysian Manufacturing. Cornell University. Photocopy (July).

Blalock, Garrick, and Paul J. Gertler. 2002. *Technology Diffusion from Foreign Direct Investment Through Supply Chain*. Working Paper. Cornell University.

Blomström, Magnus, and Ari Kokko. 1998. Multinational Corporations and Spillovers. *Journal of Economic Surveys* 12, no. 3: 247–77.

Cheung, Kui-yin, and Ping Lin. 2004. Spillover Effects of FDI on Innovation in China: Evidence from the Provincial Data. *China Economic Review* 15, no. 1: 25–44.

Dixit, Avinash, and Joseph E. Stiglitz. 1977. Monopolistic Competition and Optimum Product Diversity. *American Economic Review* 67, no. 3: 297–308.

Ethier, Wilfred J. 1982. National and International Returns to Scale in the Modern Theory of International Trade. *American Economic Review* 72, no. 3: 389–405.

Glass, Amy, and Kamal Saggi. 1999. FDI Policies under Shared Factor Markets. *Journal of International Economics* 49, no. 2: 309–32.

Hirschmann, Albert O. 1958. *The Strategy of Economic Development*. New Haven, CT: Yale University Press.

Hoekman, Bernard, and Kamal Saggi. 2000. Assessing the Case for Extending WTO Disciplines on Investment-Related Policies. *Journal of Economic Integration* 15: 629–53.

Javorcik, Beata S. 2004. Does Foreign Direct Investment Increase the Productivity of Domestic Firms? In Search of Spillovers Through Backward Linkages. *American Economic Review* 94, no. 3: 605–27.

Lall, Sanjaya. 1980. Vertical Inter-firm Linkages in LDCs: An Empirical Study. *Oxford Bulletin of Economics and Statistics* 42, no. 3: 203–06.

Lin, Ping, and Kamal Saggi. 2004. Multinational Firms, Exclusivity, and the Degree of Backward Linkages. Lingnan University and Southern Methodist University. Photocopy.

Markusen, James R. 1995. The Boundaries of Multinational Enterprises and the Theory of International Trade. *Journal of Economic Perspectives* 9, no. 2: 169–89.

Markusen, James R., and Anthony J. Venables. 1999. Foreign Direct Investment as a Catalyst for Industrial Development. *European Economic Review* 43, no. 2: 335–56.

Moran, Theodore H. 1998. *Foreign Direct Investment and Development.* Washington: Institute for International Economics.

Moran, Theodore H. 2001. *Parental Supervision: The New Paradigm for Foreign Direct Investment and Development.* POLICY ANALYSES IN INTERNATIONAL ECONOMICS 64. Washington: Institute for International Economics.

Neven, Damien, and Georges Siotis. 1996. Technology Sourcing and FDI in the EC: An Empirical Evaluation. *International Journal of Industrial Organization* 14, no. 5: 543–60.

Peres Nuñez, Wilson. 1990. *Foreign Direct Investment and Industrial Development in Mexico.* Paris: OECD.

Pack, Howard, and Kamal Saggi. 2001. Vertical Technology Transfer via International Outsourcing. *Journal of Development Economics* 65, no. 2: 389–415.

Qiu, Larry, and Zhigang Tao. 2001. Export, Foreign Direct Investment, and Local Content Requirement. *Journal of Development Economics* 66, no. 1: 101–25.

Rodriguez-Clare, Andrés. 1996. Multinationals, Linkages, and Economic Development. *American Economic Review* 86, no. 4: 852–73.

Roy, Santanu, and Jean-Marie Viaene. 1998. On Strategic Vertical Foreign Investment. *Journal of International Economics* 46, no. 2: 253–79.

Saggi, Kamal. 2002. Trade, Foreign Direct Investment, and International Technology Transfer: A Survey. *World Bank Research Observer* 17: 191–235.

Saggi, Kamal. 2004. *International Technology Transfer to Developing Countries.* Economic Paper 64. London: Commonwealth Secretariat.

UNCTAD (United Nations Conference on Trade and Development). 1996. *World Investment Report 1996: Promoting Linkages.* New York: United Nations.

UNCTAD (United Nations Conference on Trade and Development). 1997. *World Investment Report 1997: Transnational Corporations, Market Structure and Competition Policy.* New York: United Nations.

Comment

GORDON H. HANSON

A huge volume of research on the impact of foreign direct investment (FDI) on host countries now exists. The issue is of first-order policy importance. As sources of new technology and foreign capital, multinational firms have the potential to be major contributors to economic development in poor countries. In policy prescriptions for economic liberalization emanating from Washington, the recommendation to remove barriers to FDI is standard. However, the enthusiasm for FDI goes beyond the desire to liberalize capital markets. In many quarters, multinationals are seen as a catalyst for industrialization and so deserve special treatment through subsidies or tax breaks. Many countries now offer tax inducements to multinationals.

In their helpful review of the literature, Lipsey and Sjöholm begin with the observation that the enthusiasm for FDI among policymakers is puzzling. While the theoretical case for opening to FDI (and for liberalizing capital markets in general) is solid, the case for subsidizing FDI depends on strong assumptions about the existence of positive spillovers associated with multinationals. As Lipsey and Sjöholm point out, empirical support for positive FDI spillovers is mixed, at best. The empirical results in the literature are either hard to interpret (in the case of wage spillovers) or all over the map (in the case of productivity spillovers).

It is useful to consider what would be convincing empirical evidence of positive FDI spillovers. Take the case of productivity spillovers, in which the arrival of multinationals raises the total factor productivity (TFP) of domestic firms (either in the same industry, as with horizontal spillovers, or in upstream or downstream industries, as with vertical spillovers). Let

Gordon H. Hanson is professor of economics at the University of California, San Diego, and research associate at the National Bureau of Economic Research.

y_{it} be TFP in domestic firm i at time t, let x_{it} be a set of exogenous control variables for firm i, and let FDI_{it} be the multinational presence to which firm i is exposed. A positive correlation between y_{it} and FDI_{it} in the cross section—as many studies find for productivity and for wages—is not very informative. It does not reveal whether FDI raises productivity or whether multinationals are attracted to regions or industries in which domestic firms are more productive or workers are more skilled.

To remove the effects of unobserved (time-invariant) industry and region factors that affect firm productivity, a more appealing approach is to examine the correlation between the change in firm productivity and the change in FDI. The standard regression in the literature is similar to

$$\Delta y_{it} = \Delta x_{it}\beta + \Delta FDI_{it}\theta + \varepsilon_{it}$$

A positive estimate for θ is commonly interpreted as evidence of positive FDI spillovers. Since Aitken and Harrison (1999) estimated that θ was negative for their case study of Venezuela, a flood of studies attempting to overturn the result has occurred. Lipsey and Sjöholm report that the results are distressingly inconclusive. Estimates of θ vary widely, ranging from positive to negative and even zero depending on the country.

Why are the results on domestic productivity and FDI not robust? One explanation is that the standard regression equation is not identified. In the above regression, to estimate θ consistently requires that changes in FDI are exogenous to unobserved shocks to firm i's productivity. This is a tall order. There are myriad shocks to an industry or region that would both raise wages or productivity in domestic firms and attract multinationals. To identify θ, we need an alternative estimation strategy. One approach is to search for an instrument for FDI. But what factors are plausibly correlated with the attractiveness of an industry or region to FDI and uncorrelated with domestic firm productivity? An alternative approach is to search for a natural experiment. That is, to identify a control group that sweeps out the effects of unobserved shocks.

The Javorcik and Spatareanu, Blalock and Gertler, and Erdilek chapters all deal with this identification issue in a different way. Erdilek's main contribution is that it brings very disaggregated data to bear on the research and development (R&D) activities of multinational and domestic firms (in this case, in Turkey). Much previous literature fails to specify the precise channel through which multinationals affect domestic firms. Helpfully, Erdilek focuses on the single channel of R&D. He finds, not surprisingly, that multinationals engage in more R&D than do domestic firms (though there are differences between minority- and majority-owned multinationals). Erdilek's main finding is that national firms are more likely to engage in R&D when there are more multinational firms in their sector.

Is this evidence of FDI spillovers? I would suggest that the answer is "no." The random-effects estimator that Erdilek uses consistently estimates the impact of FDI on domestic R&D activity under a strong assumption: that the only source of unobserved persistence in the plant decision to undertake R&D is time-invariant features of plants that are orthogonal to observed plant characteristics and to industry FDI. This is a stronger assumption than is required in the fixed-effects estimator discussed above. By my reading, consistency in Erdilek's case would require that R&D have no fixed costs (and so no dynamic interdependence in R&D decisions). Erdilek presents some very intriguing correlations between R&D in foreign and domestic firms. It appears that foreign firms are more likely to undertake R&D, but on the basis of these results we cannot say how FDI affects domestic firms or how policymakers should treat FDI.

The Javorcik and Spatareanu study takes a quite different approach. They use survey data drawn from managers' responses to determine how multinationals have affected domestic firms (in this case, in Latvia and the Czech Republic). Javorcik and Spatareanu then examine whether firm productivity or firm employment growth is higher or lower in firms that have been more exposed to multinationals. The results are mixed. Productivity is higher in firms that learned new technologies from multinationals but it is also higher in firms that said they lost employees to multinationals. Domestic firms that are exposed to multinationals look different from other domestic firms, but we are unsure why.

What is intriguing about this study is the potential for using survey responses to look for evidence of FDI spillovers. The usefulness of survey responses hinges critically on how managers interpret questions. Consider two questions that ask about the relation between industry characteristics and foreign presence. The first question is, "Did your firm become more productive after the arrival of foreign firms?" By asking about the change in industry conditions associated with the arrival of foreign firms, the question implicitly controls for industry-fixed effects. But the question is not posed in a way that allows causal inference. We do not know whether foreign presence changed industry productivity or vice versa. The second question is, "Did the growth rate of productivity in your firm increase after foreign firms arrived in your industry?" By asking about the rate of change, the question is posed as a difference in difference. Still, it does not permit causal inference because we do not know why foreign presence increased. But if we could conduct surveys before and after events thought to trigger FDI, then we might be able to choose episodes in which the change in FDI appears driven by factors that are orthogonal to domestic firm productivity (e.g., changes in tax policy in source countries for FDI). Since manager surveys are conducted on a small scale, it might be feasible to time them to take advantage of external events that are likely to change FDI.

The Blalock and Gertler chapter is the most serious of the four about addressing identification issues associated with FDI spillovers. This study (1) identifies an explicit control group in running regressions, (2) looks for indirect effects of FDI that would be inconsistent with an endogeneity story, and (3) uses natural experiments to identify the effect of foreign ownership on firms. In the first part of the analysis, they ask whether Indonesian plants had higher TFP growth in regional industries with faster growth in downstream demand by multinationals. By controlling for region-year effects, the implicit control group is the average plant in the region. However, this specification does not account for why FDI increased, forcing us to assume that it is exogenous.

To gauge the plausibility of the exogeneity assumption, Blalock and Gertler question whether industries with faster downstream growth by multinationals experienced a larger fall in regional industry concentration or industry prices. The answer is "yes" on both counts. The opposite movements would be predicted by one source of endogeneity in FDI, in which regional demand shocks affected both firm productivity and multinational location decisions. This sort of external validation of FDI spillovers is all too rare in the literature. It is useful not just as a check on the assumption about the exogeneity of FDI but also to verify other FDI effects, which theory predicts.

In their final exercise, Blalock and Gertler ask whether, relative to domestic plants, foreign plants had higher growth after the Asian financial crisis than before. This approach makes clever use of Indonesia's financial crisis as a natural experiment to determine whether access to foreign capital affects firm performance. It does. This use of exogenous variation in the importance of FDI is also all too rare in the literature.

As international economists, what can we tell policymakers in developing countries about how they should treat multinational firms? Based on empirical work to date, the answer, unfortunately, is "not much." The literature is just beginning to seriously consider empirical issues about FDI's effect on domestic firms. Thus, the Blalock and Gertler study is a welcome addition to the literature, but it is atypical in the attention it pays to the econometric identification of FDI spillovers. Given the developing state of the field, it is important that policymakers realize that we do not know how multinational firms affect their economies. There are good reasons to liberalize capital markets, but an abundance of evidence that FDI generates positive spillovers does not exist. So far, researchers have yet to uncover robust empirical support for the kinds of subsidies that many countries have begun to offer multinational enterprises.

Reference

Aitken, Brian J., and Ann E. Harrison. 1999. Do Domestic Firms Benefit from Direct Foreign Investment? Evidence from Venezuela. *American Economic Review* 89, no. 3: 605–18.

Comment

MICHAEL P. KEANE

Any attempt to infer the effect of foreign direct investment (FDI) on the productivity of domestic firms must first confront a number of severe econometric challenges. I believe these challenges are so great that the literature has barely begun to tackle them. In particular, the econometric specifications estimated in the current literature do not seem to be closely tied to any underlying economic theory that specifies the mechanisms through which productivity spillovers might operate. Given the severe econometric problems this literature must confront, I expect that progress will require econometric modeling based rather tightly on maintained economic theory. Any inferences so obtained will then be dependent on strong a priori identifying assumptions regarding economic structure.

Of course, this situation is not unique to identifying FDI spillover effects. We always need a priori identifying assumptions in order to learn anything of interest from data, beyond perhaps the simplest of descriptive statistics. Data cannot simply "speak" and answer our questions about interesting aspects of economic behavior without our bringing some a priori information to bear.[1] However, I think the need for more a priori structure if we are

Michael P. Keane is professor of economics in the Department of Economics at Yale University.

1. By "data" I mean the joint distribution of observed variables. To use the language of the Cowles Commission,

> Suppose . . . [an econometrician] is faced with the problem of identifying . . . the structural equations that alone reflect specified laws of economic behavior. . . . Statistical observation will in favorable circumstances permit him to estimate . . . the probability distribution of the variables. Under no circumstances whatever will passive statistical observation permit him to distinguish between different

to make any progress in estimating FDI spillover effects is particularly striking.

For the most part, the existing literature on FDI spillovers takes the approach of estimating production functions in which the total factor productivity (TFP) of the domestic firms in a particular industry/country is allowed to be a function of some measure of the FDI directed by multinational corporations (MNCs) into that industry.[2] For instance, the market share of foreign-owned MNC affiliates in the industry, or the average foreign equity participation across all firms in an industry, are commonly used FDI measures. To fix ideas, consider a Cobb-Douglas production function:

$$y_{it} = A_{it} K_{it}^{\alpha} L_{it}^{\beta}$$

where y_{it} is output (or value added) of firm i at time t, A_{it} is TFP, and K_{it} and L_{it} are the capital and labor inputs, respectively. Letting TFP be determined by

$$\ln A_{it} = \pi_0 + \pi_1 F_{jt} + \eta_j + \phi_i + \varepsilon_{it}$$

where F_{jt} is the measure of foreign presence in the industry j to which firm i belongs, η_j is an industry-specific effect, ϕ_i is a firm-specific effect, and ε_{it} is a firm-/time-specific idiosyncratic productivity shock, we obtain the equation:

$$\ln y_{it} = \pi_0 + \pi_1 F_{jt} + \alpha \ln K_{it} + \beta \ln L_{it} + \eta_j + \phi_i + \varepsilon_{it} \qquad (I.1)$$

The basic approach is to estimate an equation like I.1 and to view a significant positive estimate of the coefficient π_1 on the FDI variable as evidence of spillovers.

Now, some of the key difficulties in estimating the parameters of equation I.1 are common to the literature on estimating production functions in general and are not specific to estimating FDI spillover effects. Good discussions of these problems can be found in Marschak and Andrews (1944), Griliches and Mairesse (1995), and Klette and Griliches (1996).

The most obvious problem is endogeneity of the capital and labor inputs, since these will generally be chosen in response to productivity as deter-

---

mathematically equivalent ways of writing down that distribution. . . . The only way in which he can hope to identify and measure individual structural equations . . . is with the help of *a priori* specifications of the form of each structural equation (Koopmans, Rubin, and Leipnik 1950).

2. Some studies also examine "backward linkages" by including measures of FDI in industries that are supplied by the industry in question.

mined by $\eta_j + \phi_i + \varepsilon_{it}$. The standard solutions to this problem are some combination of (i) differencing the data to eliminate the time-invariant components of productivity and/or (ii) finding instruments that are assumed to be correlated with factor input choices but uncorrelated with productivity (such as input prices). We can then estimate equation I.1 using instrumental variables (IV) to deal with the endogeneity of the factor inputs.

Instruments that might typically be used for the capital and labor inputs are measures of wage rates and the price of capital. A more recent alternative to (ii) is the Olley and Pakes (1996) procedure that uses investment as an indicator of the productivity shock.

A major problem with this general approach is the failure to deal seriously with heterogeneity in firms' production processes. As Lipsey and Sjöholm cogently point out in chapter 2 of this volume, it seems unlikely that we can make sense of FDI spillovers in a modeling framework where all they do is shift TFP. If knowledge spillovers occur, it seems likely that FDI will alter the production functions of domestic firms in much more subtle and extensive ways. For example, perhaps a knowledge spillover will lead to a more capital-intensive production process or enable a reorganization of the domestic firm so that it can take advantage of economies of scale. In such cases, spillovers will affect the share parameters in equation I.1, not just TFP. This highlights the point that no specific theory of how knowledge spillovers affect production technology underlies specifications as in equation I.1.

Furthermore, a striking aspect of equation I.1 is the assumption of fixed technology parameters even *across* industries. Yet, if we look at manufacturing industries where FDI occurs, there is ample evidence of substantial heterogeneity in firms' technologies even when we look at firms *within* narrowly defined industries. Evidence is provided in a series of studies by Feinberg and Keane (2001, 2003a, 2003b), Feinberg, Keane, and Bognanno (1998), and the chapter by Feinberg and Keane in this volume. In these studies, we find that MNC affiliates operate in very different ways even within narrowly defined industries: the shares of capital, labor, materials, and intermediates imported from parents differ quite substantially across firms.

This suggests three problems: First, if technological heterogeneity is prevalent for affiliates, it is likely to be prevalent for domestic firms as well. If share parameters are heterogeneous across firms/industries (i.e., some firms use more capital-intensive production processes than others), then an instrumental variables technique applied to equation I.1, using supply-side instruments like wage rates and the price of capital, will not generally resolve the problem of endogeneity of the capital and labor inputs. We might think that with heterogeneous coefficients we would estimate the mean coefficient values in the population of firms, which would still be of interest. However, as I discuss in the appendix, this is true only under very special assumptions that we would not expect to hold in the present case. In general, with heterogeneity on the production function parameters, the IV approach will not consistently estimate behaviorally interpretable parameters.[3]

Second, if the impact of FDI on TFP differs across firms/industries, and/or FDI has more general impact on technology than just shifting TFP, then estimation of specifications as in equation I.1 using instrumental variables procedures will not in general identify the parameter π_1, and, furthermore, it is no longer even clear how a parameter like π_1 could be interpreted.

Third, Feinberg and Keane (chapter 10 in this volume) document that MNC affiliates in developing countries are organized in very different ways. That is, if we look at affiliates within an industry/country, some are organized to use a substantial volume of imported intermediates from parents while others are not, some are organized to ship substantial volumes of intermediates back to parents while others are not, some are organized to trade heavily with the parent's affiliates in other countries while others are not, and so on. The existing econometric literature takes no account of the possibility that the form of affiliate organization may play a key a role in whether and how knowledge is transferred to local firms. This again stems from the general failure to base empirical work on specific underlying theories that specify the mechanisms through which knowledge transfer arises.

On this issue, the case study literature, such as Moran (2001), is quite informative, because it suggests that the nature of the interaction between parents and affiliates does heavily influence whether and how knowledge is transferred. As Moran (chapter 11 in this volume) notes "these investigations showed that there is a fundamental difference in performance between subsidiaries that are integrated into the global or regional sourcing networks of the parent multinationals, and subsidiaries that are oriented toward protected domestic markets. . . ."

Lipsey and Sjöholm (chapter 2 in this volume) argue that the case study literature addresses the question of whether there are examples where technology was transferred from MNCs to domestically owned firms, while the "statistical studies ask whether *on average* domestically owned firms gain . . . from the presence of foreign-owned firms." However, it is important to recognize that, when heterogeneous effects are present, an econometric analysis that assumes homogenous effects does not in general answer this "on average" question. In general, the biases induced by ignoring hetero-

---

3. Intuitively, the problem arises because, if production function coefficients differ across firms, then a model that assumes homogenous parameters will sweep the firm-specific part of the parameters, along with capital and labor input terms they multiply, into the error term. Also, with heterogeneous production function parameters, "exogenous" factor price changes will have different effects on factor inputs for different firms. Thus, changes in factor inputs induced by "exogenous" changes in the wage rate or price of capital are still correlated with the firm-specific parameters that enter the error term. The only way to deal with the problem is to model the heterogeneity explicitly. Although in a different context, Feinberg and Keane (2003a) is the only study I know of that does this.

geneity are much more fundamental (see appendix IA). I would argue instead that the case study literature might be used to help guide the development of theoretical models of the *mechanisms* through which knowledge transfers occur, and that these in turn might be used as the basis for structural economic analysis (see below).

Another general problem in the estimation of production functions that I would like to point out is what I will call the "price times quantity (PQ) problem." This problem was stressed by Griliches and Mairesse (1995) and Klette and Griliches (1996), and is also discussed by Lipsey and Sjöholm (in this volume). The main problem is that we do not actually have data on real output quantities (or real value added) y_{it} for purposes of estimating equation I.1. Rather, we typically have data only on sales revenues, meaning we see only PQ and not quantity itself.

In order to deal with the PQ problem, it has been typical in the literature on production function estimation to simply use industry-level price indices to deflate nominal sales revenue data so as to construct real output. But Griliches and Mairesse (1995) as well as Klette and Griliches (1996) have pointed out that this procedure is valid only in perfectly competitive industries, so that price is exogenous to firms. If firms have market power, then any change in inputs will shift both price and quantity, with the price effect depending both on the elasticity of demand facing the firm and the elasticity of output with respect to the input, both of which are, in general, firm specific. In the present context, the point is that, if FDI seems to shift revenue, we do not know if this is because it shifted productivity or prices. These considerations are important here because we would expect FDI to occur in industries where firms do indeed have market power. The PQ problem has received a great deal of attention recently in the industrial-organization (IO) literature (see, for example, Katayama, Lu, and Tybout 2003 and Levinsohn and Melitz 2002).

The only general solution to the problem of endogenous output prices is to estimate the production function jointly with an assumed demand system. To my knowledge, the only study where such an approach has been fully implemented is Feinberg and Keane (2003a), which estimates the production technology of US parents and their manufacturing affiliates in Canada.[4] In the FDI spillover context, one would need to estimate the production functions for domestic (i.e., host country) firms jointly with a demand system.

In this regard, Lipsey and Sjöholm (in this volume) make the interesting point that "if the foreign investors' . . . superiority consists of knowledge about . . . marketing a product . . . it will not be visible in . . . production

---

4. The solutions proposed by Katayama, Lu, and Tybout (2003) as well as Levinsohn and Melitz (2002) are somewhat more specialized and do not require complete specification of the demand system.

function comparisons." Another way to put it is that FDI spillovers may operate by affecting the demand system rather than the production function. Given the PQ problem, this means they actually *may* show up in production function comparisons, but not in any interpretable way. It is disconcerting that a knowledge spillover that enables firms to enhance market power could show up spuriously as a productivity enhancement, since the two have very different welfare implications.

Next, I focus on an issue that is more specific to the literature on estimating FDI spillover effects: FDI is likely to be endogenous. One key source of endogeneity is that MNCs may be attracted to invest in countries that have high productivity. A country's solid legal framework, low risk of appropriation (see Wang and Blomström 1992), and a relatively free/well-managed economy could make it more attractive for FDI. All these factors would presumably lead to more productive domestic firms as well. An econometric study that failed to account for these factors might falsely conclude that FDI enhanced productivity, when in fact FDI was just attracted to countries that were pursuing productivity-enhancing policies.

But there are other stories where the endogeneity bias can go either way. In the theoretical literature on FDI and spillovers (e.g., Ethier and Markusen 1996 and Petit and Sanna-Randaccio 2000), one point that is stressed is that FDI is more likely when a country/industry has better protection of intellectual property. This could lead us to see more FDI in industries/countries where spillovers are smaller, leading to a negative correlation between host country productivity and MNC penetration. On the other hand, if intellectual property protection is good for productivity-enhancing investment in general, or if it is associated with a country having a generally favorable economic climate, then MNCs' tendency to invest in countries with strong intellectual property protection could lead to a spurious positive correlation between domestic firm productivity and FDI.

Furthermore, a key point is that MNC entry into an industry will generally change the market structure, leading to either more or less competition depending on the entry and exit behavior of domestic firms. This in turn can lead to either an increase or decrease in research and development (R&D) activity by domestic firms (see Veuglers and Vanden Houte 1990). Also, if domestic firms have market power, they may engage in inefficient management practices that are reformed when foreign competition is introduced. Thus, it is perfectly possible that FDI could affect productivity of domestic firms for reasons that have nothing to do with knowledge spillovers.

Such endogeneity problems are the focus of Gordon Hanson's insightful comment in this volume. He argues that, given the endogeneity of FDI, we cannot really infer anything causal from the positive correlation between FDI and domestic firm productivity found in the literature. As Hanson discusses, one way we might try to address these endogeneity problems is to find instruments or "natural experiments" that generate exogenous changes in FDI. Such approaches are currently quite fashionable in applied economics. However, I am not optimistic that we can make much headway on estimating FDI spillover effects if we pursue this course. One basic problem is that truly exogenous factors driving FDI are hard to come by.

The theoretical literature suggests that firms choose between FDI or exports as a means to serve a foreign market based on such factors as tariffs, transport costs, wage rates, and other costs in the host country. Similar factors influence vertical FDI. But would a change in tariffs be exogenous with respect to FDI? It seems likely that tariff changes are associated with other changes in the economic environment—for example, countries that lower tariffs often engage in a broad range of economic liberalizations at the same time. In order to conclude that any change in productivity associated with a tariff-induced change in FDI was due solely to the change in FDI itself, we would have to control for all these other concomitant changes in the economic environment.

Factors like restrictions on capital investment, intellectual property protection, expropriation risk, political stability, and economic freedom are presumably important determinants of FDI as well. The data also contain a great deal of variation along these dimensions. Indeed, Lipsey and Sjöholm (in this volume) point out that more than 1,500 policy changes making regulations more favorable to FDI occurred during the 1991–2002 period, along with 100 changes making regulations less favorable. Do any of these regulator changes provide "natural experiments?" I expect not, precisely because they are likely to be accompanied by other economic policy changes and institutional changes.

Another problem with inferring causality from FDI/productivity correlations is the problem of reverse causality. FDI itself may lead to changes in regulations affecting FDI and also to changes in economic policy and/or in political/economic institutions. These policy changes might enhance productivity, quite apart from any direct effects of FDI. Thus, it seems highly implausible to me that we can ever find natural experiments where FDI is made more or less attractive while holding all other things equal.

Even if we could find a perfectly exogenous instrument that shifts FDI while not being associated with any other (unmeasured) changes in the economic environment, we would still face a number of problems. First, if production function heterogeneity exists, then the biases discussed earlier (and in the appendix) would prevent two-stage least squares (2SLS) from giving a consistent estimate of coefficient π_1.[5] Further, even if we could use such an

---

5. The popularity of the fourth approach stems, in part, from the currently prevalent view that, if we can find "natural experiments" or "clever instruments," we can learn interesting things about behavior without making strong a priori assumptions and without using "too much" economic theory. However, it is important to remember that the assumption that a variable is exogenous and a valid instrument always rests on a set of theoretical assumptions (see Marschak 1950). As Rosenzweig and Wolpin (2000) discuss, in the "natural experiment" approach, the theoretical (or behavioral) assumptions that underlie exogeneity assumptions

instrument to estimate the causal effect of FDI on productivity, we would not have isolated the mechanism through which the productivity enhancement occurred. Is it knowledge spillovers, or is it the response of domestic firms to enhanced competition, which, as we noted earlier, could lead to enhanced R&D or to adoption of more efficient management practices?

All of this suggests that we are unlikely to make progress in estimating FDI spillover effects using the simple strategy of estimating production functions with instrumental variables techniques. I believe that to make any progress we will need to model additional data beyond measures of FDI, output, and factor inputs. The preceding discussion suggests it is important to also look at industry structure (entry and exit), measures of R&D spending, and, perhaps, to attempt to form more direct measures of spillovers. Severe problems of endogeneity and reverse causality suggest that we should not attempt to model effects of FDI on productivity in a single equation framework but, rather, view both variables as endogenous outcomes that are jointly determined, along with such factors as market structure and R&D, as part of a structural system.

In this regard, I am struck by the fact that there are several parallel literatures to the FDI spillover literature that seem to simply reorganize what is on the left- and right-hand sides of the estimating equations. For instance, there is literature that examines the determinants of FDI (see, for example, Brainard 1997 and Neven and Siotis 1996), where the determinants are things like R&D intensity, labor productivity, tariff and nontariff barriers, and legal and economic institutions. There is literature in growth theory that examines the effects of such factors as institutions, the legal environment, and corruption on economic growth and/or productivity. Studies in this literature estimate equations like equation I.1 except that now the FDI measure is replaced by measures of institutions (see, for example, Acemoglu, Johnson, and Robinson 2001). There is also both theoretical and empirical literature examining how FDI and market structure influence R&D spending (see, for example, Veuglers and Vanden Houte 1990 and Wang and Blomström 1992). Furthermore, there is literature in development that examines the effect of FDI and growth on institutions.

Putting it all together, we have literature that looks at the effect of FDI on productivity, literature that looks at the effect of productivity and institutions on FDI, literature that looks at the effect of institutions on productivity, literature that looks at how FDI and market structure affect R&D,

---

are often quite strong, and they are often left implicit. The failure of wages and the price of capital to provide valid instrumental variables for the estimation of equation I.1, even if they are completely exogenous from individual firms' point of view, is a good illustration of the potential pitfalls that come from failing to explicitly record a structural model in order to examine whether an instrument is valid. As the appendix shows, wages and the price of capital are not valid instruments for estimation of this model unless a very stringent assumption on production function homogeneity is made.

and literature that looks at the effects of productivity and FDI on institutions. Perhaps it would make more sense to model how productivity, FDI, R&D, market structure, and economic institutions evolve together in a dynamic process, rather than having separate literatures that examine the determinants of each of these variables individually while treating all the others as exogenous.

Development of a dynamic structural model of FDI and productivity would obviously be a major undertaking, but one can see where it might have advantages. For instance, thinking about a dynamic model would immediately lead one to ask: Why should the contemporaneous value of FDI enter equation I.1? Knowledge transfer is presumably a gradual process, and there are costs to adopting new technologies (see Teece 1976 for a discussion). One would think that, if FDI does transfer knowledge, then it should raise productivity with a lag. These types of considerations may lead to timing restrictions that could aid identification.

In summary, I have tried to highlight some of the severe econometric problems facing the literature on FDI spillovers. Given these problems, it is very difficult to draw any reliable conclusions regarding causality from the existing econometric work in this area. I hope that by bringing additional theory and data to bear it will be possible to make further progress. In my view, the most urgently needed step is to stop treating the mapping from FDI to productivity as a black box. Researchers should attempt to formulate realistic theoretical models of the mechanisms through which FDI might generate knowledge spillovers and attempt to bring these models to the data.

Appendix IA

If the share parameters α and β in equation I.1 differ across industries, then the capital and labor inputs enter the error term of the homogenous coefficients model. That is, we can write:

$$\ln y_{it} = \pi_0 + \pi_1 F_{jt} + \bar{\alpha} \ln K_{it} + \bar{\beta} \ln L_{it}$$
$$+ \left[\tilde{\alpha}_i \ln K_{it} + \tilde{\beta}_i \ln L_{it} + \eta_j + \phi_i + \varepsilon_{it} \right] \qquad \text{(IA.1)}$$

where we have let $\alpha_i = \bar{\alpha} + \tilde{\alpha}_i$ and $\beta_i = \bar{\beta} + \tilde{\beta}_i$, where $\bar{\alpha}$ and $\bar{\beta}$ are the mean share parameters across all firms/industries, and $\tilde{\alpha}_i$ and $\tilde{\beta}_i$ are the firm i specific deviations from those means.

Note that the error term, which appears in square brackets in equation IA.1, contains the capital and labor inputs multiplied by the firm-specific share parameters. To give a simple illustration of the problems this creates, suppose that all firms face isoelastic demand functions of the form:

$$P_{it} = P_{0i} y_{it}^{-g}$$

where $0 < g < 1$, and further suppose that production is constant returns to scale (CRS), so that $\alpha_i + \beta_i = 1$. In that case, the firm's optimal choice of labor input is given by:

$$\ln L_{it} = \frac{1}{g} \{ [1 - \alpha_i(1 - g)] \ln(1 - \alpha_i) + \alpha_i (1 - g) \ln \alpha_i$$
$$+ \ln(1 - g) P_{0i} + (1 - g) \ln A_{it} - [1 - \alpha_i(1 - g)] \ln w_{it}$$
$$+ \alpha_i (1 - g) \ln \pi_{it} \} \qquad \text{(IA.2)}$$

where w_{it} is the wage rate facing firm i at time t, and π_{it} is the rental price of capital. Let us assume that the log wage and price of capital are "exogenous" in the sense that:

$$E\left[\tilde{\alpha}_i | \ln w_{it}, \ln \pi_{it} \right] = E\left[\eta_j | \ln w_{it}, \ln \pi_{it} \right] = E\left[\phi_i | \ln w_{it}, \ln \pi_{it} \right]$$
$$= E\left[\varepsilon_{it} | \ln w_{it}, \ln \pi_{it} \right] = 0$$

so these variables would, at first sight, appear to be plausible instruments.

Noting that in the CRS case we have $\beta_i = (1 - \bar{\alpha}) - \tilde{\alpha}_i$, we see that the error term in IA.1 can be written as:

$$\tilde{\alpha}_i \ln K_{it} - \tilde{\alpha}_i \ln L_{it} + \eta_j + \phi_i + \varepsilon_{it} \qquad \text{(IA.3)}$$

If we look at the term $-\tilde{\alpha}_i \ln L_{it}$, and plug in the equation IA.2 for $\ln L_{it}$, we see that the resulting expression contains a term of the form:

$\tilde{\alpha}_i [1 - \alpha_i(1 - g)] \ln w_{it}.$

Then, substituting in $\alpha_i = \bar{\alpha} + \tilde{\alpha}_i$, we see that this expression, in turn, contains a term of the form:

$$(\tilde{\alpha}_i)^2 (1 - g) \ln w_{it}.$$

This component of the error term in IA.1 is correlated with $\ln w_{it}$ unless the variance of $\tilde{\alpha}_i$ is zero (i.e., unless there is no heterogeneity in the share parameters across firms).

This argument implies that, in estimating equation IA.1, the supply price of labor is not a valid instrument for the labor input, since it will be correlated with the error term IA.3. The same type of argument shows that the supply price of capital in not a valid instrument for the capital input. In fact, given how the capital and labor inputs enter the error term, there are no valid instruments by construction. Any variable that alters firms' choices of capital and labor inputs will be correlated with the error term. The only way to deal with this problem is to actually model the distribution of the firm-specific parameters and estimate this distribution.[6]

Of course, there are conditions under which instrumental variables can be used to uncover the mean values of the coefficients in a random coefficients model. These conditions are discussed in Wooldridge (1997) and Card (1999, 1817–20). To understand why these conditions do not hold in the present case, it is useful to cast our model into their framework. Let ξ_{it} denote the composite error term in equation IA.1. Wooldridge noted that, so long as

$$E[\xi_{it}|Z_{it}] = \text{constant}$$

where Z_{it} is the vector of instruments, then 2SLS applied to equation IIA.1, using Z_{it} as the vector of instruments, will only lead to inconsistency in the estimate of the intercept. The slope coefficients of the model are still consistently estimated. However, we have seen that ξ_{it} contains the term

$$(\tilde{\alpha}_i)^2 (1 - g) \ln w_{it}$$

and we therefore have that:

$$E\left[(\tilde{\alpha}_i)^2 (1 - g) \ln w_{it}|\ln w_{it}\right] = (1 - g)\sigma_\alpha^2 \ln w_{it}.$$

Thus, the expected value of ξ_{it} varies with the potential instrument $\ln w_{it}$.

Intuitively, the real source of the problem is that the effect of the potential instrument (price of labor) on the endogenous variable (the labor input) is heterogeneous across firms, as we can see in equation IA.2. In equation

---

6. For an example, but in a different context, see Feinberg and Keane (2003a).

IA.2, the common part of the effect of the wage on the labor input just derives from the $[1 - \bar{\alpha}(1 - g)]\ln w_{it}$ term. This produces a component of ξ_{it} of the form $\tilde{\alpha}_i[1 - \bar{\alpha}(1 - g)]\ln w_{it}$, and this term is mean zero conditional on $\ln w_{it}$. Thus, we see that it is the random part of the coefficient on $\ln w_{it}$ in the labor demand function of equation IA.2 that creates the problem.

References

Acemoglu, Daron, Simon Johnson, and James Robinson. 2001. The Colonial Origins of Comparative Development: An Empirical Investigation. *American Economic Review* 91, no. 5 (December): 1369–401.

Brainard, S. Lael. 1997. An Empirical Assessment of the Proximity-Concentration Trade-Off Between Multinational Sales and Trade. *American Economic Review* 87, no. 4 (September): 520–44.

Card, David. 1999. The Causal Effect of Education on Earnings. In *Handbook of Labor Economics*, eds., Orley Ashenfelter and David Card. Amsterdam: Elsevier Science B.V.

Ethier, Wilfred, and James Markusen. 1996. Multinational Firms, Technology Diffusion and Trade. *Journal of International Economics* 41, no. 1–2 (August): 1–28.

Feinberg, Susan, and Michael Keane. 2001. US-Canada Trade Liberalization and MNC Production Location. *The Review of Economics and Statistics* 83, no. 1 (February): 118–32.

Feinberg, Susan, and Michael Keane. 2003a. *Accounting for the Growth of MNC Based Trade Using a Structural Model of U.S. MNCs*. Working Paper. College Park, MD: University of Maryland.

Feinberg, Susan, and Michael Keane. 2003b. *Tariff Effects on MNC Organization*. Working Paper. College Park, MD: University of Maryland.

Feinberg, Susan, Michael Keane, and Mario Bognanno. 1998. Trade Liberalization and 'Delocalization:' New Evidence from Firm-Level Panel Data. *Canadian Journal of Economics* 31, no. 4 (October): 749–77.

Griliches, Zvi, and Jacques Mairesse. 1995. *Production Functions: The Search for Identification*. NBER Working Paper 5067. Cambridge, MA: National Bureau of Economic Research.

Katayama, Haijime, Shihua Lu, and James Tybout. 2003. *Why Plant-Level Productivity Studies Are Often Misleading, and an Alternative Approach to Interference*. NBER Working Paper 9617. Cambridge, MA: National Bureau of Economic Research.

Klette, Tor Jakob, and Zvi Griliches. 1996. *The Inconsistency of Common Scale Estimators When Output Prices Are Unobserved and Endogenous*. NBER Working Paper 4026. Cambridge, MA: National Bureau of Economic Research.

Koopmans, Tjalling, Herman Rubin, and Roy Bergh Leipnik. 1950. Measuring the Equation Systems of Dynamic Economics. In *Cowles Commission Monograph No. 10: Statistical Inference in Dynamic Economic Models*, ed., T. C. Koopmans. New York: John Wiley & Sons.

Levinsohn, James, and Marc Melitz. 2002. *Productivity in a Differentiated Products Market Equilibrium*. Working Paper. Ann Arbor, MI: University of Michigan.

Marschak, Jacob. 1950. Statistical Inference in Economics: An Introduction. In *Cowles Commission Monograph No. 10: Statistical Inference in Dynamic Economic Models*, ed., T. C. Koopmans. New York: John Wiley & Sons.

Marschak, Jacob, and William Andrews. 1944. Random Simultaneous Equations and the Theory of Production. *Econometrica* 12, no. 3–4 (July–October): 143–205.

Moran, Theodore H. 2001. *Parental Supervision: The New Paradigm for Foreign Direct Investment and Development*. POLICY ANALYSES IN INTERNATIONAL ECONOMICS 64. Washington: Institute for International Economics.

Neven, Damien, and Georges Siotis. 1996. Technology Sourcing and FDI in the EC: An Empirical Investigation. *International Journal of Industrial Organization* 14, no. 5 (July): 543–60.

Olley, Steven, and Ariel Pakes. 1996. The Dynamics of Productivity in the Telecommunications Equipment Industry. *Econometrica* 64, no. 6 (November): 1263–97.

Petit, Maria, and Francesca Sanna-Randaccio. 2000. Endogenous R&D and Foreign Direct Investment in International Oligopolies. *International Journal of Industrial Organization* 18, no. 2 (February): 339–67.

Rosenzweig, Mark, and Kenneth Wolpin. 2000. Natural "Natural Experiments" in Economics. *Journal of Economic Literature* 38, no. 4 (December): 827–74.

Teece, David. 1976. *The Multinational Corporation and the Resource Cost of International Technology Transfer.* Cambridge, MA: Balinger Publishing Company.

Veuglers, Reinhilde, and Peter Vanden Houte. 1990. Domestic R&D in the Presence of Multinational Enterprises. *International Journal of Industrial Organization* 8:1 (March) 1–15.

Wang, Jian-Ye, and Magnus Blomström. 1992. Foreign Investment and Technology Transfer. *European Economic Review* 36, no. 1 (January): 137–55.

Wooldridge, Jeff. 1997. On Two-Stage Least Squares Estimation of the Average Treatment Effect in a Random Coefficient Model. *Economics Letters* 56, no. 2 (October): 129–33.

II

IMPACT OF FDI ON
HOST-COUNTRY GROWTH

8

Does Foreign Direct Investment Accelerate Economic Growth?

MARIA CARKOVIC and ROSS LEVINE

With commercial bank lending to developing economies drying up in the 1980s, most countries eased restrictions on foreign direct investment (FDI) and many aggressively offered tax incentives and subsidies to attract foreign capital (Aitken and Harrison 1999; World Bank 1997a, 1997b). Along with these policy changes, a surge of noncommercial bank private capital flows to developing economies in the 1990s occurred. Private capital flows to emerging-market economies exceeded $320 billion in 1996 and reached almost $200 billion in 2000. Even the 2000 figure is almost four times larger than the peak commercial bank lending years of the 1970s and early 1980s. Furthermore, FDI now accounts for over 60 percent of private capital flows. While the explosion of FDI flows is unmistakable, the growth effects remain unclear.

Theory provides conflicting predictions concerning the growth effects of FDI. The economic rationale for offering special incentives to attract FDI frequently derives from the belief that foreign investment produces externalities in the form of technology transfers and spillovers. Romer (1993), for example, argues that important "idea gaps" between rich and poor countries exist. He notes that foreign investment can ease the transfer of technological

Maria Carkovic is senior fellow in finance and Ross Levine is Curtis L. Carlson Professor of Finance at the Carlson School of Management at the University of Minnesota. We thank Norman Loayza for helpful statistical advice and Stephen Bond for the use of his DPD program. We thank participants at the World Bank conference, Financial Globalization: A Blessing or a Curse, in Washington (May 2002), and the Institute of International Economics conference, The Impact of Foreign Direct Investment on Development: New Measurements, New Outcomes, New Policy Approaches, in Washington (April 2004). We received particularly useful suggestions from Monty Graham, Marc Melitz, and Ted Moran.

and business know-how to poorer countries. According to this view, FDI may boost the productivity of all firms—not just those receiving foreign capital. Thus, transfers of technology through FDI may have substantial spillover effects for the entire economy. In contrast, some theories predict that FDI in the presence of preexisting trade, price, financial, and other distortions will hurt resource allocation and slow growth (Boyd and Smith 1992). Thus, theory produces ambiguous predictions about the growth effects of FDI, and some models suggest that FDI will promote growth only under certain policy conditions.

Firm-level studies of particular countries often find that FDI does *not* boost economic growth, and these studies frequently do *not* find positive spillovers running between foreign-owned and domestically owned firms. Aitken and Harrison's (1999) influential study finds no evidence of a positive technology spillover from foreign firms to domestically owned ones in Venezuela between 1979 and 1989. While Blomström (1986) finds that Mexican sectors with a higher degree of foreign ownership exhibit faster productivity growth, Haddad and Harrison (1993) find no evidence of growth-enhancing spillovers in other countries. As summarized by Lipsey and Sjöholm (in this volume), in some countries, researchers find evidence of positive spillovers in some industries, but country-specific and industry-specific factors seem so important that the results do not support the overall conclusion that FDI induces substantial spillover effects for the entire economy. In sum, firm-level studies do not imply that FDI accelerates overall economic growth.

Unlike the microeconomic evidence, macroeconomic studies—using aggregate FDI flows for a broad cross section of countries—generally suggest a positive role for FDI in generating economic growth, especially in particular environments. For instance, Borensztein, De Gregorio, and Lee (1998) argue that FDI has a positive growth effect when the country has a highly educated workforce that allows it to exploit FDI spillovers. While Blomström, Lipsey, and Zejan (1994) find no evidence that education is critical, they argue that FDI has a positive growth effect when the country is sufficiently wealthy. In turn, Alfaro et al. (2003) find that FDI promotes economic growth in economies with sufficiently developed financial markets, while Balasubramanyam, Salisu, and Sapsford (1996) stress that trade openness is crucial for obtaining the growth effects of FDI.

The macroeconomic findings on growth and FDI must be viewed skeptically, however. Existing studies do not fully control for simultaneity bias, country-specific effects, and the routine use of lagged dependent variables in growth regressions. These weaknesses can bias the coefficient estimates as well as the coefficient standard errors. Thus, the profession needs to reassess the macroeconomic evidence with econometric procedures that eliminate these potential biases.

This study uses new statistical techniques and two new databases to reassess the relationship between economic growth and FDI. First, based on a recent World Bank dataset (Kraay et al. 1999), we construct a panel dataset with data averaged over each of the seven five-year periods between 1960 and 1995. We also confirm the results using new FDI data from the International Monetary Fund (IMF).

Methodologically, we use the Generalized Method of Moments (GMM) panel estimator to extract consistent and efficient estimates of the impact of FDI flows on economic growth. Unlike past work, the GMM panel estimator exploits the time-series variation in the data, accounts for unobserved country-specific effects, allows for the inclusion of lagged dependent variables as regressors, and controls for endogeneity of all the explanatory variables, including international capital flows. Thus, this study advances the literature on growth and FDI by enhancing the quality and quantity of the data and by using econometric techniques that reduce biases.

Investigating the impact of foreign capital on economic growth has important policy implications. If FDI has a positive impact on economic growth after controlling for endogeneity and other growth determinants, then this weakens arguments for restricting foreign investment. If, however, we find that FDI does not exert a positive impact on growth, then this would suggest a reconsideration of the rapid expansion of tax incentives, infrastructure subsidies, import duty exemptions, and other measures that countries have adopted to attract FDI. While no single study will resolve these policy issues, this study contributes to these debates.

This study finds that the exogenous component of FDI does not exert a robust, positive influence on economic growth. By accounting for simultaneity, country-specific effects, and lagged dependent variables as regressors, we reconcile the microeconomic and macroeconomic evidence. Specifically, there is no reliable cross-country empirical evidence supporting the claim that FDI per se accelerates economic growth.

This chapter's findings are robust to

- econometric specifications that allow FDI to influence growth differently depending on national income, school attainment, domestic financial development, and openness to international trade;

- alternative estimation procedures;

- different conditioning information sets and samples;

- the use of portfolio inflows instead of FDI; and

- the use of alternative databases on FDI.

The data produce consistent results: there is not a robust, causal link running from FDI to economic growth.

This study's results, however, should not be viewed as suggesting that foreign capital is irrelevant for long-run growth. Borensztein, De Gregorio, and Lee (1998) show, and this study confirms, many econometric specifications in which FDI is positively linked with long-run growth. FDI may even be a positive signal of economic success as emphasized by Blomström, Lipsey, and Zejan (1994). More generally, "openness"—defined in a less narrow sense than FDI inflows—may be crucial for economic success, as suggested by other research (e.g., Bekaert, Harvey, and Lundblad 2001; Klein and Olivei 2000). Rather than examine these broad issues, this study's contribution is much narrower: after controlling for the joint determination of growth and foreign capital flows, country-specific factors, and other growth determinants, the data do not suggest a strong independent impact of FDI on economic growth. In terms of policy implications, this study's analyses do not support special tax breaks and subsidies to attract foreign capital. Instead, the literature suggests that sound policies encourage economic growth and also provide an attractive environment for foreign investment.

Before continuing, it is worth emphasizing this study's boundaries. We do not discuss the determinants of FDI. Instead, we extract the exogenous component of FDI using system panel techniques. Also, we do not examine any particular country in depth. We use data on 72 countries from 1960 to 1995. Thus, our investigation provides evidence based on a cross section of countries.

Econometric Framework

This section describes two econometric methods that we use to assess the relationship between FDI inflows and economic growth. We first use simple ordinary least squares (OLS) regressions with one observation per country over the 1960–95 period. Second, we use a dynamic panel procedure with data averaged over five-year periods, so that there are seven possible observations per country between 1960 and 1995.

OLS Framework

The pure cross-sectional OLS analysis uses data averaged from 1960–95. The data include one observation per country and heteroskedasticity-consistent standard errors. The basic regression takes the form:

$$\text{GROWTH}_i = \alpha + \beta FDI_i + \gamma'[\text{CONDITIONING SET}]_i + \varepsilon_i \qquad (8.1)$$

where the dependent variable, GROWTH, equals real per capita gross domestic product (GDP) growth, FDI is gross private capital inflows to a country, and CONDITIONING SET represents a vector of conditioning information.

Motivation for the Dynamic Panel Model

The dynamic panel approach offers advantages to OLS and also improves on previous efforts to examine the FDI-growth link using panel procedures. First, using panel data—that is, pooled cross-section and time-series data—to make estimates allows researchers to exploit the time-series nature of the relationship between FDI and growth. Thus, the panel approach included more information than the pure cross-country approach with positive ramifications on the precision of the coefficient estimates. Second, in a pure cross-country instrumental variable regression, any unobserved country-specific effect becomes part of the error term, which may bias the coefficient estimates (as we explain in detail below). Thus, if there are country-specific fixed effects that are not included in the conditioning set and that help explain economic growth, then the OLS procedure may produce erroneous estimates on the FDI coefficient. The panel procedures control for country-specific effects. Third, unlike existing pure cross-country studies that use instrumental variables to control for the potential endogeneity of FDI, the panel estimator controls for the potential endogeneity of *all* explanatory variables. This distinction is important. If the other growth determinants besides FDI are endogenously determined with growth, which seems likely since the other growth determinants include inflation, government size, and the black market premium, among others, and if the estimation procedure does not account for this endogeneity, then this could bias FDI's estimated coefficient and standard error. Finally, the panel estimator that we employ accounts explicitly for the biases induced by including initial real per capita GDP in the growth regression. Since initial real per capita GDP is a component of the dependent variable, economic growth, including this variable as a regressor may bias both the coefficient estimates and their standard errors, potentially leading to erroneous conclusions. For these reasons, we augment the OLS regressions with panel estimates.

Detailed Presentation of the Econometric Methodology

We use the GMM estimators developed for dynamic panel data. Our panel consists of data for a maximum of 72 countries from 1960–95, though capital flow data do not begin until 1970 for many countries. We average data over nonoverlapping, five-year periods, so that, data permitting, seven observations per country (1961–65, 1966–70, etc.) are made. Thus, we exploit the time-series, along with the cross-country, dimension of the data. Consider the following regression equation:

$$y_{i,t} - y_{i,t-1} = (\alpha - 1)y_{i,t-1} + \beta'X_{i,t} + \eta_i + \varepsilon_{i,t} \tag{8.2}$$

where y is the logarithm of real per capita GDP, X represents the set of explanatory variables (other than lagged per capita GDP), η is an unobserved country-specific effect, ε is the error term, and the subscripts i and t represent country and five-year time period, respectively. Specifically, X includes FDI inflows to a country as well as other possible growth determinants. We also use time dummy variables for each five-year period to account for period-specific effects, though these are omitted from the equations in the text. We can thus rewrite equation 8.2:

$$y_{i,t} = \alpha y_{i,t-1} + \beta' X_{i,t} + \eta_i + \varepsilon_{i,t} \qquad (8.3)$$

To eliminate the country-specific effect, take first differences of equation 8.3:

$$y_{i,t} - y_{i,t-1} = \alpha\,(y_{i,t-1} - y_{i,t-2}) + \beta'(X_{i,t} - X_{i,t-1}) + (\varepsilon_{i,t} - \varepsilon_{i,t-1})$$

Thus, this eliminates potential biases associated with unobserved fixed, country effects.

Instrument variables are required to deal with both the endogeneity of all the explanatory variables and the problem that the new error term $\varepsilon_{i,t} - \varepsilon_{i,t-1}$, which is correlated with the lagged dependent variable $y_{i,t-1} - y_{i,t-2}$, creates because of the routine inclusion of lagged values of the dependent variable as a regressor. Under the assumptions that the error term is not serially correlated, and the explanatory variables are weakly exogenous (i.e., the explanatory variables are uncorrelated with future realizations of the error term), the GMM dynamic panel estimator uses the following moment conditions, where s and t indicate the five-year period under evaluation:

$$E\lfloor y_{i,t-s} \cdot (\varepsilon_{i,t} - \varepsilon_{i,t-1})\rfloor = 0 \qquad \textit{for } s \geq 2; t = 3,\ldots,T \qquad (8.4)$$

$$E\lfloor X_{i,t-s} \cdot (\varepsilon_{i,t} - \varepsilon_{i,t-1})\rfloor = 0 \qquad \textit{for } s \geq 2; t = 3,\ldots,T \qquad (8.5)$$

We refer to the GMM estimator based on these conditions as the difference estimator.

There are, however, conceptual and statistical shortcomings with this difference estimator. Conceptually, we would also like to study the cross-country relationship between financial development and per capita GDP growth, which is eliminated in the difference estimator. When the explanatory variables are persistent over time, lagged levels make weak instruments for the regression equation in first differences. Instrument weakness influences the asymptotic and small-sample performance of the difference estimator. Asymptotically, the variance of the coefficients rises. In small samples, weak instruments can bias the coefficients.

To reduce the potential biases and imprecision associated with the usual estimator, we use a new estimator that combines in a system the regression in differences with the regression in levels. The instruments for the regression in differences are the same as above. The instruments for the regression in levels are the lagged differences of the corresponding variables. These are appropriate instruments under the following *additional* assumption: although there may be correlation between the levels of the right-hand variables and the country-specific effect in equation 8.3, there is no correlation between the differences of these variables and the country-specific effect. The following equation specifies this more formally, where p, q, and t indicate time periods:

$$E\lfloor y_{i,t+p} \cdot \eta_i \rfloor = E\lfloor y_{i,t+q} \cdot \eta_i \rfloor \ and \ E\lfloor X_{i,t+p} \cdot \eta_i \rfloor = E\lfloor X_{i,t+q} \cdot \eta_i \rfloor$$

$$for \ all \ p \ and \ q \quad (8.6)$$

The additional moment conditions for the second part of the system (the regression in levels) are:

$$E\lfloor (y_{i,t-s} - y_{i,t-s-1}) \cdot (\eta_i + \varepsilon_{i,t}) \rfloor = 0 \quad for \ s = 1 \quad (8.7)$$

$$E\lfloor (X_{i,t-s} - X_{i,t-s-1}) \cdot (\eta_i + \varepsilon_{i,t}) \rfloor = 0 \quad for \ s = 1 \quad (8.8)$$

Thus, we use the moment conditions presented in equations 8.4, 8.5, 8.7, and 8.8, use instruments lagged two periods ($t - 2$), and employ a GMM procedure to generate consistent and efficient parameter estimates.[1]

Consistency of the GMM estimator depends on the validity of the instruments. To address this issue we consider two specification tests. The first is a Sargan test of overidentifying restrictions, which tests the overall validity of the instruments by analyzing the sample analog of the moment conditions used in the estimation process. The second test examines the hypothesis that the error term $\varepsilon_{i,t}$ is not serially correlated. In both the difference regression

---

1. We use a variant of the standard two-step system estimator that controls for heteroskedasticity. Typically, the system estimator treats the moment conditions as applying to a particular time period. This provides for a more flexible variance-covariance structure of the moment conditions because the variance for a given moment condition is not assumed to be the same across time. The drawback of this approach is that the number of overidentifying conditions increases dramatically as the number of time periods increases. Consequently, this typical two-step estimator tends to induce overfitting and potentially biased standard errors. To limit the number of overidentifying conditions, we follow Beck and Levine (2003) by applying each moment condition to all available periods. This reduces the overfitting bias of the two-step estimator. However, applying this modified estimator reduces the number of periods by one. While in the standard estimator time dummies and the constant are used as instruments for the second period, this modified estimator does not allow the use of the first and second periods. We confirm the results using the standard system estimator.

Recall that we assume that the explanatory variables are "weakly exogenous." This means they can be affected by current and past realizations of the growth rate but not future realizations of the error term. Weak exogeneity does not mean that agents do not take expected future growth into account in their decision to undertake FDI—rather, it means that unanticipated shocks to future growth do not influence current FDI. We statistically assess the validity of this assumption.

and the system difference–level regression, we test whether the differenced error term is second-order serially correlated (by construction, the differenced error term is probably first-order serially correlated even if the original error term is not).

The panel procedure also has disadvantages and limitations. The major disadvantage relative to a pure cross-country comparison is that this study focuses on economic growth and seeks to abstract from business cycles and crises. To use panel procedures, however, the data are averaged over five-year periods, which may not eliminate higher frequency forces. Thus, to assess the robustness of the results, we employ both OLS techniques that use data averaged over more than 35 years and panel techniques that use data averaged over five-year periods. Furthermore, the panel procedure has limitations in that it does not solve all of the problems associated with cross-country regressions. For instance, FDI may have complex dynamic effects, such that the impact of FDI is different from the short run to the long run. We provide some sensitivity checks along this dimension by presenting results based on data averaged over both 35 years and 5 years. Nevertheless, this study does not attempt to trace the potential time-varying effects of FDI on growth. Finally, this study provides an aggregate examination. While a multitude of firm-level and industry-level studies of FDI exist, in particular countries that attempt to assess the effects of specific policies (see the chapters by Moran as well as Lipsey and Sjöholm in this volume), this study undertakes a general assessment of the relationship between FDI and growth.

Data

We collected FDI data from two sources. First, we use data from the World Bank's ongoing project to improve the accuracy, breadth, and length of national accounts data (Kraay et al. 1999). Second, we confirm the findings using the IMF's *World Economic Output* (2001) data on openness. We now define each variable.

- *FDI* equals gross FDI inflows as a share of GDP. We confirm the results using FDI inflows per capita.[2]

- *GROWTH* equals the rate of real per capita GDP growth.

---

2. Countries in the sample: Algeria (DZA), Argentina, Australia, Austria, Belgium, Bolivia, Brazil, Cameroon, Canada, Central African Republic, Chile, Colombia, Congo, Costa Rica, Cyprus, Denmark, Dominican Republic, Ecuador, El Salvador, Egypt, Finland, France, Gambia, Germany, Ghana, Britain, Greece, Guatemala, Guyana, Haiti, Honduras, Hong Kong, India, Indonesia, Ireland, Israel, Italy, Jamaica, Japan, Kenya, Lesotho, Malaysia, Malta, Mauritius, Mexico, Netherlands, New Zealand, Nicaragua, Niger, Norway, Pakistan, Panama, Papua New Guinea, Paraguay, Peru, Philippines, Portugal, Republic of Korea, Rwanda, Senegal, Sierra Leone, South Africa, Spain, Sri Lanka, Suriname, Sweden, Switzerland, Syria, Togo, Thailand, Trinidad and Tobago, Uruguay, United States, Venezuela, Zaire, Zimbabwe.

To assess the link between international capital flows and economic growth and its sources, we control for other growth determinants: *Initial income per capita* equals the logarithm of real per capita GDP at the start of each period, so that it equals 1960 in the pure cross-country analyses and, thereafter, the first year of each five-year period in the panel estimates. *Average years of schooling* equals the average years of schooling of the working-age population. *Inflation* equals the average growth rate in the consumer price index. *Government size* equals the size of the government as a share of GDP. *Openness to trade* equals exports plus imports relative to GDP. *Black market premium* equals the black market premium in the foreign exchange market. *Private credit* equals credit by financial intermediaries to the private sector as a share of GDP (Beck, Levine, and Loayza 2000).

Tables 8.1a and 8.1b present summary statistics and correlations using data averaged over the 1960–95 period, with one observation per country. There is considerable cross-country variation. For instance, the mean per capita growth rate for the sample is 1.9 percent per annum, with a standard deviation of 1.8. The maximum growth rate was enjoyed by South Korea (7.2), while Niger and Zaire suffered with a per capita growth rate of worse than −2.7 percent per annum. In the five-year periods, the minimum value is −10.0 percent growth (Rwanda 1990–95), and a number of countries experienced five-year growth spurts of greater than 8 percent per annum. The data also suggest large variation in FDI with the average of 1.1 percent of GDP. Malaysia as well as Trinidad and Tobago had FDI inflows of more than 3.6 percent of GDP over the entire 1960–95 time period, while Sudan essentially had no FDI over this period. In terms of five-year periods, the maximum value of FDI was 7.3 percent of GDP (in Malaysia from 1990–95). The variability over five-year periods is much larger than when using lower-frequency data. Although tables 8.1a and 8.1b do not suggest a simple, positive relationship between FDI and growth, we will see that many growth regression specifications yield a positive coefficient on FDI.

Results

This study estimates the effects of FDI inflows on economic growth after controlling for other growth determinants and the potential biases induced by endogeneity, country-specific effects, and the inclusion of initial income as a regressor. Moreover, we examine whether the growth effects of FDI depend on the recipient country's level of educational attainment, economic development, financial development, and trade openness.

Findings

Table 8.2 shows that the exogenous component of FDI does not exert a reliable, positive impact on economic growth. The table presents OLS and panel

Table 8.1a   Summary statistics, 1960–95

	Mean	Standard deviation	Minimum value	Maximum value
Growth rate	1.89	1.81	−2.81	7.16
School (years of school in 1960)	5.01	2.51	1.20	11.07
Inflation rate	0.16	0.18	0.04	0.91
Government size (government consumption/GDP)	0.15	0.05	0.07	0.31
Openness to trade (exports + imports/GDP)	0.60	0.37	0.14	2.32
Black market premium	0.23	0.49	0.00	2.77
Private credit	0.40	0.29	0.04	1.41
FDI (as a share of GDP)	0.011	0.010	0.000	0.043

estimates using a variety of conditioning information sets. In the OLS regressions, initial income and average years of schooling enter significantly and with the signs and magnitudes found in many pure cross-country regressions. FDI does not enter these growth regressions significantly. When we move to the five-year panel data, FDI enters three of the regressions significantly but not the other four. FDI enters the regressions significantly and positively in the regression that includes only initial income per capita and average years of schooling as control variables. FDI remains significantly and positively linked with growth when controlling for inflation or government size. However, FDI becomes insignificant once we control for trade openness, the black market premium, or financial development. In sum, FDI is never significant in the OLS regressions and becomes insignificant in the panel estimation when controlling for financial development or when controlling for international openness as proxied by either the trade share or the black market premium.[3]

Furthermore, the coefficient on FDI is unstable in the panel regressions, ranging from 323 (when controlling for initial income, schooling, and inflation) to −34 (when controlling for initial income, schooling, and financial development). Changes in the sample do not cause this instability. When the regressions are restricted to have the same number of observations, the

---

3. While some may argue that it is inappropriate to control for trade openness in assessing the relationship between FDI and growth because trade openness may be closely associated with FDI openness, we disagree. It is important to know whether there is an independent relationship between FDI and growth or whether FDI is some general proxy for openness, rather than representing a specific measure of FDI's effect on growth. Moreover, the FDI-growth results do not hold in any of the OLS regressions and the FDI-growth results vanish in the panel regressions even without controlling for trade openness or the black market exchange rate premium.

Table 8.1b Correlation matrix, 1960–95

	Growth	School[a]	Inflation[b]	Government size[a]	Openness to trade[b]	Black-market premium[b]	Private credit[a]	FDI
Growth	1							
Average years of schooling[a]	0.45*	1						
Inflation[b]	−0.28*	−0.08	1					
Government size[a]	0.24*	0.42*	−0.28*	1				
Openness to trade[a]	0.21	0.04	−0.36*	0.33*	1			
Black-market premium[b]	−0.43*	−0.40*	0.38*	−0.20	0.07	1		
Private credit[a]	0.55*	0.68*	−0.43*	0.39*	0.03	−0.60*	1	
FDI	0.17	0.12	−0.21	0.23	0.56*	−0.01	0.05	1

* = indicates significance at the 0.05 level.

Note: This table is based on a common sample of 64 countries using the average between 1960 and 1995, with one observation per country.

a. In the correlations, this variable is included as Ln(variable).
b. In the correlations, this variable is included as Ln(1 + variable).

coefficient on FDI remains unstable.[4] Note that the Sargan and serial correlation tests do not reject the econometric specification. The table 8.2
regressions do not reject the null hypothesis that FDI does not exert an
independent influence on economic growth.

We also assess whether the impact of FDI on growth depends heavily on
the stock of human capital (table 8.3). Borensztein, De Gregorio, and Lee
(1998) find that in countries with low levels of human capital the direct
effect of FDI on growth is negative, though sometimes insignificant. But
once human capital passes a threshold, they find that FDI has a positive
growth effect. The rationale is that only countries with sufficiently high
levels of human capital can exploit the technological spillovers associated
with FDI. Thus, we include the interaction term FDI*School, which equals
the product of FDI and the average years of schooling of the working-age
population.

Table 8.3 shows that the *lack* of FDI impact on growth does not depend
on the stock of human capital. In the OLS regressions, FDI and the interaction term do not enter significantly in any of the six regressions. In the panel
regressions, FDI and the interaction term occasionally enter significantly,
but even here the results do not conform to theory. Namely, when FDI and
the interaction term do enter significantly, the term on FDI is significant and
the coefficient on the interaction term is negative. This suggests that FDI is
only growth enhancing in countries with low educational attainment. These
counterintuitive results may result from including schooling, FDI, and the
interaction term simultaneously.[5] When excluding schooling, however,
the regressions do not yield robust results with a positive coefficient on
the interaction term.

Finally, we also examined the importance of human capital using an alternative specification. Instead of including the interaction term FDI*School,
we created a dummy variable, D, that takes on the value 1 if the country
has greater than average schooling and 0 otherwise. We then included the
term FDI*D. This specification also indicated that FDI's impact on growth

---

4. Also, note that the coefficient on FDI is frequently, though not always, an order of magnitude larger in the panel than the OLS regressions. We speculate that this occurs because of
more volatile data. When we restrict the sample to wealthier countries (which are also countries with less volatile growth rates), the panel coefficient on FDI is similar to the OLS regression coefficients. Similarly, when we use the IMF's *World Economic Outlook* data, which
contains fewer and very poor, highly volatile countries than the World Bank data, the panel
coefficients are closer to the coefficients from the OLS regressions. These estimates are consistent with the view that short-run fluctuations in the investment environment, and hence
FDI, are associated with large, though temporary, booms and busts in economic performance.
Thus, the use of higher frequency data produces larger (though still insignificant) coefficients
on FDI than pure cross-country regressions with data averaged over the 1960–95 period.

5. This conjecture is supported by the observation that no country passes the inflection point.
For instance, from the panel results in regression six, 351 divided by 108.6 equals 3.23, but the
highest level of school attainment is 2.4 in Denmark.

Table 8.2 Growth and FDI regressions, 5-year periods 1960–95

Conditioning information set	1 OLS	1 Panel	2 OLS	2 Panel	3 OLS	3 Panel	4 OLS	4 Panel	5 OLS	5 Panel	6 OLS	6 Panel	7 OLS	7 Panel
Constant	6.797 (0.009)	-0.723 (0.896)	7.732 (0.002)	9.324 (0.314)	7.363 (0.015)	-10.640 (0.303)	6.222 (0.074)	5.646 (0.259)	7.103 (0.006)	2.391 (0.716)	11.579 (0.000)	5.256 (0.332)	11.702 (0.000)	2.701 (0.668)
Initial income per capita[a]	-1.175 (0.008)	-0.252 (0.854)	-1.226 (0.003)	-3.026 (0.254)	-1.274 (0.005)	-1.522 (0.500)	-1.236 (0.006)	0.233 (0.822)	-1.191 (0.007)	-0.667 (0.708)	-1.414 (0.000)	0.720 (0.415)	-1.643 (0.000)	-0.508 (0.679)
Average years of schooling[b]	2.752 (0.000)	2.551 (0.407)	2.774 (0.000)	8.629 (0.182)	2.979 (0.000)	6.770 (0.195)	2.934 (0.000)	0.096 (0.967)	2.661 (0.001)	2.480 (0.556)	1.840 (0.003)	-2.576 (0.230)	2.115 (0.001)	1.617 (0.696)
Inflation[b]			-3.377 (0.034)	-0.887 (0.839)									1.398 (0.355)	-0.161 (0.949)
Government size[a]					-0.083 (0.878)	-6.461 (0.060)							-0.854 (0.127)	-2.796 (0.165)
Openness to trade[a]							0.193 (0.650)	4.830 (0.000)					0.427 (0.329)	1.664 (0.375)
Black market premium[b]									-0.292 (0.792)	-0.590 (0.645)			-1.028 (0.272)	-1.505 (0.285)
Private-sector credit[b]											1.397 (0.000)	2.262 (0.027)	1.714 (0.001)	1.250 (0.333)
FDI	12.553 (0.582)	202.167 (0.006)	2.852 (0.897)	322.933 (0.051)	16.598 (0.469)	215.245 (0.049)	10.677 (0.631)	17.045 (0.748)	12.558 (0.579)	220.854 (0.160)	14.854 (0.414)	-34.511 (0.609)	21.931 (0.238)	-9.434 (0.917)

(table continues next page)

207

Table 8.2 Growth and FDI regressions *(continued)*

Conditioning information set	1		2		3		4		5		6		7	
	OLS	Panel	OLS	Panel	OLS	Panel	OLS	Panel	OLS	Panel	OLS	Panel	OLS	Panel
Number of observations[c]	68	279	68	270	68	273	67	277	66	260	67	246	64	242
R^2 (adjusted)	0.238		0.287		0.238		0.258		0.209		0.437		0.510	
Sargan test (p-value)[d]		0.098		0.770		0.756		0.299		0.302		0.304		0.191
Serial correlation test (p-value)[e]		0.939		0.922		0.897		0.580		0.805		0.234		0.256

OLS = ordinary least squares

a. In the regression, this variable is included as Ln(variable).
b. In the regression, this variable is included as Ln(1 + variable).
c. Panel estimations use five-year periods.
d. The null hypothesis is that the instruments are not correlated with the residuals.
e. The null hypothesis is that the errors in the first-difference regression exhibit no second-order serial correlation.

Notes: Dependent variable is real per capita GDP growth. P-values are in parentheses below estimates' coefficient values.

Table 8.3 Growth, FDI, and education regressions

Conditioning information set	1 OLS	1 Panel	2 OLS	2 Panel	3 OLS	3 Panel	4 OLS	4 Panel	5 OLS	5 Panel	6 OLS	6 Panel
Constant	6.841 (0.011)	1.504 (0.857)	7.727 (0.003)	11.765 (0.252)	7.312 (0.017)	-21.189 (0.120)	6.050 (0.093)	6.882 (0.179)	7.250 (0.007)	-3.460 (0.651)	6.812 (0.029)	-4.611 (0.513)
Initial income per capita[a]	-1.175 (0.008)	-1.484 (0.451)	-1.226 (0.003)	-4.718 (0.091)	-1.281 (0.005)	-2.346 (0.295)	-1.238 (0.007)	-0.625 (0.593)	-1.190 (0.007)	-0.631 (0.738)	-1.391 (0.002)	-3.843 (0.012)
Average years of schooling[b]	2.721 (0.001)	7.025 (0.111)	2.778 (0.000)	15.183 (0.026)	3.120 (0.002)	12.607 (0.015)	3.052 (0.000)	2.612 (0.341)	2.557 (0.006)	5.520 (0.191)	3.415 (0.001)	14.161 (0.000)
Inflation[b]			-3.378 (0.035)	-2.783 (0.586)							-3.812 (0.052)	-6.959 (0.026)
Government size[a]					-0.122 (0.837)	-10.233 (0.015)					-0.555 (0.388)	-7.242 (0.013)
Openness to trade[a]							0.199 (0.644)	4.012 (0.005)			-0.078 (0.871)	1.706 (0.440)
Black market premium[b]									-0.314 (0.782)	0.690 (0.549)	0.037 (0.977)	2.256 (0.014)
FDI	7.585 (0.901)	471.575 (0.010)	3.460 (0.953)	567.935 (0.028)	35.139 (0.604)	588.334 (0.004)	28.284 (0.618)	155.478 (0.040)	-2.463 (0.970)	681.882 (0.000)	46.078 (0.485)	351.000 (0.000)
FDI*School	3.350 (0.935)	-183.992 (0.036)	-0.411 (0.992)	-161.501 (0.198)	-12.179 (0.785)	-250.233 (0.063)	-11.905 (0.756)	-48.640 (0.232)	10.084 (0.817)	-243.945 (0.000)	-23.042 (0.606)	-108.606 (0.014)

(table continues next page)

Table 8.3 Growth, FDI, and education regressions (continued)

Conditioning information set	1		2		3		4		5		6	
	OLS	Panel	OLS	Panel	OLS	Panel	OLS	Panel	OLS	Panel	OLS	Panel
Number of observations[c]	68	279	68	270	66	273	67	277	66	260	65	248
R^2 (adjusted)	0.226		0.275		0.226		0.247		0.197		0.258	
Sargan test (p-value)[d]		0.340		0.690		0.828		0.286		0.324		0.144
Serial correlation test (p-value)[e]		0.332		0.506		0.273		0.283		0.158		0.221

OLS = ordinary least squares

a. In the regression, this variable is included as Ln(variable).
b. In the regression, this variable is included as Ln(1 + variable).
c. Panel estimations use five-year periods.
d. The null hypothesis is that the instruments are not correlated with the residuals.
e. The null hypothesis is that the errors in the first-difference regression exhibit no second-order serial correlation.

Notes: Dependent variable is real per capita GDP growth. P-values are in parentheses below estimates' coefficient values.

does not robustly vary with the level of educational attainment. While some may interpret the results in table 8.3 as suggesting that the coefficient on FDI becomes significant and positive in the panel regressions when controlling for the interaction with schooling, we note that (1) the interaction terms are frequently insignificant, (2) the signs do not conform with theory, and (3) the OLS regressions suggest a fragile relationship.

Since Blomström, Lipsey, and Zejan (1994) argue that very poor countries—countries that are extremely technologically backward—are unable to exploit FDI, we reran the regressions using the interaction term, FDI*Income per capita. Table 8.4 shows, however, that a reliable link between growth and FDI when allowing for FDI's impact on growth to depend on the level of income per capita does not exist.[6]

Table 8.5 assesses whether the level of financial development in the recipient country influences the growth-FDI relationship. Better-developed financial systems improve capital allocation and stimulate growth (Beck, Levine, and Loayza 2000). Capital inflows to a country with a well-developed financial system may, therefore, produce substantial growth effects. Thus, we reran the regressions using the interaction term FDI*Credit.

Although the OLS regressions in table 8.5 suggest that FDI has a positive growth effect, especially in financially developed economies, the panel evidence does not confirm this finding. The panel regressions never demonstrated a significant coefficient on the FDI-financial development interaction term. On net, these results do not provide much support for the view that FDI flows to financially developed economies exert an exogenous impact on growth.

Table 8.6 assesses whether the relationship between FDI and growth varies with the degree of trade openness. Balasubramanyam, Salisu, and Sapsford (1996, 1999) find evidence that FDI is particularly good for economic growth in countries with open trade regimes. Thus, we include an interaction term of FDI and openness to trade in the table 8.6 regressions. The FDI*Trade interaction term does not enter significantly in any of the OLS regressions. While the FDI*Trade interaction term enters significantly at the 0.10 level in three of the panel regressions, it enters insignificantly in the other three. In sum, we do not find a robust link between FDI and growth even when allowing this relationship to vary with trade openness.

While FDI flows may go hand in hand with economic success, they do not tend to exert an independent growth effect. Thus, by correcting statistical

---

6. The only regression where the interaction enters significantly is the regression controlling only for the black market premium. Even here, however, the interaction term enters negatively, and does not alter the relationship for hardly any country in the sample because the cutoff is so high, e.g., the logarithm of real per capita GDP would have to be greater than 1114.7 divided by 110.4 equals 10.1, which is the case for only a handful of countries during the end of the sample.

Table 8.4 Growth, FDI, and income level regressions

Conditioning information set	1 OLS	1 Panel	2 OLS	2 Panel	3 OLS	3 Panel	4 OLS	4 Panel	5 OLS	5 Panel	6 OLS	6 Panel
Constant	4.609 (0.209)	-5.254 (0.459)	5.623 (0.102)	8.400 (0.446)	5.263 (0.167)	-15.806 (0.213)	4.493 (0.293)	4.792 (0.410)	5.029 (0.178)	-4.906 (0.562)	3.765 (0.368)	-3.550 (0.675)
Initial income per capita[a]	-0.880 (0.115)	0.320 (0.837)	-0.942 (0.071)	-3.356 (0.225)	-0.939 (0.101)	-1.638 (0.457)	-0.961 (0.090)	-0.247 (0.829)	-0.918 (0.100)	-0.113 (0.952)	-1.002 (0.072)	-1.340 (0.315)
Average years of schooling[b]	2.698 (0.000)	2.731 (0.377)	2.723 (0.000)	10.933 (0.075)	2.998 (0.000)	8.922 (0.057)	2.901 (0.000)	2.240 (0.391)	2.635 (0.001)	4.043 (0.327)	3.205 (0.000)	6.488 (0.018)
Inflation[b]			-3.354 (0.034)	-2.248 (0.609)							-4.078 (0.034)	-4.433 (0.124)
Government size[a]					-0.282 (0.627)	-7.663 (0.029)					-0.662 (0.288)	-4.512 (0.090)
Openness to trade[a]							0.100 (0.813)	4.034 (0.005)			-0.239 (0.618)	2.918 (0.173)
Black market premium[b]									-0.232 (0.840)	0.893 (0.572)	0.127 (0.920)	1.105 (0.257)

FDI	224.576 (0.265)	610.123 (0.055)	206.638 (0.289)	664.202 (0.149)	268.111 (0.219)	669.822 (0.178)	226.791 (0.245)	254.810 (0.421)	209.550 (0.312)	1114.655 (0.030)	322.879 (0.131)	311.729 (0.137)
FDI*Income per capita	−27.398 (0.257)	−53.443 (0.202)	−26.325 (0.262)	−46.457 (0.463)	−32.294 (0.219)	−56.910 (0.385)	−27.567 (0.241)	−22.900 (0.607)	−25.438 (0.307)	−110.359 (0.043)	−39.591 (0.125)	−30.888 (0.312)
Number of observations[c]	68	279	68	270	65	273	67	277	66	260	65	248
R^2 (adjusted)	0.237		0.286		0.240		0.257		0.206		0.367	
Sargan test (p-value)[d]		0.191		0.745		0.821		0.322		0.440		0.082
Serial correlation test (p-value)[e]		0.553		0.871		0.935		0.680		0.405		0.587

OLS = ordinary least squares

a. In the regression, this variable is included as Ln(variable).
b. In the regression, this variable is included as Ln(1 + variable).
c. Panel estimations use five-year periods.
d. The null hypothesis is that the instruments are not correlated with the residuals.
e. The null hypothesis is that the errors in the first-difference regression exhibit no second-order serial correlation.

Notes: Dependent variable is real per capita GDP growth. P-values are in parentheses below estimates' coefficient values.

Table 8.5 Growth, FDI, and finance regressions

Conditioning information set	1 OLS	1 Panel	2 OLS	2 Panel	3 OLS	3 Panel	4 OLS	4 Panel	5 OLS	5 Panel	6 OLS	6 Panel
Constant	9.236 (0.000)	4.453 (0.592)	9.380 (0.000)	-7.651 (0.146)	9.609 (0.001)	-4.337 (0.508)	8.887 (0.007)	8.217 (0.094)	9.454 (0.000)	0.383 (0.935)	9.119 (0.001)	-4.088 (0.627)
Initial income per capita[a]	-1.407 (0.000)	-0.724 (0.712)	-1.401 (0.000)	1.498 (0.215)	-1.479 (0.000)	1.780 (0.235)	-1.460 (0.001)	-0.743 (0.453)	-1.397 (0.001)	0.624 (0.620)	-1.465 (0.001)	-0.650 (0.723)
Average years of schooling[b]	2.294 (0.000)	2.087 (0.630)	2.358 (0.000)	-0.596 (0.813)	2.483 (0.001)	-1.910 (0.550)	2.477 (0.000)	2.637 (0.240)	2.162 (0.002)	-1.030 (0.746)	2.503 (0.001)	3.060 (0.458)
Inflation[b]			-1.730 (0.222)	-2.584 (0.197)							-1.118 (0.464)	-2.123 (0.475)
Government size[a]					-0.061 (0.911)	1.600 (0.326)					-0.325 (0.573)	-4.397 (0.071)
Openness to trade[a]							0.114 (0.753)	4.448 (0.001)			0.155 (0.714)	0.506 (0.824)
Black market premium[b]									-0.732 (0.336)	-4.589 (0.062)	-1.162 (0.100)	-3.900 (0.034)

FDI	152.323	−340.106	133.016	71.044	152.237	−107.266	147.760	−40.957	141.844	−237.720	119.251	−300.341
	(0.000)	(0.222)	(0.000)	(0.624)	(0.000)	(0.431)	(0.000)	(0.775)	(0.001)	(0.263)	(0.000)	(0.046)
FDI*Credit	123.541	136.398	110.615	−8.229	120.562	41.469	119.495	33.787	113.364	62.675	93.643	84.242
	(0.000)	(0.100)	(0.000)	(0.855)	(0.000)	(0.347)	(0.000)	(0.429)	(0.000)	(0.218)	(0.001)	(0.133)
Number of observations[c]	67	269	67	264	65	263	66	267	65	250	64	242
R^2 (adjusted)	0.441		0.447		0.442		0.456		0.432		0.451	
Sargan test (p-value)[d]		0.043		0.012		0.034		0.116		0.070		0.306
Serial correlation test (p-value)[e]		0.787		0.992		0.206		0.356		0.213		0.145

OLS = ordinary least squares

a. In the regression, this variable is included as Ln(variable).
b. In the regression, this variable is included as Ln(1 + variable).
c. Panel estimations use five-year periods.
d. The null hypothesis is that the instruments are not correlated with the residuals.
e. The null hypothesis is that the errors in the first-difference regression exhibit no second-order serial correlation.

Notes: Dependent variable is real per capita GDP growth. P-values are in parentheses below estimates' coefficient values.

Table 8.6 Growth, FDI, and trade openness regressions

Conditioning information set	1 OLS	1 Panel	2 OLS	2 Panel	3 OLS	3 Panel	4 OLS	4 Panel	5 OLS	5 Panel	6 OLS	6 Panel
Constant	6.462 (0.018)	4.531 (0.478)	7.563 (0.004)	10.971 (0.255)	5.700 (0.055)	-0.876 (0.918)	6.366 (0.020)	5.419 (0.330)	6.935 (0.011)	6.620 (0.376)	6.336 (0.027)	2.524 (0.706)
Initial income per capita[a]	-1.135 (0.013)	-1.120 (0.482)	-1.230 (0.004)	-3.168 (0.242)	-1.114 (0.018)	-2.698 (0.257)	-1.137 (0.014)	-0.216 (0.863)	-1.151 (0.012)	-1.393 (0.504)	-1.270 (0.005)	-5.637 (0.005)
Average years of schooling[b]	2.812 (0.000)	5.182 (0.155)	2.878 (0.000)	9.036 (0.187)	2.847 (0.000)	9.223 (0.100)	2.806 (0.000)	2.519 (0.413)	2.659 (0.001)	4.603 (0.373)	2.991 (0.000)	16.644 (0.001)
Inflation[b]			-3.057 (0.061)	-2.353 (0.529)							-3.609 (0.065)	-9.122 (0.014)
Government size[a]					-0.281 (0.598)	-4.762 (0.084)					-0.552 (0.354)	-6.782 (0.005)
Openness to trade[a]							-0.152 (0.734)	4.869 (0.001)			-0.442 (0.369)	-3.553 (0.068)
Black market premium[b]									-0.605 (0.654)	-1.823 (0.176)	-0.139 (0.919)	0.555 (0.625)

FDI	16.430 (0.458)	150.596 (0.041)	7.310 (0.746)	234.048 (0.106)	17.881 (0.435)	201.450 (0.037)	20.850 (0.473)	75.550 (0.109)	16.894 (0.417)	99.801 (0.504)	22.961 (0.424)	236.671 (0.009)
FDI*Trade	29.241 (0.491)	259.748 (0.001)	17.771 (0.670)	56.605 (0.626)	33.007 (0.445)	217.435 (0.053)	35.456 (0.479)	89.843 (0.162)	33.880 (0.370)	148.279 (0.237)	39.920 (0.361)	324.020 (0.008)
Number of observations[c]	67	276	67	267	66	270	67	275	65	257	65	245
R^2 (adjusted)	0.269		0.305		0.241		0.258		0.249		0.270	
Sargan test (p-value)[d]		0.655		0.825		0.931		0.589		0.387		0.876
Serial correlation test (p-value)[e]		0.318		0.940		0.996		0.443		0.985		0.667

OLS = ordinary least squares

a. In the regression, this variable is included as Ln(variable).
b. In the regression, this variable is included as Ln(1 + variable).
c. Panel estimations use five-year periods.
d. The null hypothesis is that the instruments are not correlated with the residuals.
e. The null hypothesis is that the errors in the first-difference regression exhibit no second-order serial correlation.

Notes: Dependent variable is real per capita GDP growth. P-values are in parentheses below estimates' coefficient values.

shortcomings with past work this study reconciles the broad cross-country evidence with microeconomic studies.

Sensitivity Analyses

We conduct a number of sensitivity analyses to assess the robustness of the results. First, we use a standard instrumental variable estimator in a pure cross-country context (one observation per country) and reexamine whether cross-country variations in the exogenous component of FDI explain cross-country variations in the rate of economic growth. We use GMM.[7] We also use *linear* moment conditions, which amounts to the requirement that the instrumental variables (Z) are uncorrelated with the error term in the growth regression in equation 8.1. The economic meaning of these conditions is that the instrumental variables can only affect *growth* through FDI and the other variables in the conditioning information set. To test this condition, we test the overidentifying restrictions, and we cannot reject the given moment conditions. The GMM results confirm this study's results.

Second, we confirm this study's findings using two alternative estimators. Instead of using Calderon, Chong, and Loayza's (2000) method of limiting the possibility of overfitting by restricting the dimensionality of the instrument set (described above), we use the standard system estimator. In addition, although the standard estimator and Calderon, Chong, and Loayza's (2000) modification are two-step estimators where the variance-covariance matrix is constructed from the first-stage residuals to allow for nonspherical distributions of the error term (and thereby get more efficient estimates in the second stage), these two-step GMM estimators sometimes converge to their asymptotic distributions slowly. This tends to bias the t-statistics upward. Nonetheless, we reran the regressions using the first-stage results, which assume homoskedasticity and independence of the error terms.

Third, we used a variety of alternative samples and specifications. As noted by Blonigen and Wang (in this volume), there may be concerns about mixing rich and poor countries in empirical studies of FDI and growth. Nonetheless, limiting the sample to developing countries—i.e., countries not classified by the World Bank as high-income economies—does not alter the findings. Also, when using a common sample across all of the regressions, the results do not change. Similarly, using the natural logarithm of FDI does not alter the conclusions. We also considered exchange rate volatility, changes in the terms of trade in the regression, and various combinations of the conditioning information set (Levine and Renelt 1992). Including these factors did not alter the conclusions. This study does not prove that FDI is unimportant. Rather, this cross-country analysis—in conjunction with

---

7. Two-stage instrumental variable procedures produce the same conclusions.

microeconomic evidence—reduces confidence in the belief that FDI accelerates GDP growth.

Fourth, we examined whether FDI affects productivity growth using the Easterly and Levine (2001) measure of total factor productivity (TFP). We found that FDI does not exert a robust impact on TFP.

Fifth, we examined portfolio inflows and found that they do not have a positive impact on growth.

Finally, we repeated the analyses using the IMF's *World Economic Outlook 2001* new database on international capital flows. The IMF cleaned the data and extended the findings through the end of 2000. The results are very similar to those reported above, so we do not report them.

Conclusion

FDI has increased dramatically since the 1980s. Furthermore, many countries have offered special tax incentives and subsidies to attract foreign capital. An influential economic rationale for treating foreign capital favorably is that FDI and portfolio inflows encourage technology transfers that accelerate overall economic growth in recipient countries. While microeconomic studies generally, though not uniformly, shed pessimistic evidence on the growth effects of foreign capital, many macroeconomic studies find a positive link between FDI and growth. Previous macroeconomic studies, however, do not fully control for endogeneity, country-specific effects, and the inclusion of lagged dependent variables in the growth regression.

After resolving many of the statistical problems plaguing past macroeconomic studies and confirming our results using two new databases on international capital flows, we find that FDI inflows do not exert an independent influence on economic growth. Thus, while sound economic policies may spur both growth and FDI, the results are inconsistent with the view that FDI exerts a positive impact on growth that is independent of other growth determinants.

References

Aitken, Brian, and Ann Harrison. 1999. Do Domestic Firms Benefit from Foreign Direct Investment? Evidence from Venezuela. *American Economic Review* 89, no. 3 (June): 605–18.

Alfaro, Laura, Chanda Areendam, Sebnem Kalemli-Ozcan, and Sayek Selin. 2003. FDI and Economic Growth: The Role of Local Financial Markets. *Journal of International Economics* 61, no. 1 (October): 512–33.

Balasubramanyam, V. N., Mohammed Salisu, and David Sapsford. 1996. Foreign Direct Investment and Growth in EP and IS Countries. *Economic Journal* 106, no. 434 (January): 92–105.

Balasubramanyam, V. N., Mohammed Salisu, and David Sapsford. 1999. Foreign Direct Investment as an Engine of Growth. *Journal of International Trade and Economic Development* 8, no. 1: 27–40.

Beck, Thorsten, and Ross Levine. 2003. Stock Markets, Banks, and Growth: Panel Evidence. *Journal of Banking and Finance* 28, no. 3 (March): 423–42.

Beck, Thorsten, Ross Levine, and Norman Loayza. 2000. Finance and the Sources of Growth. *Journal of Financial Economics* 58, no. 1-2: 261–300.

Bekaert, Geert, Campbell R. Harvey, and Christian Lundblad. 2001. *Does Financial Liberalization Spur Growth?* NBER Working Paper 8245. Cambridge, MA: National Bureau of Economic Research.

Blomström, Magnus. 1986. Foreign Investment and Productive Efficiency: The Case of Mexico. *The Journal of Industrial Economics* 35, no. 1 (April): 97–110.

Blomström, Magnus, Robert E. Lipsey, and Mario Zejan. 1994. What Explains Developing Country Growth? In *Convergence and Productivity: Gross-National Studies and Historical Evidence*, ed. William Baumol, Richard Nelson, and Edward Wolff. Oxford: Oxford University Press.

Borensztein, E., J. De Gregorio, and J. W. Lee. 1998. How Does Foreign Investment Affect Growth? *Journal of International Economics* 45, no. 1: 115–72.

Boyd, John H., and Bruce D. Smith. 1992. Intermediation and the Equilibrium Allocation of Investment Capital: Implications for Economic Development. *Journal of Monetary Economics* 30: 409–32.

Calderon, Cesar, Alberto Chong, and Norman Loayza. 2000. *Determinants of Current Account Deficits in Developing Countries*. World Bank Research Policy Working Paper 2398 (July). Washington: World Bank.

Easterly, William, and Ross Levine. 2001. It's Not Factor Accumulation: Stylized Facts and Growth Models. *World Bank Economic Review* 15: 177–219.

Haddad, Mona, and Ann Harrison. 1993. Are There Positive Spillovers from Direct Foreign Investment? Evidence from Panel Data for Morocco. *Journal of Development Economics* 42 (October): 51–74.

Klein, Michael, and Giovanni Olivei. 2000. Capital Account Liberalization, Financial Depth, and Economic Growth. Somerville, MA: Tufts University. Photocopy.

Kraay, Aart, Norman Loayza, Luis Serven, and Jaime Ventura. 1999. Country Portfolios. Washington: World Bank. Photocopy.

La Porta, Rafael, Florencio Lopez-de-Silanes, Andrei Shleifer, and Robert W. Vishny. 1999. The Quality of Government. *Journal of Law, Economics, and Organization* 15, no. 1: 222–79.

Levine, Ross, and Maria Carkovic. 2001. How Much Bang for the Buck: Mexico and Dollarization. *Journal of Money, Credit, and Banking* 33, no. 2 (May): 339–63.

Levine, Ross, Norman Loayza, and Thorsten Beck. 2000. Financial Intermediation and Growth: Causality and Causes. *Journal of Monetary Economics* 46: 31–77.

Levine, Ross, and David Renelt. 1992. A Sensitivity Analysis of Cross-Country Growth Regressions. *American Economic Review* 82, no. 4 (September): 942–63.

Romer, Paul. 1993. Idea Gaps and Object Gaps in Economic Development. *Journal of Monetary Economics* 32, no. 3 (December): 543–73.

World Bank. 1997a. *Private Capital Flows to Developing Countries: The Road to Financial Integration*. Washington.

World Bank. 1997b. *Global Development Finance 1997*. Washington.

9

Inappropriate Pooling of Wealthy and Poor Countries in Empirical FDI Studies

BRUCE A. BLONIGEN and MIAO GRACE WANG

The rapid pace of foreign direct investment (FDI) and multinational firm activity has been well documented. As with trade, the freer flow of capital, including FDI, is cited by many as an important engine of growth for the world economy, perhaps especially for the world's less developed countries (LDCs). However, systematic empirical evidence for the factors that affect FDI patterns and its effect on country-level economies is in its infancy. It is only in the past decade that reasonable data on FDI activity have become available and allowed standard statistical analysis. This is particularly true with respect to LDCs.

In fact, the vast majority of empirical FDI studies do not distinguish between LDCs and developed countries (DCs) in their analysis. In many studies, data from both types of countries are often pooled into one sample, and the estimated relationships are assumed to hold equally for both types of countries. Unfortunately, these pooled coefficient estimates may significantly misrepresent the true relationships for both sets of countries if these underlying relationships are indeed different for LDCs versus DCs. Many other studies in the literature use data only for DCs, for which data are often more readily available. The results from these DC studies then do not necessarily provide information regarding LDCs' experiences with FDI. A

Bruce A. Blonigen is Knight Professor of Social Science at the Department of Economics at the University of Oregon and research associate at the National Bureau of Economic Research. Miao Grace Wang is assistant professor at the Department of Economics at Marquette University. We thank participants of the Institute of International Economics conference that led to this book for helpful comments, particularly those of our discussant, Marc Melitz, as well as Susan Feinberg, Holger Görg, Monty Graham, Gordon Hanson, Ross Levine, Ted Moran, Fredrik Sjöholm, and Bernie Yeung.

Table 9.1 World FDI flows, 1982–2001

	Value at current prices (billions of US dollars)			Annual growth rate (percent)		
	1982	1990	2000	1986–90	1991–95	1996–2000
FDI inflows	59	203	1,300	23.6	20.0	40.1
FDI outflows	28	233	621	24.3	15.8	36.7

Source: United Nations (various years).

further concern is that the results are incorrectly assumed to be valid for LDCs as well. In fact, as we will discuss below, the theory often suggests that relationships should differ across these different types of countries.

This chapter examines the question of whether LDCs' experiences with FDI are systematically different from those of DCs. We do this by examining three types of empirical FDI studies using country-level data that typically do not distinguish between LDCs and DCs. We begin with the recent literature examining the factors that determine FDI location. We then turn to the relatively extensive literature examining whether FDI affects growth. Finally, we examine the issue of whether FDI negatively or positively affects (i.e., crowds out or crowds in) domestic investment.

The evidence may suggest that no significant differences exist and that pooling data across DCs and LDCs leads to correct inferences. We find the world is not that simple. In all three areas of FDI analysis we find substantial differences between LDCs and DCs that are both statistically and economically significant. In fact, in each we uncover surprising differences between our samples of LDCs and DCs that provide new perspectives on the existing literature. Thus, while our methodology is fairly straightforward—examining for structural differences in the coefficient estimates—the message we come away with is fairly powerful. It is inappropriate to assume that FDI plays the same role in LDCs as it does for DCs, and policy recommendations must, therefore, necessarily be different.

The next section gives a brief overview of worldwide patterns of FDI across LDCs and DCs over the past few decades. This is followed by our analysis of structural differences between LDCs' and DCs' behavior with the three different strands of the empirical FDI literature. A final section concludes by summarizing our results and providing some final thoughts on country-level FDI studies. In particular, we point out that controlling for these issues of pooling is not a panacea for other issues confronting cross-country empirical studies, including poor data and endogeneity issues.

Descriptive Differences in FDI Patterns for DCs Versus LDCs

FDI flows between nations have grown at a rapid pace in the past couple of decades. As table 9.1 shows, world FDI inflows reached $1.3 trillion in 2000

Table 9.2 Regional distribution of FDI inflows and outflows: Regions as a share of total, 1982–98

Region/country	Inflows						Outflows					
	1982–87	1988–92	1993–95	1996	1997	1998	1982–87	1988–92	1993–95	1996	1997	1998
Developed countries	**78.1**	**78.4**	**62.1**	**58.8**	**58.9**	**71.5**	**98.0**	**95.7**	**85.8**	**84.2**	**85.6**	**91.6**
Western Europe	31.5	47.4	36.0	32.1	29.1	36.9	55.3	59.7	47.0	53.7	50.6	62.6
European Union	28.2	43.9	34.0	30.4	27.2	35.7	47.4	50.1	42.7	47.9	46.0	59.5
Other Western Europe	3.4	3.5	2.0	1.8	1.9	1.2	7.9	9.6	4.3	5.8	4.6	3.1
United States	39.9	22.6	18.8	21.3	23.5	30.0	19.8	14.1	27.7	19.7	23.1	20.5
Japan	0.7	0.5	0.2	0.1	0.7	0.5	13.4	17.4	6.2	6.2	5.5	3.7
Other developed countries	6.0	7.9	7.1	5.3	5.6	4.1	9.5	4.5	5.2	4.6	6.4	4.9
Less developed countries	**21.8**	**21.6**	**38.0**	**41.2**	**41.1**	**28.4**	**1.9**	**4.3**	**14.2**	**15.8**	**14.4**	**8.4**
Africa	2.8	1.8	1.9	1.6	1.6	1.2	0.1	0.1	0.2	n.a.	0.3	0.1
Latin America and the Caribbean	8.9	6.7	9.8	12.9	14.7	11.1	0.4	0.3	1.2	1.9	3.3	2.4
Developing Europe	n.a.	0.1	0.1	0.3	0.2	0.2	n.a.	n.a.	0.0	n.a.	0.1	n.a.
Asia	10.1	12.1	23.0	22.9	20.6	13.2	1.4	3.8	12.7	13.6	10.0	5.6
West Asia	0.6	0.3	0.7	0.2	1.0	0.7	0.2	0.1	0.3	0.6	0.4	0.3
Central Asia	n.a.	n.a.	0.3	0.6	0.7	0.5	n.a.	n.a.	n.a.	n.a.	n.a.	n.a.
South, East, and Southeast Asia	9.3	11.5	21.9	22.1	18.9	12.0	1.2	3.7	12.3	13.0	9.6	5.3
The Pacific	0.2	0.2	0.1	0.1	n.a.	n.a.	n.a.	n.a.	n.a.	n.a.	n.a.	n.a.
Central and Eastern Europe	n.a.	0.9	3.2	3.5	4.0	2.7	n.a.	n.a.	0.1	0.3	0.7	0.3
World	100	100	100	100	100	100	100	100	100	100	100	100

n.a. = not available

Source: United Nations (various years).

(United Nations 2001), and the annual worldwide growth rate since the early 1980s has been over 20 percent, with almost a 40 percent growth rate in the latter 1990s. As has been well documented, the growth of FDI has easily exceeded the already fast pace of trade growth among countries.

Most world FDI flows continue to be mainly among DCs, especially the "triad" of Japan, the European Union (EU), and the United States. Table 9.2 shows the regional distribution of FDI inflows and outflows from 1982 to 1998. Over the period of 1986–2000, an average of 72.5 percent of world FDI inflows was received by DCs. However, the share of world FDI activity flowing to LDCs has been rising gradually. LDCs received 37 percent of world FDI inflows over the period of 1993–98, compared to an average of 31.2 percent from 1991–92 and an average of 17.5 percent during the second half of the 1980s. At the same time, total FDI flows into LDCs are also strikingly concentrated. For instance, during the 1990s, the five largest host countries for FDI inflows are China, Brazil, Mexico, Singapore, and Indonesia, and these five countries accounted for 55 percent of FDI inflows to all LDCs in 1998. The FDI outflows from LDCs are also concentrated in certain regions.

Of course, the biggest distinction between LDCs and DCs is that although DCs have substantial amounts of two-way FDI flows, LDCs are almost exclusively recipients of FDI. A small exception to this occurs in East and Southeast Asia, especially among Association of Southeast Asian Nations (ASEAN) countries that see some two-way flows of FDI between LDCs.

Importantly, FDI inflows are playing an increasingly important role in private capital flows to LDCs. Approximately 66.8 percent of total private capital flows to LDCs was FDI in 1998, compared with 38.5 percent in 1990.

Another interesting phenomenon in the raw numbers is the sectoral distribution of world FDI inflows (figure 9.1). The share of service FDI has been growing, while shares of manufacturing FDI and primary FDI have been declining over the past decade or so in both LDCs and DCs. However, LDCs have experienced a larger decrease in manufacturing FDI inflows and a larger increase in service FDI inflows than DCs. For DCs, the share of manufacturing FDI inflows fell from 38 percent in 1988 to 35 percent in 1997, and primary FDI inflows from 9 percent to 4 percent, while service FDI inflows went up from 43 to 54 percent. LDCs' manufacturing FDI inflows decreased from 66 percent to 50 percent, while primary FDI inflows decreased from 7 percent to 5 percent from 1988 to 1997. Service FDI inflows in LDCs increased from 25 to 41 percent of total inflows.

Estimating Determinants of FDI

In the past few decades, economists have developed ever more realistic models of FDI by multinational enterprises (MNEs). One main strand of the literature has developed models where MNEs are motivated by the desire to

Figure 9.1 Sectoral distribution of FDI inflows, 1988 and 1997
(percent)

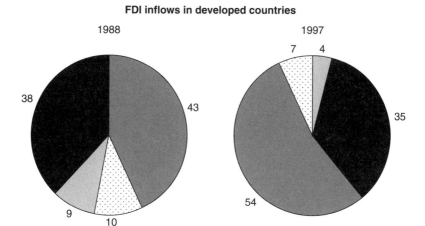

FDI inflows in developed countries

1988

1997

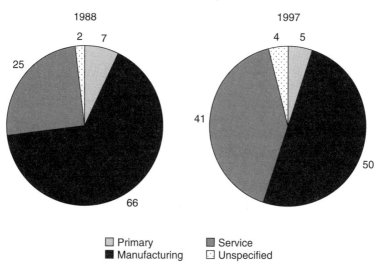

FDI inflows in less developed countries

1988

1997

- □ Primary
- ■ Manufacturing
- ■ Service
- ▢ Unspecified

Source: United Nations (various years).

outsource some of their activities to lower-cost countries. More specifically, such "vertical" FDI sees MNEs from DCs accessing less-skilled workers in LDCs to perform assembly operations at a lower wage. Formal models of vertical MNE activity stem back at least to Helpman (1984). An initially separate strand identified an alternative motivation for FDI: accessing markets in the presence of trade frictions such as tariffs or transportation costs. Such activity is horizontal since it predicts MNE FDI across larger economies that may be similar in all aspects and involves duplication of the entire production process (with the exception of headquarter services) across multiple countries. Formal modeling of horizontal MNE activity dates back to at least Markusen (1984). Recent work by Markusen et al. (1996) and Markusen (1997) combines both the vertical and horizontal motivations for FDI into one theoretical model, labeled the knowledge-capital model, and Carr, Markusen, and Maskus (CMM) (2001) have proposed and estimated an empirical specification that explains world FDI patterns based on it.[1]

While variations of a gravity model have historically been the most popular empirical framework for examining FDI activity across countries, the CMM framework is arguably the most comprehensive empirical specification we have that is grounded to some extent in theory.[2] The CMM empirical specification for the FDI from country j to country i in time period t is given by the following linear specification with a mean zero error term:

$$FDI_{ijt} = \alpha + \beta_1 SUMGDP_{ijt} + \beta_2 GDPDIFSQ_{ijt} + \beta_3 SKDIFF_{ijt}$$
$$+ \beta_4 SKDGDPD_{ijt} + \beta_5 T\_COST_{it} + \beta_6 T\_COST_{jt}$$
$$+ \beta_7 F\_COST_{it} + \beta_8 HTSKD_{ijt} + \beta_9 DIST_{ijt} + \varepsilon_{ijt} \qquad (9.1)$$

FDI represents a measure of FDI activity, typically foreign affiliate sales or the stock of FDI in the host country. The first two terms on the right-hand side control for country sizes that are most connected with the horizontal MNE aspects of the model. The first, $SUMGDP$, is defined as the sum of the two countries' real GDPs, and $GDPDIFSQ$ is defined as the squared difference between the two countries' real GDP. Since horizontal MNEs are most common between large countries of similar size, there is an expected positive correlation between $SUMGDP$ and FDI activity and an expected negative correlation between $GDPDIFSQ$ and FDI activity. The intuition is that with some positive level of trade frictions, larger and more similar sized markets better support the higher fixed costs associated with setting up production across countries (versus exporting) and lead to greater MNE activity.

The next two terms capture relative factor endowment effects and are related most to the vertical MNE aspects of the knowledge-capital model. $SKDIFF$ is a measure of the skill difference between the parent and host country and is intended to proxy for relative factor abundance differences across countries. According to the CMM interpretation of the knowledge-capital model, this variable should have a positive coefficient. The fourth term $SKDGDPD$, interacts skill difference with GDP differences between

---

1. Yeaple (2003a) also develops a model that combines vertical and horizontal motivations for FDI, though no empirical specification has yet been proposed to test this model's implications.

2. Related work by Brainard (1997) develops and tests a model of horizontal MNE activity by US firms.

the parent and host country and is predicted by CMM to have a negative coefficient.

The last five terms on the right-hand side of equation 9.1 capture trade and investment frictions. T_COST_i is the trade cost in the host country and is expected to have a positive coefficient, since higher trade costs in the host country make exporting to that market more expensive, increasing the relative benefits from FDI. T_COST_j is the trade cost in the parent country and is expected to have a negative coefficient, since higher trade costs in the parent country make it more difficult to ship goods back to the parent country from foreign affiliates, which makes vertical FDI a less attractive option. F_COST is the cost of investing in the host country, which is measured by an index based on survey data of the business environment risk in a host country. As this rises, FDI should fall. $HTSKD$ interacts host trade costs with the squared skill difference. Since host trade costs should matter less when FDI is vertical (i.e., skill differences are large), this carries an expected negative coefficient. Finally, $DIST$ is the distance between countries. Since higher distances make both trade and control of overseas FDI more difficult, the net effect is ambiguous.

Empirical results for the CMM specification are generally good, except for a key puzzle. As shown by Blonigen, Davies, and Head (2003), the skill difference term in the CMM specification has the wrong sign and is statistically significant when the variable is properly specified. Thus, the key variable identifying vertical motivations for FDI fails and suggests that observed FDI patterns are mainly connected with horizontal motivations. This is puzzling and contrasts with recent findings by Hanson, Mataloni, and Slaughter (2003) of substantial vertical FDI, or outsourcing, by US MNEs that increases with lower wages in a destination country.

A key concern is that the CMM specification is not adequate to disentangle the vertical from the horizontal motivations for FDI from the data that pools observations of FDI activity across DCs and LDCs. CMM test their model with data on bilateral FDI activity between the United States and partner countries. This includes both observations on US outbound FDI in both DCs and LDCs and inbound FDI into the United States from other parent countries (DCs and potentially LDCs). The processes behind these various combinations of host and parent country FDI activities are likely quite different and coefficient estimates from pooled data may provide estimates that are not an accurate representation of any of these activities.

To investigate this further, we take the CMM specification and explore stability of coefficients across DCs and LDCs. We use the dataset from Blonigen and Davies (2004) on US bilateral FDI activity, which provides a more comprehensive set of data on US FDI activity than CMM. This dataset spans US FDI activity with all partner countries for which data are available for the years 1970–99. Given the critique in Blonigen, Davies, and Head (2003) we look separately at US inbound and outbound FDI, since for the inbound FDI observations the parents are always skill deficient relative to the host and vice versa for outbound FDI. Details on data sources and variable construction are in appendix 9.1.

As mentioned, an implication of CMM is that we can pool all countries and directions of FDI activity and estimate coefficient estimates that are valid for the entire sample. Alternatively, we hypothesize that the vertical motivations for MNE activity will be more evident with respect to US FDI with LDCs, in particular for outbound US FDI, where the United States is a relatively skilled country potentially searching for outsourcing destinations. For MNE activity (both inbound and outbound) between the United States and other DCs, the horizontal aspects of the model are expected to be stronger. For US inbound FDI activity from LDCs, horizontal aspects should dominate as LDCs should not be looking to source low-wage activities to the United States.[3] Thus, if anything, we should see mainly horizontal motivations governing the small amount of observed FDI by LDCs into DCs—i.e., FDI motivated by the desire to access a large market in the presence of trade frictions.

Table 9.3 provides our baseline results using data on FDI stock. Our first and third columns of results report baseline estimates for US outbound and inbound FDI between all country destinations for which data are available. The results show mixed evidence for the efficacy of these base results. The R^2 statistics are reasonably high for a sample with such cross-section variation. However, only five of the eight CMM variables in the outbound regression and only four of the eight CMM variables in the inbound regression have the expected sign. Consistent with Blonigen, Davies, and Head (2003) the skill difference term (SKDIFF) has a negative coefficient, which is exactly the opposite of what CMM would predict if vertical motivations for MNE activity exist. Instead, the coefficients suggest that FDI increases as skill differences decline, which supports a purely horizontal model of world MNE activity.

An explanation for these results is that the baseline CMM specification does not encompass the different processes that govern FDI across such heterogeneous countries. To explore this, the second and fourth columns of table 9.3 add interactions of CMM variables with a dummy variable indicating whether a country is an LDC. We classify Australia, Canada, Hong Kong, Iceland, Japan, New Zealand, Norway, Switzerland, and the European Union countries (as of 2003) as DCs. All other countries are classified as LDCs. The coefficient terms on these variables give the incremental difference in the variable's effect on FDI when the observation is connected with an LDC rather than a DC. As the results show, these interactions are extremely important. The adjusted R^2 in each equation goes up dramatically and an F-test strongly supports the inclusion of these LDC interaction terms in both the inbound and outbound equations. Many of

---

3. There is a potential model of LDCs having MNEs that outsource high-skilled activities to DCs, but this model has never been proposed and is arguably inconsistent with the standard models proposed by Markusen and others.

Table 9.3 Exploring inappropriate pooling of countries in estimates of the knowledge-capital model in levels of the variables

Variable	Expected sign	Outbound FDI stock		Inbound FDI stock	
		Baseline estimates	Dummy variable interaction	Baseline estimates	Dummy variable interaction
$SUMGDP_{ij}$	+	0.04 (2.10)	7.85 (1.70)	7.28 (1.49)	17.52 (1.58)
$GDPDIFSQ_{ij}$	−	−0.0010 (0.0002)	−0.0010 (0.0003)	−0.0010 (0.0001)	−0.0020 (0.0002)
$SKDIFF_{ij}$	+	−1,904 (1,501)	−12,904 (4,865)	−11,927 (1,358)	−3,495 (2,542)
$SKDGDPD_{ij}$	−	−0.001 (0.203)	0.72 (0.54)	0.56 (0.14)	−0.03 (0.31)
T_COST_i	+	−69.15 (33.40)	−191.4 (83.6)	−2012.0 (772.0)	−2166.0 (644.8)
T_COST_j	−	−3,406.0 (1,093.0)	−3,251.0 (974.3)	−50.51 (10.94)	−76.45 (22.18)
F_COST_j	−	−323.2 (75.3)	327.3 (132.3)	−594.9 (222.8)	−898.5 (563.4)
$HTSKD_{ij}$	−	1.24 (0.79)	7.31 (4.05)	7.34 (0.84)	−0.10 (2.43)
$DIST_{ij}$	?	−2.42 (0.30)	−5.00 (0.85)	−1.34 (0.18)	−3.11 (0.35)
LDC interactions					
$SUMGDP_{ij}$ * LDC			−12.39 (1.49)		−20.72 (1.41)
$GDPDIFSQ_{ij}$ * LDC			0.0010 (0.0002)		0.0010 (0.0001)
$SKDIFF_{ij}$ * LDC			12,330 (4,877)		2,907 (2,524)
$SKDGDPD_{ij}$ * LDC			−0.60 (0.55)		0.08 (0.31)
T_COST_i * LDC			163.9 (84.1)		351.7 (118.3)
T_COST_j * LDC			31.01 (154.20)		75.20 (22.19)
F_COST_j * LDC			−383.8 (136.0)		819.2 (562.5)

(table continues next page)

Table 9.3 Exploring inappropriate pooling of countries in estimates of the knowledge-capital model in levels of the variables *(continued)*

Variable	Expected sign	Outbound FDI stock		Inbound FDI stock	
		Baseline estimates	Dummy variable interaction	Baseline estimates	Dummy variable interaction
HTSKD$_{ij}$ * LDC			−6.90 (4.06)		0.26 (2.43)
DIST$_{ij}$ * LDC			4.36 (0.86)		3.06 (0.35)
Observations		892	892	1,490	1,490
Adjusted R^2		0.30	0.47	0.35	0.62
F-test (p-value)		43.08 (0.000)	25.61 (0.000)	87.75 (0.000)	30.68 (0.000)

+ = positive correlation
− = negative correlation
? = ambiguous net effect
LDC = less developed country

Note: Robust standard errors are in parentheses.

the LDC interaction terms are statistically significant and in almost every instance are exactly opposite in sign to their counterpart noninteracted CMM terms. This evidence strongly suggests that a different process is governing MNE activity with LDCs that is not captured by the standard CMM model.

With respect to the skill difference puzzle, the LDC interaction with *SKDIFF* has a statistically significant positive coefficient for the outbound FDI regressions. However, the total direct effect of *SKDIFF* on US outbound FDI activity to LDCs—the sum of the coefficients on *SKDIFF* and *SKDIFF*LDC*—is negative and statistically insignificant (F = 1.12 with p-value = 0.28). This point estimate is also small in terms of economic significance, with a standard deviation change in skill difference reducing FDI stock by $1.4 million. Thus, while the inverse relationship between skill differences and FDI activity is no longer true for US outbound FDI to LDCs, there is no statistically significant evidence for a positive relationship that would be consistent with vertical motivations for FDI.[4]

As discussed in Blonigen and Davies (2004), researchers are concerned with the statistical properties of these estimators, which have been used to test the CMM model in all previous literature, because they are so skewed.

---

4. The total marginal effect of *SKDIFF* on FDI must also take into account the interaction terms with GDP differences. The estimated coefficients on these terms for US outbound FDI are small and statistically insignificant. At the means of the data, they yield the same qualitative comparisons of marginal effects as those reported here on only the direct marginal effects of the *SKDIFF* terms.

For example, the outbound FDI data show a mean of $10.9 billion dollars across destination countries with a standard deviation of $22.1 billion. There are many destinations with very low levels of FDI stock up to a maximum of $233.1 billion. The numbers are similarly skewed in the inbound sample as well. Not surprisingly then, a Shapiro-Wilk (1965) test easily rejects normality of the residuals and a Ramsey (1969) RESET test strongly suggests misspecification bias, even after one includes the LDC interaction terms.

Table 9.4 presents results from a log-linear model. The linear model proposed by CMM is not a structural equation derived from theory, so there is nothing inherently inconsistent with specifying a log-linear model, and this functional form transformation is often used when data are highly skewed. One issue when logging the data is dealing with negative values of the dependent variable and trade cost measures for some observations. We truncate these observations to 0.1 before taking logs although we get qualitatively similar results if we simply drop these observations. In addition, the interaction terms—*SKDGDPD* and *HTSKD*—are perfectly collinear once logged and thus are dropped from the CMM specification.

Statistically significant differences for US MNE activity between LDCs and DCs remain in the alternative log-linear model. Once again, for US outbound FDI stock we find that the vertical aspects of MNE activity show up in the *SKDIFF*LDC* variable, which has a positive coefficient. Unlike in the linear model the coefficient on this variable is statistically significant, though total skill difference effect for LDCs—the sum of the coefficients on *SKDIFF* and *SKDIFF*LDC*—is once again statistically and economically insignificant.

Table 9.4 displays other interesting differences with respect to US FDI patterns between LDCs and DCs. In the outbound regressions, increases in *SUMGDP* still have a positive impact on FDI activity, but the coefficient falls from 5.43 to 2.14 (5.43–3.29). This suggests that GDP growth in the LDC is not as important for the amount of US FDI it receives, which is again more consistent with a vertical MNE, rather than a horizontal MNE, story. The other significant difference is that FDI costs (as measured by an index of business environment risk in the host country) are much more important for LDC hosts than DC hosts. MNEs may be much more sensitive to changes in these risks for LDCs that are generally more risky.

In the inbound regressions, the most notable differences for LDCs concern the *SKDIFF* and *DIST* variables. First, greater skill differences have a slightly larger negative effect on FDI activity from LDCs into the United States than for DCs. This is likely because FDI from an LDC into the United States is often insignificant until a country has reached some threshold level of education or skills.[5] Second, distance does not seem to negatively affect LDC FDI into the United States, as it does for DCs.

---

5. As discussed below, such education thresholds also seem important for whether *inbound* FDI increases growth in LDCs.

Table 9.4   Exploring inappropriate pooling of countries in estimates of the knowledge-capital model in logs

Variable	Expected sign	Outbound FDI stock		Inbound FDI stock	
		Baseline estimates	Dummy variable interaction	Baseline estimates	Dummy variable interaction
SUMGDP$_{ij}$	+	3.73 (0.82)	5.43 (0.81)	14.71 (1.28)	12.77 (1.07)
GDPDIFSQ$_{ij}$	–	–0.67 (0.31)	–1.75 (0.32)	–4.28 (0.49)	–3.11 (0.46)
SKDIFF$_{ij}$	+	–0.10 (0.13)	–0.51 (0.13)	–4.12 (0.14)	–1.57 (0.25)
T_COST$_i$	+	–0.07 (0.04)	–0.18 (0.02)	18.89 (5.84)	13.28 (5.05)
T_COST$_j$	–	1.06 (3.97)	0.41 (3.94)	–0.15 (0.04)	–0.37 (0.04)
F_COST$_j$	–	–2.67 (0.25)	–1.22 (0.24)	–0.83 (1.19)	–0.73 (1.30)
DIST$_{ij}$	–	–1.06 (0.11)	–0.86 (0.11)	–0.50 (0.14)	–0.95 (0.11)
LDC interactions					
SUMGDP$_{ij}$ * LDC			–3.29 (0.54)		–1.38 (1.01)
GDPDIFSQ$_{ij}$ * LDC			2.08 (0.36)		–0.11 (0.53)
SKDIFF$_{ij}$ * LDC			0.95 (0.32)		–1.56 (0.37)
T_COST$_i$ * LDC			0.23 (0.06)		0.84 (0.98)
T_COST$_j$ * LDC			–0.21 (1.05)		0.39 (0.07)
F_COST$_j$ * LDC			–2.14 (0.52)		0.24 (1.80)
DIST$_{ij}$ * LDC			–0.07 (0.19)		0.83 (0.20)
Observations		892	892	1,490	1,490
Adjusted R^2		0.37	0.40	0.51	0.62
F-test (p-value)		74.87 (0.000)	85.81 (0.000)	221.57 (0.000)	388.17 (0.000)

+ = positive correlation
– = negative correlation
LDC = less developed country

Note: Robust standard errors are in parentheses.

What conclusions can we draw from these results? First, the evidence strongly suggests that the standard CMM model does not yield a comprehensive model of world MNE activity. Substantial differences in the factors that determine MNE activity between the United States and LDCs versus the United States and DCs apparently exist. This casts doubt on the CMM specification's ability to identify vertical versus horizontal MNE activity. The follow-up question is, "Where do we go from here?" Are there feasible modifications to the CMM specification that would lead to a comprehensive model or is it more fruitful to develop models that focus on DC-LDC or DC-DC FDI separately? We do not have a definitive answer, but note that our attempts to modify the CMM specification to yield residuals with nice statistical properties have been unsuccessful. These modifications (many of which are reported further in Blonigen and Davies 2004) include country fixed effects, first-difference specifications, and inclusion of short-run determinants of FDI activity, such as tax and exchange rate changes. None of these provide specifications that can pass a RESET omitted variable test or a test for normality of residuals.

Cross-country data alone may simply be insufficient to provide a full accounting of worldwide FDI patterns. For example, Yeaple (2003b) finds that interactions of an industry's relative skill intensity with a country's relative abundance of skill are important for explaining US outward FDI. Accessing low-wage countries motivates FDI most clearly for industries that are less-skilled-labor intensive. Thus, we may not be able to explain worldwide patterns of FDI based on country-level data alone. Our analysis, along with that of Yeaple (2003b) and Hanson, Mataloni, and Slaughter (2003), suggests that vertical motivations for FDI are likely more important than what is revealed by the CMM empirical specification.

FDI and Growth

One of the more important issues that economists can study is discovering which factors affect economic growth. As evidenced by the literature estimating cross-country growth equations, however, the wide variation in results across various samples and econometric methodologies calls into question our ability to definitively state which factors are important for economic growth.[6] Despite these concerns, recent studies have begun to examine whether FDI, a factor largely ignored in previous literature, has an independent impact on the economic growth of countries.

Two more well-known studies, Balasubramanyam, Salisu, and Sapsford (1996) and Borensztein, De Gregorio, and Lee (1998), examine this issue in

---

6. Important studies pointing to the fragility of cross-country growth results include Levine and Renelt (1992), Sala-i-Martin (1997), Islam (1995), and Lee, Pesaran, and Smith (1998).

the context of LDCs and find that FDI is positively correlated with economic growth, but only under certain conditions. Balasubramanyam, Salisu, and Sapsford (1996) find that the evidence for a positive FDI effect is strongest when the LDC is pursuing export-promotion policies, rather than import-substitution policies. Borensztein, De Gregorio, and Lee (1998) find that FDI positively affects economic growth in LDCs only after the country has a sufficient human capital threshold, as proxied by years of schooling of males over the age of 25. The studies' authority is based upon an economic hypothesis about when FDI should affect growth (and when it should not) for an LDC, which is confirmed by the empirical analysis.

Recent studies, however, have cast doubt on the effect of FDI on growth. For example, Choe (2003) performs Granger causality tests on a panel of countries from 1971 through 1995 and finds little evidence that FDI affects economic growth. What these results mean for the previous studies by Balasubramanyam, Salisu, and Sapsford (1996) and Borensztein, De Gregorio, and Lee (1998) is less clear, however, since they often find insignificance for a sample that includes both LDCs and DCs, while the Choe study focuses on LDCs. Indeed, Balasubramanyam, Salisu, and Sapsford (1996) and Borensztein, De Gregorio, and Lee (1998) motivate their empirical analysis with hypotheses that are arguably only valid for understanding the effect of FDI on LDCs. This calls into question whether the evidence of insignificance is coming from inappropriate pooling of the recent studies or inappropriate methodology of the previous LDC-only studies.

In this section, we examine whether it is appropriate to pool LDCs and DCs in growth regressions using a common cross-section (and panel) setting. The extant literature is particularly frustrating, because no common sample is used to explore these issues. Instead there seem to be many studies providing varying results from varying samples that preclude any direct comparison. In addition, a variety of alternative econometric techniques are employed. Statistical tests can at least provide evidence on preferred techniques, but the results may vary depending on the sample. An important choice, not often discussed, is frequency of the data. Given that FDI is a source of capital, theory would suggest that FDI stock is the appropriate measure of FDI for these growth regressions. However, FDI stock data are difficult to construct and often unavailable. Thus, some studies, such as Borensztein, De Gregorio, and Lee (1998) use FDI flows, but aggregate their data by decade. Other studies use annual observations of FDI flows. In constructing our sample, we use the former method because of concerns that highly variable annual FDI flows are much further away from our ideal measure of FDI stock.

Do we really think that such annual flows (or even one-year lagged flows) have a discernible effect on this year's growth rate? Yes, multiple observations of the same country seem essential to be able to control for unobserved country-specific heterogeneity. Many features of countries that are hypothesized to be important for growth seem largely time invariant, such as institutions and culture. Proxies for such important factors used in cross-sectional analysis are likely to have considerable measurement error. Thus, reducing omitted variable bias from these time-invariant factors through panel-data techniques seems essential.

With gracious help from Eduardo Borensztein and Jong-Wha Lee, we were able to obtain the data used in Borensztein, De Gregorio, and Lee (1998).[7] As mentioned above, these data are a panel of decade averages of the variables for only LDCs in the 1970s and 1980s. We then augmented their data by collecting observations for all the DCs for which we could get identical measures of the variables.[8] Linked to this common dataset from a well-known analysis in the area, we explored the effects of pooling LDCs and DCs on the estimate effects of FDI on growth, as well as sensitivity to panel-data techniques.

Columns 1 and 2 of table 9.5 provide seemingly unrelated regression (SUR) estimates of the determinants of per capita growth across countries for the two decades of data, 1970–79 and 1980–89. Like Borensztein, De Gregorio, and Lee (1998) we constrain all the coefficients equally across the two decades with the exception of the constant and, thus, report just one set of coefficient estimates. Column 1 of table 9.5 provides our base estimates, for which we use the same specification as Borensztein, De Gregorio, and Lee (1998) (column 1.6 of their table 1) but use a sample of both LDCs and DCs, not just LDCs. The estimated coefficients largely follow expected signs, and standard statistical measures suggest a decent goodness of fit. However, unlike Borensztein, De Gregorio, and Lee (1998), these estimates, which use data pooling LDCs and DCs, show much-reduced coefficient estimates on the FDI measures and no statistically significant effect of FDI on growth. Thus, pooling seems to have a substantial impact on the empirical evidence with respect to this issue.

This is confirmed in column 2 of table 9.5, where we include interactions of our variables with a dummy variable indicating our LDC countries.[9] A statistical test suggests that these interactions are jointly significant, though the most substantial impact occurs with the FDI variables. As in the previous section, the coefficients on the standard variables indicate the effects for DCs, while the effect for LDCs is the sum of the coefficients of the standard variables and their interactions with the LDC dummy variable. Thus, the coeffi-

---

7. We were able to gather all the data used in the Borensztein, De Gregorio, and Lee study with the exception of the data used for their institution variable. We were also able to use almost identical parameter estimates for the institution variable.

8. This added 19 additional countries: Australia, Austria, Belgium, Canada, Denmark, Finland, France, Ireland, Italy, Japan, the Netherlands, New Zealand, Norway, Portugal, Spain, Sweden, West Germany, the United Kingdom, and the United States.

9. The variables sub-Saharan African dummy, Latin American dummy, and Wars were not interacted since they are perfectly or highly collinear with an LDC dummy variable.

Table 9.5   Exploring inappropriate pooling of countries in SUR and random-effects estimates of FDI on per capita GDP growth for a panel of two decades, 1970–79 and 1980–89

Regressor	Expected sign	Seemingly unrelated regressions Base estimates	Seemingly unrelated regressions LDC dummy variable interaction	Random-effects estimates
Log of initial GDP	–	–0.012 (0.004)	–0.014 (0.005)	–0.011 (0.012)
School	+	0.002 (0.003)	–0.001 (0.006)	0.004 (0.012)
Government consumption	–	–0.065 (0.032)	0.178 (0.186)	–0.230 (0.650)
Log (1+black market premium)	–	–0.011 (0.005)	0.213 (0.386)	0.312 (0.880)
FDI	+	0.153 (0.687)	–0.987 (1.930)	1.959 (4.239)
FDI * School	+	–0.064 (0.389)	0.519 (0.857)	–1.217 (2.310)
Sub-Saharan African dummy	–	–0.020 (0.006)	–0.016 (0.006)	–0.020 (0.008)
Latin American dummy	–	–0.015 (0.006)	–0.018 (0.006)	–0.017 (0.008)
Assassinations	–	–0.014 (0.012)	0.214 (0.246)	–0.008 (0.501)
Wars	–	–0.001 (0.005)	–0.005 (0.005)	–0.004 (0.007)
Political rights (1 best, 7 worst)	–	–0.002 (0.001)	–0.000 (0.007)	–0.006 (0.015)
Financial depth	+	0.011 (0.009)	0.021 (0.022)	0.004 (0.056)
Inflation rate	–	–0.011 (0.008)	–0.247 (0.151)	0.015 (0.448)
LDC interactions				
Log of initial GDP * LDC	?		0.003 (0.005)	–0.002 (0.012)
School * LDC	?		0.004 (0.007)	–0.001 (0.013)
Government consumption * LDC	?		–0.252 (0.188)	0.142 (0.651)

(table continues next page)

Table 9.5 Exploring inappropriate pooling of countries in SUR and random-effects estimates of FDI on per capita GDP growth for a panel of two decades, 1970–79 and 1980–89 (continued)

| | | Seemingly unrelated regressions | | Random-effects estimates |
Regressor	Expected sign	Base estimates	LDC dummy variable interaction	
Log (1+black market premium) * LDC	?		−0.222 (0.386)	−0.324 (0.880)
FDI * LDC	?		−2.370 (2.242)	−4.111 (4.459)
FDI * School * LDC	?		3.339 (1.391)	4.053 (2.678)
Assassinations * LDC	?		−0.222 (0.246)	0.071 (0.502)
Political rights (1 best, 7 worst) * LDC	?		−0.003 (0.007)	0.003 (0.015)
Financial depth * LDC	?		−0.017 (0.024)	0.002 (0.058)
Inflation rate * LDC	?		0.237 (0.152)	−0.032 (0.448)
Observations		160	160	146
R^2—1970–79		0.28	0.39	
R^2—1980–89		0.35	0.40	
Goodness of fit—χ^2 (p-value)		70.59 (0.000)	101.92 (0.000)	62.98 (0.000)

+ = positive correlation
− = negative correlation
? = ambiguous net effect
LDC = less developed country
SUR = seemingly unrelated regressions

Note: Standard errors in parentheses.

cients for LDCs on FDI and *FDI*School* are −3.357 and 3.858, respectively. Both of these combined coefficients are statistically significant at the 1 percent significance level and suggest the same pattern found by Borensztein, De Gregorio, and Lee (1998). In particular, FDI has a significant impact on per capita growth only after education levels in the LDC are at a high enough threshold level. As is clear, no such relationship exists for the DCs, and pooling the data (as in column 1) obscures this important relationship.

The SUR estimates do not control for unobserved heterogeneity across countries. Given the two time periods (1970–79 and 1980–89), panel-data techniques can be applied to control for such heterogeneity, eliminating this potential source of omitted variable bias. Column 3 of table 9.5 provides random-effects estimates of the data using a specification that includes the LDC interactions.[10] In this setting, exploiting the panel nature of data does not have a substantial effect on inferences, especially with respect to the FDI variables. As with the SUR estimates, there are no statistically significant effects of FDI with respect to DCs, but there are the same types of effects of FDI for LDCs. The combined effects of FDI and *FDI*School* for LDCs are –2.152 and 2.836 with probability values of 0.12 and 0.04, respectively. The threshold level of schooling before the effect of FDI becomes positive is now 0.76, which is much closer to the Borensztein, De Gregorio, Lee (1998) estimates.

In summary, the evidence in this section suggests that inappropriate pooling of DCs with LDCs, not the introduction of panel techniques, is responsible for estimating insignificant effects of FDI with respect to per capita GDP growth. The persuasive arguments for the effects of FDI, however, have been made with LDCs in mind. That is precisely where the evidence suggests that FDI does indeed affect growth, conditioned on a sufficient level of human capital.

FDI and Domestic Investment: Crowding In or Out?

An issue related to the FDI growth question is whether FDI crowds out domestic investment or crowds it in. When foreign firms enter a country, local investors' decisions will be affected. On the one hand, FDI can crowd out domestic investment if foreign firms finance their investment by borrowing in the host country, thus increasing the host country's interest rate. Harrison and McMillan (2003) find just such evidence using a microlevel database of firms in Côte d'Ivoire. On the other hand, an increase in foreign investment can lead to an increase in domestic investment if FDI stimulates new domestic investment through forward or backward production linkages.

Borensztein, De Gregorio, and Lee (1998) use their data to explore this hypothesis. In particular, they use the same regressor matrix to explain a country's total investment as a share of GDP as they use in the growth equations. As they explain, since FDI is included in total investment, evidence of crowding in would require a coefficient greater than 1. Table 9.6 provides estimates of this hypothesis using the same pattern of specifications as in

---

10. With only two periods and limited observations, multicollinearity issues prevent us from estimating a fixed-effects model with this specification.

Table 9.6 Exploring inappropriate pooling of countries in SUR and random-effects estimates of FDI on aggregate investment rates for a panel of two decades, 1970–79 and 1980–89

Regressor	Expected sign	Seemingly unrelated regressions		Random-effects estimates
		Base estimates	LDC dummy variable interaction	
Log of initial GDP	+	0.039 (0.010)	0.040 (0.014)	0.042 (0.025)
School	+	−0.005 (0.007)	−0.008 (0.009)	−0.023 (0.019)
Government consumption	−	−0.208 (0.089)	−0.493 (0.411)	−0.495 (0.990)
Log (1+black market premium)	−	−0.001 (0.011)	−0.536 (1.017)	−1.038 (2.060)
FDI	+	−0.081 (0.753)	−2.136 (1.487)	−1.739 (2.901)
Sub-Saharan Africa dummy	−	−0.046 (0.019)	−0.043 (0.018)	−0.056 (0.021)
Latin America dummy	−	−0.044 (0.016)	−0.037 (0.017)	−0.032 (0.021)
Assassinations	−	−0.029 (0.022)	−0.219 (0.573)	−0.483 (1.039)
Wars	−	0.012 (0.011)	0.013 (0.011)	0.004 (0.014)
Political rights (1 best, 7 worst)	−	0.001 (0.003)	−0.008 (0.015)	0.004 (0.034)
Financial depth	+	0.054 (0.022)	0.044 (0.052)	0.026 (0.108)
Inflation rate	−	−0.032 (0.015)	0.487 (0.350)	0.202 (0.979)
LDC interactions				
Log of Initial GDP * LDC	?		−0.009 (0.012)	−0.015 (0.024)
School * LDC	?		0.017 (0.013)	0.021 (0.023)
Government consumption * LDC	?		0.333 (0.420)	0.360 (0.994)

(table continues next page)

Table 9.6 Exploring inappropriate pooling of countries in SUR and random-effects estimates of FDI on aggregate investment rates for a panel of two decades, 1970–79 and 1980–89 *(continued)*

Regressor	Expected sign	Base estimates	Seemingly unrelated regressions — LDC dummy variable interaction	Random-effects estimates
Log (1+black market premium) * LDC	?		0.534 (1.017)	1.032 (2.060)
FDI * LDC	?		4.284 (1.816)	4.163 (3.223)
Assassinations * LDC	?		0.188 (0.574)	0.457 (1.040)
Political rights (1 best, 7 worst) * LDC	?		0.008 (0.015)	−0.003 (0.034)
Financial depth * LDC	?		0.003 (0.059)	0.006 (0.114)
Inflation rate * LDC	?		−0.520 (0.350)	−0.250 (0.979)
Observations		160	160	146
R^2—1970–79		0.51	0.54	
R^2—1980–89		0.70	0.75	
Goodness of fit—χ^2 (p-value)		193.25 (0.000)	242.16 (0.000)	140.25 (0.000)

+ = positive correlation
− = negative correlation
? = ambiguous net effect
LDC = less developed country
SUR = seemingly unrelated regressions

Note: Standard errors in parentheses.

table 9.5. Column 1 provides the base specification of SUR estimates for a sample of pooled LDCs and DCs, column 2 adds LDC interactions, and column 3 provides random-effects estimates with LDC interactions.[11] The only alteration to the specification is omission of the *FDI*School* variable, since Borensztein, De Gregorio, and Lee (1998) did not find this interaction to be significant.

---

11. Unlike the growth specification in the previous section, we were able to estimate a fixed-effect specification, but a Hausman test suggested that the random-effects specification was more appropriate.

We discover a very similar story to that of the FDI growth hypothesis above. When we pool the data across both types of countries, we get a coefficient on the FDI variable that is very close to 0. When we allow LDC interactions in our SUR specification we get substantial differences between the effects of FDI on total investment rates for DCs (coefficient of –2.136) versus for LDCs (–2.136 + 4.284 = 2.148). The difference between these coefficients is statistically different at the 1 percent significance level and clearly suggests that FDI is much less likely to crowd out domestic investment in LDCs than in DCs. This is consistent with the notion that technology spillovers, as well as backward and forward production linkages, are more common with FDI into LDCs. While the effect of FDI on total investment is statistically different from 0 for LDCs, we cannot rule out that it takes the value of 1. Therefore, our tests do not necessarily support a "crowding-in" effect from FDI, which is consistent with the evidence found by Borensztein, De Gregorio, and Lee (1998).

In related work, Wang (2003) examines the crowding-out/-in hypothesis using annual data on FDI flows across a panel of Organization for Economic Cooperation and Development (OECD) and non-OECD countries. She also investigates lagged values of these FDI flows on domestic investment to control for endogeneity concerns. Wang's analysis provides even stronger evidence that FDI crowds in domestic investment for non-OECD (or LDC) countries than that presented here. Likewise, she finds that no such effect exists for OECD countries.

In summary, there is evidence that pooling LDCs and DCs when examining the crowding-in/-out hypothesis effect on domestic investment is inappropriate. The evidence to date suggests that FDI is much less likely to crowd out (more likely to crowd in) domestic investment for LDCs than DCs. Pooling the data is likely to obscure this potentially important relationship.

Conclusion

This study has found a variety of scenarios involving FDI in which pooling rich and poor countries in an empirical analysis leads to incorrect inferences. While these empirical analyses are often based on theories that are purportedly comprehensive representations of the entire distribution of the world's economies, the data clearly tell us that FDI in LDCs and DCs follows very different processes. We have shown this with respect to three areas of recent research interest. First, the underlying factors that determine the level of FDI activity vary systematically across LDCs and DCs in a way that is not captured by current empirical models of FDI. Second, the effect of FDI on economic growth is one that is apparently supported only for LDCs, not DCs, in the aggregate data. Third, the evidence suggests that FDI is much less likely to crowd out (more likely to crowd in) domestic investment for LDCs than DCs.

Our results must be seen as illustrative of the issue of inappropriate pooling, not a definitive statement about the exact relationship between the variables we examine. The importance of the issues of FDI patterns and its effects on host countries is matched by relatively poor data at the country level. It is not surprising that results can be found to be sensitive to a wide variety of alternative specifications when the data only includes observations in the hundreds and involve measurement issues with most of the variables. Indeed, the answer is not likely to be found in throwing ever-more sophisticated estimation techniques (particularly ones for which only asymptotic properties are known) at the data. Pooling is not a fancy econometric issue or technique, but even it is not innocuous. Pooling is often a way to increase observation size and, hence, efficiency. Thus, our recommendation to treat LDCs and DCs separately in these studies affects this margin. However, as we have shown, this margin seems to have an even larger impact on inferences than other issues (such as controlling for cross-country heterogeneity through panel data techniques).[12] Rather than despair, it is our hope that continued work on these issues from both microeconomic studies and country-level approaches will ultimately provide consensus views on these important issues involving FDI.

References

Balasubramanyam, V. N., M. Salisu, and David Sapsford. 1996. Foreign Direct Investment and Growth in EP and IS Countries. *The Economic Journal* 106, no. 1: 92–105.

Bali Online Corporation. 1999. www.indo.com.

Barro, Robert, and Jong-Wha Lee. 1996. International Measures of Schooling Years and Schooling Quality. *American Economic Review, Papers and Proceedings* 86, no. 2: 218–23.

Blonigen, Bruce A., and Ronald B. Davies. 2004. The Effects of Bilateral Tax Treaties on U.S. FDI Activity. *International Tax and Public Finance* 11, no. 5: 601–22.

Blonigen, Bruce A., Ronald B. Davies, and Keith Head. 2003. Estimating the Capital-Knowledge Model of the Multinational Enterprises: Comment. *American Economic Review* 93, no. 3: 980–94.

Borensztein, Eduardo, Jose De Gregorio, and Jong-Wha Lee. 1998. How Does Foreign Direct Investment Affect Economic Growth? *Journal of International Economics* 45, no. 1: 115–35.

Brainard, S. Lael. 1997. An Empirical Assessment of the Proximity-Concentration Trade-Off Between Multinational Sales and Trade. *American Economic Review* 87, no. 4: 520–44.

Carr, David, James R. Markusen, and Keith E. Maskus. 2001. Estimating the Knowledge-Capital Model of the Multinational Enterprise. *American Economic Review* 91, no. 3: 693–708.

Choe, Jong Il. 2003. Do Foreign Direct Investment and Gross Domestic Investment Promote Economic Growth? *Review of Development Economics* 7, no. 1: 44–57.

Hanson, Gordon H., Raymond J. Mataloni, and Matthew J. Slaughter. 2003. *Vertical Production Networks in Multinational Firms*. NBER Working Paper 9723. Cambridge, MA: National Bureau of Economic Research.

---

12. A related issue is whether even finer distinctions between samples of countries could be made and would be useful to examine—such as very poor LDCs versus newly industrializing LDCs. It would not be surprising to find that estimates in these studies are structurally different as well, though the finer detail runs into the issue of having sufficient observations for estimation.

Harrison, Ann, and Margaret S. McMillan. 2003. Does Direct Foreign Investment Affect Domestic Credit Constraints? *Journal of International Economics* 61, no. 1: 73–100.

Helpman, Elhanan. 1984. A Simple Theory of International Trade with Multinational Corporations. *Journal of Political Economy* 92, no. 3: 451–71.

Islam, Nazrul. 1995. Growth Empirics: A Panel Data Approach. *Quarterly Journal of Economics* 110, no. 4: 1127–70.

Islam, Nazrul. 1998. Growth Empirics: A Panel Data Approach—A Reply. *Quarterly Journal of Economics* 113, no. 1: 325–29.

Lee, Kevin, M. Hashem Pesaran, and Ron Smith. 1998. Growth Empirics: A Panel Data Approach—A Comment. *Quarterly Journal of Economics* 113, no. 1: 319–23.

Levine, Ross, and David Renelt. 1992. A Sensitivity Analysis of Cross-Country Growth Regressions. *American Economic Review* 82, no. 4: 942–63.

Markusen, James R. May 1984. Multinationals, Multi-Plant Economies, and the Gains from Trade. *Journal of International Economics* 16, no. 3–4: 205–26.

Markusen, James R., Anthony J. Venables, Denise Eby-Konan, and Keven Honglin Zhang. 1996. *A Unified Treatment of Horizontal Direct Investment, Vertical Direct Investment, and the Pattern of Trade in Goods and Services.* NBER Working Paper 5696. Cambridge, MA: National Bureau of Economic Research.

Markusen, James R. 1997. *Trade Versus Investment Liberalization.* NBER Working Paper 6231. Cambridge, MA: National Bureau of Economic Research.

Ramsey, J. B. 1969. Tests for Specification Errors in Classical Linear Least Squares Regression Analysis. *Journal of the Royal Statistical Society,* series B 31, no. 2: 350–71.

Sala-i-Martin, Xavier. 1997. I Just Ran Two Million Regressions. *American Economic Review* 87, no. 2: 178–83.

Shapiro, Samuel S., and Martin B. Wilk. 1965. An Analysis of Variance Test for Normality (Complete Samples). *Biometrika* 52, no. 3/4: 591–611.

Summers, Robert, and Alan Heston. 1991. The Penn World Table (Mark 5): An Expanded Set of International Comparisons, 1950–1988. *Quarterly Journal of Economics* 106, no. 2: 327–68.

United Nations. (Various years). *World Investment Report.* New York: United Nations.

Wang, Miao Grace. 2003. *Essays on Foreign Direct Investment.* Ph.D. dissertation, University of Oregon.

Yeaple, Stephen R. 2003a. The Complex Integration Strategies of Multinationals and Cross-Country Dependencies in the Structure of Foreign Direct Investment. *Journal of International Economics* 60, no. 2: 293–314.

Yeaple, Stephen R. 2003b. The Role of Skill Endowments in the Structure of U.S. Outward Foreign Direct Investment. *Review of Economics and Statistics* 85, no. 3: 726–34.

Appendix 9.1
Data Sources and Construction

For Analysis in the Third Section

These data are documented in detailed fashion in Blonigen and Davies (2004). Data on FDI stocks for nonfinancial sectors come from official statistics of the US Bureau of Economic Administration. These are publicly available at www.bea.doc.gov/bea/di1.htm. We convert these FDI stock data into millions of 1996 US dollars. Our GDP (both total and per capita in real terms) and trade openness measures are those from version 6.1 of the Penn World Tables, which are available online at pwt.econ.upenn.edu. For a detailed discussion of these measures, see Summers and Heston (1991). Our education variable is the mean years of education for adults over age 25. These data comes from the Barro-Lee dataset, which is available at www.worldbank.org/research/growth/ddbarle2.htm. Details on these data are given by Barro and Lee (1996). Distance was measured as the distance between capital cities as reported by the Bali Online Corporation. This distance calculator can be found at www.indo.com. For our measure of investment costs, we use the composite score compiled by Business Environment Risk Intelligence, S.A. (BERI). This composite includes measures of political risk, financial risk, and other economic indicators and ranges between 0 and 100, with higher numbers associated with a higher degree of openness. To compare these estimates to previously used measures of investment barriers, we define Investment Barriers as 100 minus the BERI's composite score. The data for these analyses are available from the authors upon request.

For Analysis in the Fourth and Fifth Sections

All variables in these sections of the chapter come from the identical sources and are constructed identically to those described in Borensztein, De Gregorio, and Lee (1998), with the exception of FDI data for developed countries. We obtained data on decade average flows of FDI into our developed countries from the 2001 OECD publication *International Direct Investment Statistics Yearbook, 1980–2000* (columns 1 and 2 of table 2, 13). We combined this with *International Financial Statistics* data on nominal GDP to get decade averages of FDI as a share of GDP. The data for these analyses are available from the authors upon request.

10

Intrafirm Trade of US MNCs: Findings and Implications for Models and Policies Toward Trade and Investment

SUSAN E. FEINBERG and MICHAEL P. KEANE

A large literature on spillovers from foreign direct investment (FDI) uses aggregate indicators of foreign activity in local markets to evaluate whether FDI is beneficial to host countries. Across many different contexts, researchers have found mixed results on whether FDI generates positive spillovers that improve the efficiency of host country economies. We argue that the inconclusive results of previous econometric studies on FDI spillovers may be due to the significant heterogeneity in MNC affiliate activity, which researchers have largely ignored. Indeed, FDI can take many forms, including passive foreign minority ownership, "screwdriver" plants, or research and development labs. The degree to which FDI benefits a host country should depend critically on the nature of the foreign activity in the local market.

We examine one source of important heterogeneity in foreign affiliate activity—specifically, whether multinational corporations (MNCs) that are organized to trade *intrafirm* in developing countries operate differently from MNCs with little or no intrafirm trade (IFT). In a descriptive analysis of affiliate activity in 49 developing countries from 1983 to 1996, we find that MNC

Susan E. Feinberg is assistant professor at the Robert H. Smith School of Business at the University of Maryland, College Park. Michael P. Keane is professor of economics at the Department of Economics at Yale University. The statistical analysis of the confidential firm-level data on US multinational corporations reported in this study was conducted at the International Investment Division, Bureau of Economic Analysis (BEA), US Department of Commerce, under arrangements that maintained legal confidentiality requirements. The views expressed are those of the authors and do not necessarily reflect those of the US Department of Commerce. Suggestions and assistance from William Zeile, Raymond Mataloni, Maria Borga, Ted Moran, and participants in the IIE conference on FDI and Development are gratefully acknowledged.

affiliates that are organized to trade intrafirm experience higher growth in real property, plant, and equipment (PPE) and have higher real wages than affiliates of MNCs with no IFT. From an organizational standpoint, affiliates that trade intrafirm are significantly larger in terms of total sales and come from MNCs with greater foreign activity. Affiliates that trade intrafirm also differ significantly in terms of their labor share from affiliates with no IFT. Thus there appear to be systematic and potentially important differences in the technology and organization of MNC affiliates that trade intrafirm versus affiliates that do not trade intrafirm. These differences may affect the mechanisms through which knowledge is transferred within and between firms. Hence, IFT may be an important characteristic of foreign affiliate activity that influences the magnitude and nature of spillovers from FDI to host-country economies.

The literature on FDI spillovers examines the interesting and important issue of whether activity by foreign-owned firms in the local economy is beneficial. In light of the considerable controversy around MNCs, researchers potentially have a lot to contribute to this debate. However, as other chapters in this volume argue, theoretical and empirical shortcomings in this literature have limited the degree to which researchers can speak to this issue. In particular, most current econometric studies in this area, by ignoring the considerable heterogeneity of MNC activity, obscure the mechanisms through which FDI might benefit host country firms (see Lipsey and Sjöholm in chapter 2 of this volume).

Consider the key assumption in the FDI spillovers literature—the notion that somehow foreign ownership conveys a different "class" status. All sorts of firm-specific properties are assumed to be associated with foreign ownership, especially when foreign firms are operating in developing countries. These include, for example, more advanced technology, better management practices, and better practices transferred through buyer-supplier relations. These properties of foreign ownership are assumed to exist regardless of the nationality of the foreign firms and, in many cases, regardless of the degree to which the host country firm is foreign *controlled*—e.g., when a foreign firm owns only a relatively small share of the local firm.

We argue that the diversity of MNC activity is too broad for it to be classified into "foreign market share."[1] Since MNC operations can include everything from sweatshops to research and development (R&D) labs, more attention needs to be given to the heterogeneity of MNC operations in econometric studies of FDI spillovers. As a modest first step, researchers using firm-level panel data might first investigate the nature of MNC activity

---

1. See Lipsey and Sjöholm's thorough review of the literature in this volume. Measures of foreign presence differ across studies. Examples are the ratio of foreign plants' employment to total industry employment (Kokko 1994) and foreign plants' share of total output in a four-digit industry (Kokko, Tansini, and Zejan 1996).

in the local market. For example, MNCs that undertake local R&D, or have higher local value added, might be more likely sources of knowledge transfer to local firms.

In this chapter, we focus on one aspect of MNC heterogeneity that we found associated with important intra-industry variation in MNC technology. Specifically, we examine whether MNCs that are organized to trade intrafirm in developing countries operate differently from MNCs with little or no intrafirm trade. In previous research in industrialized countries (see Feinberg and Keane 2001 and 2005; Feinberg, Keane, and Bognanno 1998), we found that MNCs that are organized to trade intrafirm differ along several important dimensions from MNCs with no IFT.

First, MNCs that are organized to trade intrafirm are considerably more dynamic technologically than MNCs with no IFT. Specifically, we found that in the context of US-Canada trade liberalization, MNCs that were initially organized to trade intrafirm experienced technical change that made it optimal to substantially increase intrafirm flows.[2] In contrast, no significant change in the factor shares of MNCs that were not initially organized to trade intrafirm occurred. These patterns were not industry specific. Indeed, as we point out in our 2001 study, there is substantial *within-industry* variation in the extent to which MNCs and their foreign affiliates are configured to trade intrafirm.

Second, we found that with increased IFT, the nature of the parent-affiliate relationship evolved. Canadian manufacturing affiliates that trade intrafirm are being transformed into production units that are more fully integrated into the MNCs' overall production process. This "deep" integration is supported by qualitative interviews we conducted with managers of MNC affiliates in Canada. These managers reported that as their affiliates became more connected with both the US parent and other foreign divisions of the MNC, more extensive communication and reporting links were established throughout the MNC. The association between IFT and more extensive communication within the firm is consistent with Moran's (2001) detailed case-based evidence on "parental supervision." For developing countries, this integration has the potential to generate dynamic benefits—namely, the transfer of best practices and greater demand for technological advances in logistics and transportation.

Third, we found that MNCs' discrete decisions to trade intrafirm persist over time, despite large reductions in tariffs and exchange rate movements. The persistence in the IFT decisions of MNCs is consistent with the large literature on firms' export decisions (e.g., Bernard and Jensen 2001; Das, Roberts, and Tybout 2001; Roberts and Tybout 1997). The relative insensitivity of IFT to changes in the economic environment implies that MNCs'

---

2. For affiliates that traded intrafirm, the production share of bilateral intrafirm shipments of intermediates increased substantially. Simultaneously, the capital share of Canadian affiliates decreased, and the labor share of US parents decreased.

production for IFT in developing countries may be less affected by local demand shocks or exchange rate variability.

Finally, Feinberg and Gupta (2004) found that MNCs with greater IFT linkages have more R&D-intensive US operations and are significantly more likely to locate R&D abroad. This finding is consistent with research on IFT in the international business literature (e.g., Kobrin 1991) that suggests that IFT in goods increases knowledge flows between MNC units. For developing-country affiliates, these relationships offer potentially significant sources of technology transfer. More importantly, affiliates that are the recipients of greater intrafirm knowledge flows may differ in both the amount and type of knowledge they could transfer to local firms.

In this study, we use confidential firm-level panel data from the Bureau of Economic Analysis (BEA) on the operations of US MNC affiliates to look at whether MNCs with and without IFT differ in terms of their employment, wage growth, and growth in capital investment across 48 developing countries during 1983–96. Our study is primarily descriptive. Estimating a model of MNCs' decisions to trade across such diverse countries over time is beyond the scope of this study. However, the rich, descriptive examination we present here provides some useful insights into the characteristics of US MNCs that trade intrafirm with their affiliates in developing countries.

We find that MNC affiliates that are organized to trade intrafirm experience higher growth in real PPE and have higher real wages than affiliates of MNCs with no IFT. From an organizational standpoint, affiliates that trade intrafirm are significantly larger in terms of total sales and come from MNCs with larger networks of foreign affiliates. Affiliates that trade intrafirm also differ significantly in terms of their labor share (defined as the ratio of affiliate employee compensation to affiliate sales). Thus there appear to be systematic and potentially important differences in the technology and organization of MNC affiliates that trade intrafirm versus affiliates that do not trade intrafirm. These differences may affect the mechanisms through which knowledge is transferred within and between firms.

The remainder of this chapter is organized as follows. In the next section, we describe the construction of our dataset. In the third section, we present descriptive features of the sample and compare the wage, employment, and capital investment growth of developing-country affiliates with high and low IFT. We discuss our results in the fourth section, and we provide a conclusion in the final section.

Data

The Benchmark and Annual Surveys of US Direct Investment Abroad, which are administered by the BEA at the US Department of Commerce, provided the dataset for this study. These surveys provide the most comprehensive data available on the activities of US-based MNCs and their foreign affiliates.

For this study, we use the BEA data disaggregated at the individual foreign affiliate level for each US MNC parent from 1983–96.

The initial universe of affiliate-year observations for this time period contains approximately 256,000 observations on 43,700 affiliates. These affiliates are located in 180 countries, which include many small island nations and "new" countries or countries that changed status from 1983–96 (e.g., Yugoslavia). Several alterations were made to the population of affiliates to construct the sample in this study. First, as we discuss in our 2001 study, reporting requirements for MNC affiliates differ between the Benchmark and Annual Surveys, and the BEA carries forward small affiliates that fill out the Benchmark Surveys but are exempt from filling out Annual Surveys.[3] In the non-Benchmark years, the BEA estimates data for these small affiliates. Since small, poor countries typically attract small affiliates, these countries tend to have higher proportions of estimated-to-reported data. In previous studies, we typically removed most, if not all, estimated data. However, such a screen would be infeasible using developing-country data, since a much larger proportion of the affiliates in developing countries fall below the reporting requirements in non-Benchmark years. Our solution to this problem was to drop countries with less than 80 total affiliate-year observations and to remove affiliates with fewer than $100,000 in total sales. These screens removed 34,000 affiliate-year observations and eliminated 77 countries from the initial population.

Affiliates submit either "short" or "long" forms to the BEA, the latter containing more detailed information. We eliminated observations on affiliates that filled out the "short" form, which removed approximately 14,800 more affiliate-year observations. Similarly, minority-owned affiliates tend to submit less detailed data, so these were also eliminated from the sample (2,000 affiliate-year observations). After these various screens, we again removed countries containing fewer than 80 affiliate-year observations and countries for which we could not obtain World Bank data. This also removed approximately 14,000 affiliate-year observations and eliminated 20 more countries from the initial universe.[4] Finally, we removed 2,500 affiliates classified in "international shipping and drilling" which the BEA defines as a code distinct from country codes. Thus, our final sample contains 186,717 affiliate-year observations on 32,600 affiliates in 78 countries. These countries are listed in the appendix.

Since our aim is to focus on developing countries in this study, we classify countries by their absolute and relative levels of development. We did not

---

3. Note that an important feature of the BEA's reporting requirements is total affiliate sales. The cut-off value that defines which affiliates are exempt from filling out the surveys differs not only between Benchmark and Annual Surveys, but also over time.

4. The countries eliminated in this round were primarily tax haven islands such as Bermuda and the Netherlands Antilles.

wish to simply classify a country as "industrialized" or "developing" since the latter group could potentially include countries as diverse as Greece and Haiti. We decided to create five development categories based upon each country's rank in real per capita gross domestic product (GDP) at the beginning and end of the time frame for this study. The categories are not quintiles, in the sense that 80 percent of all affiliate-year observations fall into the two "industrialized" country groups. Most affiliate-year observations in the first industrialized-country group are in Canada, the United Kingdom and EU countries, Japan, and Australia. The second industrialized-country group contains primarily EU countries like Greece, Portugal, Spain, and Ireland that grew quickly during the sample window and narrowed the per capita income gap with the wealthier countries in the first group.

Developing countries were classified into three groups, again based upon real per capita GDP at the beginning and end of the sample window. The wealthiest of the developing-country groups contains lower-income European countries such as Turkey and the former communist countries, as well as more developed Latin American countries such as Chile, Mexico, and Brazil, along with industrializing Asian countries such as Thailand and Malaysia. The second developing-country group includes middle-income South and Central American countries (e.g., Peru and Guatemala), wealthier African countries such as South Africa, Morocco, and Egypt, and lower-income Asian countries such as Indonesia and the Philippines. The poorest countries in South Asia, the Americas, and Africa (e.g., Pakistan, Haiti, and Zambia) are in the third developing-country group.

The BEA collects several different types of trade data: data on trade in goods with the United States (imports and exports, both intrafirm and arm's-length), and data on distribution of affiliate total revenue by type (goods, services, and investment income) and destination (local market, United States, and other countries). The actual countries in the "other country" category are not collected in non-Benchmark years (see Zeile 1997 for a detailed examination of the BEA's intrafirm trade data). The three destinations are further divided into intrafirm versus arm's-length sales.

We construct three IFT flows from the data: affiliate intrafirm sales to US parents, affiliate intrafirm sales to other foreign affiliates of the same MNC, and US parent intrafirm sales to foreign affiliates.[5]

Affiliates report cost and revenue data in (thousands of) current US dollars. We deflate this using the 1992 US GDP deflator.

---

5. We note that parent intrafirm sales to affiliates is explicitly only for sales of goods, whereas affiliate intrafirm sales to parents and other affiliates potentially captures the sales of goods, services, and investment income. In the present study, this distinction does not create serious comparability problems because we primarily examine the IFT of affiliates in manufacturing industries, which is nearly all sales of goods.

Empirical Results

Trends in Intrafirm Trade and Features of the Sample

Figures 10.1a and 10.1b show the trends in the IFT/sales of manufacturing affiliates in developing and industrialized countries, respectively. We define manufacturing as BEA industry codes 200–400. These correspond quite closely to Standard Industrial Classification codes. We define "developing countries" as groups three to five and "industrialized countries" as groups one and two (see appendix 10.1).

As illustrated in figure 10.1a, for affiliates in developing countries, there is an upward trend in all three trade flows. Intrafirm trade from parents to affiliates increases from 11 percent to 17.6 percent of affiliate sales in developing countries. Affiliate sales to parents and affiliate-to-affiliate sales more than double as a percent of total affiliate sales between 1983 and 1996, the former increasing from 9.1 percent to 20.7 percent of affiliate sales, and the latter increasing from 5.1 percent to 10.1 percent of affiliate sales.

In figure 10.1b, the intrafirm trade of affiliates in industrialized countries shows the strongest upward trend for affiliate-to-affiliate trade. This flow increases from approximately 13.5 percent to 18 percent of affiliate sales between 1983 and 1996. In contrast, the flows to and from affiliates and US parents both remain fairly constant at approximately 8 percent of affiliate sales. Note that affiliate-to-affiliate trade is by far the largest of the three trade flows for affiliates in industrialized countries, whereas it is the smallest of the three flows for affiliates in developing countries This is due to the predominance of affiliates in EU countries (where there is large intraregional trade) in the industrialized-country sample.[6]

Table 10.1 gives descriptive statistics for the affiliates in our sample. The first column contains observations on the full sample of affiliates in all industries and development groups. The second and third columns describe affiliates in industrialized countries and the subset of industrialized-country affiliates in manufacturing industries. The fourth and fifth columns give similar breakdowns for affiliates in developing countries.

Note that, in the last row of table 10.1, we can see that approximately 80 percent of all affiliate-year observations (149,524 of the total 186,717) are in

---

6. Not surprisingly, Canada and Mexico have much larger bilateral affiliate-parent trade flows.

Figure 10.1 Trends in affiliate intrafirm trade/manufacturing sales, 1983–96

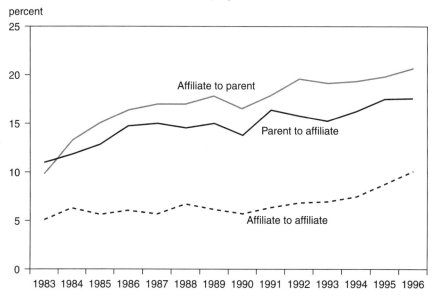

a. In developing countries

percent

Affiliate to parent

Parent to affiliate

Affiliate to affiliate

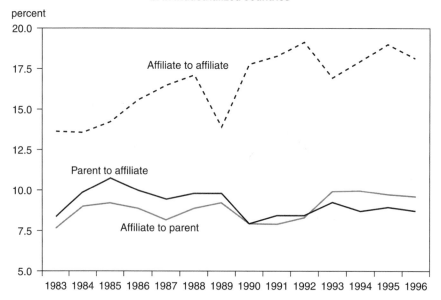

b. In industrialized countries

percent

Affiliate to affiliate

Parent to affiliate

Affiliate to parent

Source: BEA Benchmark and Annual Surveys on US Direct Investment Abroad.

industrialized countries. This is broadly representative of US FDI. Nearly 60 percent of all affiliate-year observations are in Canada and the European Union.

In columns 2 through 5, we can see that the developing- and industrialized-country subsamples differ along several interesting dimensions. First, the average developing-country affiliate is part of an MNC with a significantly larger network of foreign affiliates than the average affiliate in an industrialized country (row 4). Similarly, the average developing-country affiliate's US parent sales (row 2) and total foreign affiliate sales (row 3) are also significantly larger.[7] For US MNCs, FDI in developing countries is still a relatively new and small phenomenon undertaken primarily by the largest, most experienced international firms.

The magnitude and destination of intrafirm trade flows also differs significantly between developing and industrialized countries. As mentioned above, affiliates in the industrialized-country subsample (manufacturing industries) trade intrafirm much more with other affiliates (as a percent of sales) than with US parents. In contrast, affiliates in the developing-country subsample (manufacturing industries) export only 4.5 percent of their total sales intrafirm to other affiliates, but send 7.3 percent of their total sales intrafirm to US parents. US parent sales to foreign affiliates are approximately 8 percent of total affiliate sales in both the developing- and industrialized-country subsamples.[8]

Finally, note that the average annual wage—defined as employee compensation divided by number of employees—is $36,920 in the full sample of industrialized-country affiliates, but is substantially smaller, $32,890 among industrialized-country affiliates in manufacturing industries. Similarly, the average developing-country wage is $15,160 for all affiliates, but at $12,160 the wage is again substantially smaller for manufacturing affiliates in developing countries. At first glance, the developing country wage might seem quite large. However, more than 60 percent of the affiliate-year observations in the developing-country subsample are in the highest income group. Fewer than 10 percent of affiliate-year observations are in the lowest income group. The wage gap between manufacturing affiliates in the highest and lowest income groups is quite large—$12,700 versus $7,800, respectively.

---

7. Total foreign affiliate sales is the sum of the sales of all the foreign affiliates of the same US parent.

8. The differences in the means in table 10.1 from the annual means in figures 10.1a and 10.1b result from the method of calculation. In figures 10.1a and 10.1b, sales and trade flows are aggregated at the country level. In table 10.1, means are calculated from the entire set of affiliate-year observations. Since so many affiliates have no trade flows, the means calculated from the micro data are much smaller.

254

Table 10.1 Descriptive statistics for sample affiliates

	Full sample	Industrialized countries		Developing countries	
		All	Manufacturing	All	Manufacturing
Affiliate sales	84,597 (432,719)	92,971 (475,357)	124,099 (634,751)	50,931 (173,714)	53,837 (177,575)
Parent sales	7,030,261 (14,300,000)	6,492,353 (13,900,000)	5,165,212 (120,000,000)	9,192,811 (15,800,000)	7,920,680 (15,900,000)
Sales of all affiliates in the MNC network	6,049,347 (16,600,000)	5,280,490 (15,400,000)	4,150,722 (13,000,000)	9,140,319 (20,500,000)	6,724,940 (15,800,000)
Number of affiliates in the MNC network	39 (42)	36 (41)	35 (40)	51 (44)	48 (41)
Affiliate PPE	35,469 (239,202)	36,489 (255,333)	53,152 (318,723)	31,370 (158,508)	27,440 (106,256)
Affiliate labor share (employee compensation/sales)	0.191 (0.152)	0.194 (0.151)	0.204 (0.119)	0.177 (0.157)	0.184 (0.147)
Affiliate employment	372 (1,538)	342 (1,593)	503 (1,884)	495 (1,285)	699 (1,543)
Affiliate wage (employee compensation/employment)	32.54 (19.30)	36.92 (18.18)	32.89 (15.15)	15.16 (12.07)	12.16 (9.42)
Affiliate IFT to affiliates/total affiliate sales	0.060 (0.168)	0.064 (0.171)	0.097 (0.193)	0.042 (0.154)	0.045 (0.147)

Affiliate IFT to parents/total affiliate sales	0.028 (0.119)	0.022 (0.096)	0.041 (0.128)	0.050 (0.183)	0.073 (0.217)
Parent IFT to affiliates/total affiliate sales	0.083 (0.166)	0.088 (0.170)	0.081 (0.143)	0.072 (0.149)	0.078 (0.150)
Affiliate IFT to affiliates	10,461 (120,062)	12,202 (133,141)	20,886 (187,168)	3,462 (32,251)	3,808 (32,825)
Affiliate IFT to parents	5,770 (122,613)	5,489 (133,126)	11,074 (203,098)	6,898 (64,996)	9,535 (77,182)
Parent IFT to affiliates	6,865 (112,012)	7,237 (122,994)	11,244 (185,817)	5,370 (46,564)	8,215 (62,700)
Percent of affiliate-year observations with IFT to affiliates	36.7 (48.2)	38.4 (48.6)	54.7 (49.8)	30.1 (45.9)	40.7 (49.1)
Percent of affiliate-year observations with IFT to parents	21.9 (41.3)	22.8 (42.0)	41.4 (49.3)	17.9 (38.4)	26.8 (44.3)
Percent of affiliate-year observations with parent IFT to affiliates	49.2 (50.0)	49.0 (50.0)	64.5 (47.9)	50.2 (50.0)	62.5 (48.4)
Number of affiliate-year observations	186,717	149,524	62,891	37,193	19,895

IFT = intrafirm trade
MNC = multinational corporation
PPE = property, plant, and equipment

Notes: All sample means in the industrialized- and developing-country subsamples differ at the 1 percent level. Dollar figures are in thousands of 1992 US dollars.

Source: BEA Benchmark and Annual Surveys on US Direct Investment Abroad.

Characteristics of Developing-Country Affiliates with High and Low IFT

In tables 10.2a through 10.2c, we focus on differences between developing-country manufacturing affiliates with no IFT versus affiliates at the 75th percentile of intrafirm trade/sales (IFT/sales) for the 1983–86, 1989–91, and 1993–96 periods.[9] We construct averages by affiliates over 3–4-year time intervals, to smooth the sample, and we include three time periods to examine changes in levels over time. Interesting differences are evident both between high- and low-trade affiliates for a given trade flow and across the three different trade flows.

Affiliate-to-Affiliate IFT

In table 10.2a, we see that developing-country affiliates with high IFT to other MNC affiliates are approximately twice the size of low-trade affiliates in each of the three time periods. Affiliates with high IFT to other affiliates also tend to be part of much larger MNC networks. Indeed, in the 1993–96 time period, the MNCs of high-trade affiliates have 10 more affiliates on average than the MNCs of low-trade affiliates. Interestingly, the network size of the high- and low-trade affiliates is virtually the same in the first time period.

Several other interesting differences between the high- and low-trade affiliates in developing countries can be seen in table 10.2a. First, the labor share (defined as an affiliate's employee compensation to sales) of the low-trade affiliates is higher and increases slightly over time, from 18.4 percent in 1983–86 to 21 percent in 1993–96. In contrast, the high-trade affiliates' labor share decreases slightly from 16.5 percent to 15.8 percent and is considerably lower than the labor share of affiliates with no IFT.

As shown by the percent of affiliate-year observations with IFT, affiliates with high IFT to other affiliates are significantly more likely to have IFT with US parents—in both directions. Affiliates in the high-trade subsample see their sales to other affiliates increase from 11 percent to 25 percent of total sales from the first to the third time periods.

Affiliate-to-Parent IFT

Table 10.2b compares developing-country manufacturing affiliates with high versus low IFT to US parents. Similar to the affiliates with high IFT to

---

9. We do not contrast the 75th percentile with the 25th percentile of IFT/sales since the median affiliate has no IFT for two of the three trade flows. This is evident in the percent of affiliate-year observations with IFT, reported in tables 10.1 and 10.2a through 10.2c. Although affiliates have non-zero IFT *from* parents at the median, the 25th percentile is zero. Hence, the "high-trade" affiliates in tables 10.2a through 10.2c are defined at the 75th percentile, whereas the "low-trade" affiliates have zero IFT. This explains the much larger *n* in the low-trade subsamples (see bottom row of tables 10.2a through 10.2c).

Table 10.2a Characteristics of developing-country manufacturing affiliates with high intrafirm trade to other affiliates versus developing-country manufacturing affiliates with no intrafirm trade

	1983–86		1989–91		1993–96	
	High	Low	High	Low	High	Low
Affiliate sales	69,115 (179,865)	29,534 (84,212)	85,495 (225,082)	34,183 (116,208)	90,874 (263,962)	44,618 (166,031)
Parent sales	7,052,977 (13,000,000)	8,096,538 (16,600,000)	7,084,218 (11,800,000)	8,799,354 (17,700,000)	8,982,267 (17,400,000)	8,680,828 (18,200,000)
Sales of all affiliates in the MNC network	5,095,551 (12,200,000)	4,838,088 (12,900,000)	6,870,591 (14,900,000)	7,308,478 (16,900,000)	9,742,890 (19,700,000)	8,263,058 (18,100,000)
Number of affiliates in the MNC network	45 (33)	42 (35)	51 (36)	43 (37)	61 (50)	51 (51)
Affiliate PPE	41,024 (149,724)	17,253 (58,220)	46,175 (157,465)	17,336 (63,293)	44,613 (163,704)	22,259 (64,027)
Affiliate PPE growth	0.000 (0.290)	−0.025 (0.446)	0.049 (0.342)	0.048 (0.419)	0.091 (0.358)	0.094 (0.418)
Affiliate labor share	0.165 (0.098)	0.184 (0.151)	0.169 (0.113)	0.198 (0.169)	0.158 (0.116)	0.210 (0.187)
Affiliate employment	940 (2,258)	529 (911)	982 (2,040)	610 (1274)	895 (2,030)	671 (1,695)
Affiliate employment growth	0.007 (0.319)	−0.019 (0.481)	0.041 (0.376)	0.047 (0.386)	0.020 (0.305)	0.025 (0.375)
Affiliate wage	10.36 (7.01)	10.40 (6.71)	12.27 (8.45)	10.53 (8.13)	15.07 (11.89)	13.65 (11.29)

(table continues next page)

Table 10.2a Characteristics of developing-country manufacturing affiliates with high intrafirm trade to other affiliates versus developing-country manufacturing affiliates with no intrafirm trade *(continued)*

	1983–86		1989–91		1993–96	
	High	Low	High	Low	High	Low
Affiliate IFT to affiliates/total affiliate sales	0.112 (0.187)	0 (0)	0.168 (0.251)	0 (0)	0.252 (0.295)	0 (0)
Affiliate IFT to parents/total affiliate sales	0.072 (0.188)	0.034 (0.161)	0.078 (0.179)	0.118 (0.291)	0.075 (0.183)	0.111 (0.278)
Parent IFT to affiliates/total affiliate sales	0.103 (0.160)	0.064 (0.138)	0.080 (0.135)	0.083 (0.176)	0.087 (0.144)	0.079 (0.169)
Affiliate IFT to affiliates	9,756 (30,620)	0 (0)	12,598 (43,240)	0 (0)	21,721 (95,959)	0 (0)
Affiliate IFT to parents	10,962 (58,060)	5,115 (27,261)	13,254 (72,147)	8,337 (47,856)	8,351 (60,666)	12,819 (90,730)
Parent IFT to affiliates	9,562 (43,759)	4,650 (24,810)	11,728 (80,949)	6,726 (46,527)	9,358 (48,963)	9,995 (69,016)
Percent of affiliate-year observations with IFT to parents	38.6 (48.7)	11.0 (31.3)	44.2 (49.7)	25.3 (43.5)	41.8 (49.3)	23.1 (42.1)
Percent of affiliate-year observations with parent IFT to affiliates	78.3 (41.2)	62.4 (48.5)	71.4 (45.2)	54.2 (49.8)	63.0 (48.3)	45.6 (49.8)

IFT = intrafirm trade
MNC = multinational corporation
PPE = property, plant, and equipment

Notes: All sample means in the industrialized- and developing-country subsamples differ at the 1 percent level. Dollar figures are in thousands of 1992 US dollars.

Source: BEA Benchmark and Annual Surveys on US Direct Investment Abroad.

Table 10.2b Characteristics of developing-country manufacturing affiliates with high intrafirm trade to US parents versus developing-country manufacturing affiliates with no intrafirm trade

	1983–86		1989–91		1993–96	
	High	Low	High	Low	High	Low
Affiliate sales	78,304 (180,576)	30,389 (96,128)	91,852 (264,876)	33,819 (84,717)	109,711 (361,087)	42,901 (96,916)
Parent sales	10,700,000 (21,600,000)	6,256,943 (11,500,000)	12,300,000 (23,800,000)	6,716,153 (11,100,000)	10,400,000 (23,000,000)	7,904,053 (14,800,000)
Sales of all affiliates in the MNC network	5,841,403 (14,200,000)	4,484,997 (12,500,000)	9,979,956 (22,600,000)	6,267,550 (13,700,000)	8,859,554 (21,400,000)	8,444,485 (17,000,000)
Number of affiliates in the MNC network	39 (32)	45 (35)	39 (38)	50 (37)	42 (50)	60 (49)
Affiliate PPE	57,502 (174,032)	13,129 (38,334)	50,872 (158,579)	14,595 (50,899)	49,595 (153,835)	19,927 (68,737)
Affiliate PPE growth	0.046 (0.261)	−0.042 (0.405)	0.072 (0.339)	0.036 (0.441)	0.070 (0.339)	0.104 (0.442)
Affiliate labor share	0.238 (0.173)	0.160 (0.105)	0.266 (0.206)	0.154 (0.107)	0.253 (0.206)	0.165 (0.136)
Affiliate employment	1,419 (2,384)	385 (676)	1,438 (2,341)	399 (757)	1,381 (2,706)	450 (942)
Affiliate employment growth	0.051 (0.485)	−0.024 (0.375)	0.044 (0.426)	0.043 (0.363)	0.011 (0.291)	0.028 (0.381)
Affiliate wage	8.80 (6.31)	10.89 (6.57)	9.61 (7.81)	11.85 (8.36)	12.37 (10.85)	15.34 (11.68)

(table continues next page)

Table 10.2b Characteristics of developing-country manufacturing affiliates with high intrafirm trade to US parents versus developing-country manufacturing affiliates with no intrafirm trade (continued)

	1983–86		1989–91		1993–96	
	High	Low	High	Low	High	Low
Affiliate IFT to affiliates/total affiliate sales	0.050 (0.132)	0.021 (0.093)	0.041 (0.115)	0.042 (0.152)	0.070 (0.170)	0.061 (0.187)
Affiliate IFT to parents/total affiliate sales	0.188 (0.297)	0 (0)	0.382 (0.378)	0 (0)	0.361 (0.364)	0 (0)
Parent IFT to affiliates/total affiliate sales	0.132 (0.202)	0.057 (0.110)	0.157 (0.237)	0.055 (0.118)	0.135 (0.206)	0.063 (0.133)
Affiliate IFT to affiliates	7,033 (28,469)	908 (7,271)	6,794 (33,913)	1,390 (11,588)	11,123 (83,915)	3,039 (22,814)
Affiliate IFT to parents	22,758 (66,110)	0 (0)	33,312 (101,405)	0 (0)	48,454 (215,148)	0 (0)
Parent IFT to affiliates	17,627 (54,943)	1,158 (4,925)	25,191 (107,244)	1,187 (3,765)	35,291 (164,324)	1,816 (7,053)
Percent of affiliate-year observations with IFT to affiliates	60.4 (48.9)	37.8 (48.5)	39.7 (48.9)	33.0 (47.0)	43.9 (49.6)	35.6 (47.9)
Percent of affiliate-year observations with parent IFT to affiliates	74.2 (43.7)	68.3 (46.5)	62.9 (48.3)	59.3 (49.1)	60.3 (48.9)	50.8 (50.0)

IFT = intrafirm trade
MNC = multinational corporation
PPE = property, plant, and equipment

Notes: All sample means in the industrialized- and developing-country subsamples differ at the 1 percent level. Dollar figures are in thousands of 1992 US dollars.

Source: BEA Benchmark and Annual Surveys on US Direct Investment Abroad.

Table 10.2c Characteristics of developing-country manufacturing affiliates with high intrafirm trade from US parents versus developing-country manufacturing affiliates with no intrafirm trade

	1983–86		1989–91		1993–96	
	High	Low	High	Low	High	Low
Affiliate sales	42,074 (123,054)	33,667 (105,280)	61,900 (231,606)	31,913 (72,892)	84,641 (338,733)	41,528 (89,055)
Parent sales	9,940,715 (20,500,000)	6,809,006 (9,689,754)	11,900,000 (23,400,000)	7,230,282 (11,800,000)	9,627,087 (21,300,000)	9,179,145 (16,300,000)
Sales of all affiliates in the MNC network	6,015,993 (14,900,000)	4,231,254 (10,100,000)	9,836,720 (21,600,000)	6,510,113 (13,800,000)	8,868,892 (20,700,000)	8,900,515 (16,900,000)
Number of affiliates in the MNC network	44 (35)	43 (36)	44 (36)	48 (39)	48 (48)	61 (53)
Affiliate PPE	24,530 (95,105)	17,300 (42,903)	27,899 (96,150)	16,597 (68,546)	32,532 (121,998)	21,485 (70,548)
Affiliate PPE growth	0.012 (0.261)	−0.063 (0.576)	0.036 (0.465)	0.054 (0.409)	0.085 (0.346)	0.103 (0.418)
Affiliate labor share	0.212 (0.163)	0.182 (0.132)	0.214 (0.180)	0.181 (0.158)	0.210 (0.177)	0.191 (0.175)
Affiliate employment	731 (1,432)	585 (1,018)	903 (1,627)	578 (1,178)	984 (2,566)	604 (1,156)
Affiliate employment growth	0.028 (0.349)	0.005 (0.352)	0.043 (0.366)	0.051 (0.450)	0.017 (0.348)	0.033 (0.380)

(table continues next page)

Table 10.2c CCharacteristics of developing-country manufacturing affiliates with high intrafirm trade from US parents versus developing-country manufacturing affiliates with no intrafirm trade (continued)

	1983–86		1989–91		1993–96	
	High	Low	High	Low	High	Low
Affiliate wage	9.74 (7.12)	9.22 (6.68)	11.20 (8.40)	9.90 (7.91)	16.01 (12.35)	12.65 (11.16)
Affiliate IFT to affiliates/total affiliate sales	0.041 (0.120)	0.036 (0.134)	0.035 (0.101)	0.060 (0.200)	0.049 (0.129)	0.085 (0.233)
Affiliate IFT to parents/total affiliate sales	0.109 (0.260)	0.026 (0.127)	0.175 (0.318)	0.108 (0.280)	0.127 (0.268)	0.100 (0.268)
Parent IFT to affiliate/total affiliate sales	0.248 (0.192)	0 (0)	0.289 (0.217)	0 (0)	0.292 (0.197)	0 (0)
Affiliate IFT to affiliates	4,778 (24555)	2,054 (12488)	5,279 (31068)	1,730 (7,428)	8,446 (81,031)	3,132 (17,172)
Affiliate IFT to parents	17,746 (65,097)	1,286 (7,189)	26,585 (100,794)	2,185 (8,793)	37,262 (211,867)	4,092 (29,981)
Parent IFT to affiliates	17,788 (52,848)	0 (0)	27,126 (106,970)	0 (0)	38,664 (163,610)	0 (0)
Percent of affiliate-year observations with IFT to affiliates	51.6 (50.0)	32.0 (46.6)	36.5 (48.2)	26.1 (43.9)	42.2 (49.4)	29.0 (45.4)
Percent of affiliate-year observations with IFT to parents	29.9 (45.8)	10.2 (30.3)	41.7 (49.3)	23.3 (42.3)	39.7 (48.9)	21.3 (41.0)

IFT = intrafirm trade
MNC = multinational corporation
PPE = property, plant, and equipment

Notes: All sample means in the industrialized- and developing-country subsamples differ at the 1 percent level. Dollar figures are in thousands of 1992 US dollars.

Source: BEA Benchmark and Annual Surveys on US Direct Investment Abroad.

other affiliates, affiliates with high IFT to parents are between two and three times the size of affiliates with no IFT to parents. However, affiliates with high IFT to parents come from considerably smaller MNCs, in terms of number of affiliates, than the low-trade affiliates. Although the high-trade affiliates come from MNCs with a smaller number of foreign affiliates, these MNCs are typically larger in terms of sales—both parent sales and the total sales of foreign affiliates. MNCs with extensive affiliate-to-parent IFT appear to have fewer, but larger, foreign subsidiaries as compared to MNCs with extensive affiliate-to-affiliate IFT. The high-trade affiliates' labor share is approximately 25 percent versus 16 percent (during 1994–96) for affiliates with no IFT to parents. Note the interesting contrast between high-trade affiliates in this group versus the high-trade affiliates in table 10.2a. Affiliates with high IFT *to other affiliates* have significantly smaller labor share than affiliates that do not trade intrafirm with other affiliates.

In the high affiliate-to-parent IFT subsample, affiliates with high IFT to parents have high *bilateral* trade with parents. They purchase approximately 14 percent of total sales intrafirm from parents versus 6 percent for the low-trade affiliates. Affiliates in the high-trade subsample see their sales to US parents increase from 19 percent to 36 percent of total sales from the first to the third time periods.

Parent-to-Affiliate IFT

Table 10.2c compares developing-country manufacturing affiliates with high IFT *from* US parents and affiliates that purchase no goods from US parents. Similar to the high-trade affiliates in tables 10.2a and 10.2b, affiliates with high intrafirm purchases from US parents are approximately twice the size of affiliates with no IFT from parents (in the second and third periods). The size characteristics of high- and low-trade affiliates in table 10.2c resemble those in table 10.2b in the sense that affiliates with high intrafirm purchases from parents come from MNCs that are larger in terms of parent and total affiliate sales, but smaller in terms of number of foreign affiliates.

Affiliates with high intrafirm purchases from US parents have fairly constant IFT with other MNC affiliates—approximately 4 percent of sales. Affiliates with high intrafirm purchases from parents are about twice as likely to have some intrafirm sales to parents as affiliates that purchase no goods from parents. Interestingly, affiliates that purchase no inputs from US parents have large increases in their sales *to* US parents from the first to the third time periods—from 2.6 percent to 10 percent of sales.

Finally, parent intrafirm trade to affiliates in the high-trade subsample increases from 25 percent to 29 percent of affiliate sales from the first to the second time period, but remains constant at 29 percent of sales in the third time period.

Wage, Employment, and PPE Growth of High- Versus Low-Trade Affiliates

Figures 10.2a through 10.2c show the growth in real wages for the high- and low-trade affiliates in tables 10.2a through 10.2c (i.e., manufacturing affiliates in developing countries). Recall that real wages are measured as real employee compensation/employment. Total employee compensation includes all employment-related expenses, and the resulting wages are measured in thousands of (1992) US dollars.

Figure 10.2a shows the wage growth in affiliates with high and low IFT to other affiliates for the three time periods given in tables 10.2a through 10.2c (i.e., 1983–86, 1989–91, and 1993–96). Note that the real wages of low-trade affiliates remain stagnant at approximately $10,000 in the first and second periods, while the (initially same) real wages of high-trade affiliates grow to more than $12,000 in the second period. The real wages of both groups of affiliates grow from the second to the third period, but the high-trade affiliates' wages grow to $15,070, and the low-trade affiliates' wages reach only $13,650 in the third period.

Figure 10.2b plots the wage growth for affiliates with high and low IFT to US parents. Wages in both groups of affiliates grow approximately 40 percent from the first to the third period. However, the real wages of high-trade affiliates are lower than the wages of affiliates that have low intrafirm sales to parents. The real wages of high-trade affiliates grow from $8,800 to $12,370 but the real wages of low-trade affiliates grow from $10,890 in the first period to $15,340 in the third period.

Finally, figure 10.2c shows the real wages of affiliates with high and low intrafirm purchases from US parents. Again, as in the first chart, the real wages of affiliates with no intrafirm purchases from parents remain nearly constant from the first to the second period. In contrast, the real wages of affiliates with high intrafirm purchases from parents grow 15 percent from the first to the second periods. Of all the groups of affiliates shown in figures 10.2a through 10.2c, those with high intrafirm purchases from US parents have the highest real wage—$16,010 in the third period. This contrasts with the significantly lower third-period real wage of $12,650 for affiliates that purchase no inputs from US parents.

In all, real wage growth is the same or greater for affiliates with high IFT versus low IFT. The levels of real wages are higher for affiliates with high IFT to other affiliates and high intrafirm purchases from US parents. Although affiliates with high sales to US parents experience significant growth in wages over time, the wages of these affiliates are lower, on average, than the wages of affiliates with no intrafirm sales to US parents.

Table 10.3 shows changes in the three intrafirm trade flows as well as average annual changes in employment and real PPE for the full sample of affiliates and grouped by development category. We also examine changes in employment and real PPE for high-trade affiliates, as defined in tables

**Figure 10.2   Real wages of manufacturing affiliates in the top
and bottom quartiles of intrafirm sales**

a. To other foreign affiliates

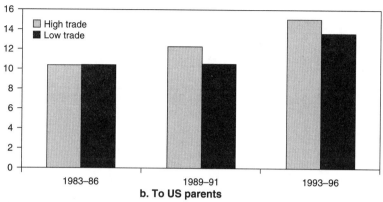

thousands of 1992 US dollars

High trade
Low trade

1983–86   1989–91   1993–96

b. To US parents

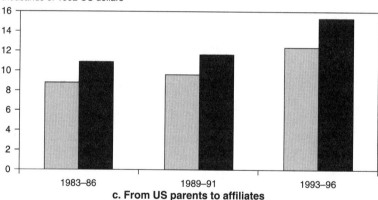

thousands of 1992 US dollars

1983–86   1989–91   1993–96

c. From US parents to affiliates

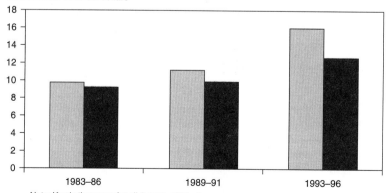

thousands of 1992 US dollars

1983–86   1989–91   1993–96

Note: Key is the same for all 3 parts of this figure.

Source: BEA Benchmark and Annual Surveys on US Direct Investment Abroad.

Table 10.3 Average annual changes in intrafirm trade, employment, and PPE of developing-country affiliates

	Changes in intrafirm trade*			Average annual change in affiliate employment**				Average annual change in affiliate real PPE***			
	To parents	To affiliates	From parents	All affiliates	High P sales	High A sales	High P to A sales	All affiliates	High P sales	High A sales	High P to A sales
Full sample	0.072 (0.269)	0.121 (0.543)	0.056 (0.252)	0.010 (0.368)	0.011 (0.383)	0.013 (0.335)	0.011[a] (0.337)	0.055 (0.489)	0.059[b] (0.395)	0.069[a] (0.435)	0.055 (0.418)
Development subsamples											
Most developed											
1	0.024[c,d] (0.090)	0.025[a] (0.108)	0.010[c] (0.089)	0.008[b,e] (0.354)	0.007 (0.325)	0.010[c,f] (0.320)	0.011[c] (0.321)	0.058[b] (0.492)	0.057 (0.408)	0.073[a] (0.434)	0.056 (0.425)
2	0.018 (0.317)	0.035[c] (0.143)	−0.024[c] (0.151)	0.011 (0.382)	0.024[c] (0.304)	0.011 (0.332)	0.017 (0.311)	0.060 (0.471)	0.086[b] (0.357)	0.076[b] (0.346)	0.073[b] (0.350)
3	0.049[c] (0.097)	0.040[c] (0.136)	0.028 (0.078)	0.022[a] (0.389)	0.026 (0.388)	0.024 (0.343)	0.022 (0.349)	0.061[c] (0.447)	0.062 (0.335)	0.071[c] (0.383)	0.057 (0.391)
4	0.071 (0.144)	0.177 (0.349)	0.059 (0.225)	0.002[c] (0.396)	0.016 (0.333)	0.017[b] (0.355)	0.005 (0.304)	0.005[a] (0.483)	0.018[a] (0.363)	0.024[b] (0.391)	0.000 (0.367)
Least developed											
5	0.270 (0.477)	0.428 (1.207)	0.221 (0.510)	0.016[a] (0.409)	−0.030[c] (0.422)	0.048[b] (0.378)	0.046[b] (0.380)	0.043 (0.511)	0.077[c] (0.314)	0.075[c] (0.448)	0.059 (0.559)

A = affiliate; IFT = intrafirm trade; P = parent; PPE = property, plant, and equipment

* Changes in IFT are the average of annual percentage changes in each trade flow/sales in the relevant development subsample.
** Changes in affiliate employment are calculated as the log (annual) change in employment averaged over all affiliates in each development subsample.
*** Changes in affiliate PPE are calculated as the log (annual) change in real PPE averaged over all affiliates in each development subsample.

Differences in means significant (two-tailed tests):
a. At 1 percent.
b. At 5 percent.
c. At 10 percent.

d. T-tests in the "Intrafirm trade" panel compare the mean within each development subsample to the full sample means in row one.
e. T-tests in the "All affiliates" column in panels two and three compare the mean employment change and PPE growth for each development subsample with the overall sample means in row one.
f. T-tests in the "High-trade" columns compare the means for affiliates above the 75th percentile of the relevant trade flow within each development subsample with the development subsample means.

Note: Full sample = 186,717 affiliate-year observations; 1 = 136,227; 2 = 13,297; 3 = 23,658; 4 = 10,015; 5 = 3,520.

Source: BEA Benchmark and Annual Surveys on US Direct Investment Abroad.

10.2a through 10.2c. The first column in panels two and three gives the average change in employment and PPE for all affiliates in the given development group. The next three columns give the average change, within each development group, for affiliates with high IFT to parents, high IFT to other affiliates, and high intrafirm purchases from parents. Year-to-year changes are calculated at the affiliate level.

Focusing on panel two in table 10.3, there are no obvious differences in employment growth between the development categories. Further, we see no systematic differences in employment growth within development categories. Although the point estimates are generally higher for employment growth of affiliates with high intrafirm sales to other affiliates and high intrafirm purchases from US parents, only about half of these are significantly different from the average employment growth for the relevant development group.

In contrast, real PPE growth is consistently higher for affiliates that export goods intrafirm. Note, in particular, that affiliates with high intrafirm sales to parents and sales to other affiliates have significantly higher PPE growth than the average for the relevant development group. Affiliates with high intrafirm sales to US parents have higher real PPE growth in the full sample and in four of the five development groups. Affiliates with high intrafirm sales to other affiliates have higher real PPE growth in all development groups and in the full sample. Only affiliates with high intrafirm purchases from US parents do not differ significantly from their development group in real PPE growth.

Discussion of Results

The descriptive statistics highlight the following interesting characteristics of affiliate activity. Focusing on affiliates in the developing country subsample, IFT is increasing rapidly as a percent of affiliate sales. Affiliates tend to trade more bilaterally with US parents than with other affiliates. However, affiliate-to-affiliate IFT doubled as a percent of affiliate sales between 1983 and 1996.

In the developing-country subsample, affiliates with high IFT flows are quite different from affiliates that do not trade intrafirm. Affiliates with high IFT/sales tend to be larger, and have generally higher real wages and PPE growth than affiliates that have no IFT. Affiliates with high IFT tend to have larger US parents with greater international activity (as measured either by number of affiliates in the network or by total foreign affiliate sales).

We also find evidence that, for high-trade affiliates, the direction of the IFT flow (i.e., to other affiliates, *from* parents, *to* parents) seems to have systematic consequences for affiliate organization and technology. For example, affiliates with high IFT to other affiliates have a much smaller labor share (as a percent of sales) than affiliates with high IFT to US parents—approximately

16 percent versus 25 percent, respectively. Similarly, affiliates with high intrafirm sales to US parents (as a percent of total sales) actually have lower real wages on average than affiliates with no IFT to parents. In contrast, affiliates with high intrafirm *purchases* from US parents have the highest real wages of any group of affiliates.

Finally, compared with affiliates with high affiliate-to-affiliate trade, affiliates that trade extensively with US parents (in either direction) come from MNCs with a smaller network of much larger affiliates. Again, the direction of trade flows seems to matter not only to the organization of the affiliate itself, but to the configuration of the MNC.

Conclusion

The descriptive nature of our study raises many questions. Are the observed differences in affiliate and MNC structure explained by industry? In an earlier study (Feinberg and Keane 2001), we find evidence of substantial *within*-industry variation in the degree to which MNCs are organized to trade intrafirm. However, we do not know if this holds in a developing-country context.

What explains the different characteristics of affiliates that have high levels of a particular IFT flow? Are goods traded intrafirm among affiliates more likely to be of the "horizontal" variety (i.e., differentiated products) while the goods traded intrafirm between affiliates and parents are more likely to be "vertical" intermediate goods? What explains the different characteristics of affiliates that have high sales to parents versus high purchases from parents? It may seem surprising, in light of anecdotes about low-value-added "screwdriver" plants in developing countries, that affiliates that *import* more from US parents have such high real wages. Are these imports technology- or capital-intensive goods?

Clearly, MNC affiliates that trade intrafirm are organized differently from affiliates that produce primarily for sales in the local market. We believe that IFT may be an indicator of a substantively different kind of technological configuration in the local market—one that may be more likely to generate "spillovers." This integration may be even more important than FDI, per se, in the sense that best practices may come from investment in technology within the firm, or from closer vertical linkages between unrelated and geographically distant firms, as has been documented in the auto industry.[10]

---

10. Moran (2001, 17) studied the effect of Japanese FDI in Thailand's auto industry. He notes that many Thai auto parts manufacturers with no ownership ties to Japanese firms received technical assistance from buyers in the course of achieving original equipment manufacturer certification. This example has two important implications for research on spillovers. First, the industries of the MNCs and the firms benefiting from "spillovers" may differ. In this ex-

In the international business literature, Kobrin (1991) suggests that IFT in goods likely signals the presence of greater knowledge flows within the firm. This is strongly supported by Moran (2001; also see chapter 11 in this volume). It seems reasonable to expect that foreign affiliates engaged in such activities may be better sources of knowledge transfer than foreign-owned firms whose practices are essentially indistinguishable from domestic firms.

IFT is only one source of heterogeneity in MNC activity that seems relevant to the issue of whether FDI is beneficial to host countries. Given how diverse the activities of MNC affiliates are in host countries, we argue that using variables such as "foreign market share" to capture this activity not only results in noisy measures, but obscures the mechanisms through which knowledge is transferred (see Keane, in the commentary for section I in this volume).

To advance the literature on FDI spillovers, the questions "What kind of FDI?" and "What is the nature of MNC activity in the local market?" need to be addressed. Researchers with micro panel data on MNCs and local firms might start by considering a priori important sources of heterogeneity and the mechanisms through which these might affect knowledge transfers. Javorcik's (2004) examination of spillovers between firms with buyer-supplier linkages is an example of such a study. Moreover, Javorcik and Spatareanu's (chapter 3 in this volume) survey on managers' perceptions of the effect of MNC activity (in the same sector) on their firms' performance also sheds light on mechanisms through which knowledge is transferred between MNCs and local firms.

From a policy standpoint, IFT appears to be an important development issue in the sense that affiliates that trade intrafirm are generally growing faster and paying higher real wages than affiliates that do not trade intrafirm. Additionally, MNCs' increasing use of IFT in production implies that the macro effects of changes in exchange rates may be more difficult to predict. If US MNCs are engaging in bilateral IFT to produce finished goods for the US market, it is not clear how their operations would be affected by real appreciations or depreciations of the dollar.

Finally, in a recent working paper (Feinberg and Keane 2004), we find that IFT is relatively insensitive to trade liberalization and other price changes.

---

ample, autos and auto parts are closely related. However, many other less obvious industries also supply the auto industry (e.g., chemicals, rubber, paints, etc.). Firms in these industries may also receive similar technical assistance from foreign firms. Second, vertical relationships between unaffiliated firms may be more important than FDI for "spillovers" to occur. In the extreme, one could imagine a scenario in which Japanese auto makers give technical assistance to Thai parts suppliers without the former having any physical investment in Thailand. In such a case, close integration between local and foreign firms may transfer more knowledge than foreign presence in the local market.

This is consistent with Das, Roberts, and Tybout's (2001) findings on the relative insensitivity of firm exports to different trade policy regimes. This implies that it would probably not be useful from a policy standpoint to undertake direct measures to try to encourage FDI by MNCs that trade intrafirm. Instead, the optimal policy mix may be a liberal trade and FDI regime in which MNCs could organize production most efficiently.

References

Bernard, Andrew, and J. Bradford Jensen. 2001. *Why Some Firms Export*. NBER Working Paper 8349. Cambridge, MA: National Bureau of Economic Research.

Das, Sanghamitra, Mark Roberts, and James Tybout. 2001. *Market Entry Costs, Producer Heterogeneity, and Export Dynamics*. NBER Working Paper 8629. Cambridge, MA: National Bureau of Economic Research.

Feinberg, Susan E., and Anil K. Gupta. 2004. Knowledge Spillovers and the Assignment of R&D Responsibilities to Foreign Subsidiaries. *Strategic Management Journal* 25: 823–45.

Feinberg, Susan E., and Michael P. Keane. 2001. US-Canada Trade Liberalization and MNC Production Location. *The Review of Economics and Statistics* 83, no. 1 (February): 118–32.

Feinberg, Susan E., and Michael P. Keane. 2004. *Tariff Effects on MNC Organization*. Working Paper.

Feinberg, Susan E., and Michael P. Keane. 2005. *Accounting for the Growth of MNC-based Trade Using a Structural Model of US MNCs*. Working Paper.

Feinberg, Susan E., Michael P. Keane, Mario F. Bognanno. 1998. Trade Liberalization and Delocalization: New Evidence from Firm-Level Panel Data. *Canadian Journal of Economics* 31, no. 4 (October): 749–77.

Javorcik, Beata Smarzynska. 2004. Does Foreign Direct Investment Increase the Productivity of Domestic Firms? In Search of Spillovers Through Backward Linkages. *American Economic Review* 94 (3): 605–27.

Kobrin, Steven J. 1991. An Empirical Analysis of the Determinants of Global Integration. *Strategic Management Journal* 12 (Summer): 17–32.

Kokko, Ari. 1994. Technology, Market Characteristics and Spillovers. *Journal of Development Economics* 43 no. 2: 279–93.

Kokko, Ari, Ruben Tansini, and Mario C. Zejan. 1996. Local Technology Capability and Productivity Spillovers from FDI in the Uruguayan Manufacturing Sector. *Journal of Development Studies* 32, no. 4: 602–11.

Moran, Theodore H. 2001. *Parental Supervision: The New Paradigm for Foreign Direct Investment and Development*. POLICY ANALYSES IN INTERNATIONAL ECONOMICS 64. Washington: Institute for International Economics.

Roberts, Mark J., and James R. Tybout. 1997. The Decision to Export in Colombia: An Empirical Model of Entry with Sunk Costs. *American Economic Review* 87: no. 4 (September): 545–64.

Zeile, W. J. 1997. US Intrafirm Trade in Goods. *Survey of Current Business* (US Department of Commerce) 77, no. 2 (February): 23–38.

Appendix 10.1　Countries in each development subsample

Country	Development category	Country	Development category
Australia	1	Malaysia	3
Austria	1	Mexico	3
Belgium	1	Oman	3
Brunei	1	Panama	3
Canada	1	Poland	3
Denmark	1	Russian Federation	3
Finland	1	Thailand	3
France	1	Trinidad and Tobago	3
Germany	1	Turkey	3
Hong Kong	1	Uruguay	3
Italy	1	Venezuela	3
Japan	1	Bolivia	4
Luxembourg	1	Colombia	4
Netherlands	1	Côte d'Ivoire	4
New Zealand	1	Dominican Republic	4
Norway	1	Egypt, Arab Republic	4
Singapore	1	El Salvador	4
Sweden	1	Gabon	4
Switzerland	1	Guatemala	4
United Arab Emirates	1	Indonesia	4
United Kingdom	1	Jamaica	4
Bahrain	2	Lebanon	4
Cyprus	2	Morocco	4
Greece	2	Papua New Guinea	4
Ireland	2	Peru	4
Israel	2	Philippines	4
Korea, Republic of	2	South Africa	4
Kuwait	2	Tunisia	4
Portugal	2	Cameroon	5
Saudi Arabia	2	China, People's Republic of	5
Spain	2	Haiti	5
Argentina	3	Honduras	5
Bahamas	3	India	5
Barbados	3	Kenya	5
Brazil	3	Liberia	5
Chile	3	Nicaragua	5
Costa Rica	3	Nigeria	5
Czech Republic	3	Pakistan	5
Ecuador	3	Zambia	5
Hungary	3	Zimbabwe	5

Note: Industrialized countries are development categories 1 and 2; developing countries are development categories 3, 4, and 5.

Comment

MARC J. MELITZ

In parallel to the trade and growth debate, a related research agenda has analyzed the cross-country linkages between foreign direct investment (FDI) and development. The two chapters by Blonigen and Wang and Carkovic and Levine offer new insights into this momentous debate. At first glance, these chapters could be summarized as reaching opposite conclusions concerning the impact of FDI on development. However, I will argue that the main findings in both chapters can be reconciled into a unified assessment of the cross-country links between FDI and development.

Before turning to the potential impact of FDI on development, Blonigen and Wang analyze the cross-country determinants of FDI. They focus on the fundamental differences in the processes governing the location and effects of FDI between developed and developing countries. As they report in some initial descriptive statistics, almost all of the world's FDI originates from parent companies in developed countries (with a minor exception for some FDI flows between countries in Southeast Asia). Most of this investment is also located in other developed countries. Such investments are predominantly driven by foreign market access and classified as "horizontal" FDI: the entire manufacturing process (but not necessarily the distribution/retailing of the good) is reproduced in a foreign location in proximity to major foreign markets. However, a substantial and growing amount of FDI now also flows to developing countries. Some of this investment undoubtedly also reflects horizontal FDI in the big (and growing) developing markets. Yet, another form

Marc J. Melitz is associate professor of economics at Harvard University and researcher at the National Bureau of Economic Research and the Centre for Economic Policy Research.

of "vertical" FDI is also prominent in developing countries: such investment reflects the breakup of the production chain into processes with different factor intensities. The unskilled labor–intensive production processes are then located in low-wage (hence, developing) countries. These foreign-owned production facilities often import intermediate inputs from their parents and reexport most—in some cases all—of their output.

Given the fundamental differences between horizontal and vertical FDI, it is, therefore, natural to expect these different types of FDI to be attracted by different country characteristics and then engender different consequences for the local economy. Blonigen and Wang show that this is indeed the case. Given their availability, data on US outward and inward FDI are commonly used for cross-country studies. Among such data, only the US outward FDI to developing countries would capture a substantial proportion of vertical FDI. Blonigen and Wang show that this distinction is important when analyzing the determinants of US outward FDI. In particular, theoretical models predict that a country's level of development (and hence its relative skill abundance) will have opposite effects on its ability to attract horizontal and vertical FDI: Lower skill abundance (entailing lower labor costs for unskilled labor–intensive processes) would attract vertical FDI but simultaneously make horizontal (market access–seeking) FDI less attractive. These predictions are confirmed by Blonigen and Wang: US outward FDI to developed countries (predominantly horizontal FDI) is strongly attracted to countries with higher skill abundance.[1] However, this effect is reversed for US outward FDI to developing countries—although this overall effect is not statistically significant.

In any event, Blonigen and Wang clearly show that a country's skill abundance has a very different impact on the FDI pattern of US firms in developing countries relative to developed countries. This difference is both economically and statistically significant. Furthermore, the overall insignificant effect of skill abundance on FDI location for developing countries can be attributed to the combined measurement of both horizontal and vertical FDI (which respond in opposite ways to skill abundance) in some developing countries. This effect is confirmed by Yeaple (2003), whose study finds that US outward FDI in unskilled labor–intensive sectors (most likely to represent vertical FDI) is significantly higher in less skill abundant countries. However, these countries also attract significantly less US FDI in skilled labor–intensive sectors (most likely to represent horizontal FDI).

The effect of a country's skill abundance on its acquisition of US outward vertical FDI has also been more directly substantiated in a recent

---

1. To conform to some previous work, Blonigen and Wang use a measure of skill difference with the United States as their independent variable. It should be noted that, when US outward FDI is separated from US inward FDI (as is the case here), the effect of this variable is identical to one measuring the negative of the recipient country's skill abundance measure: the effect of US skill abundance is subsumed in the regression constant.

study by Hanson, Mataloni, and Slaughter (2003). They use a much more direct gauge of vertical FDI, measured as the share of a US affiliate's cost spent on imported (from the US) intermediate inputs for further processing. They find that such a measure significantly responds to differences in the wages of unskilled workers across countries: countries with lower unskilled wages attract disproportionately more of this vertical FDI. More importantly, for the subsequent analysis of FDI and economic growth, Hanson, Mataloni, and Slaughter (2003) also find that this measure of vertical FDI strongly and significantly responds to lower trade barriers: vertical FDI increases with the presence of export processing zones, lower trade costs (by sector), and proximity to the United States (the location of the parent company). This confirms the prediction of theoretical models of vertical FDI: trade is a needed complement for this type of FDI, as intermediate inputs are imported by the affiliate and the processed product must then be reexported. In contrast, horizontal FDI mainly serves as a substitute for trade: affiliate production and sales replace export sales from the parent's domestic production facilities.

Turning to the effect of FDI on growth, Blonigen and Wang investigate the cross-country relationship between decade averages of total FDI inflows and per capita GDP growth. Since they have data for only two decades (the 1970s and 1980s), they cannot control for unobserved country characteristics that are correlated with inward FDI (a fixed-effects specification). Therefore, they investigate the effects of observed country characteristics, controlling for those unobserved characteristics that are uncorrelated with FDI (the random-effects specification). Blonigen and Wang find that a country's level of development and education are very important controls: inward FDI has a statistically significant effect on growth only for those developing countries above a certain education level. This clearly demonstrates a correlation— among developing countries with higher education levels—between FDI levels and economic growth.

As with the trade and growth debate, a nagging question over causation persists. In particular, could some unobserved country characteristics be driving both FDI flows and growth? Carkovic and Levine address this issue by using a longer time series (35 years from 1960 to 1995 averaged over 5-year intervals) and new panel data estimation techniques. Their Generalized Method of Moments (GMM) estimation controls for such unobserved country characteristics (including those correlated with FDI inflows) as well as the endogeneity of other regressors (in particular, the use of initial per capita GDP as a control). Their baseline results, including controls for initial per capita GDP, skill abundance, inflation, and government size confirm the findings of Blonigen and Wang: the significant correlation between FDI and growth persists after controlling for unobserved country characteristics. Put differently, within countries, above (historical) average levels of FDI are significantly correlated with above average growth rates. Carkovic and Levine reach negative conclusions about the link between

FDI and growth based upon the results including controls for trade openness (either directly or via the black market premium) and domestic financial credit. Carkovic and Levine then show that the independent effect of
FDI is no longer significant. Although these subsequent results impose
some strong qualifications on the relationship between FDI and growth,
I disagree with the authors' final assessment on the absence of such a link.

As I previously noted, vertical FDI and trade are necessary complements
and are thus jointly determined by a country's overall policy toward international trade and investment (as well as other country-specific factors).
Changes in the latter would then move both vertical FDI and trade in the
same direction. Carkovic and Levine's results suggest that such joint
changes in both FDI and trade are significantly correlated with growth.
Thus, increases in FDI that are associated with increases in trade (as theory
predicts should be the case for vertical FDI in developing countries) lead
to higher growth rates. In this qualified interpretation, the link between
FDI and growth remains present. Nevertheless, this interpretation should
be applied cautiously: as Carkovic and Levine point out, there is no evidence that increases in FDI alone (not associated with increases in trade)
lead to higher growth rates. How should one interpret such independent
changes in FDI, especially in developing countries, and why do they not
contribute separately to economic growth?

Moran's chapter in this volume provides some illuminating answers by
carefully studying different policies toward foreign investment in developing countries. He documents how certain countries (in certain sectors and
time periods) bundle FDI policies with restrictive and burdensome regulations concerning affiliate ownership (e.g., forbidding majority ownership,
and imposing joint ventures), domestic content requirements, onerous (rent
shifting) taxes, and import barriers. These policies are often designed for
import substitution, where the foreign-owned plant is restricted to serve the
protected domestic market. Moran further documents how these restrictive
policies hinder or even preclude the integration of the foreign-owned affiliate into the parent's international sourcing network, leading to substantial
performance penalties (e.g., smaller plant size, worse efficiency and quality, lower investment) relative to foreign affiliates in developing countries
with more liberal policies toward FDI. It is therefore not surprising to expect
these different policies to substantially affect or even reverse the links
between FDI and growth. In addition, these liberal investment policies also
lead to joint increases in FDI and trade, as the affiliates integrated into their
parent's network import intermediates from, and reexport back to, this
network. However, increases in FDI in countries with restrictive investment policies will not be associated with increases in trade—and may
even be linked with decreases in trade as imports are substituted with
affiliate production.

Naturally, more formal econometric evidence is needed to confirm that
such overly restrictive investment policies are behind the subaverage per-

formance of developing countries that attract FDI without concurrently increasing their trade levels. At the same time, the evidence presented by Carkovic and Levine still supports—but does not confirm—the view that increases in vertical FDI associated with increases in trade (which supports the foreign affiliate's integration into the parent's international network) are linked to higher growth rates. As with the trade and growth literature, the evidence on these links between FDI and development leaves enough room for some fairly different interpretations. Blonigen and Wang contribute to this literature by showing how developing countries attract different types of multinational activity than developed countries, and that this multinational activity is correlated with higher growth rates in developing countries that attain certain education threshold levels. Carkovic and Levine further contribute to this debate by showing that this correlation is not driven by unobserved country characteristics. Nevertheless, they also show that independent increases in FDI inflows are not likely to enhance growth. Countries experiencing concurrent increases in FDI, trade, and domestic credit are the most likely to enjoy the largest growth-enhancing benefits. Identifying the right mix of policies that generate such changes remains a crucial—and hotly debated—area for further research.

References

Hanson, Gordon H., Raymond J. Mataloni, and Matthew J. Slaughter. 2003. *Vertical Production Networks in Multinational Firms.* NBER Working Paper 9723. Cambridge, MA: National Bureau of Economic Research.

Yeaple, Stephen R. 2003. The Role of Skill Endowments in the Structure of US Outward Foreign Direct Investment. *Review of Economics and Statistics* 85, no. 3 (August): 726–34.

III

DESIGNING POLICIES TO CAPTURE BENEFICIAL EFFECTS

11

How Does FDI Affect Host Country Development? Using Industry Case Studies to Make Reliable Generalizations

THEODORE H. MORAN

One dollar of FDI is worth no more (and no less) than a dollar of any other kind of investment.

—Dani Rodrik (2003)[1]

Volkswagen requires that plants producing the four components of the 'basic vehicle plat-form' (engines, axles, chassis, and gear boxes), which the parent manufactures separately from assembly sites in Brazil, Mexico, Argentina, and Eastern Europe, be designed to receive simultaneous engineering improvements online within 16 hours of each other.

—Kristian Ehinger (1999)

As with the studies of wage and productivity spillovers, those of the effects of FDI inflow on economic growth are inconclusive . . . one cannot say from these studies that there are uni-versal effects.

—Robert E. Lipsey (2002)

What is the impact of foreign direct investment (FDI) in manufacturing and assembly on host countries in the developing world? When do the opera-tions of foreign manufacturing and assembly firms have the most positive impact on the growth and welfare of the host economy? When do they have the least positive—or possibly negative—impact? What policies should those host countries that want to maximize the benefits, and avoid the haz-ards, from FDI adopt?

This chapter begins by examining the answers I derived from an initial set of industry case studies in a limited number of countries. The third sec-

Theodore H. Moran is Marcus Wallenberg Professor of International Business and Finance at the School of Foreign Service, Georgetown University.

1. Dani Rodrik, Appel Inaugural Lecture, Columbia University, March 27, 2003.

tion probes how robust and generalizable the observations contained in those case studies appear to be. The fourth section then investigates why other approaches have failed to come to the same conclusions. Sections five and six conclude with suggestions for further research, with implications for policies toward FDI and development.

Initial Answers from a Limited Number of Case Studies

When the Institute for International Economics first asked me to investigate the impact of nonextractive FDI on development, I chose to focus on the two industries—the automotive industry and the high-performance electronics industry (e.g., computers, telecommunications equipment, and semiconductors)—where flows of FDI have been among the largest in the manufacturing sector and where globalization of production has been most extensive (Moran 1998). The countries where the industry analysis was most thorough included Mexico, Brazil, and Thailand for the automotive industry, and Mexico, Malaysia, and Thailand for high-performance electronics.

The advantage of selecting case studies of these industries in these countries was that the empirical sources were most probing and the detail extraordinarily rich. The disadvantage, of course, was that the results might not be generalizable, might be misleading, or might be useless—as the story of the proverbial drunk, searching for lost car keys under the lamppost because the light there was best, constantly warns.

These investigations showed that a fundamental difference in performance exists between subsidiaries that are integrated into the global or regional sourcing networks of the parent multinationals, and subsidiaries that are oriented toward protected domestic markets and prevented by mandatory joint venture and domestic content requirements from being so integrated. They differ in terms of size of plant, proximity of technology and quality control procedures to the international frontier, rapidity with which technology and quality control procedures are upgraded, efficiency of operations, and cost of output.

FDI to Build an Integrated Corporate Supplier Network

When the international auto and electronics companies built plants upon whose operations their competitive position in international markets depended, the parent companies designed them to capture all economies of scale and used cutting-edge technology and quality control techniques. They insisted upon whole or majority ownership, and upon freedom from mandatory local content requirements. From a dynamic perspective, the parent companies upgraded technology and quality control procedures on a continuous near-real-time basis, a process (by their own testimony) that served the larger corporate self-interest.

The popular term "outsourcing," which seems to imply shopping around for cheap inputs, fails to capture the potent interaction between parent and subsidiary when the fate of the former depends upon the performance of the latter. Engines produced at the General Motors (GM) export plants in Brazil were designed to be interchangeable with engines produced at the Pontiac plant in upstate New York. Engines produced at Ford export plants in Brazil were perfect substitutes for engines manufactured in Lima, Ohio and received the company's highest quality rating. Foreign-owned telecommunications and semiconductor plants in Malaysia incorporated high precision manufacturing and quality control techniques as soon as they were developed: "As far as assembly and testing are concerned," observed a Texas Instruments executive, "We have more expertise here than we have in the US" (Lim and Eng Fong 1991, 115). Once Mexico acceded to IBM's demand for 100 percent ownership, the parent built an export-oriented plant supplying its western hemisphere network nine times larger than any other computer plant in the protected domestic market.

The foreign investors in these industries provided jobs paying more than other employers, and generated millions—sometimes billions—of dollars worth of exports. To anticipate an area of controversy that will become important in the fourth section's assessment of appropriate and inappropriate ways to measure the impact of FDI on the host economy, multinational auto firm exports of vehicles and parts from Mexico grew from a very small base in the mid-1970s to some $7 billion in 2000, for example, with employment reaching more than 354,000, remunerated at a level second only to the petroleum sector.

With regard to backward linkages and spillovers, the automotive and electronics multinationals in Mexico, Brazil, Malaysia, and Thailand assiduously avoided horizontal technology transfer, insisting upon whole or majority ownership of their plants to keep what they called "leakage" of technology and management procedures to a minimum. In the vertical direction, however, they worked closely with suppliers in the host country (foreign-owned and indigenously owned suppliers) to increase those suppliers' productivity, ensure low rejection rates for their inputs, generate lower prices, improve management, and build team spirit.[2]

More than 400 auto parts producers in Mexico, Brazil, and Thailand qualified—under foreign investor supervision—for Original Equipment Manufacturer (OEM) or Replacement Equipment Manufacturer (REM)

---

2. As Javorcik and Spatareanu point out in this volume, some aspects of the foreign investor–host supplier relationship fall easily into the category of direct assistance (such as advance payment and financing); other aspects might be better characterized as a "positive productivity shock" (such as having to pass a technical audit or acquire ISO 9000 quality certification to win a supplier contract).

status (Peres Nuñez 1990; Doner, Noble, and Ravenhill 2002). Almost without exception the most prominent indigenous electronic-component producers in Thailand and Malaysia originated as contract manufacturers to foreign plants, with production-to-spec leading to joint design of a growing array of inputs. Early country studies complained about a lack of backward linkages, with later reports documenting the spread of contract manufacturing among suppliers (Lim and Eng Fong 1991; Ernst 1999). The evidence supports the contention that foreign investors take time to learn how to take advantage of potential suppliers, and that local businesses must pass certain basic thresholds to qualify.

The backward linkages from foreign investors into the host economy extended to supporting industries as well as input suppliers: seven of the nine largest machine tool manufacturers in Malaysia began by providing tooling services to the international telecommunications and semiconductor investors; each of their founders started their careers as local managers at the foreign plants, and 10 percent of their workers had prior experience as employees (Rasiah 1995).

To help host country suppliers achieve economies of scale, the foreign automotive or electronics investors sometimes provided export coaching, a process that began with sales to sister subsidiaries of the investors but led some indigenous firms to penetrate international markets on their own. In Malaysia, QDOS Microcircuits, for example, got started as a supplier to Motorola, won contracts for similar products from the affiliates of Siemens and Hewlett-Packard in Penang, added sales to factories owned by these three multinationals in Thailand and Indonesia, and then began to export to other buyers in the Southeast Asia region.

FDI to Serve a Protected Host-Country Market

Foreign investment flows oriented toward serving protected host country markets offer a much different picture. The automotive plants in Mexico, Brazil, and Thailand built to accommodate the import substitution (IS) policies of the host authorities were one-tenth—or less—the size of assembly lines built to capture all economies of scale. They did not employ the same production processes as assemblers producing output for world markets; instead, they put together completely knocked-down (CKD) or semiknocked-down (SKD) "kits" of automotive components. The automotive plants did not and could not use the same automated technologies and quality control procedures as world-class plants, substituting hand welding for precision computer-assisted welding. Their production costs were 30–80 percent higher than the full-scale assemblers. The term "tariff jumping investment," which might imply replication of plants of similar size and sophistication across borders, does not adequately capture the dissimilarities in management and production processes.

These projects did pay higher than average host country manufacturing wages, but creating employment in the local economy came at a high price: the cost per job created in the protected market ran as high as $300,000 apiece.

However, the small size and inefficient production techniques did not necessarily mean that the parent corporations found foreign investment in the protected host market to be unappealing, or unprofitable. Chrysler's Mexican affiliate during that country's IS phase was the corporation's most profitable operation in the world, and the parent fought *against* the liberalization of the Mexican automotive sector in order to preserve what its managers described as a "cash cow" (Samuels 1990, 148).

In high-performance electronics, Mexico also provides detailed information about the characteristics of plants designed to comply with a protectionist informatics regime prior to the liberalization of 1985. As in the automotive sector, the IS plants of Hewlett-Packard, Compaq, Apple, and other foreign investors again were boutique operations. Required to accept a Mexican joint venture partner and to meet specific levels of local content, the foreign affiliates produced computers two and three years behind the newest models in the United States—a strategy deliberately aimed at reaping a second round of oligopoly rents from previous-generation products without fear of turning local partners into rivals or being challenged by imports of newer and cheaper substitutes—for prices 130–170 percent of the external price (Harvard Business School 1990). The miniature dimensions of the assembly processes prevented the joint venture (JV) companies from using the most advanced high-precision construction of circuit boards and "large batch" quality control monitoring.

In both the automotive and the electronics industries, the small size of the protected plants constrained the generation of backward linkages. Throughout the country's IS period, upstream auto parts suppliers in Mexico were concentrated in simple operations where scale economies were small (e.g., springs, coils, and stamped plastic articles) and not in operations requiring larger production runs to be efficient (e.g., catalytic converters, fuel injection assemblies, or exhaust systems) (Peres Nuñez 1990). Computer component companies in Mexico resorted to hand soldering of connections rather than automated assembly techniques. To meet domestic content requirements, Hewlett-Packard and Compaq had to settle for local purchases of fiberglass housings for their computers, because the operations of Mexican suppliers were not large enough to support the use of advanced plastics and composites.

For both economic and technological reasons, attracting foreign investment to serve a protected local market failed to serve as an effective infant industry strategy. The plants built to replace imports of autos or computers could not be used as building blocks for launching internationally competitive operations. Creating a viable host country base in each industry required the construction of new plants with new and different assembly lines and quality control procedures—plants that the parent investors insisted be wholly owned and free from specific restrictions on the sourcing of inputs.

Once Mexico approved IBM's proposal to operate a wholly owned facility (allowing Hewlett-Packard to shed its Mexican partner as well), and eliminated specific domestic content requirements, for example, the interaction between foreign affiliate size and potential for backward integration became apparent: both companies built cutting-edge export-oriented plants approximately nine times larger than any previous facility and began to purchase larger amounts of local inputs than they did when required to meet domestic content targets. The degree of integration within the domestic industry actually increased as imports as a percentage of host country production declined (Peres Nuñez 1990).

On the basis of these case studies of the automotive and electronics industries, which focused on the experiences of four countries, I concluded that FDI that was integrated into the global sourcing network of the parent multinationals would provide diverse positive impacts on the host economy (see the fifth section for a schematic inventory of positive impacts, some of which include externalities and some of which do not). I also concluded that FDI that was oriented toward protected domestic markets and prevented from being integrated into the parent's global sourcing network by mandatory joint venture and domestic content requirements would not have such a positive effect (or would be much less beneficial).

How generalizable are the observations from these case studies, and how reliable are the conclusions about when FDI is most likely to make a strong positive contribution and when it is not?

Avoiding Selection Bias and Allowing Generalization from Country and Industry Case Studies

Case study analysis is often referred to as "anecdotal" evidence, suggesting that lessons drawn might be easily discredited or disproved by any other handful of observations. Moreover, the small and specially selected number of observations—as indicated earlier—may provide misleading suggestions about what is occurring more generally. It is important, therefore, to expand the number of observations and to take careful precautions to check for selection bias (King, Keohane, and Verba 1994; Scarbrough and Tanenbaum 1998; George and Bennett 2004). To accomplish this I examined the extent to which the same outcomes seem to occur in the same industries in different countries and over different periods of time. Next, I tried to investigate the extent to which the same outcomes seem to occur in other industries.

If the findings in the case studies appear to be supported by similar results across geography and time as well as in observations from the same industry and observations from other industries—complete with similar testimony about the motivation for the different outcomes and backed by solid theoretical models to explain the "good" and "bad" outcomes—then it should be reasonable to conclude that the case study findings can be considered quite robust.[3]

But this still leaves open the question of why other researchers using other methodologies do not report similar results—a puzzle to be addressed after first assessing the generalizability of the original case study analysis.

Comparing the Experience of Automotive Investors in Different Countries and Over Different Periods of Time

In the automotive industry the earliest observations of the contrast in size of plant, type of technology, degree of productivity, and relative cost between foreign investors producing for protected host country markets and plants oriented to international markets begin in the 1970s and extend to the contemporary period.[4] They derive from Latin America and Southeast Asia as well as from Eastern Europe and South Africa.

In her classic study of import substitution in the Indian automobile industry in 1975, Anne Krueger discovered that foreign automotive firms were operating with much smaller size and much lower efficiency than companies producing for world markets (Krueger 1975). Of those studied, 27 of 34 assemblers and associated suppliers required effective levels of protection of 50 percent to remain in business.

In a survey of 16 countries with protected auto industries in the mid-1980s, Bale and Walters (1986) found plants that were consistently less than half the size of developed-country assembly operations. The size penalty, coupled with mandatory domestic content requirements, led to price levels 1.5 to 2 times higher than the cost of imports. Over the course of the 1980s, the differentiation of production technologies between full-scale assembly operations with increasing levels of automation, and boutique fabrication of SKD and CKD "kits," became standard throughout the industry.

The penalties in efficiency from small plant size and kit assembly technology have not changed over time. In 1992 GM built a new 15,000-car-per-year plant to serve the Hungarian domestic market (Klein 1995). Its CKD production line peaked with an output of 8 Opels per hour in 1995, in comparison to 90 vehicles per hour in the company's full-scale assembly operations (200,000 units per year) elsewhere in Europe. The plant required a 22.5 percent tariff, plus other subsidies, to remain profitable.

---

3. The summary of evidence that follows amplifies what was first reported in Moran (2001).

4. In this volume, Robert Lipsey and Fredrik Sjöholm point out that putting in controls for scale of operation in microdata regressions may conceal the advantages that foreign firms operating with international sourcing networks have to offer. The same might be true of controls for other operating characteristics.

Evidence from Turkey and Indonesia reinforces the demonstration of the negative effects of using FDI for import substitution in the automotive sector (Okamoto and Sjöholm 2000; Basri, Aswicahyono, and Hill 2000; Erdilek 1982).

The boutique plants that Mitsubishi and Daewoo built in Vietnam in 1995 with designated Vietnamese partners required that each automobile body be assembled individually from 30 to 100 components that arrived in containers, with the parts temporarily held together with jigs as they were hand-welded (Ngo and Conklin 1996, app. 3).[5] The engine, transmission, seats, and other interior parts were placed by hand in the auto body. This contrasted with home country plants in Japan and South Korea that feature highly automated assembly lines in which robots perform much of the welding and assembly. To make the Vietnamese kit assembly viable required tariff protection of 200 percent. Despite a legal requirement to increase domestic content by 5 percent each year, the proportion of local goods and services used in vehicle manufacturing had reached only 10 percent by 2002, limited to "simple technology chains" for welding, painting, and installation (*Vietnam Investment Review* 2002).

In a background study of the Association of Southeast Asian Nations' (ASEAN) proposed Common Effective Preferential Tariff (CEPT) regime, the Japan Research Institute estimated that a small car imported from an ASEAN neighbor at a price of $16,500 would cost $34,340 if assembled from a CKD kit at one of the joint venture plants in Vietnam.[6]

South Africa presents a "before-and-after" picture as import substitution was replaced by export promotion as the basic strategy toward FDI in the automotive sector. During the period of economic isolation associated with apartheid, South Africa experienced problems of high cost and low productivity at domestic car assembly plants (Henri E. Cauvin, "A Quest to Promote the Quality of Cars Made in South Africa," *The New York Times*, November 24, 2001). After the election of Nelson Mandela, DaimlerChrysler, BMW, and Volkswagen (VW) took the decision to make South Africa a world production center to serve the right-hand driving markets of Australia, Japan, and the United Kingdom with the Mercedes-Benz C-Class sedan, the BMW 3-Series sedan, and the VW Golf 4 hatchback.

To "make the leap from a low-volume accident of history to a high-volume asset of the future" (quoted from Cauvin's article) required building highly automated production lines that reduced the number of hours needed

---

5. It is important to note the difference between foreign direct investors freely choosing a local partner to help penetrate a host country market, and foreign direct investors required to form a joint venture as a condition of entry. Multinational corporations (MNCs) frequently partner with a local firm to help penetrate a local economy, and then take full control if they decide to incorporate the host site into the parent's internal sourcing network.

6. "Vietnam Auto Industry Gears Up for CEPT," Japan Research Institute, February 6, 2003 at *asia.news* (accessed June 16, 2004).

to build a car from 100 to less than 60. As for quality, to ensure that each Mercedes rolling off the assembly line in East London was "every bit as good as those coming out of the plant at Bremen, Germany," DaimlerChrysler reported sending hundreds of workers to Germany for training, flying in dozens of experts from Germany, and spending millions of dollars on vocational instruction. Ford took complete ownership of its local subsidiary and designated South Africa as the sole production site for one engine line. Other foreign-owned parts exports expanded as well, led by plants producing catalytic converters.

Anticipating the end of tariff protection with Hungary's accession to the European Union, GM simply shut down its small Opel kit assembly plant in 1999 rather than undertake the major new investment associated with constructing a world-scale assembly site (Kalotay 2002). Instead, GM concentrated on export-oriented manufacture of engines, cylinder heads, and gearboxes for inclusion in the Opel model assembled in Germany, Spain, and Britain, reaching a capacity of more than 800,000 units per year in 2002. To ensure that the Hungarian components were indistinguishable from other parts in the parent's supply chain, operations at the GM plant were designed to accept continuous real-time changes and improvements without having to rebuild the production line. To qualify for employment, Hungarian workers were required to pass a 12-week course in quality control. Hungarian managers were rotated through other GM plants in Europe as part of their promotion cycle.

GM entered Hungary as majority shareholder (67 percent) in a joint venture with a local parts producer (Raba) and the Hungarian State Development Institute. As GM abandoned local kit assembly and expanded the operations supplying components for the parent's EU supply network, the company bought out its partners and terminated the relationships. GM showed the same preference for complete control over operations when the parent solicited bids for the first auto assembly plant to serve the entire Southeast Asia region, insisting that the winning host country—which turned out to be Thailand—allow the venture to be wholly owned. In both Eastern Europe and Southeast Asia GM required that export-oriented plants be free from domestic content requirements.

In China, the requirement that foreign investors operate with a local partner led to the use of production processes during the 1990s that were, by industry estimates, an average of ten years behind the frontier of best practices (*Wall Street Journal*, February 11, 1998, 1). According to Chrysler, the refusal of foreign firms to introduce cutting-edge procedures derived from a fear that the Chinese JV firms would take them over, as when Audi's partner in the First Automobile Works "expropriated" the production technology after the European parent's license expired in 1997. And GM's operations have been bedeviled by ongoing "piracy problems" with its designated joint venture partners (Danny Hakim and Keith Bradsher, "China Lowers the Wall for US Cars and Parts," *The New York Times*, November 13, 2003, 1).

Comparing the Experience of High-Performance Electronics Investors in Different Countries and Over Different Periods

While there is less information about relative plant size in high-performance electronics, the evidence across countries and across time shows a clear distinction between FDI oriented toward protected domestic markets and FDI serving the parent's global sourcing network. Even more than in the automotive sector, the issue of operating with wholly owned subsidiaries stands out in high-performance electronics.

In the computer sector, Brazil's informatics policy limiting foreign ownership to 30 percent in designated sectors—and excluding foreign investment altogether in other sectors—led those investors who would participate to use older technology in less capable products priced at $2\frac{1}{2}$ to 3 times more than potential imports (Cline 1987). Besides costing consumers approximately $500 million per year in the 1980s, Brazilian efforts at national self-sufficiency put a drag on the competitiveness of the country's indigenous industries, leading Embraer (aerospace) and Petrobras (petroleum exploration and development) to become leading critics of the policy. Industrial users in Brazil complained that the lag in introducing new capabilities, such as CAD-CAM technology, was a greater burden than the excess cost.

In India, the lag between introducing new computer capabilities in developed countries and introducing similar capabilities in the domestic market steadily widened during the country's IS period (Grieco 1984). IBM withdrew from the protected Indian market altogether when the host authorities insisted that foreign computer investors form joint venture partnerships.

Throughout Southeast Asia—not just in Malaysia and Thailand—there was a contrast between US computer firms building international sourcing networks and Japanese firms producing for protected local markets, which kept the home market in Japan relatively unpenetrated from offshore sites until well into the 1990s (Encarnation 1992). The difference showed up in the speed of technology transfer between parent and subsidiary. Michael Borrus observed (1994, 134–35):

> Because their Asian affiliates were integrated into production operations serving advanced country markets, US firms upgraded their Asian investments in line with the pace of development of the lead market being served, the US market. In essence, they upgraded in line with the United States rather than local product cycles. By contrast, Japanese firms were led to upgrade the technological capabilities of their Asian investments only at the slower pace necessary to serve lagging local markets.

In the disk drive industry, Seagate, Read-Rite, and other assemblers operated exclusively via wholly owned subsidiaries to minimize coordination problems in ramping up new generations of products and to prevent technology escaping horizontally to potential competitors in Singapore and

China as well as Malaysia and Thailand (McKendrick, Donner, and Haggard 2000). Vertically they farmed out increasing amounts of subcontractor work (printed circuit boards, motor assemblies, and actuator arms) to host country suppliers, utilizing contract manufacturing with supervision from the parent.

In the semiconductor industry, Intel similarly eschewed joint ventures or partnerships in its assembly and test facilities in Costa Rica, China, and the Philippines, just as in its wafer fabrication plants in Ireland and Israel (Spar 1998).

Evidence from Other Industries

What evidence is there from FDI in other sectors of developing-country economies to corroborate the differences between projects oriented toward international markets and projects oriented toward protected domestic markets?

Using cost-benefit analysis and valuing inputs and outputs at world market prices, Dennis Encarnation and Louis T. Wells, Jr. (1986) offer a reexamination of three major attempts to measure the impact of specific foreign investment projects on the host economy, comprising 83 foreign investment projects in 30 developing countries over more than a decade. The sectors include industrial equipment, agribusiness, textiles, pharmaceuticals, chemicals, and petrochemicals as well as automotive equipment and electrical equipment. A majority of the projects—ranging from 55 to 75 percent, depending upon the shadow-price assumptions—made a positive contribution to host national income. But a large minority—from 25 to 45 percent—used resources in a way that created fewer goods and services for the host economy than the cost of those resources. There was a consistent rank-order correlation between the effective rate of protection and the proportion of projects with a deleterious impact on the host economy.[7]

In another study with a similar methodology, looking in detail at one country, Bernard Wasow (2003) calculated the costs and benefits in use of national resources when 14 foreign-owned firms produced 35 diverse goods in Kenya under IS policies in the late 1980s. He found that only 3 of the 35 created benefits for Kenya in excess of their costs. Of these, a single one—a large exporter of processed fruit—made a substantial contribution to host country welfare. More than half generated no foreign exchange saving or earnings at all; instead, they drained foreign exchange from the economy.

---

7. Encarnation and Wells, Jr. (1998) did not explicitly assess plant size, plant ownership structure, or technology flows from the parent. A theoretical case for negative effects from FDI in protected markets can be found in Brecher and Dias Alejandro (1977).

Many of these foreign firms operated with considerable excess capacity.[8] Wasow calculated that if the firms had produced closer to full capacity, the drain on the s economy would have been proportionately greater.[9]

In a survey of 15 FDI projects in petrochemicals, Peter Gray and Ingo Walter (1984) found that scale of plant output was decisive for the operation's success. Six projects built for IS purposes were subscale and inefficient, and did not serve as building blocks to move from infant industry to competitive status. Two of the six ended up as failures by parent investors' estimates, with one—a mandatory joint venture in South Korea—being sold at a loss to the local partners as the MNC withdrew. The other four required ongoing trade protection to stay in business.

V. N. Balasubramanyam, M. Salisu, and David Sapsford (1996) found that the effect of FDI was most strongly positive when the host country pursued export promotion policies rather than import substitution.

Is there corroboration outside the automotive and high-performance electronics sectors that joint venture or other technology-shifting requirements affect the flow of technology or intimacy of interaction between parent and subsidiary?

Investigating technology flows between parent and subsidiaries in 2 separate studies some 16 years apart, Edwin Mansfield and Anthony Romeo (1980) and J.-Y. Lee and Edwin Mansfield (1996) found that technology introduced into joint ventures across a variety of industries in developing countries was 3 to 4 years older than technology introduced into wholly owned subsidiaries.[10] In 14 sectors as diverse as chemicals, medical products, metal products, rubber, food, textiles, transportation equipment, and electrical goods, Vijaya Ramachandran (1993) discovered that technology transfers and the interchange of managers and technicians between parent and subsidiary were significantly higher for wholly owned subsidiaries than for joint venture partnerships or licensees. In this volume, Long Guoqiang finds that wholly owned and majority-owned foreign affiliates in China are much more likely to use the most advanced technology available to the parent corporation than 50-50 ownership or domestic majority ownership affiliates.

Like mandatory joint venture requirements, technology transfer mandates also appear counterproductive for bringing technology into the host economy. Magnus Blomström, Ari Kokko, and Mario Zejan (1992) report

---

8. For a theoretical analysis of why trade protection, domestic content requirements, or other restraints on competition are likely to lead to a proliferation of subscale and inefficient plants, see Eastman and Stykolt (1970). Potential success for domestic content mandate schemes requires complicated assumptions about potential for internal rent shifting.

9. Wasow did not look explicitly at domestic content requirements, ownership structure, or technology flows from parent to subsidiary.

10. Mansfield and Romeo (1980) lumped together joint ventures and licensees.

a negative correlation between host country requirements that foreign investors provide access to the parent's patents, transfer skills to local personnel, perform research and development (R&D) onsite, or use the most advanced technology available and technology inflows to the host economy. For Japanese investors, Shujiro Urata and Hiroki Kawai (2000) observed that technology requirements imposed on international companies as a condition to establish a local affiliate led to a negative coefficient for intrafirm technology transfer. Across Eastern Europe and the former Soviet Republics, Beata Smarzynska Javorcik and Kamal Saggi (2004) find that foreign investors with more sophisticated technologies and marketing skills (relative to other firms in their industry) prefer direct entry to joint ventures, because joint ventures are associated with less sophisticated technological and marketing capabilities.

According to Keith E. Maskus (2000), unless host countries provide foreign investors with the right to operate with wholly owned facilities, the degree of protection of intellectual property rights does not, on its own, have a significant impact on where international investors choose to locate.

The evidence that whole ownership limits opportunistic behavior, prevents appropriation of proprietary assets, and allows parent companies to minimize transaction costs associated with trying to control the actions of local partners is quite abundant (Gomes-Casseres 1989; Beamish and Delios 1997). Mihir A. Desai, C. Fritz Foley, and James R. Hines, Jr. (2002) note that over the past two decades US multinationals have shown a growing preference for wholly owned or majority-owned affiliates. Using data from 1982–97, they find that whole or majority ownership is most common when the parent firms coordinate integrated production operations among different international sites, when the parent firms transfer technology and other intangible property among affiliates, and when the parent firms coordinate tax planning worldwide. Desai, Foley, and Hines show, in addition, that when a host country liberalizes ownership restrictions, US investors trade more with their affiliates in that market: each 4 percent increase in sole ownership of affiliates is associated with 3 percent higher intrafirm trade volumes.

From this survey, it would appear that the conclusions initially based on evidence from the automotive and high-performance electronics sectors in a handful of countries appear quite robust in light of similar findings from the same industries and from other industries, in other countries, across time. Indeed, if used properly, many political scientists are prepared to argue that case study analysis can be used to provide a deeper and richer insight into causal relationships than mere statistical correlations (King, Keohane, and Verba 1994; George and Bennett 2004). As the fifth section will point out, however, further research is needed in at least three areas where predicted outcomes may not be as straightforward as the results summarized here.

But first it is necessary to investigate why other studies have not reported the same findings as the investigations reviewed to this point.

Why Have Other Studies Not Come to the Same Conclusions?

Dani Rodrik's (1999) contention that FDI brings no special benefits to host country development in comparison to other kinds of investment derives from the analysis of plant-level data from two countries: Brian Aitken and Ann Harrison's (1999) study of Venezuela and Mona Haddad and Ann Harrison's (1993) study of Morocco.

How well do these two studies provide a test of the impact of FDI on host country development? Why do they not show results similar to those observed in the industry case studies summarized earlier?

The data on industrial plants in Aitken and Harrison's Venezuelan study cover 1976 through 1989 (Aitken and Harrison 1999). During this period, Venezuela followed a determined IS development strategy with, as Aitken and Harrison acknowledge, a heavy layer of controls on foreign investment.[11] Foreign firms were discriminated against in a number of ways: They faced higher income taxes than domestic firms (50 percent versus 35 percent); they were obliged to exchange bolivares at the official exchange rate rather than the free market rate; they had restrictions on repatriation of profits; and they were restricted from exercising confidentiality and exclusive use-of-trade-secrets clauses in joint ventures.

The Venezuelan Superintendencia de Inversiones Extranjeras exercised substantial discretion in regulating the inflow of foreign investment into three ownership compartments: less than 20 percent foreign ownership, 20–49.9 percent foreign ownership, and majority foreign ownership. In evaluating Venezuela's investment regime during the 1980s, the Business International index of "openness" used the descriptors "strict joint venture requirements/only foreign minority position tolerated and this on a limited basis" to describe the country's policy toward foreign ownership, and "general requirements for specified percentage of local content/strictly enforced requirements for fully utilizing local components and materials" to describe the country's policy toward domestic content (Wheeler and Mody 1992).

Aitken and Harrison (1999) investigated whether rising levels of foreign equity participation were correlated with increases in productivity for recipient plants and discovered a robust positive relationship only for small enterprises. Searching for spillovers from joint ventures to plants with no foreign investment, they found that foreign investment was negatively correlated with the productivity of domestically owned firms in the same industry. The gains from foreign investment appeared to be entirely captured by the foreign joint ventures. On balance, they concluded that the net effect of foreign investor participation in the Venezuelan economy was quite small, with pos-

---

11. On Venezuela's IS strategy, see Balasubramanyam, Salisu, and Sapsford (1996).

itive effects from foreign-owned firms only slightly outweighing negative effects on domestic firms.

These findings are surprising not because they fail to show a strongly beneficial FDI impact on the host economy, including vibrant spillovers from foreign firms to domestic counterparts, but because they show results that appear to be beneficial at all.

The trade and investment regime in Venezuela during this period quite closely resembles those conditions under which Encarnation and Wells, Jr. (1986) and Wasow (2003) found that FDI made a negative net contribution to host country welfare, when all inputs and outputs were valued at world market prices. One would predict that Venezuela was quite probably experiencing a mix of beneficial and adverse foreign investor operations in a highly distorted setting, but this is impossible to know from the way the analysis is designed. Aitken and Harrison (1999) do not control for export-oriented FDI (if any) versus import-substitution FDI; for foreign investors free to source from wherever they wish (if at all) versus foreign investors operating with domestic content requirements; or for foreign investors obliged to operate as minority shareholders versus foreign investors with whole or majority ownership.[12]

Without these controls, the Aitken-Harrison (1999) study is designed like a medical experiment exploring the impact of minerals on patient health after the patient receives dosages of calcium and iron mixed with dosages of mercury and lead. With the intake of some minerals proving helpful to the body and the intake of others generating internal disorders, it is difficult to see how the analysis could arrive at a meaningful single aggregate assessment of the minerals' effect on the patient's physical condition.

Mona Haddad and Ann Harrison's (1993) investigation of FDI in Morocco may offer a clearer insight into FDI's impact on development. Prior to 1983, Morocco had a regulatory regime for FDI even more restrictive than Venezuela, mandating that all foreign firms not only have local joint venture partners but that they accept less than 50 percent foreign ownership. Between 1983 and 1985 the foreign investment regulations were liberalized, allowing foreign firms in industrial sectors to have an equity participation of more than 49 percent. There was also a degree of trade reform, so one might hope that the Moroccan case would offer a chance to test how the behavior of foreign investors responds under conditions of simultaneous trade and investment liberalization.

But "trade reform" during this period in Morocco was limited to phasing out quantitative restrictions while leaving in place a complicated tariff system that was structured to provide effective rates of protection considerably higher than nominal rates and that rose with each processing

---

12. However, Aitken and Harrison did find a coefficient on foreign ownership within the plant that was positive and statistically significant.

stage. Except for basic metals, tariff rates ranged by sector from 17 percent to 44 percent. Other researchers (Balasubramanyam, Salisu, and Sapsford 1996) continued to characterize the Moroccan trade regime during this period as "IS." Haddad and Harrison (1993, 56, n. 4) acknowledge that after 1985 Morocco was "still far from being an open economy."

The data on foreign investor behavior in the Moroccan investigation cover four years, 1985 through 1989. During this period new inflows of FDI that might be structured to take advantage of the permission to allow majority ownership were quite limited, raising the foreign share of manufacturing assets by 2 percentage points, from 13 percent in 1985 to 15 percent in 1989. Changes in the share of foreign ownership by sector were also small: 5 percentage points in leather, 4 percentage points in scientific instruments, and 3 percentage points in machinery, textiles, and apparel. Only in chemicals (phosphates) was there a substantial FDI inflow, with the foreign share rising by 7 percentage points. By far the bulk of the FDI stock had been established to respond to the earlier minority foreign ownership IS regime. With the given data, it is impossible to know how much reorientation—if any— occurred among firms whose operations had been set up prior to 1985.

Controlling for firm size, Haddad and Harrison (1993) found that foreign investors did not exhibit higher levels of labor productivity or greater outward orientation for most sectors than their domestic counterparts. Firms with foreign ownership demonstrated higher levels of total factor productivity than their domestic counterparts, but the rate of productivity growth was higher for the latter because—as Haddad and Harrison show—the domestic firms were better prepared to cope with the distortionary effects of protected markets.[13] There was no significant relationship between higher productivity growth in domestic firms and greater foreign presence in the sector, suggesting that foreign investment did not bring positive spillovers to the host economy. When Haddad and Harrison varied measures of relative trade protection, technology spillovers from foreign investors to domestic firms remained insignificant and generally negative.[14] Overall, Haddad and Harrison found that foreign investors did not make a large or dynamic contribution to the development of the Moroccan economy.

Thus the Rodrik-led contention that a dollar of FDI is worth no more and no less than a dollar of any other kind of investment rests on four years of observing a host economy whose foreign investment base had been built as

---

13. The data from Morocco show a positive and statistically significant relationship between the extent of foreign ownership of a firm's assets and firm-level productivity: each increase by one standard deviation in the extent of foreign ownership of a given firm brought that firm 4 percent closer to best practices in the industry. Harrison (1996) tested the Moroccan data in a later analysis. In the original study of Morocco, Haddad and Harrison (1993) had suggested that firms with majority foreign ownership behaved generally in the same way as firms with minority foreign ownership.

14. Haddad and Harrison (1993) tested only for horizontal spillovers, not vertical spillovers.

part of an IS strategy, with no large numbers of new investors arriving and significant trade distortions remaining in place. The 1985–89 Morocco case study would seem to be a less than compelling basis on which to generalize that FDI brings no special benefits to host country growth and welfare.

A second approach assessing FDI's impact on development compares the economic performance of FDI-heavy developing countries with less FDI-heavy countries. However, it also fails to discern positive results. Ted Truman (2002) reviews the economic performance of 12 major emerging market economies from 1980–2000: South Korea and Thailand achieved a "high" growth score over the period; Malaysia and India achieved a "good" growth score; Egypt and Turkey were a step behind with a "moderate" growth score; Mexico, Brazil, Argentina, and the Philippines received a "weak" growth score; and Nigeria and Venezuela had a "negative" growth score.

Truman then examines FDI as a percent of GDP for the 12 countries. He points out that for this 20-year period, the two economies with superior growth performances, South Korea or Thailand, were at the opposite ends of the scale of FDI as a percentage of GDP: Thailand was a bit above the group average, while South Korea was toward the low end. Of the two countries with "good" growth performance, Malaysia had a high rate of FDI, but India had the lowest. The two countries with "moderate" growth performance had only average (Egypt) or below average (Turkey) reliance on FDI. The four countries with "weak" growth performance (Mexico, Brazil, Argentina, and the Philippines) had average participation of FDI. The two countries with "negative" growth performance had average (Venezuela) or above average (Nigeria) ratios of FDI to GDP. Thus, Truman (2002, 16) concludes that, "on the whole, this is not a very convincing picture in favor of FDI as providing a valuable and stable stimulus to growth."

But is this formulation—for example, arguing that Mexico's average amount of FDI as a proportion of GDP, but weak aggregate economic performance, demonstrates that FDI does not contribute much to growth—the appropriate way to specify the counterfactual?

As indicated earlier, over this period the largest FDI flows into Mexico occurred in the automotive industry, with consequences that included exports of vehicles and parts growing from a negligible level in the mid-1970s to $7 billion in 2000; employment reaching more than 354,000 (earning wages second only to the petroleum sector); and plants in several cities winning world-best quality awards by independent tracking agencies supported by more than 300 indigenous Mexican suppliers of inputs and accessories.

Is it logical to conclude on the basis of the overall performance of the Mexican economy between 1980–2000 that this automotive-sector FDI did not make a positive contribution to Mexican economic performance?

Or would it make more sense to rephrase the counterfactual: Why has Mexican economic performance over this period been so relatively poor, *despite* the benefits of automotive-sector investment? Might not Mexican economic performance have been *even weaker* in the absence of FDI?[15]

Similarly, why should the outside observer want to generalize in the way that the Truman study does—arguing on the basis of *Mexican* economic performance that the massive FDI in the *Malaysian* electronics industry was unimportant for the behavior of the Malaysian economy?

Is it more plausible to conclude that trade and investment liberalization are *not* significant factors for Indian economic growth, or that India's "good" economic performance would probably have been *even better* if Indian trade and investment liberalization had proceeded more vigorously?

Implications for Further Research

The preceding sections suggest that future research will be more valuable—and more convincing—if the researchers do not mix data from foreign investment projects oriented toward protected domestic markets with export-oriented foreign investment projects, or mix data from projects burdened with domestic content and/or joint ownership requirements with projects free from such requirements.

Similarly, future assessments of the contribution of FDI to development will be particularly valuable if the investigators try to assess how the economic performance of a given host country with a given configuration of FDI would compare with the economic performance of that same host country in the absence of that FDI, rather than simply compare the economic performance of more foreign investment–heavy developing countries with less foreign investment–heavy developing countries.

There are three specific areas, however, where the studies reviewed above suggest that well-structured future research might provide interesting amplifications of or variations on—even divergences from—the results generally observed thus far. These involve:

- examining the differences in impact between FDI that allows a host economy to undertake completely new activities, and foreign investment that allows a host economy to improve the activities that it conducts;

- exploring the difference in impact between FDI in middle-income developing countries, and FDI in poorer developing countries with "low absorptive capacity"; and

---

15. This suggested methodology is similar to efforts of Görg and Strobl (in this volume) to simulate the evolution of the host economy—and, in their case, to calculate what would have happened to the population of domestic plants—in the absence of MNC investment. For the background on how macro mismanagement and failures in institutional reform in Mexico have offset the benefits of growing investment and trade flows during the North American Free Trade Agreement (NAFTA), see Sidney Weintraub (2004).

■ investigating what measures host governments might take to expand backward linkages and spillovers from foreign investors to local firms.

FDI in "New" Versus Improvement in Current Host Economy Activities

The industries that provided the basis for my initial research at the Institute for International Economics—automotive and high-performance electronics—fit quite well into the distinction formulated by Paul Romer (1993a, 1993b, 1994), as a precursor to "endogenous growth theory," between introducing goods and services into a host economy that help a country carry out activities that it already does more efficiently and importing "ideas" (via FDI) that enable a country to undertake entirely new kinds of activities altogether.

It is possible to make a case that Brazil and Mexico had rudimentary indigenous automotive companies, and that Malaysia and Thailand had simple indigenous electrical companies, prior to the arrival of the major US and European multinational firms. But the multinational computer, telecommunications, semiconductor, and auto investors introduced a combination of technology, management, and quality control procedures that gave these host economies a new "endowment" of productive activities, capable of competing in these sectors internationally for the first time.

In cases such as these, foreign investors differ from domestic firms not only because they operate on different production functions, but because they allow the creation of an entirely new production possibility frontier for the host economy. But many foreign investment projects may not accomplish this. Instead they may simply allow the host country to use its resources more efficiently in carrying out activities already present in the economy. Future research might contrast the impact of these two different kinds of FDI across the entire inventory of potential contributions from FDI, including backward linkages and externalities, as sketched out in box 11.1.

There may be many cases that resemble primary contribution category (3) more closely than category (4). In category (3) foreign investors differ from domestic firms either because they operate with different production functions or because they operate at different points on the same production function, but their primary potential impact is to allow the host economy to operate more efficiently rather than to engage in entirely new types of activities.

Category (3) foreign investments may be found in mature industries where the pace of innovation is slower, economies of scale are smaller, and/or product differentiation is less pronounced—such as basic chemicals and paints, household appliances and furniture, off-patent and generic pharmaceuticals, industrial equipment, tires and rubber products, electrical fixtures and devices, unbranded garments and apparel, and processed

Box 11.1 Inventory of potential FDI contributions to a host economy

FDI can contribute to host country development in many ways even when the foreign firms do not necessarily provide externalities.

Primary contributions may add to host country growth and welfare whether or not externalities are generated.

1. The foreign investor brings new products, improved quality, and/or lower prices to consumers in the host country.

2. The foreign investor provides additional resources (capital, technology, and management) to raise the level of domestic output. For example, an investor in London acquires a chain of restaurants in Baghdad, providing capital to help with reconstruction.

3. The foreign investor provides technologies, management techniques, and quality control processes that potentially allow the host economy to engage in existing activities more efficiently and offer better/cheaper goods to consumers or inputs to producers. For example, Sherman Williams makes an investment in Brazil to produce the Sherman Williams basic line of house paints.

4. The foreign investor provides technologies, management techniques, and quality control processes that allow the host economy to undertake completely novel activities. For example, Seagate builds a plant in Thailand to assemble high-speed disk drives; Intel builds a plant in Costa Rica to produce semiconductors.

5. The foreign investor provides technologies, management techniques, and quality control of types (2) and (3) above that enable the host economy to penetrate international markets and earn foreign exchange and/or allow competitive substitution of imports.[1] For example, Brazil reduces its importation of house paints as a result of the Sherman Williams investment and/or Sherman Williams supplies the Southern Cone from its Brazilian plants; GM expands its Hungarian plant to supply 1.6-liter Audi engines to its assembly sites throughout the European Union.

Secondary contributions via backward linkages may add to host country growth and welfare without necessarily providing externalities.

6. The foreign investor provides new demand from its local subsidiary for host country suppliers to meet, using operations they already know how to undertake. For example, Ericsson's plant in the Philippines purchases boxing and shipping materials from Philippine suppliers.

7. The foreign investor provides new demand from foreign subsidiaries for host country suppliers to meet, with coaching from the foreign subsidiaries about how to provide inputs at cheaper cost or with more reliability. For example, Motorola

(box continues next page)

foods and beverages. Category (3) foreign investments might be found in larger and more advanced developing countries with more extensive indigenous business communities.

It would be useful to contrast the contributions from foreign investments in category (3) with foreign investments in category (4). One might find that foreign investments in category (3) appear less valuable than those in category (4), since the presumed intangible benefits from foreign ownership are

Box 11.1 *(continued)*

farms out printed circuit board (PCB) assembly to two electrical firms in Singapore to which it provides instructions about what machinery to purchase and how to carry out quality control procedures.

Externalities

8. The presence of foreign investors generates leakage of personnel, management techniques, or technologies from the foreign firms to host country firms. For example, Citibank's training program alumni in Brazil spread throughout the Brazilian financial sector. In some cases, the trained employees establish their own banks or financial service firms.

9. The foreign investor introduces new technologies, management techniques, and quality control into existing sectors in the host economy that either allow host country competitors to upgrade their own operations by *imitation* and/or force host country competitors to upgrade their own operations via *competition*. For example, BASF produces nonrun bleach-resistant textile dyes in India, which signals to Indian dye producers the new chemicals needed to achieve the same results and puts pressure on them to remain competitive.

10. The foreign investor provides host country firms that become suppliers the opportunity to offer the new goods and services to other buyers in the host economy.[2] For example, after Motorola farms out PCB assembly to two firms in Singapore, the two firms extend their sales of PCBs from Motorola to Philips and Texas Instruments.

11. The foreign investor provides host country firms that originate as suppliers new opportunities to become producers of goods and services to other buyers in the international economy (with or without export coaching from the original foreign investor).[3] For example, Malaysian machine tool firms that originated selling equipment and services to Intel in Malaysia follow the MNC to China, and begin to sell equipment and services to US, European, and Japanese firms in the Chinese market.

---

1. General equilibrium considerations would suggest that primary contribution categories (1), (2), (3), and (4) will have export-import implications by allowing host country resources to be used more efficiently. To the extent that "market penetration" is a barrier to entry to a particular industry, or an intangible asset of an MNC, category (5) merits separate consideration.

2. Rather than explicit "coaching," the foreign investor may provide a "positive productivity shock" in the form of a required technical audit or ISO 9000 certification in order for an indigenous firm to qualify as a supplier.

3. See footnote 1 regarding general equilibrium considerations.

more often offset by special knowledge and customization advantages of indigenous producers. In the examples given in the "inventory" above, Sherman Williams house paint production in Brazil or BASF nonrun bleach-resistant textile dye production in India might not prove to be far superior— if superior at all—to local competitors.

In addition, while foreign investments in category (3) might appear to be of higher productivity than other investments in the host economy, genuine problems in deciphering the direction of causality may exist: a pre-existing high-productivity sector might simply attract high-productivity foreign participants whose performance does not have much to add, complicating the measurement of spillovers.

In contrast, for foreign investments in category (4), reverse causality is simply not plausible: Seagate did not happen to locate in a disk drive sector in Thailand that was already populated with high-productivity indigenous disk drive firms, nor did Intel happen to locate in a semiconductor sector in Costa Rica that was already populated with high-productivity indigenous semiconductor firms.

It is logical to imagine that FDI's impact on category (3) might differ appreciably from its impact on category (4). For foreign investment of category (3), the externalities of category (9) might be larger than those associated with category (4), since there is less of a technological gap between the foreign investor and the indigenous counterparts, leading to horizontal spillovers as all firms "catch up" via competition and imitation to the same best practices.[16] For the same reason, backward linkages of categories (6) and (7) might be greater from the foreign firms of category (3) in a vertical direction to indigenous suppliers than from foreign firms of category (4), although whether these backward linkages from the foreign firm were greater than those from the indigenous counterparts would bear examination. So, too, externalities of category (10) might be larger from foreign investors in category (3) than from foreign investors in category (4).

Providing some confirmation of such a contrast, Robert Lipsey (2000) examined the evolution of the electrical machinery industry, consisting primarily of consumer electronics likely qualifying for category (3), in Southeast Asia.[17] In 1977, the subsidiaries of US and Japanese multinationals produced more than half of the exports; by the mid-1990s, their share of exports had fallen to 22 percent even while their absolute level steadily rose. This represented, in his view, a "maturing of the industry" as indigenous producers overtook the initial superiority of the foreign investors. In the nonelectrical machinery industry, consisting primarily of computers and accessories—likely qualifying as category (4), in contrast—where the level of technological sophistication was greater and the pace of innovation faster, the subsidiaries of US and Japanese multinationals increased their share as well as their absolute levels of exports substantially between 1977 and 1995.

At the same time, some observations about foreign investor performance—and some implications for host country policy—might apply equally well to investors in category (3) as well as category (4). In the case of

---

16. Kokko (1994), Blomström and Wolff (1994), and Kathuria (2001) suggest that additional horizontal spillovers and faster convergence between foreign and domestic firms are likely when there are lesser initial technology gaps or differences in capital intensity or science intensity between them.

17. The countries included Hong Kong, China, Indonesia, South Korea, Malaysia, Philippines, Singapore, Thailand, and Taiwan.

domestic content requirements and import substitution, the studies surveyed earlier by Encarnation and Wells, Jr. (1986) and by Wasow (2003) included foreign investment in more mature industries of the kind likely found in category (3) as well as foreign investment in cutting-edge operations of the kind likely to be found in category (4). They concluded that foreign investment of all kinds in their samples is more efficient and more likely to make a positive contribution to host country growth and welfare when the investors are not protected by trade or other barriers to competition, and less efficient and likely to be detrimental to host country growth and welfare when they are so protected.

Similarly, with regard to joint venture requirements and technology sharing mandates, the studies surveyed earlier by Mansfield and Romeo (1980), Lee and Mansfield (1996), Ramachandran (1993), and Blomström, Kokko, and Zejan (1992) also included foreign investment in more mature industries of the kind likely to be found in category (3) as well as foreign investment likely to be found in category (4). They found that parent firms in all categories deploy newer technology and provide more training when local plants are wholly or majority owned and not subject to technology sharing requirements than when local plants are minority owned or bound by technology sharing mandates.

FDI in Poorer Developing Countries with "Low Absorptive Capability"

The observations about the globalization of the automotive and high-performance electronic industries presented earlier originated in middle-income developing countries. Several of the best-known aggregate statistical efforts to evaluate the impact of FDI on the host economy have found that the potentially beneficial effects tail off, or disappear, at the lowest levels of development. Borensztein, De Gregorio, and Lee (1998) found a strong complementary interaction between FDI and human capital, with the positive contribution of FDI to economic growth dependent upon a minimum threshold stock of human capital. A survey of 11 studies by de Mello (1997) reports stronger positive effects of FDI inflows on host country growth as a function of the host country's level of development as well as openness and greater attention to export promotion.

This seems to suggest a kind of Catch-22 trap—that poorest and least developed countries with lowest levels of human capital can utilize FDI to enhance their domestic growth only by becoming less poor and more developed with higher levels of human capital—thereby appearing to exclude them from using FDI to move up from the lowest to the middle ranks of developing countries.

What does the case study evidence show about whether the poorest and least developed countries with lowest levels of human capital can utilize FDI for development? Is there a path that the poorest countries can follow that begins with foreign investment in least-skilled, labor-intensive activities and moves toward the more skilled labor–intensive operations of the kind shown earlier in the automotive and high-performance electronics sectors?

To be sure, the historical flows of FDI to the developing world have been quite concentrated. Over the past few decades, 20 countries—none of them the poorer developing countries that lack favorable natural resource endowments—have accumulated 83 percent of the total stock of FDI in the developing world and economies in transition (UNCTAD 2003). In 2002, 20 countries—again, none of them the poorer developing countries that lack favorable natural resource endowments—received 82 percent of all FDI flows in the developing world and economies in transition.

Not only are the relative amounts of nonextractive FDI to poorer developing countries small, but the efforts of would-be new hosts among the least developed to break into the ranks of those successfully using FDI for development are filled with stories of failure (Madani 1999). Business-unfriendly regulatory systems, red tape and bribery, overvalued exchange rates, and lack of reliable infrastructure hinder FDI's attraction and frustrate the expansion of investor activities when they arrive.

But the evidence from least developed regions—"even" from Africa and "even" from the tropics—does *not* support the proposition that poorer countries are unable to use FDI for development.

Indeed the country that caught Paul Romer's eye as the model for transforming a nation's development trajectory by importing "ideas" via FDI (Romer 1993b) was Mauritius, whose prospects were so poor that inhabitants with any skills had been advised by the British to emigrate to escape the stagnant economy (Meade 1961).

When a new government in 1982 turned away from protecting local industry to a strategy of foreign investor export-led growth, backed by a more realistic exchange rate, however, Mauritius turned itself into one of the more formidable success stories. Led by textile investors from Hong Kong, Mauritius achieved an average annual growth rate in manufactured products over the next two decades that placed it seventh—in the calculations of Steven Radelet (1999)—among the 15 leading exporters of manufactured products among low- and middle-income countries around the world. By 2000, 70 percent of all exports were manufactured goods, earning some $1.2 billion annually and generating 80,000–90,000 jobs (International Monetary Fund, or IMF 2001).

Deliberately copying Mauritius, Madagascar established the same unexceptional package of reforms in 1989—macroeconomic stability, a realistic exchange rate, and a determination to facilitate foreign investor export-led growth—and managed to attract 120 foreign firms in the first five years. By 2000, the foreign investor–dominated export sector employed almost 40,000 workers and generated $64 million in foreign sales (Economist Intelligence Unit 2000).

In both countries, foreign investor–employed workers received wages and benefits not just better than alternatives in the rural areas from which they came but higher than comparable jobs across the economy. Holding education level, work experience, and length of tenure constant, Mireille Razafindrakoto and François Roubaud (1995) found that export processing zone (EPZ) workers in Madagascar earned 15–20 percent more than other workers throughout the country. In Mauritius, real wages within the export-oriented manufacturing sector rose by more than 50 percent between the late 1980s and the late 1990s (Radelet 1999). In general, foreign direct investors paid more than domestic employers, with appropriate controls for plant size and worker skill level, in poorer as well as mid-level developing countries.[18]

More detailed research is needed on how other poorer countries—including the Dominican Republic, Honduras, El Salvador, and the Philippines—have achieved similar results, generating tens of thousands of jobs and tens if not hundreds of millions of dollars in exports. A first glance at the requirements for success in these cases suggests that the levels of macro, micro, and institutional reforms that were required were modest and—while politically difficult—not at all impossible.[19] The countries did not have to rise to the top of the Institutional Investor's charts or the Davos competitiveness index to do well.

The case study evidence from lesser and least developed countries does not suggest that an initial strategy of allowing foreign investors only into the lowest-skilled activities is necessarily devoid of externalities. In the early stages of export-led growth, foreign firms owned virtually all of the outward-oriented manufacturing facilities in Mauritius. As workers and managers gained experience in the foreign plants, they left to start up their own firms (Rhee, Katterback, and While 1990). Within 15 years indigenous investors represented 50 percent of the total equity capital in companies with EPZ status throughout the country. In the Dominican Republic, local firms took advantage of the favorable business setting provided for the foreigners, established operations alongside them, and accounted for 35 percent of all manufacturing exporters by 2000. For the Philippines, the comparable figure was 20 percent at the end of the 1990s. It would be useful to have a detailed look at the interaction between, and possible spillovers among, the foreign investors and the indigenous exporters.[20] Responding primarily—according

---

18. For surveys of evidence and methodologies, see Lim (2001) and Brown, Deardorff, and Stern (2002).

19. For an initial effort at this research, see Moran (forthcoming 2005).

20. In Mexico, Aitken, Hanson, and Harrison (1997) found that the probability of an indigenous Mexican plant engaging in exports is positively correlated with the proximity of that plant to foreign investors but uncorrelated to the overall presence of exporters in the region, suggesting that the presence of the foreign investors helps local firms to export rather than some geographical comparative advantage for exporting in general.

to investor surveys—to the presence of workers with basic high school and vocational school skill levels, foreign investors in electronics, auto parts, industrial products, medical devices, data processing, and business services initiated operations alongside plants producing garments and footwear, paying wages two to five times higher.[21]

This points to the third area in which further research would be particularly valuable: What measures can host countries take to stimulate the expansion of backward linkages and spillovers?

Host Country Policies to Expand Backward Linkages and Spillovers

A preliminary examination of the country cases listed above suggests that the challenge of expanding backward linkages and spillovers from local firms to foreign investor operations in poorer developing countries—as in richer developing countries—has some straightforward dimensions. Above all, it requires providing local firms with the same kind of liberalized environment that foreign investors demand for themselves: one cannot expect indigenous companies in the midst of hostile regulatory systems, burdened with high-priced inputs, lacking access to low-cost imports, required to buy from and sell to designated customers, dependent upon unreliable infrastructure, and used to favors and having to bribe to obtain timely services, to become first-class suppliers—let alone competitors—to foreign multinationals.

Beyond this, however, the question of how to enlarge backward linkages and spillovers becomes more tricky, and requires much more extensive research. There is an incipient literature on "vendor development" efforts that offers a model program in which host authorities contribute to the salary of a manager in certain foreign affiliates, who acts as a "spotter" to identify potential local suppliers and prescribe the machinery needed for their success. Host country agencies then provide special loans for the equipment required by the designated firms and special training for workers (UNCTAD 2001b; McKendrick, Donner, and Haggard 2000). These loans can then be paid back from the proceeds of foreign supplier contracts.

Even the most imaginatively constructed "vendor development" programs, however, raise complicated questions of targeting, separating winners from losers, avoiding cronyism, and escaping the rent-seeking behavior associated with industrial policy. Is there sufficient justification

---

21. Country studies for the Dominican Republic, Madagascar, Mauritius, and the Philippines can be found in Moran (2002). There the hypothesis that foreign investors pay higher wages to attract and retain better workers as their plant output grows more sophisticated and must meet higher quality control standards to compete in international markets is tested, with positive results. The surprising discovery is that as lower-skill–intensive plants and slightly higher-skill–intensive plants are mixed worker treatment across all plants improves dramatically.

for host governments to provide specialized services and subsidized loans to potential indigenous suppliers to MNCs rather than to all indigenous firms? Should small and medium-sized indigenous firms be favored over larger firms, or the reverse? Should resources for vocational and technical training of workers be devoted to meeting the needs of potential suppliers rather than to improving educational services for the population at large?

Implications for Policies Toward FDI

The preceding analysis has important implications for the trade and investment agenda in the Doha Round of the WTO, for the use of incentives to attract and hold multinational investor activities, and for the reconceptualization of the "Washington consensus" toward FDI and development.

Developing Country Policies Toward FDI and the Trade and Investment Agenda in the Doha Round

The differentiation of nonextractive FDIs into positive and negative categories has important policy implications not just for individual host countries but for the multilateral community at large.

Host country development objectives are not served by the attempt to use FDI for import substitution, or to generate backward linkages and spillovers by imposing domestic content, joint venture, and other technology sharing requirements. Many individual developing-country governments are coming to this conclusion on their own. Some leading developing-country representatives to the Trade and Investment Working Group of the Doha Round, however, have asserted just the opposite with the aim of reopening the Trade Related Investment Measures (TRIMs) Agreement in the World Trade Organization (WTO 2002).

The TRIMs agreement from the Uruguay Round has required all WTO members to eliminate domestic content requirements and import-export balancing requirements placed upon foreign firms. Developing countries that have petitioned for extensions of the 5–7-year phase-out period have been granted longer time periods in return for a specific schedule for removal. The logical conclusion from the previous analysis would be that developing country self-interests would be served by reaffirming the TRIMs agreement in the Doha Round and extending it to include mandatory joint venture and technology sharing requirements as well.

Instead some key developing countries are proposing to revisit, and rescind, the TRIMs agreement, arguing in one case that domestic content requirements are an "extremely useful and necessary tool" for promoting growth, and in another that "measures to encourage the use of products of domestic origin" should be allowed as a tool to expand the industrial base of the host country (UNCTAD 2001a). The proposed objectives for trade-and-investment negotiations in the Doha Round include "imposition of manufacturing requirements on foreign investors, protection of domestic producers, use of binding obligations on technology transfer, and avoiding crowding out of domestic firms" (WTO 2002).

The failure of the Trade Ministerial in Cancún in September 2003 has made it unlikely that investment issues will be included in the Doha Round negotiations. Whatever the outcome, the preceding analysis shows clearly that the self-interest of the developing world will not be served by backsliding on the TRIMs Agreement prohibition of domestic content requirements.

More broadly, it is important to the policy debate that analytic agnosticism about the impact of FDI on development be replaced with a clear recognition of both positive and negative potential contributions from foreign investors as spelled out in this study.

Locational Incentives and Subsidies to Attract FDI

A second important policy issue concerns whether it makes sense for host countries in the developing world to provide incentives and subsidies to attract FDI.

On the one hand, the evidence reviewed above shows that foreign investment projects integrated into the global supply networks of the parent companies not only contribute to host economic growth but generate genuine spillovers and externalities that might justify a certain degree of subsidy on the part of the recipient country.

On the other hand, there is growing evidence that using incentive packages to either attract multinational investors or prevent them from leaving continues to increase and shows no signs of abating.

The conventional wisdom in business economics literature has long been that international companies do not base their basic global strategy for production on tax considerations. It gradually became apparent in the 1990s, however, that MNCs searching for a new plant site in the developing world would identify several roughly alternative production locations and then stimulate an incentive bidding war among the hosts that acted as—in the words of GM—a "tie breaker" (Harvard Business School 1993).

Somewhat more surprising, it has become evident that the competition between developed- and developing-country sites has been growing, and that multinational firms have become more responsive to various kinds of investment incentives—tax concessions, free land, and subsidized factory space—over time. Analyzing data from 14 home countries and 34 host countries over the past 20 years, Altschuler, Grubert, and Newlong (1998) show that the locational decisions of international direct investors have become increasingly sensitive to differential subsidy considerations. John

Mutti (2004) has found that the siting of export-oriented FDI is particularly responsive to host country tax breaks, and that this responsiveness is even greater with regard to developing-country sites than for developed-country locations. Developing countries regularly provide locational incentives to international investors, but they do not do so as massively or as effectively as the countries of Ireland, Portugal, and southern Italy, or the states of Alabama, South Carolina, and Kentucky (Thomas 2000, Shah 1995).

Rather than the current practice in which alternative host sites try to match the giveaways of others in a prisoner's dilemma game of massive proportions, the ideal public policy approach—however politically difficult to achieve—would be a global agreement to limit and roll back the incentive competition. If direct subsidies, free land and factory space, and tax breaks could be brought under control, whatever resources developing countries might want to devote to attracting externality-laden foreign investment could then be focused on creating effective educational and vocational training programs, efficient infrastructure, and effective public bureaucracies with low levels of red tape and corruption.

Revising the "Washington Consensus" on FDI and Development

During the heyday of the "Washington consensus," conventional wisdom held that FDI—as long as it did not pollute the environment or blatantly abuse workers—was "good" for development, and "the more the better." But the evidence presented here shows that this approach is far too complacent.

FDI in manufacturing, agribusiness, and other processing industries can make a positive contribution to development only if it occurs in a reasonably open setting, not protected and sheltered from competition. Therefore, public authorities and researchers alike must pay careful attention to the policy context within which FDI occurs, to determine whether the investment projects are likely to prove beneficial—or detrimental—to development.

References

Aitken, Brian J., and Ann E. Harrison. 1999. Do Domestic Firms Benefit from Direct Foreign Investment? Evidence from Venezuela. *American Economic Review* 89, no. 3 (June): 605–18.

Aitken, Brian J., Gordon H. Hanson, and Ann E. Harrison. 1997. Spillovers, Foreign Investment, and Export Behavior. *Journal of International Economics* 43, no. 1–2 (August): 103–32.

Altschuler, R., H. Grubert, and S. Newlong. 1998. *Has US Investment Abroad Become More Sensitive to Tax Rates?* NBER Working Paper 6383. Cambridge, MA: National Bureau of Economic Research.

Balasubramanyam, V. N., M. Salisu, and David Sapsford. 1996. Foreign Direct Investment and Growth in EP and IS Countries. *Economic Journal* 106, no. 434 (January): 92–105.

Bale, Jr., Harvey E., and David Walters. 1986. *Investment Policy Aspects of US and Global Trade Interests: Looking Ahead.* NPA Pamphlet 9. Washington: National Planning Association.

Basri, M. C., H. Aswicahyono, and H. Hill. 2000. How Not to Industrialize: Indonesia's Automotive Industry. *Bulletin of Indonesian Economic Studies* 36, no. 1 (April): 209–41.

Beamish, Paul W., and Andres Delios. 1997. Incidence and Propensity of Alliance Formation by US, Japanese, and European MNEs. In *Cooperative Strategies: Asian-Pacific Perspectives*, ed., Paul W. Beamish and J. Peter Killing. San Francisco: New Lexington Press.

Blomström, Magnus, Ari Kokko, and Mario Zejan. 1992. *Host Country Competition and Technology Transfer by Multinationals*. NBER Working Paper 4131. Cambridge, MA: National Bureau of Economic Research.

Blomström, Magnus, and Edward N. Wolff. 1994. Multinational Corporations and Productivity Convergence in Mexico. In *Convergence of Productivity: Cross-National Studies and Historical Evidence*, ed., William Baumol, Richard Nelson, and Edward N. Wolff. Oxford: Oxford University Press.

Borensztein, E., J. De Gregorio, and J. W. Lee. 1998. How Does Foreign Direct Investment Affect Economic Growth? *Journal of International Economics* 45, no. 1 (June): 115–35.

Borrus, Michael. 1994. Left for Dead: Asian Production Networks and the Revival of US Electronics. In *Japanese Investment in Asia: International Production Strategies in a Rapidly Changing World*, ed., Eileen M. Doherty. San Francisco: Asian Foundation and Berkeley Roundtable on International Economics.

Brecher, Richard A., and Carlos F. Dias Alejandro. 1977. Tariffs, Foreign Capital and Immiserizing Growth. *Journal of International Economics* 7, no. 4 (November): 317–22.

Brown, Drusilla K., Alan V. Deardorff, and Robert M. Stern. 2002. *The Effects of Multinational Production on Wages and Working Conditions in Developing Countries*. University of Michigan Research Seminar in International Economics, Discussion Paper 483 (August 30). Ann Arbor, MI: University of Michigan.

Cline, William R. 1987. *Informatics and Development: Trade and Industrial Policy in Argentina, Brazil, and Mexico*. Washington: Economics International.

De Mello, Jr., Luiz R. 1997. Foreign Direct Investment in Developing Countries and Growth: A Selective Survey. *Journal of Development Studies* 34, no. 1 (October): 1–33.

Desai, Mihir A., C. Fritz Foley, and James R. Hines, Jr. 2002. *International Joint Ventures and the Boundaries of the Firm*. NBER Working Paper 9115 (August). Cambridge, MA: National Bureau of Economic Research.

Doner, R. F., G. W. Noble, and J. Ravenhill. 2002. *Production Networks in East Asia's Automobile Parts Industry*. Background paper for the Project on East Asia's Economic Future. Washington: World Bank.

Eastman, H., and S. Stykolt. 1970. A Model for the Study of Protected Oligopolies. *Economic Journal* 70: 336–47.

Economist Intelligence Unit. 2000. *EIU Country Profile 2000: Madagascar*. New York.

Ehinger, Kristian. 1999. FDI Policy and Individual Country Experiences: The Volkswagen Experience. Paper presented at the OECD Conference on the Role of International Investment in Development, Paris (September 20).

Encarnation, Dennis J. 1992. *Rivals Beyond Trade*. Ithaca, NY: Cornell University Press.

Encarnation, Dennis J., and Louis T. Wells, Jr. 1986. Evaluating Foreign Investment. In *Investing In Development: New Roles for Private Capital?* ed., Theodore H. Moran Washington: Overseas Development Council.

Erdilek, Asim. 1982. *Direct Foreign Investment in Turkish Manufacturing: An Analysis of the Conflicting Objectives and Frustrated Expectations of a Host Country*. Tübingen: Mohr.

Ernst, D. 1999. Globalization, Convergence, and Diversity: The Asian Production Networks of Japanese Electronics Firms. In *Rivalry or Riches: International Production Networks in Asia*, ed., M. Borrus, D. Ernst, and S. Haggard. Cornell, NY: Cornell University Press.

George, Alexander, and Andrew Bennett. 2004. *Case Studies and Theory Development*. Cambridge, MA: MIT University Press.

Gomes-Casseres, Benjamin. 1989. Ownership Structures of Foreign Subsidiaries: Theory and Evidence. *Journal of Economic Behavior and Organization* 11, no. 1 (January): 1–25.

Gray, H. Peter, and Ingo Walter. 1984. Investment-Related Trade Distortions in Petrochemicals. *Journal of World Trade Law* 17, no. 4 (July/August): 283–307.

Grieco, Joseph M. 1984. *Between Dependency and Autonomy: India's Experience with the International Computer Industry.* Berkeley: University of California Press.

Haddad, Mona, and Ann Harrison. 1993. Are There Positive Spillovers from Direct Foreign Investment? Evidence from Panel Data for Morocco. *Journal of Development Economics* 42, no. 1 (October): 51–74.

Harrison, Ann. 1996. Determinants and Effects of Direct Foreign Investment in Cote d'Ivoire, Morocco, and Venezuela. In *Industrial Evolution in Developing Countries: Micro Patterns of Turnover, Productivity, and Market Structure,* ed., Marc J. Roberts and James R. Tybout. New York: Oxford University Press for the World Bank.

Harvard Business School. 1990. *Mexico and the Microcomputers.* Case 9-390-093. Cambridge, MA: Harvard Business School.

Harvard Business School. 1993. *Adam Opel AG,* Case 9-392-100, 101, 127. Cambridge, MA: Harvard Business School.

IMF (International Monetary Fund). 2001. *International Financial Statistics: Mauritius.* Washington: International Monetary Fund.

Javorcik, Beata Smarzynska, and Kamal Saggi. 2004. Technological Asymmetry Among Foreign Investors and Mode of Entry. Working Paper.

Kalotay, Kalman. 2002. Central and Eastern Europe: Export Platform for Investors? *The Journal of World Investment* 3, no. 6 (December): 1042–49.

Kathuria, Vinish. 2001. Productivity Spillovers from Technology Transfer to Indian Manufacturing Firms. *Journal of International Development* 12: 343–69.

King, Cary, Robert O. Keohane, and Sidney Verba. 1994. *Designing Social Inquiry: Scientific Inference in Qualitative Research.* Princeton, NJ: Princeton University Press.

Klein, Karen. 1995. *General Motors in Hungary: The Corporate Strategy Behind Szentgotthard.* Washington: Georgetown University, Pew Economic Freedom Fellows Program.

Kokko, Ari. 1994. Technology, Market Characteristics, and Spillovers. *Journal of Development Economics* 43, no. 4: 279–93.

Krueger, Anne O. 1975. *The Benefits and Costs of Import Substitution in India: A Microeconomic Study.* Minneapolis: University of Minnesota Press.

Lee, J.-Y., and Edwin Mansfield. 1996. Intellectual Property Protection and US Foreign Direct Investment. *Review of Economics and Statistics* 78, no. 2: 181–86.

Lim, Linda Y. C. 2001. *The Globalization Debate: Issues and Challenges.* Geneva: International Labor Organization.

Lim, Linda Y. C., and Pang Eng Fong. 1991. *Foreign Direct Investment and Industrialization in Malaysia, Singapore, Taiwan and Thailand.* Paris: Organization for Economic Cooperation and Development.

Lipsey, Robert E. 2000. Affiliates of US and Japanese Multinationals in East Asian Production and Trade. In *The Role of Foreign Direct Investment in East Asian Economic Development,* ed., Takatoshi Ito and Anne O. Krueger. Chicago: University of Chicago Press for the National Bureau of Economic Research.

Lipsey, Robert E. 2002. *Home and Host Effects of FDI.* NBER Working Paper 9293 (October). Cambridge, MA: National Bureau of Economic Research.

Madani, Dorsati. 1999. *A Review of the Role and Impact of Export Processing Zones.* World Bank PREM-EP Working Paper (August). Washington: World Bank.

Mansfield, Edwin, and Anthony Romeo. 1980. Technology Transfer to Overseas Subsidiaries by US-Based Firms. *Quarterly Journal of Economics* 95, no. 4: 737–50.

Maskus, Keith E. 2000. *Intellectual Property Rights in the Global Economy.* Washington: Institute for International Economics.

McKendrick, David G., Richard F. Donner, and Stephan Haggard. 2000. *From Silicon Valley to Singapore: Location and Competitive Advantage in the Hard Disk Drive Industry.* Stanford, CA: Stanford University Press.

Meade, James. 1961. Mauritius: A Case Study in Malthusian Economics. *Economic Journal* b71 (September): 521–34.

Moran, Theodore H. 1998. *Foreign Direct Investment and Development: The New Policy Agenda for Developing Countries and Economies in Transition.* Washington: Institute for International Economics.

Moran, Theodore H. 2001. *Parental Supervision: The New Paradigm for Foreign Direct Investment and Development.* POLICY ANALYSES IN INTERNATIONAL ECONOMICS 64. Washington: Institute for International Economics.

Moran, Theodore H. 2002. *Beyond Sweatshops.* Washington: Brookings Institution.

Moran, Theodore H. 2005. *Foreign Direct Investment and the Development of Low Income Poorly Performing States.* Center for Global Development. Forthcoming.

Mutti, John. 2004. *Foreign Direct Investment and Tax Competition.* Washington: Institute for International Economics.

Ngo, H., and D. Conklin. 1996. *Mekong Corporation and the Viet Nam Motor Vehicle Industry.* The University of Western Ontario: Richard Ivey School of Business, 96-H002.

Okamoto, Y., and Fredrik Sjöholm. 2000. Productivity in the Indonesian Automotive Industry. *ASEAN Economic Bulletin* 17: 1–14.

Peres Nuñez, Wilson. 1990. *Foreign Direct Investment and Industrial Development in Mexico.* Paris: Organization for Economic Cooperation and Development.

Radelet, Steven. 1999. *Manufactured Exports, Export Platforms, and Economic Growth.* Harvard Institute for International Development, CAER II Discussion Paper 43 (November). Cambridge, MA: Harvard University.

Ramachandran, V. 1993. Technology Transfer, Firm Ownership, and Investment in Human Capital. *Review of Economics and Statistics* 75, no. 4: 664–70.

Rasiah, R. 1995. *Foreign Capital and Industrialization in Malaysia.* New York: St. Martin's Press.

Razafindrakoto, Mireille, and François Roubaud. 1995. Les Entreprises Franches à Madagascar: Economie d'Enclave ou Promesse d'Une Nouvelle Prospérité? Nouvel Exclavage ou Opportunité pour le Développement du Pays? *Economie de Madagascar,* no. 2.

Rhee, Yung Whee, Katharina Katterback, and Jeanette While. 1990. *Free Trade Zones in Export Strategies.* Washington: World Bank, Industry Development Division (December).

Rodrik, Dani. 1999. *The New Global Economy and Developing Countries: Making Openness Work.* Washington: Johns Hopkins University Press for the Overseas Development Council.

Romer, Paul. 1993a. Idea Gaps and Object Gaps in Economic Development. *Journal of Monetary Economics* 32, no. 1: 543–73.

Romer, Paul. 1993b. Two Strategies for Economic Development: Using Ideas and Producing Ideas. In *Proceedings of the World Bank Annual Conference on Development Economics.* Washington: World Bank.

Romer, Paul. 1994. New Goods, Old Theory, and the Welfare Costs of Trade Restrictions. *Journal of Development Economics* 43, no. 3: 5–38.

Samuels, Barbara C. 1990. *Managing Risk in Developing Countries: National Demands and Multinational Response.* Princeton, NJ: Princeton University Press.

Scarbrough, Elinor, and Eric Tanenbaum. 1998. *Research Strategies in the Social Sciences: A Guide to New Approaches.* Oxford: Oxford University Press.

Shah, Anwar, ed. 1995. *Fiscal Incentives for Investment and Innovation.* New York: Oxford University Press for the World Bank.

Spar, Debora. 1998. *Attracting High Technology Investment: Intel's Costa Rican Plant.* Foreign Investment Advisory Service Occasional Paper 11. Washington: World Bank Group.

Thomas, Kenneth P. 2000. *Competing for Capital: Europe and North America in a Global Era.* Washington: Georgetown University Press.

Truman, Edwin M. 2002. How Far Have We/They Come? Performance Scorecard for Major Emerging Market Economies. The Bretton Woods Committee, Scorecard Symposium, Washington (April 19).

UNCTAD (United Nations Conference on Trade and Development). 2001. *World Investment Report 2001: Promoting Linkages.* Geneva: United Nations Conference on Trade and Development.

UNCTAD (United Nations Conference on Trade and Development). 2001. Host Country Operational Measures. *UNCTAD Series on Issues in International Investment Agreements.* Geneva.

UNCTAD (United Nations Conference on Trade and Development). 2003. *World Investment Report 2003: FDI Policies for Development: National and International Perspectives,* (Annex table B.1.). UNCTAD FDI/TNC database www.unctad.org/fdistatistics.

Urata, Shujiro, and Hiroki Kawai. 2000. Intrafirm Technology Transfer by Japanese Manufacturing Firms in Asia. In *The Role of Foreign Direct Investment in East Asian Economic Development,* ed., Takatoshi Ito and Anne O. Krueger. Chicago: University of Chicago Press for the National Bureau of Economic Research.

Vietnam Investment Review. 2002. Automobile Sector in a Spin, no. 548 (April 15–21).

Wasow, Bernard. 2003. The Benefits of Foreign Direct Investment in the Presence of Price Distortions: The Case of Kenya. Photocopy (May).

Weintraub, Sidney. 2004. Ten Years Hence: Is NAFTA Succeeding? *Texas Business Review* (June): 1–5.

Wheeler, David, and Ashoka Mody. 1992. International Investment Location Decisions: The Case of U.S. Firms. *Journal of International Economics* 33: 57–76.

WTO (World Trade Organization). 2002. Development Provisions. Note by the WTO Secretariat to the Working Group on the Relationship between Trade and Investment (June 11).

12

China's Policies on FDI: Review and Evaluation

GUOQIANG LONG

Foreign direct investment (FDI) has been one of the most discussed topics in the drive for economic globalization. Multinational corporations (MNCs) consider FDI an important means to reorganize their production activities across borders, in accordance with their corporate strategies and the competitive advantages of host countries. Host countries regard inflow of FDI as a significant opportunity for integrating their economies into the global market and promoting their economic development. To maximize FDI's benefits in economic development, host country governments employ a variety of policies and measures. Performance requirements might serve as an important policy tool in this regard, since they help enhance the benefits brought along by, and address those concerns in relation to, FDI inflow. However, the effectiveness of performance requirements still remains a controversial issue: A number of developing countries believe that performance requirements require foreign-invested enterprises' (FIE) compliance with host countries' development objectives, while critics, especially those hailing from developed countries, question their effectiveness. Though some performance requirements were called off after China's accession to the World Trade Organization (WTO), certain voluntary performance requirements remain.

Since 1993, China has been boasting the largest amount of FDI inflow of all developing countries, with about 90 percent of it brought in by green-

Guoqiang Long is senior research fellow and deputy director general of the Department of Foreign Economic Relations, the Development Research Center of the State Council of the People's Republic of China. Opinions presented in the paper are those of the author and should not be attributed to the institute that the author belongs to.

field investment. FDI has played an important role in contributing to the country's economic/trade development and institutional reform. In fact, the Chinese government has already formulated a series of FDI policies, such as tax incentives and the Guiding Directory on Industries Open to Foreign Investment.

This study evaluates FDI's impact in China and the effectiveness of China's policies governing FDI with regard to export trade and technological advancement. The second section briefly describes the evolution of FDI in China, and the third section summarizes China's FDI policies. The fourth section then evaluates the influence exerted by FDI policies upon export performance requirements, while the fifth section aims to evaluate the effectiveness of technological performance requirements. It ends with a summary conclusion in the sixth section.

The Evolution of FDI in China

Basic Patterns

Since 1993 China has been the biggest developing host country in the world. In fact, by the end of 2003, China had accumulated more than $500 billion in FDI (figure 12.1).[1] FDI in China occurs through joint ventures,[2] cooperative enterprises,[3] and solely foreign-owned enterprises (table 12.1). However, solely foreign-owned enterprises were not permitted unless they either adopted advanced technology and equipment or exported a majority of their products.[4] In 2001, China removed these restrictions, which were also contrary to their WTO commitments, and encouraged foreign-owned enterprises to usher in advanced technology and increase their export volume.[5] As a result, solely foreign-owned enterprises replaced joint ventures as the most popular form of FDI in China.

---

1. Throughout the chapter, all dollar amounts are based on the US dollar unless otherwise noted.

2. Joint ventures refer to enterprises composed of joint investments by foreign companies, enterprises, and other economic organizations or individuals and Chinese companies, enterprises, or other economic organizations. In China, however, foreign parties are required to contribute at least 25 percent of the total capital, which is higher than the 10 percent required by the Organization for Economic Cooperation and Development (OECD) countries and others.

3. Cooperative enterprises are also called "agreement-based partnership businesses," since they are based on cooperative terms and conditions agreed upon by foreign companies, enterprises, and other economic organizations or individuals together with Chinese companies, enterprises, or other economic organizations.

4. See the 1990 *Detailed Implementing Rules for the Law of the People's Republic of China on Wholly Foreign-Owned Enterprises.*

5. See the 2001 *Detailed Implementing Rules for the Law of the People's Republic of China on Wholly Foreign-Owned Enterprises.*

Figure 12.1   FDI in China, 1984–2003

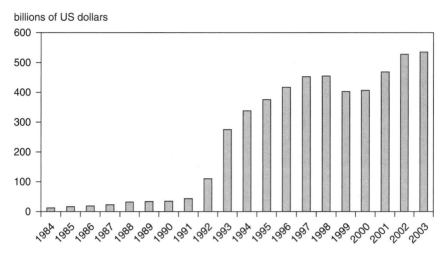

billions of US dollars

Source: China Ministry of Commerce.

Sources of FDI in China

East Asia, particularly Hong Kong, is the most important origin of China's FDI. In 2002, Hong Kong's accumulated paid-in FDI amounted to $204.9 billion. Based on official statistical data, Taiwan is also a pivotal origin of China's FDI with an accumulated $33.1 billion. In fact, quite a few Taiwanese businessmen invested in mainland China via such springboards as Hong Kong, the Virgin Islands, and the Cayman Islands in order to avoid the multiple restrictions exerted by the incumbent Taiwan authority. Indeed, the actual amount of Taiwan-originated investment in mainland China may be two to three times the amount publicly acknowledged. Therefore, it is unsurprising that Taiwan ranks as the second most important place of origin of FDI in China. In addition, the United States, Japan, and some developed countries in Europe have also contributed to FDI in China (see table 12.2). It is worth pointing out that renowned FIEs from developed countries have been the primary investors in China, and they fund large-scale capital- and technology-intensive projects. The presence of these FIEs, such as IBM, GE, GM, Motorola, Sony, and Samsung, is particularly significant for China since it signals the greater possibility of even more future foreign investment.

Distribution of FDI in Various Chinese Industries

More than 80 percent of FDI in China is greenfield investments, and most FDI is in the manufacturing industry. At the end of 2001, FDI in manu-

Table 12.1 Proportional relationship among different patterns of FDI in China (cumulated to 2002 dollars)

	Number of projects	Ratio (percent)	Contract amount (billions of dollars)	Ratio (percent)	Amount realized (billions of dollars)	Ratio (percent)
Joint venture	225,883	53.25	326	39.56	192	42.91
Cooperative	52,965	12.49	163	19.72	83	18.48
Solely foreign owned	145,165	34.22	333	40.16	166	36.97
Others	183	0.04	5	0.56	7	1.64
Total	**424,196**	**100.00**	**828**	**100.00**	**448**	**100.00**

Source: China Ministry of Commerce (2003, 127).

facturing industry constituted 70 percent of total FDI projects, 56 percent of the aggregate amount of FDI, and 60 percent of the aggregate amount of registered capital in FDI in China. In the services sector, FDI is mainly poured into the real estate industry. The investment in the primary industry occupies a rather low proportion of the total investment amount (table 12.3). A majority of FDI has gone into the manufacturing industry because China possesses a competitive edge thanks to its lower costs of production and relatively powerful ability to supply supporting parts. In contrast, China has strictly controlled the flow of FDI into the services sector for a long period.

China's FDI Policies

For the last 25 years, China has aggressively shaped a relatively complete range of laws and regulations governing foreign investment. They include the Law of the People's Republic of China upon Foreign Wholly Owned Enterprises, Law of the People's Republic of China upon Sino-Foreign Joint Ventures, Law of the People's Republic of China upon Sino-Foreign Cooperative Enterprises, and the Guiding Directory on Industries Open to Foreign Investment. China's laws and regulations on FDI also include related preferential policies and stipulations for special economic zones in the country.

In a nutshell, China encourages favorable FDI policies. Therefore, FIEs enjoy preferential treatment when compared to domestic enterprises. In fact, FIEs are entitled to markedly different treatments depending on the region and industry, and this differential treatment is outlined by policies. Furthermore, the Chinese government has stipulated different FDI performance requirements depending on these distinctions.

China has designated certain parts of the country as special economic areas and each is governed by different policies. China has also enforced two policies called Develop China's West at Full Blast and Strategy of

Table 12.2   Top 15 sources of FDI in China (cumulated to the end of 2002 dollars)

	Number of projects	Share (percent)	Contract amount (billions of dollars)	Share (percent)	FDI realized (billions of dollars)	Share (percent)
Hong Kong	210,876	49.71	373.8	45.14	204.9	45.73
United States	37,280	8.79	76.3	9.21	39.9	8.90
Japan	25,147	5.93	49.5	5.98	36.3	8.11
Taiwan	55,691	13.13	61.5	7.42	33.1	7.39
Virgin Islands	6,659	1.57	49.3	5.96	24.4	5.44
Singapore	10,727	2.53	40.1	4.85	21.5	4.79
South Korea	22,208	5.24	27.5	3.32	15.2	3.39
United Kingdom	3,418	0.81	19.6	2.37	10.7	2.39
Germany	3,053	0.72	14.3	1.73	8.0	1.78
France	2,033	0.48	7.2	0.87	5.5	1.24
Macao	7,827	1.85	10.8	1.34	4.7	1.07
Netherlands	1,065	0.25	9.0	1.08	4.3	0.97
Cayman Islands	706	0.17	9.5	1.14	3.8	0.85
Canada	6,040	1.42	10.4	1.25	3.4	0.75
Malaysia	2,538	0.60	6.2	0.75	2.8	0.63
Others	28,928	6.82	63.0	7.61	29.4	6.55
Total	**424,196**	**100.00**	**828.1**	**100.00**	**448.0**	**100.00**

Source: China Ministry of Commerce (2003, 131).

Reviving Rusty Industrial Bases to encourage FDI into its western and northeast regions. Therefore, FDI policies in China's western region entitle foreign enterprises to even more preferential treatment than in other regions of the country.

The Chinese government pays much attention to industrial guidance on FDI. In June 1995, China first promulgated the Provisional Regulations upon Guidance for Foreign Investment Orientations and the Guiding Directory on Industries Open to Foreign Investment. Furthermore, the different preferential treatments granted to enterprises in various industries have mainly been determined under the Guiding Directory. This Guiding Directory was revised first in December 1997, and then again in April 2002 because of China's accession to the WTO. The Guiding Directory is important because it divides FDI-involved projects into four categories: projects that were encouraged, allowed, restricted, and prohibited. These categories are then subdivided even further. For instance, 262 types of encouraged projects, 75 types of restricted projects, and 34 types of prohibited projects exist.

China currently encourages FDI for the purposes of

■ transforming traditional agriculture, developing modern agriculture, and promoting the industrialization of agriculture;

■ producing transportation infrastructure, energy sources, and raw materials, and other basic industries;

Table 12.3 Distribution of accumulated FDI in different industries in China (to the end of 2001)

Sector	Number of companies		Investment amount		Registration capital amount		By foreign investors	
	Number	Share (percent)	Millions of dollars	Share (percent)	Millions of dollars	Share (percent)	Millions of dollars	Share (percent)
Agriculture	4,752	2.35	9,135	1.04	6,180	1.22	4,763	1.32
Mining	1,047	0.52	3,282	0.38	2,317	0.46	1,462	0.41
Manufacturing	141,668	70.03	491,322	56.15	305,250	60.35	214,931	59.76
Electricity, gas, and water	1,268	0.63	49,505	5.66	20,039	3.96	11,606	3.23
Construction	5,139	2.54	21,547	2.46	11,862	2.35	7,743	2.15
Geology investigation	128	0.06	4,237	0.48	1,545	0.31	1,412	0.39
Logistics and communication	3,499	1.73	41,442	4.74	20,432	4.04	15,163	4.22
Distribution	12,249	6.05	24,592	2.81	15,585	3.08	11,311	3.14
Finance and insurance	74	0.04	2,089	0.24	1,965	0.39	1,415	0.39
Real estate	11,925	5.89	149,094	17.04	72,244	14.28	55,536	15.44
Social services	16,169	7.99	56,274	6.43	34,020	6.73	23,188	6.45
Health and sports	469	0.23	2,774	0.32	1,543	0.31	1,128	0.31
Education, culture, and films	530	0.26	1,390	0.16	982	0.19	675	0.19
R&D and technology service	1,851	0.91	4,334	0.50	2,752	0.54	2,171	0.60
Others	1,538	0.76	13,994	1.60	9,079	1.80	7,179	2.00
Total	202,306	100.00	875,011	100.00	505,793	100.00	359,683	100.00

Sources: China Statistical Yearbook 2002, tables 17–19. Percentages were calculated by the author.

- tapping into cutting-edge, technology-oriented industries such as electronic information, bioengineering, new materials, and aviation and aerospace, as well as establishing local R&D centers;

- encouraging foreign businesses to utilize advanced and applicable techniques to transform traditional industries such as machinery, textiles, and consumption goods manufacturing industries as well as to upgrade their equipment and facilities;

- using raw and renewable resources comprehensively, initiating environmental protection projects, and modernizing public utilities;

- encouraging export-oriented FDI projects; and

- building up the industries in China's western region.

In the past, China's FDI laws included some performance requirements. However, to meet WTO membership requirements, within a year of its entry into the organization China revised its three laws and removed the FDI requirements regarding such criteria as export proportion, local contents, balance of foreign exchanges, technology transfer, and creation of R&D centers. The remaining restriction limited ownership share on projects falling in the "restricted" category.[6] However, in practice, the Chinese partners of some joint ventures or cooperatives privately require technology sharing or transfer from FIE foreign investors.

Export Performance Requirement Policies' Influence on FDI

China's FDI policies are complicated. When designing such a set of policies, multiple objectives must be met, including

- strengthening the country's industrial base and increasing the domestic value added,

- promoting linkages,

- generating and increasing the level of exports,

- balancing trade,

- promoting regional development, and

- transferring technology.

---

6. There is no definition of the "restricted" category. Projects falling in this category, such as small electricity stations, usually face some difficulties in securing the approval of the government.

Among these criteria, promoting exports and transferring technology (technological advancement) are China's two most important FDI objectives. This chapter examines whether China's FDI policies regarding these two objectives are effective.

Before China became a member of the WTO, its FDI policies regarding exports could be divided into three categories: compulsory, neutral, and voluntary.

Compulsory policies required that "FDI shall be able to keep a balance of exchanges, or make sure the proportion of their domestically made products in the total number of products reaches a certain benchmark, or a certain percentage of their products must be exported."[7] However, since such requirements are inconsistent with the WTO Agreement on Trade-Related Investment Measures (TRIMs), these compulsory provisions were eliminated.

Neutral polices tried to create fair conditions for exports to compete internationally. For example, the tariff and VAT exemptions on reexport processing imports would level the ground for China's companies to compete in overseas markets. Voluntary policies to promote exports were encouraged. For example, an enterprise with 70 percent of export products is entitled to a 50 percent cut in corporate income tax. Thus, major exporters enjoy more favorable treatment in terms of trade, and these policies have been linked with increasing the level of export performance of enterprises.

This chapter next will analyze the following data to evaluate the effectiveness of China's FDI policies to promote exports.

Export Performance of FDI

After a lapse of 25 years, in 2003 China ranked 4th among other countries in the world's international trade chart, which was a major improvement from its 32nd rank in 1978. China's rapid rise as a trading power has been considered a global economic miracle, and FDI has played a crucial role in developing China's foreign trade.

Table 12.4 displays the development of China's foreign trade as well as the export and import performance of FIEs. As illustrated in the table, the export value registered by FIEs made up only 1.94 percent of China's total export value in 1986, but had climbed up to 54.81 percent in 2003. Between 1986 and 2003, FIEs contributed up to 58.8 percent to China's total increase of export and 62 percent to its increase of import value.

---

7. Law on Foreign-Invested Enterprises, PRC.

Table 12.4 Development of China's foreign trade by FIEs, 1986–2003 (billions of dollars, percent)

Year	Foreign trade turnover			Export			Import		
	Total	By FDI	Percent of FDI	Total	By FDI	Percent of FDI	Total	By FDI	Percent of FDI
1986	73.8	3.0	4.07	30.9	0.6	1.94	42.9	2.4	5.59
1987	82.7	4.6	5.56	39.4	1.2	3.05	43.3	3.4	7.85
1988	102.8	8.3	8.07	47.5	2.5	5.26	55.3	5.8	10.49
1989	111.7	13.7	12.26	32.5	4.9	15.08	79.2	8.8	11.11
1990	115.4	20.1	17.42	62.1	7.8	12.56	53.3	12.3	23.08
1991	135.7	29.0	21.37	71.9	12.0	16.69	63.8	17.0	26.65
1992	165.5	43.7	26.40	84.9	17.4	20.49	80.6	26.3	32.63
1993	195.7	67.1	34.29	91.7	25.2	27.48	104.0	41.9	40.29
1994	236.6	87.6	37.02	122.1	34.7	28.42	114.5	52.9	46.20
1995	280.8	109.8	39.10	148.8	46.9	31.52	132.0	62.9	47.65
1996	289.9	137.1	47.29	151.1	61.5	40.70	138.8	75.6	54.47
1997	325.1	152.6	46.94	182.7	74.9	41.00	142.4	77.7	54.56
1998	323.9	157.7	48.69	183.8	81.0	44.07	140.1	76.7	54.75
1999	360.6	174.5	48.39	194.9	88.6	45.46	165.7	85.9	51.84
2000	474.3	236.7	49.91	249.2	119.4	47.91	225.1	117.3	52.11
2001	509.7	259.1	50.83	266.1	133.2	50.06	343.6	125.9	36.64
2002	620.8	330.2	53.19	325.6	169.9	52.18	295.2	160.3	54.30
2003	851.2	472.2	55.47	438.4	240.3	54.81	412.8	231.9	56.18

FIEs = foreign-invested enterprises

Source: China General Custom, *Custom Statistics, 2003;* China Ministry of Commerce (2003).

Reasons for China's Predominantly Export-Oriented FDI

On the whole, transnational investment can be divided into two categories: In "domestic-market seeking" investment, investors seek to enter the host country's local market. In "export-oriented" or "efficiency-pursuing" investment, investors establish production bases in the host country but export most of their products to the global market. In the past, China's domestic market was small, and the country's restrictive FDI policies prohibiting FIEs from selling locally made sense. Furthermore, China was an ideal low-cost production location to manufacture goods to export. For instance, the wage levels in the United States, Japan, South Korea, and Taiwan are 47.8 times, 29.9 times, 12.9 times, and 20.6 times, respectively, those of China. Today, compared with developed and even developing countries, China has lower production costs, and, equally important, its domestic market has enormous potential for growth. Moreover, China implemented an import substitution strategy between 1949 and 1979, established a relatively complete industrial base, and trained a large number of skilled workers. All of these factors make China an ideal base for production, particularly for East Asia's FIEs. In fact, in 2002, the Japan External Trade Organization (JETRO) (2003) surveyed the overseas branches of Japanese companies and found that the percentage of surveyed companies exporting more than 70 percent of their products is 61.6 percent in China overall, with a staggering 82.5 percent in southern China, compared with the average 55.9 percent for those located in all of Asia. Another 2002 survey, conducted by the Japan Bank for International Cooperation (JBIC), found that 68.9 percent of Japanese enterprises invested in China because of its cheaper labor cost, 25.2 percent considered the country an ideal production base to export products to the global market, and 26.8 percent thought it was an ideal location to export to Japan.

The constant inflow of FDI into China has actually strengthened its capacity to be a production base for manufacturing exports. A "domino effect" inevitably occurs when FIEs in the same industry compete with one another, particularly if they are concentrated in the same region. The competition boosts the development of some supporting industries, improves the general economic climate within these supporting industries, and essentially establishes an important industrial cluster. For example, China's Pearl River Delta and Yangtze River Delta regions have emerged as world-class information technology (IT) clusters. The formation of such industrial clusters helps China absorb an ever increasing amount of FDI, which in turn attracts more foreign investment. Thus, it is unsurprising to find that a 2003 American Chamber of Commerce in China survey of its members found that 56 percent chose to invest in the country because of its ideal location as a production base for global exports and its growing domestic market.

Table 12.5 Export tendency: A comparison of domestic enterprises and FIEs 1998–2002 (billions of dollars)

Year	Export by domestic enterprises	Industrial output of domestic enterprises	Export tendency of domestic enterprises (percent)	Export by FIEs	Industrial output of FIEs	Export tendency of FIEs (percent)
1998	85.32	509.8	16.74	67.23	167.6	40.12
1999	88.23	537.5	16.41	73.54	189.5	38.80
2000	107.73	622.1	17.32	99.10	234.6	42.24
2001	110.31	682.3	16.17	110.56	272.2	40.62
2002	129.23	784.8	16.47	141.02	319.3	44.17

Export tendency = export's share in industrial output
FIEs = foreign-invested enterprises

Note: Industrial output of domestic enterprises refers to that of all state-owned enterprises (SOEs) and non-SOEs with an industrial output higher than 5 million renminbi (equivalent to about $600,000). Data of industrial output for all domestic enterprises are not available after 1999 due to adjustments made by the competent Statistics Authority. Thus, the exporting trend of domestic enterprises is overrated. For example, the exporting tendency of domestic enterprises using data of industrial output for all enterprises is 8.32 percent, only about half of that shown in the table.

Sources: China Statistical Abstract 2003; China Customs Statistics, various years; Jiang (2002).

Effectiveness of China's Export Promotion Policies

China's policies for promoting the exports of FDI have been increasingly effective. As noted earlier, before China's membership in the WTO, there were a number of restrictive policies governing FDI that diverted many potential investors to other countries, especially since the domestic market was small and largely unavailable to FIEs. Those who did invest in China despite the restrictions did so primarily for its lower production costs and to export its products (table 12.5).

China's processing trade policy, which exempts input imports for reexport from tariff and value-added tax (VAT), has improved the country's export value tremendously. Two kinds of processing trade exist in China: processing trade with imported materials (PTI) and processing trade with materials supplied by clients (PTS).[8]

Prior to China's WTO membership, the country maintained a relatively high tariff level (e.g., the average level was 55.6 percent in 1982 and

---

8. Under the PTS pattern, FIEs provide domestic enterprises with intermediate materials such as spare parts and also pay them processing fees. Under the PTI pattern, domestic enterprises purchase imported spare parts and other intermediate materials themselves and then export the finished products after processing and assembling.

43.2 percent in 1992). After China reformed its tax system in 1994,[9] imports were subject to a new 17 percent VAT; and certain imports (e.g., the automobile industry) are further subject to a 10 percent excise tax. Under such a high tariff/VAT system, without any exemptions on imports for PTI or PTS, there would be an incredible decrease in Chinese exports. In order to eliminate this possibility, China implemented the exemption policy immediately after initiating its reform and open policies. Thus, imported raw materials and spare parts used in the export processing industry are exempt from tariff and VAT from the outset and any verification will occur after the finished goods have been exported. However, if the products are not exported and are sold domestically, FIEs will be charged the relevant tariff and VAT taxes. However, China's policy, in order to encourage domestic value added of exports, allows imported raw materials and spare parts to be sold to downstream processing enterprises without levying tariffs/VAT, as long as the processed materials are eventually exported.

Thus, China's processing trade policy has played an important role in helping China attract FDI and expand its exports. Without these exemptions, most of China's early foreign investors would not have invested in the country. In fact, processing trade has always remained the principal mode of FIE exports, and it currently contributes 80 percent of the total export value by FIEs.

Policy factors have also had a significant influence on FIE domestic purchases. As domestic supporting industries have evolved and improved and VAT reimbursement has been implemented, the percentage of local content of China's exports in the processing trade has markedly increased. In 1993, the "domestic value increment rate"[10] recorded in PTI was 17.3 percent, while it was 18.5 percent for PTS. In 2003, the domestic value increment rates of FIE exports climbed to 23.3 percent for PTI and 31.4 percent for PTS. What factors led to the difference between the domestic value increment rates of these two different trading modes? The most viable explanation for the difference lies in the "VAT reimbursement for exports" policy, noted earlier, that China implemented toward these two different trading modes: domestically purchased materials used in PTI may be reimbursed but not in PTS. Essentially, companies engaged in PTI can receive a tax rebate equal to 17 percent of the value of domestically purchased materials, but PTS companies cannot. Such a cost difference is large enough to force enterprises to make a prudent decision on where to purchase materials: domestically or abroad. Although initiated to provide equal footing for domestic raw materials, the opposite effect has occurred. The difference between PTI and PTS in terms of the domestic value increment rate has indicated that the VAT

---

9. Since this 1994 reform, the VAT imposed upon domestically purchased materials can be reimbursed for PTI; however, the "VAT reimbursement for exports" policy does not apply to PTS.

10. Domestic value increment rate = (export − imported inputs)/export*100%.

reimbursement for exports policy has effectively impacted purchasing decisions of FIEs toward imported raw materials and spare parts.

China's policies to promote exports have also affected FDI. For example, an FIE with an export ratio higher than 70 percent receives a 50 percent corporate income tax "discount." In fact, in a survey I conducted in 2001, 121 enterprises, or 27 percent, with higher than 70 percent export ratios received a corporate income tax "discount." Although not precise, the finding illustrates that China's policies have affected FDI and export performance. For example, as figure 12.2 illustrates, when enterprises were asked what the most important factor that influenced their decision to conduct processing trade in China was, most stated that the country's favorable FDI policies were the main factor (8.4 points out of a total 11 points).

FDI's Contribution to Advancing China's Technological Capability

Like many other developing countries, one of China's major goals for FDI is to advance its technological capability. With its FDI policies, China not only encourages technology into the country, but also seeks to establish more R&D centers. China also seeks to use FDI to transform its traditional industries through advanced and applicable technology.

Introducing Advanced Technology

FDI's contribution to advancing China's technological capability can be divided into three types: filling in the technological gaps, introducing advanced technology, and improving existing technology. According to several investigations, FDI has introduced a significant amount of advanced technology. Dr. Xiaojuan Jiang (2002, 52) chaired a survey of 127 FIEs that showed 83 respondents, or 65 percent of FIEs, adopted some technology that filled in certain technological gaps in China while 44 respondents, or 35 percent of FIEs, used domestically advanced technology. In another two surveys that Professor Zhile Wang (1995) chaired, similar results were found. One survey of 33 global FIEs found that 52 percent employed some technology that filled in the technological gaps in China (Zhile Wang 1995); the second survey of 40 Japanese enterprises in China found that 95 percent either employed some technology that filled in certain technological gaps in China or adopted some advanced technology (Zhile Wang 1998). In yet another survey, among all the FDI projects in Beijing's industrial sector, 81 percent ushered in advanced technology from abroad, which helped advance its domestic technological skill level by about 15 years (He and Zhang 1999). I also chaired a survey (Long et al. 2003) of 442 FIEs engaged in China's processing trade. The survey found that 26.8 percent

Figure 12.2 Factors affecting the decision of FIEs doing export processing in China

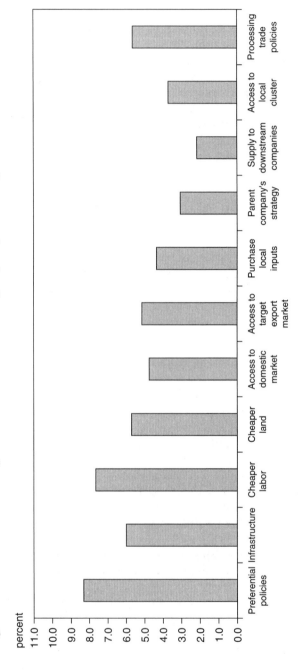

Source: Long et al. (2003, 162).

Table 12.6   Difference of technology used by type of FDI (percent)

Type of FDI	1	2	3	4	5
Domestic majority-owned joint ventures	5.8	2.3	52.3	5.8	33.7
Equally shared joint ventures	22.6	0	41.9	9.7	25.8
Foreign majority-owned joint ventures	39.7	1.3	26.9	17.9	14.1
Solely foreign-owned	31.7	1.7	29.4	23.3	16.7
Cooperative foreign-owned	28.0	6.0	32.2	2.0	24.0
Total foreign-owned	26.8	2.1	34.8	15.3	21.2

Columns:
1. The most advanced technology in parent companies.
2. Technology not available in China.
3. Equal to the most advanced technology used in China before the surveyed company was established.
4. Ordinary technology in parent companies, less advanced than 3.
5. Technology broadly used in China, the least advanced level.

Source: Long et al. (2003).

of the enterprises used the most advanced technologies of their parent companies, while 2.1 percent used technology not previously used in the country and 34.8 percent adopted technology that measured up to China's most advanced level. Unsurprisingly, foreign wholly-owned and majority-owned FDI tend to use more advanced technologies (table 12.6).

FDI in China has constantly upgraded the country's technological level as result of increasing competition. According to the results of the same survey I chaired (Long et al. 2003) 29.9 percent of the 442 FIEs registered "great technological advancement," 61.5 percent registered "some certain technological advancement," and 7.3 percent registered "no technological advancement," while 1.3 percent posted "some technological backslide." According to the findings of a tracing investigation chaired by Dr. Jiang (Jiang 2002) among FIEs surveyed in 2002, 60 percent employed advanced technology (i.e., technology at the same level as employed by their parent companies), while 40 percent adopted relatively advanced technology (i.e., lagged by 2 to 3 years behind the technology of their parent companies). In contrast, these two figures in 1997 were 13 percent and 54 percent, respectively (table 12.7).

Establishing R&D Centers

Since 1999, China's official FDI policies have encouraged foreign investors to establish their R&D centers in the country. For example, major policies include:

■ any imported equipment and supporting technology confined to the FIE's laboratory and used for pilot experiments (and not production) are exempt from tariff and other import taxes;

Table 12.7 Technological skill level of FIEs in China (percent)

Level	1997	2002
Technology at the same level as their parent company	13	60
Technology lagging 2–3 years behind their parent company	54	40
Technology that their parent company has washed out	33	—

FIEs = foreign-invested enterprises

Source: Jiang (2004).

- income from the transfer of technology that has been developed solely by an FIE is exempt from sales tax;

- an FIE with technological development expenses at least 10 percent over its previous year is entitled to a 50 percent discount of its total technological development expenses in the current year's corporate income tax (subject to approval by the taxation authority); and

- FIEs with R&D centers in China are allowed to import and sell a small quantity of high-tech products on a trial basis in the local market, if they are goods produced as a result of the R&D by their parent companies (China Ministry of Commerce 2003, 107).

In addition, China's regional governments offer multiple preferential policies for FIEs in a number of ways, including reduced land use fees and assistance with employee recruitment.

As 2002 official data showed, about 400 FIEs have established independent R&D centers in China; Microsoft, GE, Motorola, Intel, GM, Honda, Siemens, Nortel, and Volkswagen head the list. Earlier, these R&D centers were mainly engaged in technological R&D activities geared toward transforming products for local market consumers. Recently, particularly in the last two years, some strategic-minded FIEs such as Microsoft and GE began to initiate R&D activities in their China R&D centers for the global market (Jiang 2004). Most FIEs establish R&D centers within their respective companies. According to the findings of the survey I chaired (Long et al. 2003), of the 442 FIEs engaged in the processing trade, 1.27 percent not only meet their own demands but also sell technology patents, 48.28 percent can meet most of their own demands, and 22.06 percent can meet some of their own demands. However, 28.59 percent of the surveyed FIEs do not have an R&D center (Long et al. 2003, 76).

FIEs establish R&D centers in China for a number of reasons. First, they do so in order to meet their business needs. As noted earlier, China has become an increasingly important market and/or production base so products need to be redesigned to meet local demand. Thus, R&D and manufacturing become more intricately entwined. Second, FIEs can readily take advantage of China's wealth of scientific research and technological talent. FIEs have established their R&D centers in regions where colleges and universities exist so they can recruit talent at lower cost than in other countries. In fact, these R&D FIE centers work cooperatively with many Chinese scientific research organizations. For example, the Swiss Novartis Company works with Shanghai Institute of Materia Medica under the Chinese Academy of Sciences to study and develop new types of drugs made of natural ingredients. Last, setting up R&D centers in China is a policy criterion that improves relations between governments. For seeking a long-term presence in China, establishing R&D centers in the country not only wins favor from the Chinese government but also helps the FIEs' business by helping them tailor products to the local market. It is a win-win situation for everyone involved.

Generating Technological Spillover Effects

Host countries must try their best to prevent crowding-out effects toward domestic enterprises from FIEs' R&D and to make full use of their spillover effects.

FIEs generate technology spillover effects most often when: developing and producing new products in the local market, providing technical assistance to supporting enterprises to meet new technology requirements, collaborating for developing technology, training and then losing staff to domestic companies, and providing domestic enterprises with a manufacturing base from which to develop new products. As a developing country, China has lagged behind developed countries in terms of developing new products. For instance, when the mobile communication market emerged, equipment and mobile phones were all either imported or produced by FIEs in China. Thus, FIEs helped develop this market. The market's quick growth and high profitability drove local Chinese enterprises to quickly and successfully engage in the industry by working with FIEs through joint ventures and cooperative companies. China is regarded as the world's largest mobile communications market, and in the mobile phone market, domestic brand products make up more than 60 percent of the total market share.[11]

After entering the Chinese market, FIEs typically develop a "vertical division of labor" with domestic enterprises. For example, Motorola is supplied by up to 80 supporting enterprises in Tianjin, where it established a plant, and also by 170 other supporting enterprises outside Tianjin. In order to ensure consistent product quality, FIEs often stipulate specific ordering requirements to their local suppliers. These requirements are

---

11. China's domestic enterprises began producing mobile phones in 1999. In 1999, the market share of domestic brand mobile phones was 2 percent and has increased significantly in a short time. Market share of domestic brand mobile phones was 8 percent in 2000, 15 percent in 2001, 30 percent in 2002, and 60 percent in the first 10 months of 2003 (*Beijing Newspaper,* December 22, 2003, tech.tom.com/1121/2069/20031222-72485.html).

often met after FIEs send drawings or even personnel to offer technical guidance to domestic enterprises.

As noted earlier, FIEs have successfully collaborated with domestic enterprises and scientific research institutions to develop new technology. In fact, most Chinese partners have already been leading competitors in the local industry when they enter into a joint venture. For example, the Lenovo Group worked with Oracle to develop ERP software to meet the demands of small and medium-sized companies; the Langchao Group cooperated with LG to develop company-used Composite Solutions software; and TCL worked with French Alcatel to develop new mobile communication technologies. These collaborations not only developed new technologies for both also enhanced their respective competitiveness in the market. But more importantly, domestic enterprises developed their technological capabilities, and FIEs tapped into China's high-caliber scientific research institutions and employee pool and worked with them to conduct technological cooperation.

What about the human factor? The results of the survey I chaired (Long et al. 2003, 82) show that 85.4 percent of 442 enterprises engaged in the processing trade have trained their employees in China, 21.3 percent trained their employees abroad, and only 8.89 percent did not train any of their employees. Training was offered to managerial staff members, technical specialists, and ordinary workers as well. As these employees left FIEs to either start up or work for rival companies,[12] the training has contributed to the benefit of the entire society.

Foreign investment has also provided China's domestic enterprises with a manufacturing base from which to develop new products. This technological spillover has been particularly beneficial in certain regions. For example, ZTE Telecommunications Co. Ltd., an emerging telecommunications equipment manufacturer based in Shenzhen, has taken advantage of the Pearl River Delta region to develop and produce a huge quantity of highly competitive ITC products.

"Crowding Out" and "Spillover Effects"

Throughout the world, FDI's affects on host countries vary. Crowding out and technology spillover effects inevitably occur, however, and they are often compared.

In many developing countries, FDI generates crowding-out effects upon the host country's market, preventing domestic enterprises from developing. In China, FDI's crowding-out effects occur in two ways. First, FIEs

---

12. According to the same survey (Long et al. 2003), 90 percent of FIE-trained employees left to work for other organizations, with some senior management staff members and technological development specialists working for rival Chinese companies.

have easily recruited scientifically and technologically talented workers with higher wages. In the mid-1990s, this scenario was common since SOEs maintained rigid infrastructures and were unable to provide advancement opportunities or high wages for their employees.[13] Similarly, China's private domestic enterprises were just emerging and were equally unable to attract large numbers of talented employees.

However, changes began at the end of the 1990s. First, a large number of SOEs were restructured to meet current market requirements and aggressively recruited talented job seekers. Second, as Chinese private enterprises (e.g., Huawei, ZTE, TCL, etc.) have developed and become leading technology providers, they have attracted large numbers of extremely talented tech personnel. Third, as the Chinese market grows ever larger and is globally targeted, Chinese students who have studied abroad have returned home to either establish their own businesses or work in domestic enterprises. Consequently, domestic enterprises have increased their technological capabilities. Furthermore, these changes have significantly offset FDI's crowding-out effects.

Second, FDI's crowding-out effects in China occur because foreign investors restrict any technological development by their Chinese partners through their controlling interest in joint ventures. In fact, foreign investors' better understanding of intellectual property rights' (IPRs) importance gave them the upper hand when stipulating stronger control of IPRs under joint venture contracts.[14] Also, since most parent companies of FIEs controlled R&D and produced most of the goods from joint ventures, domestic investors in JVs were unable to establish independent R&D centers. China's automobile industry is a prime example of this crowding-out effect. In recent years, China's automobile industry has developed quickly. In 2003, the number of cars produced in China reached 2.069 million, up by 80.7 percent from the preceding year, and the number of cars sold amounted to 2.04 million, up by 92.8 percent from 2002. Unsurprisingly, all major worldwide automobile makers have established joint ventures in China. In these joint ventures, although foreign investors possess no more than 50 percent of the total share capital, they usually control developing technology so that domestic partners must obtain their approval for any technological improvements to existing car models. Therefore, some domestic private enterprises, after overcoming government restrictions, have entered the automobile industry with new car models they have developed without establishing JVs with foreign partners. Thus, despite MNCs' restrictions in joint ventures, overall, FDI's spillover effects in China's automobile industry have been positive.

---

13. However, SOEs did provide such fringe benefits as medical insurance coverage, housing allowances, and retirement pensions, but well-educated young employees preferred a high salary.

14. Unsurprisingly, many domestic brands disappeared after these joint ventures broke up.

However, it is important to note the difference between China's automobile industry and others (e.g., the IT industry). Domestic automakers were restricted by overprotective government policy and their technological innovation abilities were also underdeveloped. The local market offered little or no motivation to compete. However, after China's membership in the WTO, many restrictions on the automobile industry were removed, import tariffs were drastically reduced, and a decrease in car prices has rapidly increased demand for cars. Thus, competition in the market has increased the quality and quantity of cars in China.

On the whole, FDI's spillover effects have appeared more eye-catching than its crowding-out effects. When comparing China's development with other developing nations across industries this is particularly apparent. Several factors affect this result. First, big market scale leaves enough growing space for domestic enterprises despite fierce competition from FIEs. In a small economy, big FIEs usually deprive the opportunities of domestic enterprises. Second, if the industrial foundation in the host country has been poorly developed, MNC considers the host country as nothing more than a production base and therefore rarely establishes links with domestic enterprises. The "enclave-featured economy" of FIEs limits "spillover effects." However, if the host country's industrial foundation is well developed, like China in recent years, FIEs are encouraged to purchase as many domestically made raw materials and spare parts as possible. Consequently, FIEs establish strong links and cooperate with domestic enterprises, which causes significant technology spillover. Third, competition between FIEs and domestic enterprises spurs technology spillover.

China's FDI policies of performance requirements have only introduced limited technology. China implemented a "swap market for technology" strategy, which essentially required foreign investors to "import" advanced technology in return for entering the domestic market. To return to the automobile industry as an example, China requires its foreign investors to operate in joint ventures with domestic automobile enterprises. These joint ventures, as noted earlier, require that FIEs own no more than 50 percent in total shares and that they transfer technology to their domestic partners. FIEs thus introduce new car models and manufacturing techniques from their parent companies, which are more advanced than those of their domestic partners. However, the "swap market for technology" strategy backfires since the government must control access to the domestic market—namely, by restricting other enterprises from entering the market. In order to do so, higher tariffs are imposed and nontariff barriers are erected to protect the domestic market, which essentially prohibits competition. Consequently, foreign investors are no longer motivated to pursue technological advances since lack of competition makes it unnecessary. For example, in 1985 when Volkswagen entered the domestic market through a joint venture, the VW Santana introduced more advanced technology than the domestically made cars. This outdated and unimproved model continued to be produced by Shanghai Volkswagen.

As the automobile industry example illustrates, it is not enough to effect compulsory policies concerning introduction and transfer of technology. Equally important are policies that promote competition, IPR protection, and the like. Essentially, the entire domestic market must be developed in such a way that FIEs become an integral part of the economy.

Conclusion

China introduced foreign direct investment over 20 years ago and has progressively pursued foreign investment while adjusting its FDI policies. Since 1993, China has attracted the largest amount of FDI of all developing countries while increasing its levels of both exports and technological advancement.

To increase its level of exports, China has implemented compulsory, neutral, and voluntary FDI policies. Compulsory policies required that "FDI shall be able to keep a balance of exchanges, or make sure the proportion of their domestically made products in the total number of products reaches a certain benchmark, or a certain percentage of their products must be exported."[15] Interested foreign investors have to meet such requirements before receiving approval for investing in China. As China has ameliorated its balance of payments constantly, these compulsory requirements, have, in practice, played a decreasingly important role. In fact, authorities would rather pursue other policy-front objectives (such as ushering in technology). After China's membership in the WTO, the government eliminated most of these compulsory requirements to conform with the TRIMs Agreement. China has already attracted a huge amount of FDI and exports a high level of manufactured products. Simultaneously, China has implemented neutral (such as refunding of VAT for export) and voluntary policies (such as tax preference and trade facilitation) to promote exports. China's favorable FDI policies have apparently played an important role in improving the country's level of exports (as evident in the number of supporting survey results cited earlier). Like many other developing countries, China's major FDI policy objective is to introduce advanced technology. China's former compulsory FDI policies and a number of its voluntary policies have helped make this a reality with the added bonus of establishing a large number of R&D centers in the country as well. However, as a host country, China should pay close attention to technology spillover effects and less to crowding-out effects from FDI, particularly given its growing domestic market.

---

15. Laws on foreign direct investment in China.

Market competition is a much stronger force for sustaining technological advancement than FDI policies stipulating performance requirements. If we compare the progress of technology in an overprotected industry, such as the automobile industry, with a competitive one, it is evident that a number of supporting policies must exist beyond compulsory or voluntary FDI policies to advance technological progress. As China's automobile industry illustrates, the most important factor is to create a market climate that is conducive to full competition, since only competition will drive enterprises to embrace enduring technological advancement. As noted earlier, it is also necessary to create an environment that protects and encourages technological innovation by reinforcing the protection of IPRs as well as intensifying the effects of education and training.

It is also important to promote competition and links between FIEs and domestic enterprises so that FIEs blend seamlessly into the local economy and become an integral part of it. Simultaneously, domestic enterprises will constantly enhance their technological innovation capabilities.

References

American Chamber of Commerce, People's Republic of China. 2003. *American Business in China*. White Paper.
China Ministry of Commerce. 1990. Detailed Implementing Rules For the Law of the People's Republic of China on Wholly Foreign-Owned Enterprises. www.mfocom.gov.cn.
China Ministry of Commerce. 2001. Detailed Implementing Rules For the Law of the People's Republic of China on Wholly Foreign-Owned Enterprises. www.mfocom.gov.cn.
China Ministry of Commerce. 2003. *Foreign Investment Report 2003*. www.mfocom.gov.cn.
Bing He, and Siqiang Zhang. 1999. Study of Technological Innovation Issues in Beijing's Industrial Sector with Regard to Utilization of Foreign Investment. Working paper of Research Topic II of Beijing International Trade Society.
Japan External Trade Organization (JETRO). 2003. *Japanese-Affiliated Manufacturers in Asia, Survey 2002 Summary* (March). www.jetro.go.jp/ec/e/stat/surveys/manufacturers_asia.pdf.
Xiaojuan Jiang. 2002. *China's FDI Economy*. Beijing: University of China Press.
Xiaojuan Jiang. 2004. On the Influence Exerted by Absorption of FDI toward China's Drive for Technological Advancement and Enhancement of Its R&D Capabilities. In *The Collection of Speeches Delivered on the Symposium "Review and Perspective of China's Strategy of Ushering in Foreign Capital."* Beijing: Chinese Academy of Social Sciences.
Guoqiang Long, Liping Zhang, Lei Feng, and Yue Pan. 2003. *Processing Trade in China: A New Path of Industrialization*. Beijing: China Development Press.
Zhile Wang, ed. 1995. *Investments in China of World Famous FIEs*. Beijing: China Economic Press.
Zhile Wang, ed. 1998. *Japanese Investment in China*. Beijing: China Economic Press.

13

Is Africa's Skepticism of Foreign Capital Justified? Evidence from East African Firm Survey Data

TODD J. MOSS, VIJAYA RAMACHANDRAN, and MANJU KEDIA SHAH

The world has increasingly recognized that private capital has a vital role to play in economic development. The United Nation's (UN) Millennium Declaration explicitly calls for greater foreign direct investment (FDI) to Africa. Over the course of the 1990s, African countries significantly liberalized the environment for foreign investment. Nearly all countries revised their national laws governing FDI, and the vast majority lifted controls on capital (UNCTAD 1998).

Despite these substantial changes, Africa has not received the levels of FDI that reformers had expected. At the same time, within Africa, a deeply rooted skepticism toward foreign investment remains, owing to historical, ideological, and political reasons. These sentiments have manifested themselves through a range of barriers to foreign investment, including nationalization of foreign firms, heavy state intervention in the economy, direct legal restrictions on foreign investment, and a host of indirect barriers. Some of the early ideological objections to foreign capital have eroded over time, and most of the legal restrictions have been removed as countries have pursued economic policy reforms over the past two decades. Nevertheless, some constraints remain in place, and many of the indirect barriers remain significant obstacles to higher flows to the continent.

Todd Moss is research fellow at the Center for Global Development. Vijaya Ramachandran is assistant professor at Georgetown University. Manju Kedia Shah is consultant at the World Bank. We thank Robert Lawrence and Ted Moran for helpful comments on an earlier draft and Alicia Bannon for excellent research assistance. All judgments, opinions, and errors are those of the authors alone and do not represent the views of the Center for Global Development, Georgetown University, the World Bank, or their respective staffs or boards of directors, nor the countries that the executive directors of the World Bank represent.

At least part of the lingering antiforeign-capital climate is rooted in specific concerns that purported benefits of foreign investment are not being realized. This chapter outlines the context of Africa's view of foreign capital and then uses new data from firm surveys conducted in Kenya, Tanzania, and Uganda as part of the World Bank's Regional Program on Enterprise Development (RPED) to assess some of these specific concerns about the effects of FDI in poor countries.

Foreign Investment in Sub-Saharan Africa

The literature on the effects of FDI in developing countries lists a range of prospective benefits to the recipient country. At the macroeconomic level, FDI by definition brings new capital for investment, contributing to the balance of payments, adding to the country's capital stock, and potentially adding to future economic growth. FDI is also cited as a more stable type of capital flow, and thus is arguably more appropriate and development friendly for low-income countries than portfolio flows. There is also some evidence that foreign investment can contribute to raising exports and integrating into global economic networks. At the microeconomic level there are also a range of purported benefits, especially higher productivity through new investment in physical and human capital, increased employment, enhanced management, and the transfer of technology. Foreign investment also is thought to have important spillover effects on local firms through supply and distribution chains, trading, and outsourcing (see, among many, e.g., Blomström and Kokko 1997, 1998; Markusen and Venables 1997).

Partly as a result of the growing recognition that FDI can play an important role in economic growth and development, low-income countries have increasingly engaged in competition to attract foreign investment. Most low-income countries have undergone some type of policy reform designed to reduce barriers and attract investment and most also now have some explicit kind of investment promotion agency. Because a range of studies looking at determinants of FDI has pointed to the business environment as a key factor,[1] countries have typically moved toward macroeconomic stability, enhanced contract enforcement, and other measures thought to be investment friendly.

Africa has also been part of this trend. Many countries have taken steps to liberalize the environment for FDI, gradually allowing foreign investors to operate in an increasing number of sectors. Indeed, whereas countries used to list those specific sectors open to foreign investment, now the norm is to assume a legally open regime with restricted sectors listed as the

---

1. See, for example, Goldsborough et al. (1996), MIGA (2002), Pigato (2001), and Asiedu (2003). For Africa, see Morisset (2000).

Figure 13.1 Inward FDI to Africa, 1970–2002
(three-year running averages)

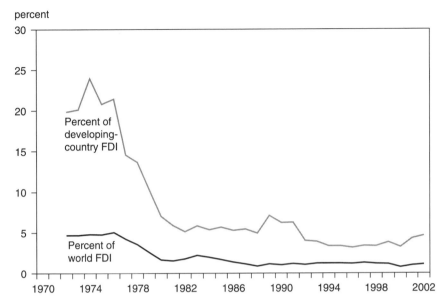

percent

Note: These figures are based on totaling 48 sub-Saharan African country figures and thus are not the same as UNCTAD's reported "Africa" aggregate total, which includes North African countries. In this study, Sudan is considered to be a sub-Saharan nation.

Source: UNCTAD FDI database.

exceptions. There have also been some policies actively designed to attract investment, such as tax holidays, reduced import and customs controls, infrastructure investment, and labor law reform.

The response to Africa's investment policy changes has been mixed. Inward FDI to Africa has been marked by three general trends over the past three decades. First, levels have generally increased over time in nominal absolute terms. Average annual flows in the 1970s to sub-Saharan Africa averaged just $907 million. In the 1980s, this figure rose only slightly to $1.3 billion, but jumped to $4.3 billion in the 1990s. In the most recent three years for which data are available (2000–02), the average inward FDI to sub-Saharan Africa has more than doubled again to $9.3 billion per year.

Despite these increases, total world FDI has grown much faster. As a result, Africa's relative share of global FDI, which averaged around 5 percent in the early 1970s, fell to 1 percent by the early 1980s—and has not recovered above this level (see figure 13.1). This loss in FDI share has coincided with other developing regions attracting much higher levels of FDI, also pushing down Africa's relative share. Africa's portion of all FDI to

Table 13.1   Inward FDI: Sub-Saharan Africa, 1998–2002
(annual average)

Rank		Net flows (millions of US dollars)	Percent of sub-Saharan total	Cumulative percent
1	South Africa	2,099	24.1	24.1
2	**Angola**	**1,584**	**18.2**	42.4
3	**Nigeria**	**1,074**	**12.4**	54.7
4	**Sudan**	**478**	**5.5**	60.2
5	**Equatorial Guinea**	**384**	**4.4**	64.6
6	Tanzania	344	4.0	68.6
7	Mozambique	283	3.3	71.8
8	**Chad**[a]	**266**	**3.1**	74.9
9	Côte d'Ivoire	260	3.0	77.9
10	Uganda	238	2.7	80.6
21	Kenya	62	0.7	95.0
22–48	Bottom 27 countries	433	5.0	100.0

a. Chad data are based on a four-year average because of missing data for 2001.

Note: Bold indicates countries whose FDI is mainly oil related.

Source: UNCTAD FDI database; authors' calculations.

developing countries has followed a similar trend, plummeting in the late 1970s from above 20 percent to around 5 percent and hovering near or below that level for the past two decades. In 2002, it was still 5 percent.

The third trend is a strong concentration of inward FDI in a few countries. In the most recent five-year period, just three countries (South Africa, Angola, and Nigeria) accounted for 55 percent of the total (table 13.1). The top fifth (10 out of 48 countries) account for 80 percent, and the bottom half account for less than 5 percent. This trend has held for at least the last three decades, with the top 10 countries accounting for more than 75 percent of the continent's total FDI inflows. Additionally, there has been a long-standing concentration in the extractive sectors, particularly petroleum. Nearly all of the investment going to Angola, Nigeria, Equatorial Guinea, Sudan, and Chad is oil related, with the bulk invested in offshore facilities. In the most recent five-year period, these five countries accounted for 43.5 percent of Africa's total FDI (roughly matching oil concentration in previous periods). In addition, much of the foreign investment in Ghana, Zambia, Namibia, Botswana, and South Africa, and more recently Tanzania, has been in large mining projects.

For our purposes here, the oil and mining investment concentration is relevant in two ways. A large portion of FDI to Africa has been in enclave projects, which may limit their integration with local firms and the local economy. At the same time, this isolation means these projects are typically better situated to avoid some of the barriers to foreign investment, especially security issues or infrastructure weaknesses. The large size of foreign oil and mining firms also means that they are often able to negotiate directly with the government, and thus may be able to avoid bureaucratic bottlenecks or other regulations that might affect smaller enterprises or those integrated into the local economy. This suggests that nonextractive FDI, especially in smaller firms in manufacturing or services, faces a very different environment.

African Skepticism Toward Foreign Investment

Despite the growing competition for FDI and Africa's ability to attract only modest amounts outside of the extractive industries, the continent still has a strong historical skepticism toward foreign capital. Much of the prevailing attitude toward foreign investment is rooted in history, ideology, and the politics of the postindependence period. There is also a set of specific concerns that the benefits of FDI are not forthcoming and that certain kinds of government intervention are necessary to correct market failures. This discussion will lead directly to some of the outcomes of these attitudes—the direct and indirect barriers to FDI—in the following section.

Africa's early experiences with foreign companies continue to affect official and public perceptions of FDI. The arrival of European capitalism in West Africa, first by the Portuguese in the 15th century and later by the Dutch, French, and British, is indelibly linked in the public mind to the slave trade and as a precursor for colonialism. The use of European companies as proxies for the sovereign has helped link international business in the public's mind with imperial expansion. In 1652 Jan van Riebeeck arrived on the Cape on behalf of the Dutch East India Company. In the late 19th century, Cecil Rhodes claimed swaths of southern Africa on behalf of the British South Africa Company. Through the company, Rhodes secured mining concessions in gold, copper, and diamonds, playing the dual roles of entrepreneur and representative of the British crown. Harsh conditions and maltreatment of laborers further linked foreign companies with exploitation, particularly in the mines (e.g., under the Witwatersrand Native Labor Association) and plantations (see, e.g., Hochschild 1999 for conditions on rubber plantations in the Belgian Congo). As with the United Fruit Company in Latin America, foreign companies in Africa are frequently thought of as agents of imperialism and exploitation.

Although the colonial period ended more than a generation ago, it has also remained a central factor in Africa's skepticism over joining the global economy. Reflecting a common sentiment even today, Zambia's leading daily recently editorialized:

> Since when has global capitalism been concerned about equality, fairness and genuine justice or the lives of those it affected? From the days of mercantile capitalism and its slave trade, through classical colonialism with its crude extraction of raw materials from our countries, to today's neo-colonialism the situation of our people is basically or fundamentally the same—marginalised, exploited, ignorant, diseased, hungry and generally poor. (*The Post*, April 26, 2003)

Perhaps just as importantly, most of Africa's anticolonial movements were heavily supported by the Soviet Union and its satellites. This encouraged the popularity of socialism and an ideological bias against foreign (or, more specifically, Western) capital. These leftist leanings were closely complemented by dependency theory, which argued that capitalism in general, and foreign companies in particular, were agents of underdevelopment and merely continuing colonialism in another guise (Leys 1975, Senghaas-Knobloch 1975, Rodney 1981). Although dependency theory has been widely discredited, it continues to flourish among certain academic circles, many nongovernmental organizations (NGOs), and in some political circles today and contributes to the current climate of distrust of foreign investors.

Although there has been substantial turnover of political leadership in Africa over the past decade, many of the current decision makers (including those frequently hailed as reformers) have held political positions for decades and were trained on the socialist model steeped in antiforeign investment ideology. Indeed, nearly every African leader, no matter how liberal he is considered today, began his career as a socialist or Marxist. Even as most of Africa's finance ministers have become both increasingly convinced that economic openness can be beneficial for their countries and fluent in the language of international capitalism, many of their cabinet colleagues remain unreconstructed economic nationalists. Some of the ideological opposition to foreign investment is part of a general critique of capitalism—and more recently of globalization—and foreign capital remains an easy target.

Ideas of economic nationalism affected sentiment toward foreign investment, and they continue to influence policy today. Kenneth Kaunda's view that "political independence is meaningless without economic independence," shaped not only Zambian investment policy but also the policies of his entire generation of leaders (Tangri 1999; Kaunda, Adedeji, and Tambo 1979). Botswana, one of the African countries that has pursued more orthodox economic policies, has not been immune. Kenneth Koma, leader of the opposition, recently cautioned against privatization because "lack of managerial skills and capital among Botswana will lead to a situation where the economy will be in the hands of foreigners which will ultimately impact on the policy of the country. . . . It is like a man who marries a rich woman. He will lose control over the affairs of his house."[2]

Leaders frequently sought a symbolic break with foreign players that were closely identified with colonialism or external control. On a more practical level, political elites also did not want to be constrained by foreigners who might control key strategic sectors of the economy or their access to foreign exchange. Although FDI may be considered more stable than other types of capital flows, the flip side is that foreign investors with a greater

---

2. *Mmegi,* March 5, 2000.

stake in the long term might be more inclined to get involved in influencing policy or, in the extreme, supporting opposition political groups.[3]

Tangri (1999, 19–22) aptly summarizes the political underpinnings:

> Strong feelings of 'economic nationalism' stemmed from the weakness and subordinate status of African private enterprise as well as from the fact that African economies at independence were largely in the hands of foreigners. Public sector enterprise was seen as enabling the state to carry out the activities that African private entrepreneurs could not perform and also to reduce the dominance of foreign enterprise. Throughout the continent, political leaders sought to secure greater indigenous ownership of the economy, especially of the activities a country depended on for its foreign-exchange earnings. They also sought to achieve greater local control of the economy, particularly to ensure that economic decisions were consonant with governmental interests. Foreign economic control posed constraints on state personnel exercising decisions affecting the economy; it also made the possibility of foreigners intervening in domestic politics much more likely. On nationalistic and political grounds, therefore, government leaders desired economic independence.

Fourth, many of the purported benefits of FDI are frequently challenged directly, on both ideological and empirical grounds. There is a common critique that foreign investors crowd out local firms that cannot compete because of size, financing, marketing power, or some other unfair advantage (Dunning 1993, ActionAid 2003). The government-owned *Times of Zambia* (March 4, 2004), for example, recently argued, "The uneven playing field has led to local industry and products failing to compete effectively . . . there are far too many cases of investors coming into the country and diverting into ventures that should be best left to the locals. . . . It is such issues that investment legislation needs to address."

There are complaints that foreign firms merely exploit local labor and make no contribution to the wider economy, either by creating jobs, training workers, or using local suppliers (Oxfam 2003b). A frequent grievance against foreign investment is that, although the theory suggests capital inflows, in practice FDI can be a drain on foreign exchange. This is because foreign firms may be more likely to import materials (Chudnovsky and Lopez 2002) and remit profits (Oxfam 2003a). More broadly, there is considerable concern that the interests of foreign firms will diverge from social development objectives or constrain governments' ability to promote economic development (Chudnovsky and Lopez 2002, South Centre 1997, Kolodner 1994).[4]

---

3. Tangri (1992) shows that this dynamic could under certain circumstances work in the opposite way. Under Jerry Rawlings (1981–2000), Ghana's government was less suspicious of foreign business than it was of domestic business, which had been closely aligned with the main opposition party. Despite Rawlings' populist streak, his policies were an example of bias toward foreign investors over local ones as the former were seen as less likely to be involved in domestic politics.

4. Two other common criticisms of FDI that we do not address are the impacts on environmental management and on the indigenous population (e.g., see Oxfam 2003a). See Grabel (1995) for an attack on portfolio investment for constraining the ability of governments to set national priorities and Moss (2003, chapter 6) for a rebuttal.

African Barriers to FDI

As a direct result of these historical and political issues, African governments have constructed a series of barriers to foreign entry. The notion that Africans needed to seize control of their economies after independence manifested itself in several ways that continue to affect foreign investment. Even though early concerns were directed at large European and small South Asian investors,[5] the more recent influx of investment from East Asian (Brautigam 2003) and South African investors (Daniel, Naidoo, and Naidu 2003) has helped to sustain some of these issues.

Economic nationalism was used to justify extensive state intervention in the economy, including the creation of parastatals, heavy regulation, and often nationalization or expropriation (Kobrin 1984). Although these affected both local and foreign firms, many of the largest exporting firms had been foreign owned and operated and thus intervention was directly targeted at them. Many of the nationalized companies have, of course, since returned to foreign private ownership, such as Ghana's Ashanti Goldfields and the Tanzania Cigarette Company, which were both nationalized in the 1960s and then privatized in the mid-1990s (although the governments retain substantial minority stakes in each). Nevertheless, the threat of expropriation remains ever present. As we argue below, even where privatization has been actively pursued, governments have also continued to play a strong interventionist role in the economy, affecting the business environment in direct and indirect ways.

In many countries there was, and continues to be, a deliberate policy of Africanization, whereby state intervention is justified in order to transfer ownership of firms from foreigners (or indigenous minorities) to locals (e.g., Adedeji 1981, Boone 1993). In its most extreme cases widespread and violent expropriation forces such transfers, as occurred in Uganda under Idi Amin or, more recently, with commercial farms in Zimbabwe. But many countries, including Kenya and Zambia, pursued less violent but nonetheless explicit forms of encouraging ownership transfer to locals. This policy continues in some forms today, especially with privatization, which tends to include special dispensations to encourage local ownership through legal biases or awarding bids or even through share set-asides or discounts (Craig 2002).

---

5. Throughout East Africa many Africans of Asian descent are still considered "foreigners" and when officials speak of "foreign capital," they are at times referring to minority local investors (Himbara 1993). There is a large literature on minority entrepreneurs in Africa (e.g., Winder 1962, Brennan 1999, Mengistae 2001, Vandenberg 2003; in the popular press see Sowell 1994; Kotkin 1994). Although many of the measures taken or biases against foreigners are also directed at minority groups, for the purposes of this chapter "foreign" is considered a citizenship rather than racial issue.

There are direct de jure barriers to foreign participation in the economy. Explicit legal restrictions on foreigners have diminished substantially as economic reform and liberalization have been implemented, but some limitations still exist. Most obviously, most African stock markets have legal limits on the amount of equity owned by nonresident foreigners (Moss 2003). Although this mostly affects portfolio investors, any share above 10 percent is considered FDI, so this is a direct limitation for any publicly listed company and a potential reason not to list on the local exchange.

Many African countries still have restricted sectors in which foreigners are not allowed to own businesses. In some cases, this is tied directly to parastatal monopolies, so liberalization has occurred alongside privatization, but not in all instances. Ethiopia legally excludes foreigners from the financial sector, and Tanzania allowed foreign bank entry only since the early 1990s. Ghana, which has undergone significant liberalization since beginning economic reform two decades ago, still bars foreigners from certain trading and services sectors.

Many countries have legal requirements for (or have given officials wide discretionary powers to add) performance requirements, such as local employment, local partnership, or local inputs. Concerns over protecting these conditions led to considerable African (and NGO) resistance to reforms aimed at universalizing national treatment or limiting the ability to impose certain requirements, such as the Multilateral Agreement on Investment (MAI) and more recently at the World Trade Organization (WTO) (Graham 2000). Oxfam (2003a), for example, claims that a WTO agreement on investment could be "disastrous." ActionAid (2003) also warns against including investment in multilateral trade negotiations because "Developing countries need to regulate investment in order to protect sensitive sectors from liberalisation and to maximise the positive benefits for poor people. Yet it is precisely these measures which would be threatened by a WTO investment agreement because host governments would be restricted in their ability to regulate in favour of the poor." The overall effect is that, despite the trend of investment liberalization and privatization throughout much of Africa, substantial lingering legal biases against foreign investment still exist in many countries.

Perhaps most importantly, a range of indirect obstacles related to the business climate that act as de facto barriers to FDI exist.[6] Morisset (2000) and Basu and Srinivasan (2002) found that certain African countries have been able to attract FDI not because of natural resources but through a broad

---

6. There is a rich literature on the determinants of FDI, looking at a range of variables, such as income, infrastructure, labor costs, taxes, openness, and political stability. Singh and Jun (1995), for example, find that export orientation is a large attraction for FDI. Goldsborough et al. (1996) emphasize macroeconomic stability and reforms. For an overview of the various studies that use cross-country regressions to identify country characteristics, see table 3 in Asiedu (2002).

improvement in the business environment and deliberate image-enhancing campaigns.[7] Although most African countries have undertaken substantial economic reform, Asiedu (2004) finds that the decline in African FDI as a ratio of total FDI is partly because improvements in policy environment have not been large relative to reforms in other regions. In addition, Africa has been especially prone to "partial reform syndrome," where many reforms are only partially implemented or where only parts of a basket of policy changes are pursued, undermining the intended effect (Gordon 1993, van de Walle 2001).

Indirect barriers typically include bureaucratic and other informal impediments to foreign investment, such as ambiguous regulatory approval, delays in customs clearance, limited visas for expatriate workers, or weaknesses in the legal system. Many of these barriers are captured in the broader business climate, affect domestic firms as well, and could be considered unintentional. However, these factors are different for foreign firms in two important ways. Data from the RPED investment climate assessments suggest that foreign firms face dissimilar environmental constraints from domestic firms (see below), which implies that public policy actions to remedy these problems could be inherently biased for or against foreign firms.

Critically, it is also not always clear that such barriers are in fact unintentional; rather, they may be used as deliberate impediments to foreign entry or operation. Political economists have frequently found that excess bureaucracy, erratic economic policy, and other problems associated with weak business environments have strong political logic (Bates 1981, Lewis 1996, Chabal and Daloz 1999, van de Walle 2001). Because political elites and business elites are typically allied in Africa (or often are one and the same), foreign investors could threaten market positions of privileged domestic firms. Indeed, inefficient industries and policies have often been a good source of rents for the state or for particular individuals. Monopolistic positions by influential businessmen, political leaders, or their families are frequently threatened by foreign competition. Much of the nationalist resistance to liberalization, including worries of foreign domination or the displacement of local firms, has narrow rent-seeking roots, designed to benefit certain people or groups. In this way, clearance of investment projects may be rejected out of the "national interest" or imported equipment may be inexplicably delayed or lost, but in practice this is used to protect politically connected competitors. Tangri (1999, 14) concludes, "The political nature of the state-foreign business relations is an important reason why sub-Saharan Africa has failed to attract much foreign direct investment since independence."

---

7. Morisset (2000) found this was true for Mali and Mozambique. Basu and Srinivasan (2002) found this was true for Mozambique and Uganda.

Figure 13.2   FDI inflows: Kenya, Tanzania, and Uganda, 1970–2002

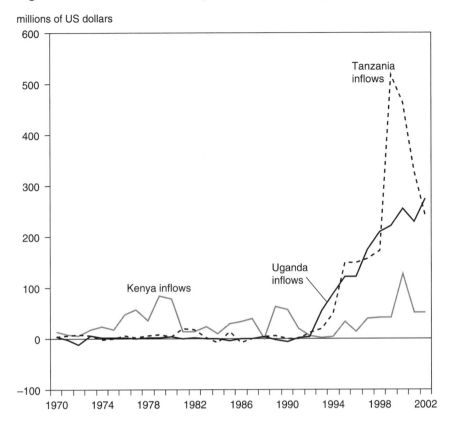

millions of US dollars

Source: UNCTAD FDI database.

Background: Foreign Investment in East Africa

Given this context, we turn now to three case studies in East Africa: Kenya, Tanzania, and Uganda. Each of these countries has seen a recent improvement in FDI flows (see figure 13.2) and each is undergoing some process of policy reform and liberalization. None has any meaningful oil-related foreign investment, but Tanzania's recent inflow surge has been largely driven by greenfield investment in its rapidly growing gold mining sector.

Each of the three countries has been substantially affected by its colonial experience and suffered postindependence traumas of some kind that affect their present attitudes toward foreign investment. All three are former British colonies, although mainland Tanzania was German prior to World War I. Kenya was designated a settler colony and had a substantial European business and farmer class, whereas Tanzania and Uganda were managed under indirect colonial rule and thus had smaller European populations. All three countries have significant populations of South Asian origin that date to the colonial period.

Kenya. After independence, Kenya chose to align with the West in the Cold War. Although ostensibly allied with market capitalism, in practice the government followed a statist strategy that increasingly deteriorated into narrow rent seeking and corruption. Partially because of the large colonial settler population, there was a substantial foreign presence in the country, much of which remained after independence. Large foreign banks, for instance, have continued operations. For the most part, legal barriers to foreigner investment have been minimal. Kenya officially encourages foreign investment and grants national treatment to foreign investors.[8] Nevertheless, Kenya's political elites believed "reliance on external actors was . . . potentially unreliable, economically risky, and most importantly, politically unacceptable" (Himbara 1994, 470). Therefore, the government used state enterprises to deliberately promote African entrepreneurs at the expense of both foreign and local Asian investors (Jaffee 1992; Himbara 1993, 1994; Holmquist 2002). At times antiforeigner sentiment, fuelled by government officials, led to violence, including widespread looting of Asian-owned businesses in the early 1980s. Legal restrictions on equity investors also exist, with foreign investors capped at 40 percent of Nairobi stock exchange–listed companies.

Despite its western–orientation and rhetorical commitment to capitalism, Kenya has not been immune to some of the nationalist-populist arguments against foreign investors. Parliamentarian Stephen Ndicho, waving a copy of the constitution, recently declared, "This document says Kenya is a sovereign state, but we are not and we now live at the mercy of these multinationals."[9] Another member of parliament, Mirugi Kariuki, recently implored the government to "chase away any investor who perceives Kenya as a place where cheap labor is available and whose intention is to exploit workers with impunity."[10]

More broadly, there has been wide regulatory discretion, with significant informal biases against foreign firms and minority-owned firms. Over time, the deteriorating business environment, especially poor governance, growing corruption, and, more recently, crime, has contributed substantially to low inflows of FDI.

Kenya's current business environment is in flux following the defeat of the Kenya African National Union (KANU) in December 2002, ending its nearly four decades in power. The new government of President Mwai Kibaki is thought to be reformist, and ran on an anticorruption platform.

---

8. WTO, Trade Policy Reviews, first press release on Kenya. Press/TPRB/124, January 19, 2000.

9. *The Nation*, December 7, 2000.

10. *The Monitor*, June 26, 2003.

In theory, this should benefit foreign investors as the government tackles one of the most prominent barriers to greater inflows. However, the new ruling coalition also has its antiforeign tendencies. In the late 1960s Kenya's official campaign of discriminating against Asian businessmen in favor of indigenous Africans was led by a then-obscure commerce minister, Mwai Kibaki (Himbara 1994). Raila Odinga—currently a cabinet minister, but also a possible successor to Kibaki and the leading candidate to become prime minister if proposed constitutional changes are implemented—has anti-FDI leanings. In 1999, Odinga suggested that Kenya was receiving too much FDI rather than too little, claiming, "The government must protect local industries against undue competition from multinationals to speed up industrialization. . . . [N]o country could industrialize with foreign investment alone."[11]

Tanzania. Under Julius Nyerere, Tanzania attempted a socialist transformation that saw widespread nationalization of property, including the seizure of foreign assets. Foreign investment was legally and effectively banned. This was widened in the 1970s to include most Asian-owned businesses and an (unevenly enforced) expropriation of any property valued at greater than $15,000. Capitalism and foreign capital in particular were considered un-African, whereas *ujamaa* was considered more "authentic" and appropriate.[12]

More recently the climate has changed considerably. Economic reforms began slowly in 1986 and accelerated after an economic crisis in the mid-1990s, substantially altering the government's stance on foreign investment. The privatization program, which included many nationalized firms previously owned by foreign companies, facilitated the return of foreign firms to the country. Mining reforms in the early 1990s allowed major new investment by foreign firms, especially Ghana's Ashanti Goldfields and South Africa's AngloGold. Foreign banks were allowed entry after 1993, and several large South African and British banks began operations soon thereafter. Legal changes in 1997 lifted most of the remaining sectoral restrictions on foreign investment on the mainland (although many regulations remain in place in semiautonomous Zanzibar). Previous demands of government equity have also been lifted for all sectors, except petroleum (UNCTAD 2002). Otherwise, foreign investors are generally afforded nation-al treatment, including protection of fiscal incentives, guarantee of repatriation, and importing expatriate staff. Remaining legal biases are relatively minor, for example, the minimum capital investment to qualify for approval is three times the local requirement.

---

11. *The Nation*, April 22, 1999.

12. The closest translation of the Swahili word *ujamaa* is "family," but Nyerere and others used it as a synonym for his concept of "African socialism."

Despite the reforms and increased inflows, residual resentment against foreign capital remains. For Tanzania we provide specific evidence of skepticism toward foreign capital: Although solid polling data on such attitudes is unusual in Africa, in 2001 Michigan State University specifically asked about whether the government should encourage foreign investment or "be wary of foreigners because they may gain control of our national wealth." Two-thirds of the people polled in Tanzania felt the latter, with 57 percent strongly so, while only 23 percent strongly agreed that government should encourage foreign investment (Afrobarometer 2003).[13]

Other indicators of attitude toward foreign capital also suggest doubt. The stock exchange operated for its first three years with a complete ban on foreign participation. Only in 2003 did it allow nonresident foreigners to buy shares, but only up to 60 percent of total equity. "Africanization" continues officially, although implementation has been piecemeal. The privatization program did not overtly penalize foreign firm bids, but there were special financing terms for local investors buying smaller firms. Although there are no blanket legal requirements for local partners, officials have hinted that such a provision was possible. Iddi Simba, then minister for trade and commerce, said, "Foreign companies which want to invest in Tanzania will be compelled to identify local partners. If they cannot do so, the government will help them identify partners because we are now aiming at localising and promoting local participation in investments."[14]

Bureaucracy also remains a problem in business. Most of the current officials and bureaucrats were trained during socialist times and the reflex has been to overregulate and resist ceding control. For example, one privatized manufacturing firm was under investigation after it tried to lease some of its space, because its business plan did not include real estate transactions (Temu and Due 1998). The Tanzanian public has also retained some of its old reservations. Despite the large inflows of mining investment, even the business press has complained. For example, the *Business Times* recently asked:

> [W]hat is the percentage of the so-called 'economic contribution' of the mining companies to Tanzania vis-à-vis what they are reaping from their operations under decidedly lopsided agreements? True, the sector has grown rapidly since 1997. But, for whom has it been growing, pray? How much has Tanzania as a nation-state, and its impoverished people, gained from that growth? . . . it is an officially sanctioned rape of Tanzania's mineral wealth. (September 26, 2003)

Uganda. Uganda has seen the most extreme swings in sentiment toward foreigners. Idi Amin nationalized foreign businesses and in 1972 forcibly expelled 80,000 Asians. His successor, Milton Obote, was little better.

---

13. The Afrobarometer is a joint project of the Institute for Democracy in South Africa, the Ghana Centre for Democratic Development, and Michigan State University, which polls attitudes on democracy and markets in Africa. They polled in Uganda in 2000, but did not include this specific question on foreign investors.

14. *The East African*, February 18, 1999.

However, the government of Yoweri Museveni, which came to power in 1986, began one of Africa's most wide-ranging economic reform programs, reopening the economy to foreign investment. In the 1990s Museveni actively sought foreign investment and successfully invited Asians back to the country to reclaim lost property.

Ironically, Uganda's investment code is technically restrictive on foreigners, insisting on a license that could be denied for any number of ambiguous reasons, including anything deemed "contrary to the interests of Uganda." In practice, however, the licensing process has become automatic, and the national-interest clause has never been formally invoked against a prospective foreign investor (UNCTAD 2000). The only restricted sector is agriculture, although agroprocessing has been allowed, and the cabinet has approved some exceptions in the case of foreign investment in tea estates. Privatization has also encouraged foreign investment in a range of sectors. Uganda opened a stock market in 1999 with no restrictions of any kind on foreigners.

Despite the general openness in Uganda, performance requirements can be imposed on foreigners. For any foreign majority–owned business, officials have legal rights to impose employment, local input, or technology conditions on the license. There are also minor biases against foreign firms in finance, since the central bank may impose restrictions on access to domestic credit, and foreign-owned banks and insurance companies are subject to higher capital requirements. Foreign investors are also allowed leasehold on land, but are not permitted freehold land title.

Foreign Investment in East Africa: New Results from Firm Surveys

In this context, the results of a new firm-level investment climate database from the World Bank's RPED are illuminating. The firm surveys, which cover 300–400 manufacturing firms of various sizes, classes, and types of ownership in Kenya, Tanzania, and Uganda, were undertaken during 2002–03. A series of variables describe various characteristics of firms, including the inputs and outputs of the production process, access to finance, wages and other characteristics of workers, and types of technology and learning in the firm. The surveys also measure the amount of foreign equity in each firm surveyed.[15] Two key results emerge: foreign firms often operate

---

15. The World Bank's RPED, based in the Africa Private Sector Group, has conducted firm-level surveys in Africa for over a decade. In recent years, a new round of African data has been collected as part of the Bankwide Investment Climate Initiative. In the past two years, firm surveys have been conducted in Mozambique, Eritrea, Kenya, Tanzania, Uganda, and Zambia. Surveys are currently under way in South Africa, Lesotho, Mauritius, Madagascar, Senegal, and Mali. More information on these surveys and the survey methodology is available at www.worldbank.org/rped or www.worldbank.org/privatesector.

Table 13.2 East Africa's business environment respondents' evaluation of general constraints to operation

(percent of firms evaluating constraint as "major" or "very severe")

General constraints to operation	Uganda		Tanzania		Kenya	
	Foreign	Domestic	Foreign	Domestic	Foreign	Domestic
Corruption	55	33	58	50	81	72
Macroeconomic instability	58	41	51	41	49	52
Regulatory policy uncertainty	38	24	27	33	60	52
Customs and trade regulations	38	23	36	30	45	41
Crime, theft, and disorder	37	24	18	27	73	71
Access to land	25	16	18	26	23	24
Tax administration	42	35	58	55	47	53
Electricity	49	43	67	57	53	47
Anticompetitive or informal practices	34	30	29	23	72	62
Telecommunications	6	5	11	12	67	40
Transportation	29	21	24	22	54	38
Cost of financing (e.g., interest rates)	54	62	48	60	66	77
Tax rates	43	50	78	72	55	69
Access to financing (e.g., collateral)	37	48	35	52	36	49
Skills and education of available workers	25	32	24	25	31	27
Labor regulations	12	10	22	10	17	24
Business licensing and operating permits	13	9	22	28	13	17

Source: World Bank, RPED.

in a very difficult business environment and, despite the obstacles they face, these foreign firms are more productive and invest more in the production than domestic firms. The overall results suggest that FDI brings many of the claimed benefits, including some of those specifically challenged by critics.

We begin by looking at the business environment for firms operating in Uganda, Kenya, and Tanzania. We see that both foreign and domestic firms face several constraints that impede their day-to-day operations (table 13.2). Apart from the somewhat predictable complaints about the cost of finance and tax rates, firms complain about macroeconomic instability, the poor availability of reliable electric power, corruption, inefficient tax administration, and crime. A higher proportion of foreign firms complain about corruption in all three countries, suggesting that foreign firms bear a greater burden of nonofficial payments, or at least are more sensitive to their prevalence.

Looking at the case of Uganda in more detail, the uncertainty in the business environment is of concern to both domestic and foreign-owned firms. Corruption is of greater concern to foreign firms; they pay almost 4 percent

Table 13.3 Corruption in Uganda (as reported by respondent firms)

Dimension	All firms	Large	Small	Foreign	Domestic	Exporter	Non-exporter
Percent of revenues needed for informal payments	2.4	1.1	2.6	3.9	1.9	3.0	2.3
Percent saying gift/payment required for:							
Mainline telephone connection	18.3	28.6	16.4	18.4	18.5	18.2	17.6
Electrical connection	21.5	21.4	21.5	18.2	22.3	24.0	21.2
Construction permit	12.3	20.0	11.1	10.0	13.2	5.6	14.8
Import license	3.6	0.0	4.3	5.3	2.8	0.0	4.5
Trading license	4.2	3.4	4.3	3.8	4.3	2.7	4.5
Percent of revenue reported for tax purposes	76.7	87.3	75.2	81.3	75.3	86.1	74.7

Source: World Bank (2004).

of revenues in informal payments compared with less than 2 percent for domestic firms (table 13.3). The data indicate that between 4 and 22 percent of respondents make a nonofficial payment for telephone connections, electrical connections, construction permits, and import and trading licenses. Finally, it is interesting to note that foreign firms are able to compensate to a greater extent for poor services than local firms (table 13.4). Both foreign and domestic firms experienced about 40 power outages in the year preceding the survey. However, foreign firms are able to offset these losses to some extent. About 68 percent of foreign firms have their own generators and 28 percent have a well, compared to 26 percent and 9 percent respectively for domestic firms.

Table 13.5 shows the regulatory burden and administrative delays that firms face in Uganda. Again, it is clear that both foreign and domestic firms operate in a very difficult business environment. Only 40 percent of firms in Uganda report that regulations are interpreted in a consistent and predictable manner. Almost 4 percent of foreign firms report that payments are made to "get things done" compared to 2 percent of domestic firms. It can be argued that these estimates are downward biased, however, the differential between foreign and domestic firms is likely accurate. Foreign firms also spend significantly more time on inspections and meetings with officials (26 days per year versus 9.7 for local firms), yet report a higher percentage of their revenues for tax purposes.

Despite the constraints in the operating environment described above, our data indicate that foreign firms make a substantial contribution to the African private sector. Foreign firms invest a greater share of profits back into the firm than local firms. They report a higher percentage of revenue for tax purposes than do domestic firms. Firms with foreign equity are also

Table 13.4 Infrastructure indicators in Uganda

Indicator	All firms	Large	Small	Foreign	Domestic	Exporter	Non-exporter
Frequency of power outages (number of times last year)	38.6	54.2	36.5	40.3	38.0	38.3	37.7
Production lost due to power outages (percent)	6.3	4.5	6.5	7.4	5.9	3.7	6.7
Own generator (percent)	35.3	69.4	30.7	67.7	26.0	53.3	31.9
Built own well (percent)	13.0	30.6	10.6	27.9	8.7	24.4	10.6
Number of days to obtain a telephone connection	33.2	23.1	35.1	17.7	39.3	35.1	32.8
Number of days to obtain an electricity connection	38.3	39.1	38.3	46.8	36.2	48.7	36.6

Source: World Bank (2004).

substantially larger than local firms. Within the sample, the average foreign firm employs 391 workers versus 102, and this disparity held for each country, with Uganda showing a nearly 10 to 1 ratio (see figure 13.3). It is clear from these data that foreign firms are a very significant source of employment in East Africa.

Foreign firms also report higher productivity; value added per worker is significantly higher in foreign versus local firms (figure 13.4). This may be explained by the greater managerial skills and experience in foreign firms (figure 13.5). More than half of the foreign firms reported the general manager had a university degree, but this was true in less than one-quarter of domestic firms. The manager also reported an average of 11 years' experience in foreign firms versus 7 in a domestic firm, although this did not show up in Kenya. Thus, management skills is also potentially relevant to spillover effects, since other studies have found that experience in foreign firms is associated with higher productivity in new local firms started by managers after leaving the foreign firm.[16]

Worker training may also be a factor. Foreign firms are nearly twice as likely to have a formal training program (figure 13.6). Investments in training have been shown to produce large gains for African manufacturing (Biggs, Shah, and Srivastava 1995). For firms and the economy as a whole, this adds to human capital, productivity, and output. For individual workers, training adds to their skills. Thus, worker training not only offers a reason why foreign firms might have higher productivity, but also challenges

---

16. See World Bank (2004) for Uganda and Görg and Strobl (2004) for Ghana.

Table 13.5   Regulatory burden and administrative delays in Uganda

Dimension	All firms	Large	Small	Foreign	Domestic	Exporter	Non-exporter
Consistent and predictable interpretations of regulations (percent disagreeing)	40.0	33.3	41.0	36.4	41.0	31.1	41.4
Senior management's time spent dealing with regulations (percent)	0.04	0.07	0.04	0.06	0.04	0.05	0.04
Revenues typically paid to officials to "get things done" (percent)	2.4	1.1	2.6	3.9	1.9	3.0	2.3
Total firm revenues typically reported for tax purposes (percent)	76.7	87.3	75.2	81.3	75.3	86.1	74.7
Inspections							
Total days spent in inspections or required meetings with officials	13.4	25.6	11.8	26.0	9.7	18.2	12.6
Percent of meetings/ inspections by local authorities	19.4	7.6	21.4	8.9	23.0	16.3	20.1
Total cost of fines or seized goods (percent of sales)	0.1	0.3	0.0	0.2	0.0	0.2	0.0
Percent of interactions in which informal payment was requested	6.7	9.4	6.3	6.8	6.7	7.3	6.6
If yes, value? (percent of sales)	0.3	0.6	0.3	0.4	0.3	0.4	0.3
Imports							
Average number of days to clear customs	5.8	5.5	5.9	5.6	6.1	5.3	6.0
Longest delay to clear customs (days)	11.2	10.1	11.5	12.5	9.8	10.9	11.3
Exports							
Average number of days to clear customs	3.5	4.2	3.2	3.5	3.6	3.3	3.7
Longest delay to clear customs (days)	6.0	6.3	5.9	6.5	4.8	5.8	6.2

Source: World Bank (2004).

Figure 13.3   Firm size (employment)

average number of workers

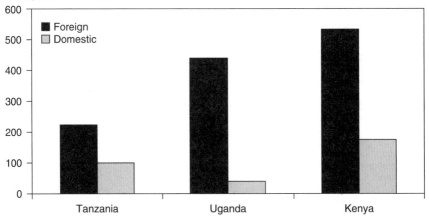

Source: World Bank, RPED.

the notion that they do not invest in their workers. Combined with the finding that foreign subsidiaries are on average three years older than domestic firms, this does not suggest mobile FDI associated with exploiting short-term low-cost labor.

The results for the likelihood of exporting are also quite different between foreign and domestic firms. Foreign firms are much more likely to export their output and be able to purchase necessary imported inputs (figure 13.7). This suggests that foreign firms are more connected to global markets. The results also show that foreign firms, although they report importing on average 56 percent of their inputs, rely on domestic suppliers for the other 44 percent. This suggests substantial linkage to the local economy although, as one might expect, to a lesser degree than domestic firms.

The survey also highlights foreign-domestic differences in their investments in infrastructure (figure 13.8). On average, 80 percent of foreign firms report owning their own generator, compared with less than half of local firms. Foreign firms were also nearly twice as likely to have their own well or to have built their own roads. Within each country, these patterns held, except for the case of roads in Tanzania, where domestic firms were more likely (11 percent versus 9 percent). These investments in infrastructure suggest three implications. First, this could be viewed as a positive sign that companies are investing for the long-term and are contributing to the country's infrastructure development. Second, this confirms that foreign firms find the general business environment a significant barrier to operation. Third, the greater relative investment also suggests that foreign firms are better capitalized to overcome these deficiencies than local firms.

Figure 13.4   Productivity (value added per worker)

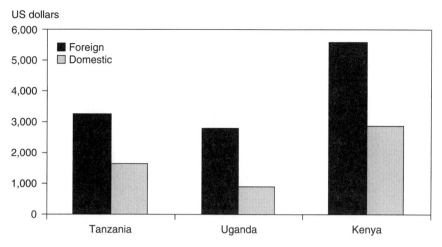

US dollars

Source: World Bank, RPED.

Finally, it is interesting to note the differences between foreign and domestic firms with respect to health benefits (table 13.6). Foreign firms are three times more likely to provide health insurance in Uganda and almost twice as likely to do so in Tanzania. Similarly, the provision of on-site medical care is much higher in all three countries as is accident compensation or insurance (except Kenya for the latter). Foreign firms are also more likely to carry out preemployment health checks than domestic firms.

Factors Determining Foreign Ownership: A Simple Econometric Test

Thus far, the discussion has examined the constraints to foreign investment in Africa, and the differences in the behavior of foreign versus domestic firms. Key problems in political attitude and pressures, weak infrastructure, and unfavorable business environment deter foreign firms from locating in sub-Saharan Africa. For firms that have chosen to locate in East Africa, we see that they invest more in local infrastructure, are more likely to train their workers, and are larger and more capital intensive than local enterprises. They also tend to have higher market power: they control a greater percentage of the local market for their products compared to local enterprises.

In this section we examine the economic factors distinguishing foreign firms from local enterprises within a simple econometric framework. Any firm's decision to operate is governed by its potential profit; foreign firms that choose to locate in sub-Saharan Africa do so because they expect that

Figure 13.5 Management skills

a. Firms with college graduate as manager

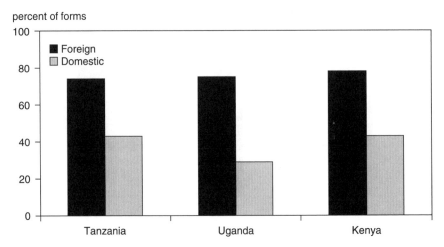

percent of forms

Source: World Bank, RPED.

b. Experience of general manager

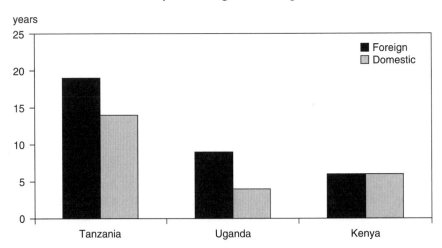

years

Source: World Bank, RPED.

despite the structural constraints, revenues from operations will exceed
their costs. By definition,

$$Profit = (P * Q \, C * Q)$$

where P = unit price, Q = quantity, C = unit cost. Higher profits can be
achieved by raising the unit price through oligopolistic or monopolistic
behavior, and/or by lowering cost the unit cost through greater efficiency.

Figure 13.6 Forms with formal worker training programs

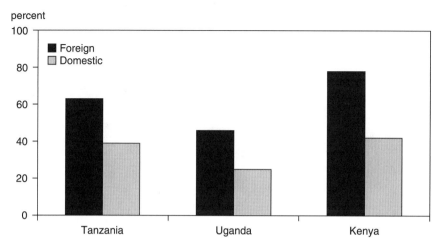

Source: World Bank, RPED.

A common economic criticism of foreign firms has been that they enter the local markets to drive out competitors, raising prices and exploiting local resources. Others have argued that these firms are more efficient than the locals and improve the competitive environment in their host countries.

Using our East African data, we test the following hypotheses:

- *Hypothesis I:* Foreign firms exercise strong market power by creating local monopolies and crowding out domestic investment—i.e., the "economy will be in the hands of foreigners." This hypothesis is tested in our model by using a measure of market share.

- *Hypothesis II:* Foreign firms are profitable because they are more productive. This is measured by labor productivity, managerial education, and worker training variables.

- *Hypothesis III:* FDI is a drain on foreign exchange, because foreign firms are more likely to use imported raw materials. We test this by including the percentage of raw materials imported in our model. We also include the percentage of output exported.

The probit model is used, which measures the likelihood of a firm being a foreign enterprise (see table 13.7). We try two specifications for the left-hand variable—the first model examines the distinguishing characteristics between foreign and local firms, where foreign firms are defined as those that have any foreign equity. In the second specification, model II, we define foreign firms as only those with majority foreign equity—where foreign equity is greater than 50 percent. The dependent variable, 0/1, is set

Figure 13.7 Firm exports and imports

a. Exports/output

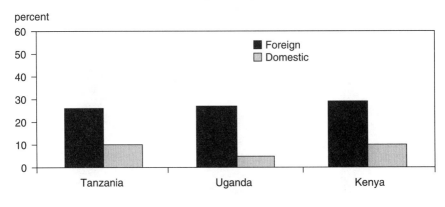

b. Imports/inputs

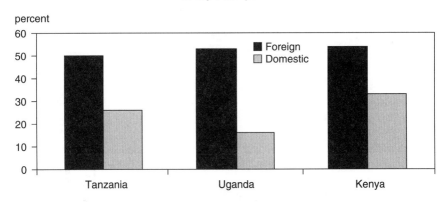

Source: World Bank, RPED.

to 1 in model I if the firm has any foreign equity and is set to 1 in model II if the firm has more than 50 percent foreign equity.

As expected, we see that foreign firms are significantly larger than local enterprises. After controlling for firm size, we see that the two other key factors distinguishing foreign firms from locals are percentage of output exported and labor productivity. Foreign firms, even within the same size class, are more likely to export their products than local firms (hence bringing in foreign exchange; the import dummy is insignificant) and have a more productive labor force indicating greater efficiency. The market share variable is not significant, indicating that market power is not the key driving force for greater profits for these firms. Thus, we reject hypotheses I and III, but cannot reject hypothesis II that foreign firms have higher productivity.

Figure 13.8   Infrastructure investment by private firms

Own generator

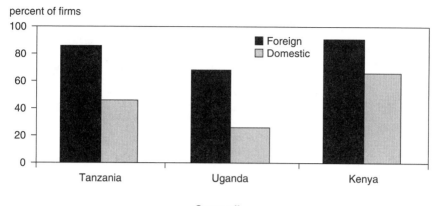

Own well

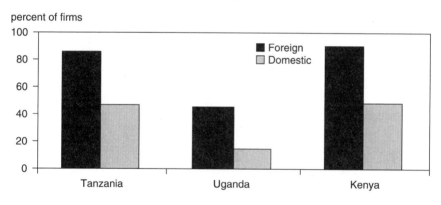

Invest in roads

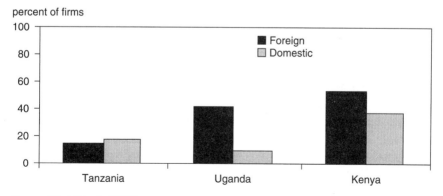

Source: World Bank, RPED.

Table 13.6 Health benefits: Foreign versus local firms
(percent of firms providing benefits)

Benefit	Uganda		Kenya		Tanzania	
	Local	Foreign	Local	Foreign	Local	Foreign
Health insurance	11.1	37.5	45.2	64.8	24.8	42.8
Medical care at company clinic	14.8	59.3	29.5	62.2	22.5	48.2
Accident compensation/ insurance	23.5	93.8	90.4	83.8	62.3	73.7
Other health/medical benefit	15.4	21.9	40.4	40.5	41.8	50.0
Preemployment check	17.3	34.4	29.5	48.6	47.1	69.6

Source: World Bank (2004).

Conclusion

Foreign investment can play an important role in developing countries, but African countries have, for the most part, not received much FDI. At least part of this poor performance is a result of deep-seated sentiments against foreign capital reinforced by political factors that militate against FDI. These factors have manifested themselves in many ways, including a range of business environment factors that impede greater foreign flows. Although much of the ideological resistance has faded, a number of specific challenges to the purported benefits of FDI have been successful in preventing more active liberalization and the removal of indirect barriers. Data from firm surveys in Kenya, Tanzania, and Uganda suggest that important and positive FDI effects for both the host economies and the workers in foreign-owned firms exist. Based on our three-country sample, foreign firms are more productive, bring management skills, invest more heavily in infrastructure and in the training and health of their workers, and are more connected to global markets. At the same time, they do not appear to succeed by seizing market share and crowding out local industry. These results suggest that many of the objections to foreign investment are exaggerated or false. Therefore, Africa, by not attracting more FDI, is failing to fully benefit from the potential of foreign capital to contribute to economic development and integration with the global economy.

Table 13.7   Foreign ownership probit results

Variable	Model I (Foreign if equity > 0)	Model II (Foreign if equity > 50)
Intercept	−3.20* (0.55)	−3.16* (0.58)
Lwork	0.25* (0.08)	0.18* (0.08)
Tanzania	−0.21 (0.25)	−0.31 (0.26)
Kenya	−0.68* (0.24)	−0.76* (0.25)
Pctexp	0.006* (0.003)	0.007* (0.003)
Pctimp	0.001 (0.002)	0.004 (0.003)
Mktsh	0.004 (0.003)	0.003 (0.003)
Train	0.14 (0.21)	0.11 (0.22)
Unived	0.28 (0.21)	0.32 (0.22)
LVal	0.14* (0.06)	0.14* (0.07)
N	301	301

* = coefficient is statistically significant
N = number of firms in the sample

Kenya: Country dummy for Kenya, Uganda is the excluded category.
LVal: Log of value added per worker, measuring labor productivity.
Lwork: Log of total workers employed by the firm (capturing the firm-size effect).
Mktsh: Percent of industry output for the product that is supplied by the firm.
Pctexp: Percent of total output exported.
Pctimp: Percent of total raw materials imported.
Tanzania: Country dummy for Tanzania; Uganda is the excluded category.
Train: A 1/0 dummy, 1 if the firm has a formal training program for its workers.
Unived: A 1/0 dummy, 1 if the manager has a university degree.

Note: Figures in parentheses are standard errors.

Source: Authors' calculations.

References

ActionAid. 2003. Unlimited Companies: The Developmental Impacts of an Investment Agreement at the WTO. London: ActionAid.

Adedeji, Adebayo, ed. 1981. *Indigenization of African Economies*. London: Hutchinson University Library for Africa.

Afrobarometer. 2003. Attitudes to Democracy and Markets in Tanzania, March–April and August 2001. Data prepared by Wonbin Cho and Virginia Parish, Michigan State University (August).

Asiedu, Elizabeth. 2002. On the Determinants of Foreign Direct Investment to Developing Countries: Is Africa Different? *World Development* 30, no. 1 (January): 107–19.

Asiedu, Elizabeth. 2003. Foreign Direct Investment to Africa: The Role of Government Policy, Governance and Political Instability. Department of Economics, University of Kansas. Photocopy (July 8).

Asiedu, Elizabeth. 2004. Policy Reform and Foreign Direct Investment to Africa: Absolute Progress but Relative Decline. *Development Policy Review* 22, no. 1 (January): 41–48.

Basu, Anupam, and Krishna Srinivasan. 2002. *Foreign Direct Investment in Africa—Some Case Studies*. IMF Working Paper WP/02/61. Washington: International Monetary Fund.

Bates, Robert. 1981. *Markets and States in Tropical Africa: The Political Basis of Agricultural Policies*. Berkeley: University of California Press.

Biggs, Tyler, Manju Kedia Shah, and Pradeep Srivastava. 1995. *Training and Productivity in African Manufacturing Enterprises*. Regional Program on Enterprise Development Discussion Paper. Washington: World Bank.

Blomström, Magnus, and Ari Kokko. 1997. *How Foreign Investment Affects Host Countries*. Policy Research Working Paper WPS 1745. Washington: World Bank.

Blomström, Magnus, and Ari Kokko. 1998. Multinational Corporations and Spillovers. *Journal of Economic Surveys* 12, no. 3 (July): 247–77.

Boone, Catherine. 1993. Commerce in Côte d'Ivoire: Ivoirianisation without Ivoirian Traders. *Journal of Modern African Studies* 31, no. 1 (March): 67–92.

Brautigam, Deborah. 2003. Close Encounters: Chinese Business Networks as Industrial Catalysts in Sub-Saharan Africa. *African Affairs* 102, no. 408 (July): 447–67.

Brennan, James R. 1999. South Asian Nationalism in an East African Context: The Case of Tanganyika, 1914–1956. *Comparative Studies of South Asia, Africa and the Middle East* 19, no. 2: 24–38.

Chabal, Patrick, and Jean-Pascal Daloz. 1999. *Africa Works: Disorder As Political Instrument*. Bloomington: Indiana University Press.

Chudnovsky, Daniel, and Andres Lopez. 2002. *Globalization and Developing Countries: Foreign Direct Investment, Growth and Sustainable Human Development*. UNCTAD Occasional Paper. Geneva: United Nations.

Craig, John. 2002. *Privatisation and Indigenous Ownership: Evidence from Africa*. Working Paper 13 (January). Manchester, UK: Centre on Regulation and Competition, University of Manchester.

Daniel, John, Varusha Naidoo, and Sanusha Naidu. 2003. Post-Apartheid South Africa's Corporate Expansion into Africa. *Traders: African Business Journal*, no. 15 (August–November).

Dunning, John. 1993. *Multinational Enterprises and the Global Economy*. Wokingham, UK: Addison-Wesley.

Goldsbrough, D., et al. 1996. *Reinvigorating Growth in Developing Countries: Lessons from Adjustment Policies in Eight Economies*. IMF Occasional Paper 139. Washington: International Monetary Fund.

Gordon, David. 1993. Debt, Conditionality, and Reform: The International Relations of Economic Restructuring in Sub-Saharan Africa. In *Hemmed In: Responses to Africa's Economic Decline*, ed., Thomas Callaghy and John Ravenhill. New York: Columbia University Press.

Görg, Holger, and Eric Strobl. 2004. Spillovers from Foreign Firms through Worker Mobility: An Empirical Investigation. Photocopy (January). University of Nottingham and Catholic University of Louvain.

Grabel, Ilene 1995. Marketing the Third World: The Contradictions of Portfolio Investment in the Global Economy. *World Development* 24, no. 11 (November): 1761–76.

Graham, Edward. 2000. *Fighting the Wrong Enemy: Antiglobal Activists and Multinational Enterprises.* Washington: Institute for International Economics.

Himbara, David. 1993. Myths and Realities of Kenyan Capitalism. *Journal of Modern African Studies* 31, no. 1 (March): 93–107.

Himbara, David. 1994. The Failed Africanization of Commerce and Industry in Kenya. *World Development* 22, no. 3 (March): 469–82.

Hochschild, Adam. 1999. *King Leopold's Ghost.* New York: Houghton Mifflin.

Holmquist, Frank. 2002. *Business and Politics in Kenya in the 1990s.* Centre of African Studies Occasional Paper. Copenhagen: University of Copenhagen.

Jaffee, Steven. 1992. *How Private Enterprise Organized Agricultural Markets in Kenya.* Policy Research Working Paper WPS 823. Washington: World Bank.

Kaunda, Kenneth, Adebayo Adedeji, and O. R. Tambo. 1979. *Africa's Economic Independence.* Lusaka, Zambia: Government of Zambia.

Kobrin, Stephen. 1984. Expropriations as an Attempt to Control Foreign Firms in LDCs: Trends from 1960 to 1979. *International Studies Quarterly* 28, no. 3 (September): 329–48.

Kolodner, Eric. 1994. *Transnational Corporations: Impediments or Catalysts of Social Development?* United Nations Research Institute for Social Development, Occasional Paper No. 5. World Summit for Social Development. Geneva: United Nations Research Institute for Social Development.

Kotkin, Joel. 1994. *Tribes: How Race, Religion and Identity Determine Success in the New Global Economy.* New York: Random House.

Lewis, Peter. 1996. From Prebendalism to Predation: The Political Economy of Decline in Nigeria. *Journal of Modern African Studies* 34, no. 1 (March): 79–103.

Leys, Colin. 1975. *Underdevelopment in Kenya: The Political Economy of Neo-Colonialism, 1964–71.* London: Heinemann.

Markusen, James, and Anthony Venables. 1997. *Foreign Direct Investment as a Catalyst for Industrial Development.* NBER Working Paper 6241. Cambridge, MA: National Bureau of Economic Research.

Mengistae, Taye. 2001. *Indigenous Ethnicity and Entrepreneurial Success in Africa: Some Evidence from Ethiopia.* Policy Research Working Paper WPS 2534. Washington: World Bank.

MIGA (Multilateral Investment Guarantee Agency). 2002. *Foreign Direct Investment Survey 2002.* Washington: World Bank.

Morisset, Jacques. 2000. *Foreign Direct Investment in Africa: Policies Also Matter.* Policy Research Working Paper WPS 2481. Washington: World Bank.

Moss, Todd. 2003. *Adventure Capitalism: Globalization and the Political Economy of Stock Markets in Africa.* London: Palgrave Macmillan.

Oxfam. 2003a. *The Emperor's New Clothes.* Oxfam Briefing Paper 46 (April). Oxford, UK: Oxfam International.

Oxfam. 2003b. *Running into the Sand.* Oxfam Briefing Paper 53 (August). Oxford, UK: Oxfam International.

Pigato, Miria. 2001. *The Foreign Direct Investment Environment in Africa.* Africa Region Working Paper 15. Washington: World Bank.

Ramachandran, Vijaya, and Manju Kedia Shah. 1997. *The Effects of Foreign Ownership in Africa: Evidence from Ghana, Kenya, and Zimbabwe.* RPED Paper 81. Washington: World Bank.

Rodney, Walter. 1981. *How Europe Underdeveloped Africa.* Washington: Howard University Press.

Senghaas-Knobloch, Eva. 1975. The Internationalization of Capital and the Process of Underdevelopment: The Case of Black Africa. *Journal of Peace Research* 12, no. 4: 275–92.

Singh, Harinder, and Kwang W. Jun. 1995. *Some New Evidence on Determinants of Foreign Direct Investment in Developing Countries.* Policy Research Working Paper WPS 1531. Washington: World Bank.

South Centre. 1997. *Foreign Direct Investment, Development and the New Global Economic Order: A Policy Brief for the South.* Geneva: South Centre.

Sowell, Thomas. 1994. *Race and Culture: A World View.* New York: Basic Books.

Tangri, Roger. 1992. The Politics of Government-Business Relations in Ghana. *Journal of Modern African Studies* 30, no. 1 (March): 97–111.

Tangri, Roger. 1999. *The Politics of Patronage in Africa.* Trenton, NJ: Africa World Press.

Temu, Andrew, and Jean M. Due. 1998. The Success of Newly Privatized Companies: New Evidence from Tanzania. *Canadian Journal of Development Studies* 19, no. 2: 315–41.

UNCTAD (United Nations Conference on Trade and Development). 1998. *World Investment Report 1998: Trends and Determinants.* Geneva: United Nations.

UNCTAD (United Nations Conference on Trade and Development). 1999. *National Treatment.* Geneva: United Nations.

UNCTAD (United Nations Conference on Trade and Development). 2000. Investment Policy Review: Uganda. Geneva: United Nations.

UNCTAD (United Nations Conference on Trade and Development). 2002. Investment Policy Review: The United Republic of Tanzania. Geneva: United Nations.

Vandenberg, Paul. 2003. Ethnic-Sectoral Cleavages and Economic Development: Reflections on the Second Kenya Debate. *Journal of Modern African Studies* 41, no. 3 (September): 437–55.

van de Walle, Nicolas. 2001. *African Economies and the Politics of Permanent Crisis, 1979–99.* Cambridge: Cambridge University Press.

Winder, R. B. 1962. The Lebanese in West Africa. *Comparative Studies in Society and History* 4, no. 3 (April): 296–333.

World Bank. 2004. *Competing in the Global Economy: An Investment Climate Assessment for Uganda.* Africa Private Sector Group (May). Washington: World Bank.

Comment

ROBERT Z. LAWRENCE

How does foreign direct investment (FDI) affect host country development? The three chapters in this section reveal the considerable differences in the way people answer this question. The chapter by Moss, Ramachandran, and Shah chronicles in considerable detail the negative views held by many Africans. It also indicates that despite recent movements toward policy liberalization in East Africa, numerous obstacles to FDI remain. Apparently, FDI is still widely seen as exploitative and risky, bringing few gains to the local community, and these attitudes have affected policies. Moss, Ramachandran, and Shah use survey evidence to show that treatment of foreign firms in East Africa remains discriminatory.

By contrast the chapter by Guoqiang Long describes the effort of the Chinese to attract FDI and their positive experiences and perceptions. By and large, foreign investors have been treated more favorably than private domestic firms, particularly in the initial period of domestic reforms. This preferential treatment actually created incentives for domestic firms to try, through "round ripping," to become foreign firms. Overall, the chapter argues, the FDI experience has been favorable. The Chinese experience seems to have involved a virtuous cycle. Once China succeeded in attracting some foreign firms other countries have sought similar advantages. In attracting foreign firms, has China succeeded in encouraging technological development and diffusion. The chapter paints a positive picture. It presents impressive evidence on how much research and development (R&D) is accomplished by foreign firms in China. It also describes the role

Robert Z. Lawrence, senior fellow, is Albert L. Williams Professor of Trade and Investment at the John F. Kennedy School of Government at Harvard University.

of foreign firms in: demonstrating and introducing new products; making demands by placing orders and providing technical assistance to suppliers; training and research in collaboration with domestic firms and ins-titutions; and providing a manufacturing platform for local firms to participate. While acknowledging the possible dangers of crowding out as well as poaching talented people from local firms and appropriating intellectual property through joint ventures, Guoqiang Long concludes that overall FDI "spillover effects appear more eye-catching than the effects of crowding out."

In his chapter, Ted Moran draws on case studies of many countries to suggest that the different perceptions in these two locations are quite typical of existing FDI literature. Case studies show that FDI has led to impressive performance and results in some countries while it has failed in others.

Why are these perceptions and results so different? Moran's chapter provides one answer: the impact of FDI depends critically on the overall context in which it occurs. If FDI is motivated by the desire to service a protected and distorted domestic market, the effects could well disappoint. Foreign firms may find it profitable to operate, but they may do so without bringing the best technologies and/or using the country as part of their international supply networks. By contrast, impact will likely be positive when FDI is motivated by the desire to participate fully in the international sourcing networks of the parent multinational, and operations are unrestricted by rules on ownership and local content. If the Moran hypothesis is correct, therefore, the divergent perspectives presented in Moss, Ramachandran, and Shah and Guoqiang Long are easily explained: Africa's disappointing experience stems from the fact that its FDI has taken place in distorted and protected markets while China's positive experience results from the fact that it has by and large been directed toward increased global integration.

I find Moran's hypothesis plausible. Its implications for policy and empirical research are important. In fact, Moran's hypothesis about FDI applies to other sources of economic growth such as trade and education. It highlights the importance of the incentives under which such activities occur. For example, if there is one message that comes out very clearly from microeconomic theory, it is that the answer to the question "Is free trade good or bad?" is "It depends." In the face of imperfect markets and the wrong price signals free trade could well make things worse. To be sure it *could* still make things better, but in a second-best world we cannot be sure. If, for example, a country fails to force export industries that pollute to take account of the costs they impose on the environment, more trade has an ambiguous impact on welfare: the social gains from expanding trade and more export production could be more than offset by the social losses from pollution. Likewise, the returns from investing in education could well disappoint if the labor market fails to provide workers with the opportunities to use their knowledge in productive ways. For example, if you hire many of them for government positions, as was the case in Egypt, or recruit them for Soviet Union firms, the labor market will not see much impact. However, if you hire them for firms in the United States or South Korea, the results could be very different. Failure to control for the impact of such regimes could well lead researchers to draw the wrong conclusions.

However, as the other two chapters reveal, actually implementing Moran's insight is not easy. One issue relates to how we measure contributions to development, and the second issue relates to how we identify liberal and distorted regimes. Consider these issues in turn.

How should the results of FDI be measured? The Moss, Ramachandran, and Shah chapter on Africa, for example, argues that the negative views held by Africans are actually misguided. The authors claim that foreign firms do not crowd out domestic firms in East Africa. Instead, foreign firms favorably affect the economy: foreign firms are bigger, have more skilled managers, and are more likely to have worker training programs. They are likely to export more abroad and invest more locally. Contrary to African perceptions, foreign-owned firms also appear to be fairly well embedded in the domestic economy and to make considerable use of local inputs. Foreign firms also have higher value added per worker that the authors argue, based on econometric evidence, reflects their higher productivity rather than their monopolistic power. Implicitly, therefore, Moss, Ramachandran, and Shah claim that even though African economies remain highly distorted and policies toward foreign investors are discriminatory, FDI already contributes positively to African development. Whereas the Moran hypothesis is that FDI will disappoint in a hostile environment, Moss, Ramachandran, and Shah believe it has succeeded despite the context.

To be sure, one way to reconcile this claim with the Moran hypothesis is to argue that while the net effects of FDI have already been positive in Africa, they would be even more positive in a regime that had fewer distortions. But it is also possible that despite the evidence supplied by Moss, Ramachandran, and Shah, FDI still hurts African welfare given current policies. In particular, even though—as Moss, Ramachandran, and Shah have found—foreign-owned firms are relatively large, train their workers, and have higher value added per worker than domestic firms, their operations could nonetheless reduce host country welfare. For example, Moran quotes a study by Bernard Wasow in which only 3 of 35 products made by foreign-owned firms in Kenya in the 1980s actually created benefits to the national economy in excess of their costs. Hopefully this is no longer the case, but if foreign firms are still misallocating resources because prices are wrong, the country might have been better off if they were smaller and invested less!

This question of how to measure success is present in all three chapters. In particular, evidence that foreign firms use local inputs, use the latest technologies, are larger, invest more, pay higher average wages, export more, and have higher value added per worker are generally viewed as positive behavior. Moran, for example, lists ways FDI contributes to host country development even when foreign firms do not provide externalities. Contributions to development include whether they add resources, technology, and management as well as whether they introduce new activities, earn foreign exchange, and/or boost competitive substitution of imports in the host country. But these effects are not necessarily linked to increased welfare and well-being.

It might be more or less efficient to behave in these ways. In countries with different factor prices, for example, efficiency might dictate using different technologies and not always the latest. Higher value added per worker could reflect higher markups and the use of more capital rather than more productive technologies. Bigger is not always better. Firms could be too large as well as too small. The central idea here is that association does not imply causation. The fact that most industrial countries produce steel, for example, does not imply that the best way to industrialize is to produce steel. Thus, instead of the broad range of indicators used in the chapters, I would prefer the use of criteria grounded in economic theory.

A second issue relates to how government policy is characterized. Moran has drawn on case study literature to support his hypothesis. It is tempting to suggest that a variable depicting the nature of the government policy be inserted into a more aggregative cross-sectional study of growth just as some studies do with openness. However, problems summarizing the nature of a regime with a single measure occur. Indeed, this issue has long plagued the debate over the "East Asian miracle." According to some views, for example, South Korean success stems from the country's relatively neutral policies. For others, however, the key was that they "got prices wrong" and explicitly promoted exports. Similarly, Guoqiang Long's chapter reveals that China's policies toward foreign investors have not exactly been those of laissez-faire. Although China targeted and succeeded in attracting FDI, it is not a story of policy neutrality. Instead China used both carrots and sticks to attract FDI. On the one hand, favored foreign investors have been given special benefits such as tax preferences and favorable treatment with respect to the use of imported inputs and equipment for exporters; on the other hand, performance requirements have been imposed. Prior to China's recent entry into the World Trade Organization (WTO) these included performance requirements for local content, export performance, and foreign exchange balancing. Again the Moran view can be reconciled with the Chinese evidence by stating that the Chinese succeeded despite the sticks rather than because of them. It appears that over time, China has moved increasingly toward treating foreign investors more neutrally. While FDI in China was successful, perhaps the Chinese would have been even more successful had they applied more neutral policies earlier. But this country example shows that in practice it may actually be quite difficult to implement Moran's distinction between distorted and liberal regimes in cross-sectional studies. Is China an example of a liberal regime or one that has engaged in considerable government intervention? Clearly it is a combination of the two.

In sum, therefore, all three are stimulating chapters. Taken together they highlight the importance of the overall context in which FDI occurs. However, much work is still needed to improve measurement of both outcomes and policy regimes.

IV

CONCLUSIONS AND IMPLICATIONS FOR POLICY

14

Conclusions and Implications for FDI Policy in Developing Countries, New Methods of Research, and a Future Research Agenda

THEODORE H. MORAN, EDWARD M. GRAHAM, and MAGNUS BLOMSTRÖM

How do the results presented in this volume help answer the question, "What is the impact of foreign direct investment (FDI) on development?"[1] The evidence gathered in this volume demonstrates that a search for a "universal result" of FDI on a developing-country economy is simply misguided. FDI can have dramatically differing impacts—both positive and negative.

On the positive side, when FDI occurs under reasonably competitive conditions—in particular, with low barriers to trade and few restrictions on operations—foreign firms, or multinational corporations (MNCs), can help the host country conduct activities its economy is already engaged in more efficiently. Or—even more valuable—FDI can bring entirely new kinds of activities into the host economy, changing the production possibility frontier—the development trajectory—available to the country. Far beyond simply adding more capital to a host economy, FDI can be the conduit to the cutting edge of research and development (R&D), production technology, and management expertise in use around the world. FDI truly becomes "trade on steroids" with strongly favorable—not harmful—implications for host country development.

---

1. The conclusions and policy implications presented in this chapter represent the views of the editors—Theodore H. Moran, Edward M. Graham, and Magnus Blomström. There has been no attempt to have the contributors to this volume come to a "consensus view."

FDI can generate spillovers and externalities in a horizontal and—more often—in a vertical direction. FDI can increase competition in individual sectors and demonstrate to local firms how to meet that competition. FDI can even impart "positive productivity shocks" to motivate indigenous firms to raise their performance and improve their quality.

FDI can provide explicit assistance and coaching to local firms that want to become suppliers. As part of this assistance, foreign investors can introduce host country companies to members of the investors' network in other countries and to international markets more generally. Furthermore, FDI can lower input prices, increase demand, and improve local firm profitability as well as bring new, better, and cheaper goods and services to consumers. When accompanied by increases in trade, larger flows of FDI can enhance economic growth.

To be sure, these outcomes may not happen in a uniform way in every case, and—as discussed later—when host countries undertake multiple liberalizing reforms simultaneously, it is likely to be difficult to separate out just exactly what specific benefits derive from specific sources. FDI does not guarantee that all of these positive results will occur in all countries—they may be subject to varying human resource, financial system, and institutional constraints.

On the negative side, FDI in protected host country markets leads to an inefficient use of local resources and subtracts from local economic welfare. Foreign investors in countries with domestic content, joint venture, and technology sharing requirements deploy production techniques lagging far behind the frontier in international industry. Foreign affiliates with older technology and less efficient plants are not good candidates to develop from an infant industry to a robust world competitor.

Investment restrictions and trade restrictions affect foreign investors' backward linkages into the host economy. Local firms that sell to foreign affiliates in protected markets are often subscale in size and inefficient in operation; they seldom have strong exports. FDI under restrictive and distortionary conditions is not associated with developing a world-class supplier network in the host economy similar to the kind found under more competitive conditions. In fact, investment restrictions combined with trade restrictions hinder host country growth.

Implications for Policy Toward FDI

The dichotomy in outcomes in the studies gathered in this volume provides a framework to address the policy issues that opened this volume—namely, whether host country development is best promoted by imposing performance requirements on foreign investors and requiring them to share technology with indigenous firms, simply by allowing foreign investors access to all (or most) domestic sectors, or by providing special incentives and subsidies to lure foreign investors to choose the host economy as a base for operations.

The studies collected in this volume provide clear guidance for the first of these queries: The evidence cannot in any way be taken to support the contention that host country development objectives would be served by levying performance requirements or imposing other restrictions on FDI or on trade and investment together.

Quite to the contrary, the kinds of measures resurrected by some developing countries (i.e., domestic content requirements, joint venture mandates, and technology sharing regulations) are precisely the kinds of host policies most likely to interrupt the "intrafirm trade" and "parental supervision" shown in this volume to be so potent for host development. These restrictive measures lead to outdated technology, inefficient production processes, and wasteful use of host country resources.

Most strikingly, as Robert Lawrence reads the evidence presented here, in protected and distorted economies, a little bit of FDI is likely to worsen the economic welfare of the host a little, while a lot of FDI is likely to worsen the economic welfare of the host a lot more.

What about the latter two queries: To serve their interests most effectively, should host governments simply open their economies up to greater trade and investment, or expend resources to attract and fulfill foreign investor demands? The answer to whether to expend resources to attract and fulfill foreign investor demands is more complicated than a simple yes or no.

The Question of Providing Incentives and Subsidies to Foreign Investors

In chapter 4, Garrick Blalock and Paul J. Gertler provide the most extensive exposition of the argument that externalities justify providing incentives and subsidies to foreign investors. The creation of externalities means that foreign investors cannot appropriate for themselves all of the benefits that their activities bring to the host economy. From the host country's perspective, under these conditions, MNCs tend to underinvest in comparison to what would be optimal from the host's point of view. Thus, the host country's policy goal should be to expend resources to move the foreign investors toward that optimal level of investment. The introduction to this volume noted, however, that the analysis of providing incentives to attract foreign investors—even when externalities are present, as shown in the Blalock and Gertler data—should not be limited to whether or not a host country should merely push money toward MNCs (Blomström and Kokko 2003).

Investment flows depend upon macro, micro, and institutional reforms—low inflation rates, realistic exchange rates, reasonably efficient legal and regulatory systems that protect property and reward savings and investment, low levels of corruption—that create favorable conditions for business operations in general.[2] Beyond this, there are three broad categories of "investment promotion" expenditures that are regularly associated with host efforts to attract foreign direct investors.

The first category of expenditures focuses on providing information to potential investors in an effective and timely manner—including the creation of an efficient investment promotion agency, which is staffed to provide customized investment proposals, ready to brief MNCs at their headquarters, and backed by up-to-date Web sites with current economic and legal data as well as links to established investors ("satisfied customers").

The second category of "investment promotion" expenditures needed to make a host country a serious contender for foreign investment includes modernly equipped industrial parks, well-functioning infrastructure, and effective vocational and skill-training institutions suited to the investors' generic (if not industry-specific) human resource needs.

To complete the list, the third category of "investment promotion" expenditures involves meeting foreign investor demands to provide tax breaks and direct subsidies at least equivalent to other host countries in the region.

China, for example, introduced what was to become a highly successful model of investment promotion beginning in the middle 1980s, via the establishment of its "special economic zones" designed to attract foreign investors (Graham 2004). Originally, these zones were meant to be experiments with economic reform, at a time when Chinese economic policy remained quite Communist in direction even though the Deng Xiao Ping "reformist" faction shared power in Beijing with the more orthodox Li Peng faction. Over time, these zones became what amounted to havens for foreign investors, where these investors received special treatment, including most importantly insulation from the stultifying regulations associated with Communist doctrine. The zones also provided much-upgraded infrastructure, particularly in telecommunications and logistics, than was available elsewhere in China. At the same time, the Chinese central government in Beijing allowed local governments to engage in "policy experimentation" in the zones in their territories, with this experimentation turning into effective "policy competition" as each zone tried to make itself more attractive to foreign investors than competing zones. This included some positive incentives for investors, including tax relief, duty-free importation of capital goods, and provision of trained workers. Finally, it included insulation from much of the corruption that had become endemic in the largely state-owned industrial sector of China. In short, the zones provided each of the three types of investment promotion discussed above.

---

2. See the *International Country Risk Guide 2004*, *Institutional Investors Ratings 2004*, *Competitiveness Indicators of the World Economic Forum 2004*, and *Transparency International 2004*.

During the late 1980s, these zones attracted cumulatively at least $6 billion in FDI, small figures compared with recent flows to China but enormous by the standards of the 1970s or even the early 1980s. By 1990, a number of new zones had been created, some of these designated as "economic and technical development zones" for which the legal framework was somewhat different than for the original special economic zones. In 1991, acting largely on the basis of the success of the special economic zones and the economic and technical zones in attracting FDI, China removed many restrictions on foreign investment elsewhere in the economy so that the benefits of location in these zones to foreign investors was reduced. Even so, to this day, a large percentage of FDI to China flows into the zones or into newer industrial parks located close to the zones, largely because these zones and proximate areas still provide better infrastructure than available in most other areas of China.

An examination of the most thoroughly researched case of a developing country's attempt to attract foreign investment—the case of Costa Rica and Intel in 1996—suggests that these three types of expenditures noted above need to be evaluated separately (Spar 1998). To "market" the country, Costa Rican authorities suspected from the beginning that they would have to grapple with less than perfect information markets.[3] Costa Rica had an unusual reputation for political stability in comparison to other Central or Latin American countries. In the early 1990s, the country already had an FDI base concentrated in low-skilled garment factories. But Costa Rican officials nonetheless doubted that their economy would pop up automatically on the horizon of the more advanced manufacturing investors with no experience in their country that they hoped to recruit, in contrast to China, which by 1996 was on the horizon of just about every such investor.

To launch the search for MNCs in medium- and higher-skilled activities, Costa Rica devoted up front resources to restructure the country's investment promotion agency, CINDE (Coalición Costarricense de Iniciativas para el Desarrollo), by staffing it with high-paid personnel, specially trained to prepare feasibility studies tailored to meet the needs of the new target companies. The government realized that CINDE would need operating and travel funds for several years before any concrete results could appear.

In the effort to catch Intel's attention, Costa Rica discovered—as predicted—that the country was not even on the long list of prospective production sites Intel was considering until CINDE pushed its national name into view. Even then—despite what Debora Spar calls "assiduous" campaigning with unsolicited project proposals—it took more than two

---

3. Eduardo Alonso, *Trade and Investment Promotion: The Case of CINDE in Costa Rica, 2000*, presentation at the Inter-American Development Bank, Washington, September 18, 2001.

years even to wrangle an appointment with senior Intel management, traveling (of course) at CINDE's own expense to the semiconductor MNC's headquarters in California.

As for host country expenditures on infrastructure and on worker training, Costa Rica had to address Intel's concern about the risks associated with operating in an untried locale where delays in shipment, production downtime, or inadequate staffing would not only cost the parent money but reduce the "lead time over rivals."[4] To qualify for a spot on Intel's "short list" of production sites for assembly and testing of its latest Pentium microprocessors, the government committed itself to construct a new cargo terminal at the national airport, to build a new electric substation dedicated to meeting the power needs at Intel's plant, and to create special vocational training programs designed jointly by Intel and the Costa Rican Institute of Technology.

In closing the deal, Costa Rica provided tax breaks to Intel: full exemption from income taxes for the first eight years of operation and a 50 percent exemption for the next four. CINDE asserted that it had no choice but to match the tax treatment available from the other alternative sites Intel was considering (Indonesia, Thailand, Brazil, Chile, and Mexico) (Alonso 2001).

CINDE hoped that securing the Intel plant would have a "signaling" or "demonstration effect" that would influence the decisions of other foreign investors. As it turned out, Costa Rica tripled its stock of foreign investment in the subsequent three years, to a total of $1.3 billion, with exports totaling $3.3 billion annually—allowing the country to overtake Chile as the most export-intensive country in Latin America. A survey of 61 foreign multinationals showed that 72 percent (36 in electronics, 13 in medical devices, 3 in business services, and 9 in other sectors) weighed Intel's choice of Costa Rica heavily in their own calculations (Larraín, Lopez-Calva, and Rodriguez-Clare 2001).

Costa Rica's government acted—the investment promotion authorities admitted (Alonso 2001)—without any but the most intuitive calculation of the potential for positive spillovers from Intel's operations to local firms, workers, and communities and later from the operations of Motorola, Abbott Laboratories, Baxter Healthcare, Procter & Gamble, FedEx, and others. The only concrete point of reference was that the new Intel factory would employ approximately 3,500 workers with average wages approximately 50 percent higher than elsewhere in the domestic manufacturing sector ($3.36 per hour at Intel versus $2.21 elsewhere).

Should other developing countries follow what has come to be known as "the Costa Rica model"?

---

4. Intel manager quoted in Spar (1998, 5).

With regard to providing up-to-date information tailored to meet investor needs, Dani Rodrik and Ricardo Hausmann (2004) argue that host country public spending on foreign investment feasibility studies provides "informational externalities" that the market does not supply on its own. The Foreign Investment Advisory Service of the World Bank Group has found that the social returns from reducing search costs for foreign direct investors, enhancing credibility of information, and facilitating site comparisons are quite high: a net present value of almost four dollars for every dollar spent.[5]

With regard to expenditures on infrastructure and skill-building institutions, host authorities trying to attract first-time investors in nontraditional sectors face a challenge similar to a used car dealer trying to help a buyer overcome the fear of making an expensive purchase and being stuck with a potential "lemon" (Akerloff 1970). Unlike used car dealers, however, host governments cannot eliminate the investor's risk by offering a warranty, but host authorities can reduce the investor's risk by addressing the most likely sources of trouble (e.g., port congestion, power failures, and skilled-manpower shortages). Faced with making "irreversible commitments under uncertainty," Avinash Dixit and Robert Pindyck (1994) find that calculations of high profitability may be a relatively weak motivator of new corporate investment in comparison to concrete actions by the host that narrow the scope of uncertainty surrounding the project.[6] The rationale for public expenditures on improvements in infrastructure and in vocational education to attract foreign firms is strengthened by the likelihood that they will improve the business environment for indigenous firms as well.

What about awarding tax breaks to foreign investors?

The Costa Rican case highlights a policy dilemma of increasing importance to both developing and developed countries. Over the past two decades, there has been an escalation in the packages of tax breaks, incentives, free land, below-market-priced office space, and other subsidies that both developed and developing countries have been offering to attract multinational investors, and/or to keep home country investors in place (Thomas 2000).

Developed—and not developing—countries have led the increase in incentive packages. Ireland was a leader, awarding special incentive packages to more than 1,200 foreign firms between 1980 and 2000. German grants to firms settling in the former East Germany have grown to exceed the already generous treatment European Union (EU) members awarded

---

5. See Wells, Jr. and Wint (2000). A survey of 25 African investment promotion agency Web sites, in contrast, showed a lack of up-to-date economic or legal information, and few usable links to key ministries or existing investors.

6. See Dixit and Pindyck (1994). As shown in the Costa Rica case, such host country expenses may play both a risk-reducing and a signaling role.

to investors in lagging regions. US locational subsidies to national and international firms from state and local governments have risen from $27,000 per job created in the mid-1980s to approximately $200,000 per job created in the late 1990s.

Developing countries have been drawn into this competition for FDI. However, although the availability of tax breaks and direct subsidies has grown, the amounts are not as large and the deployment is not as effective as in the developed economies (Shah 1995).

Traditional analysis assumed that multinational investors did not base their locational decisions on tax considerations, and that there was little competition between developed-country and developing-country production sites. Both of these assumptions are being challenged by contemporary econometric research that shows multinational investors becoming more responsive to locational incentives and competition growing between developed- and developing-country sites (Mutti 2003; Altshuler, Grubert, and Newlong 2001). Using data from 48 developed and developing countries, John Mutti shows that over the past two decades the responsiveness of international investors to locational incentives has grown, and that sensitivity to tax competition is particularly pronounced for production destined for international markets.

In fact, the propensity of MNCs to base their decisions about locations on host country tax policy is strongest for plants producing manufactures for export from the developing world. Here Mutti finds that tax measures to reduce the cost of capital by 1 percent raise MNC production in the manufacturing sector of the host country by approximately 3 percent.

This escalation of revenue giveaways has made the need for a public policy solution increasingly apparent: developed and developing countries have a common interest in working together to cap and control tax breaks and locational subsidies on an international basis. Past efforts to impose restraints on host country treatment of potential investors—within an Organization for Economic Cooperation and Development (OECD) context—have had, at best, only very modest success (Thomas 2000). It would be mutually advantageous for developed and developing countries to try again with new vigor imposing limits within a multilateral framework. Developing countries might be allowed two tiers of locational incentives, with least developed hosts graduating to middle-level status according to an automatic formula (Mutti 2003, chapter 4).

Instead of competing to match whatever tax treatment was available from other jurisdictions, developing countries could devote more of those resources available for investment promotion to overcome imperfections in the supply of information, make infrastructure improvements, and launch education and training initiatives that can benefit foreign and indigenous firms alike.

Besides international agreement to limit competition in tax giveaways, the analysis presented here—in particular, the differentiation between "harmful" FDI and "beneficial" FDI—points to two other areas in which developed- and developing-country interests overlap.

Developed Country Support for Outflows of "Harmful" FDI?

As illustrated in this volume, the "Washington consensus"—that FDI is "good" and more is always better than less—was, and is, incorrect. It is not in developing countries' interest to have FDI that depends upon trade restrictions and/or other protection from competition to survive. Nor is it in developed countries' interest to have inefficient, welfare-harming—and trade-reducing—FDI flowing from the home economy to the host.

Yet a survey of national political risk insurance agencies in 21 OECD countries whose mission is to support outward flows of FDI to developing countries shows that 19 (including the Overseas Private Investment Corporation of the United States, and equivalents in the United Kingdom, Canada, France, Germany, Italy, and Japan) do not screen projects to eliminate those that require protection to survive.[7] The Multilateral Investment Guarantee Agency (MIGA) and International Finance Corporation (IFC) of the World Bank Group, as well as the investment guarantee programs of the Inter-American Development Bank, the Asian Development Bank, the European Bank for Reconstruction and Development, and the African Development Bank must be added to this list.

These official and quasi-official political risk insurance agencies look at the commercial viability of the project—as well as other environmental and social criteria such as compliance with core labor standards—to qualify it for coverage. But "commercial viability" can be misleading. Protected FDI projects are often highly profitable. In fact, protected investors value political risk coverage, especially breach of contract coverage, to preserve their status quo arrangements. As Moran notes in chapter 11, Chrysler's boutique auto assembly plant in Mexico during the country's import-substitution period was the company's most profitable operation anywhere in the world. Hewlett-Packard, Apple, and Compaq lobbied *against* the liberalization of Mexico's computer sector in order to preserve their ability to exact a second round of oligopoly rents from 2- to 3-year-old technology for models priced 130 to 170 percent higher than world prices.

But taxpayers in developed countries do not have any reason to back government-supported political risk insurance for FDI projects that lower developing-country welfare and impede trade expansion. The interests of both developed and developing countries would be served by a joint agreement among official political risk insurance agencies to screen out, and not support, FDI projects that are launched with trade protection.

---

7. The 2004 Commitment to Development Index, Foreign Policy Magazine/Center for Global Development, *Foreign Policy,* May/June 2004.

A Common Developed- and Developing-Country Agenda for Trade and Investment Negotiations Within the WTO Framework

The trade and investment agreement that emerged from the Uruguay Round—the Trade Related Investment Measures (TRIMs) Agreement—committed all countries to phase out domestic content requirements and import-export balancing requirements imposed upon foreign affiliates. Developed countries had two years to end the use of these measures, while developing countries had five years and least developed countries had seven years.

Both developing and least developed countries were allowed to petition to extend their phaseouts. Concerned that foreign affiliates with domestic content requirements would be uncompetitive—a concern that the evidence presented in this volume has shown to be well founded—several developing countries have requested more time to deal with the inevitable dislocations and adjustments, including the Philippines, Malaysia, Thailand, Romania, and Chile. For these petitions, the World Trade Organization (WTO) Council on Trade in Goods has permitted a longer phaseout period in exchange for a specific schedule for eliminating the domestic content or trade-balancing requirement.

The TRIMs Agreement provided for a self-review to begin in 2000. During this review, some developing-country negotiators have continued to assert that domestic content requirements are a useful and necessary means to create local industries and promote host country growth. At the WTO Ministerial Conference in 2003 in Cancún, the developing countries indicated—under the rubric of "development provisions"—that they wished to reopen the TRIMs Agreement.[8]

The evidence presented in this conference volume shows clearly that domestic content requirements, and the implicit trade protection associated with imposing such requirements, do not create efficient local industries or promote host country growth. Weakening or undoing the TRIMs Agreement would not serve the self-interest of developing countries. Quite to the contrary, reaffirming the TRIMs Agreement and adding multilateral prohibitions on joint venture and technology sharing requirements would serve the self-interest of developing countries.

While it appears that the Singapore issues—including trade and investment (as well as competition and government procurement)—will not be included in the Doha Round, the WTO Working Group on the Relationship between Trade and Investment will continue to address the contentious

---

8. Communication by Brazil and India on the need to amend the TRIMs Agreement, in *Foreign Direct Investment and Performance Requirements: New Evidence from Selected Countries*, Geneva, UNCTAD, 2003, 38–39. See also Development Provisions, WTO Secretariat note to the Working Group on the Relationship between Trade and Investment, June 11, 2002.

arguments involved (*Inside US Trade* 22, no. 32, August 6, 2004, 1). The evidence demonstrates clearly that in these working group discussions, the trade and investment agenda of the developing and the developed countries should overlap with regard to performance requirements: the existing TRIMs Agreement should be endorsed, not weakened, and the roster of prohibited practices should be expanded to include mandatory joint venture and technology sharing requirements.

Implications for Future Research Methodology

The studies assembled in this volume make important contributions to the understanding of how to disentangle the diverse impact of FDI on the host economy and how to identify spillovers and externalities in a more rigorous fashion. These chapters, and commentaries by Gordon Hanson, Michael P. Keane, Marc Melitz, and Robert Lawrence, explore in some detail the challenges that remain.

Three particular challenges stand out for researchers attempting to use econometric techniques to test for externalities—challenges concerning endogeneity, the market power of firms, and heterogeneity in firms' production functions.

Endogeneity

As Gordon Hanson points out in his commentary, many factors affect an industry or region that might, on the one hand, stimulate FDI, on the other hand, raise wages or productivity in domestic firms. Finding a correlation between an increase in foreign investment and an increase in domestic firm wages or productivity and concluding a causal relationship from it would not necessarily be justified.

For example, a host country might take the decision to make a number of business-friendly reforms simultaneously. These reforms might serve to attract foreign firms into the country while providing a setting in which domestic firms could operate more productively. Thus, inferring that the entry of foreign firms led to improved domestic firm productivity would be incorrect.

A particularly tricky case, Michael P. Keane points out, could arise in investigating what happens when a country improves its intellectual property rights (IPR) protection. Better IPR protection might make the country more attractive to foreign investors, since they could exercise greater control over their technology, leading to fewer knowledge spillovers into the host economy. Thus, the result would be a negative correlation between domestic firm productivity and foreign penetration. Or the result might be enhanced attraction of foreign investors and greater ability of domestic firms to exercise greater control over their own technology, producing a positive (but spurious) correlation between domestic firm productivity and foreign penetration.

The contributors to this volume do not offer any miraculous solutions to the problems of endogeneity. The principal challenge, rather, is for future researchers to replicate Garrick Blalock and Paul J. Gertler's careful and creative analysis. Their study investigated whether Indonesian plants had higher total factor productivity (TFP) growth in regional industries where there was more rapid downstream demand by multinationals. Hanson points out that by isolating region-year effects, Blalock and Gertler establish the average plant in the region as the control group. They then examine whether there was a larger fall in either regional industry concentration or industry prices in sectors where downstream growth by multinationals was larger. Positive answers in both cases, Hanson argues, preclude external factors from determining domestic firm productivity outcomes and foreign investor location outcomes simultaneously. Blalock and Gertler's demonstration that foreign entrants transfer technology to suppliers to reduce cost and improve quality and that diffusion of technology induces competition in both the supply sector and other downstream buyer sectors—creating welfare gains for both consumers and firms—remains robust.

Market Power of Firms

Michael P. Keane labels dealing with the market power of firms "the PQ problem"—researchers must use sales revenues (price times quantity, or PQ) without information on quantity itself. If FDI appears to change the revenue results for firms in an industry, it is not clear whether this change in revenue derived from shifts in productivity or in prices since FDI is expected to occur in industries where firms have market power (this is more likely to be a concern in a horizontal direction than in a vertical direction). A knowledge spillover that enables firms to enhance market power could be mistakenly interpreted as a productivity enhancement.

The only general solution, argues Keane, is to estimate the production function jointly with an assumed demand system, as he and Susan E. Feinberg have calculated for US MNCs and their manufacturing affiliates in Canada (Feinberg and Keane 2004). Levinsohn and Melitz (2002) and Katayama, Lu, and Tybout (2003) have also attempted to deal with the "PQ" problem.

Heterogeneity in Firms' Production Functions

The standard econometric approach to search for spillovers is to estimate production functions in which the total factor productivity (TFP) of the domestic firms in a particular industry/country is taken to be the function of some measure of FDI brought into the industry/country by MNCs (usually market share of MNC affiliates in the industry, or the average foreign equity participation across all firms in an industry). But, as Robert Lipsey and Fredrik Sjöholm point out, knowledge spillovers are likely to alter the production functions in important ways that go beyond shifts in TFP, like changing the capital intensity of the operation or the marketing strategy of the firm, as shown in the materials gathered. Or FDI may generate reorganization—as Feinberg and Keane observe—that allows the firm to take advantage of economies of scale. Therefore, Lipsey and Sjöholm and Keane conclude that it is far too narrow to concentrate the search for spillovers by simply looking for shifts in TFP.

Heterogeneity in production functions within industries, as Feinberg and Keane observe, and between industries complicates the investigation of spillovers in other ways as well.

The limitations of econometric tests for spillovers lead Keane to conclude that economists should devote closer attention to the case study literature to trace the mechanisms through which knowledge transfers occur. Gordon Hanson adds that surveys of firm managers can be improved in ways that will help remedy the difficulties in the use of econometrics encounters in establishing causality. These possibilities are explored next.

Case Studies and Survey Results

Economists frequently refer to case studies as "anecdotal" evidence, with the pejorative connotation that they present results that are one-off observations whose implications are liable to be negated the next time any other observation is reported. This flimsy result may occur from using case studies, but need not be.

As the political science and political economy literature demonstrate, small numbers of cases can be chosen and structured comparisons carefully carried out in order to specify counterfactuals, test hypotheses, and provide conclusions that can be further tested and independently verified (King, Keohane, and Verba 1994; George and Bennett 2004). Larger numbers of case studies can be gathered so as to avoid selection bias and provide generalizable results. This is the approach Theodore H. Moran undertakes in investigating the performance differences between affiliates that are tightly linked into the parent MNC's production network and affiliates that are prevented by domestic content and joint venture requirements from being so linked. Moran tests the hypothesis in a handful of industries and in a handful of countries during a defined time period, then moves the analysis across industries, across countries, and across time periods, matching the case study results with other statistical investigations.

Case study analysis has the advantage of being rich in detail, and allowing the researcher to examine directly what statistical analysis can only infer. For instance, an important analytical question is whether a foreign investor will provide explicit assistance to suppliers if the investor cannot capture all the benefits for himself—or whether a foreign investor will provide explicit assistance even if some of the improved supplier performance might be spread to competitors. Moran's case studies and Blalock and Gertler's interviews show that the answer is frequently "yes," with the investors explaining that they want host country suppliers to achieve economies of scale, produce items of reliable quality, and capture the lowest price even if this benefits rivals. Moreover, foreign investors realize that they cannot hold their suppliers to exclusive commercial relationships in the real world.

Similarly, the case study evidence introduced in this volume can make an important contribution to the debate about whether host country suppliers to MNCs "learn" how to export from the MNCs, or whether more capable host country firms become suppliers to MNCs and also—coincidentally—begin to send products abroad. In Malaysia, Thailand, and Indonesia—as recounted in the surveys in part I and the case studies in part III—indigenous firms on the path to becoming "contract manufacturers" for the electronics industry reported that they first entered export markets by being taken by the hand by the foreign investor in their home country and set up in a purchase relationship with a sister affiliate in a neighboring country. Afterward, these indigenous firms began to sell their output in that neighboring country and in external markets more broadly.

In both examples above, as Lipsey and Sjöholm point out, the case studies demonstrate that foreign investors do provide spillovers and externalities to host countries in the developing world. However, the case studies do not demonstrate that this outcome occurs in the "average" case let alone every case. But—as indicated above—if there are similar results across countries, industries, and time periods, researchers can be increasingly confident of the results.

Blalock and Gertler's manager interviews and Javorcik and Spatareanu's survey results offer some of the same advantages for research on FDI–host economy impacts, subject to the caveats they note about sampling techniques. An "intriguing" possibility, as Hanson suggests, is to try to structure manager interviews and firm surveys in a manner that overcomes the problem of endogeneity.

The question "Did your firm become more productive after the arrival of foreign firms?," Gordon Hanson argues, implicitly controls for industry fixed effects, but leaves open the possibility that some external factor "caused" both a growing foreign presence and a rising domestic firm productivity. A more useful question then might be, Did the growth rate of productivity in your firm increase after foreign firms arrived in your industry?—or rather, Did the foreign presence lead to a difference in domestic firm productivity? But the causal inference is still incomplete without knowing why the foreign presence increased. The solution, Hanson concludes, might be more frequent surveys timed around events likely to trigger FDI.

With sufficient care, manager interviews and firm surveys might also be helpful in investigating questions about the market power of firms (whether changes in sales revenues of domestic firms associated with FDI inflows can be attributed to changes in productivity or in prices) and about heterogeneity in firms' production functions (whether knowledge spillovers from foreign investors change the capital intensity of operations or the marketing strategy of domestic firms). Thus, taken together, case studies and survey results can increase the confidence the research community has in statistical studies where inference is the only causal link. For example, Brian Aitken, Gordon Hanson, and Ann Harrison (1997) show that the probability of an indigenous Mexican plant engaging in exports is positively correlated with the proximity of that plant to multinational investors but uncorrelated with the concentration of exporters in the region in general, suggesting that some "learning" or "triggering" mechanism is at work.[9] Case studies and management surveys can add confidence to the inference about causation.

Priority Areas for Further Research

There are many areas in which further research on FDI's impact on the host economy is sorely needed. Three of the most important involve expanding the analysis of the contribution of FDI and trade to host country growth, investigating whether FDI can help the poorest developing countries where human resource levels are very low, and exploring how host countries might enhance their prospects for spillovers and externalities from foreign investors.

The Contribution of FDI and Trade to Host Country Growth

In part II of this volume, Maria Carkovic and Ross Levine offered a reassessment of whether FDI accelerates economic growth. They critiqued the research of Borensztein, De Gregorio, and Lee (1998), whose work showed a positive relationship between FDI and host country growth, since their own research suggested that FDI did not accelerate growth as a general proposition.

Bruce Blonigen and Miao Grace Wang countered by arguing that inappropriate pooling of data from developed and developing countries was

---

9. Aitken, Hanson, and Harrison (1997) find that the relationship between the presence of foreign plants and exports on the part of domestic plants is independent of proximity to national borders, independent of proximity to the capital city, and independent of the existence of other exporters. This means, they argue, that the superior export performance of these particular Mexican firms cannot be attributed to some local comparative advantage from where they are situated, but must rather come (somehow) from proximity to the foreign investors.

responsible for results indicating that FDI does not significantly affect per capita growth. When inappropriate pooling of data is avoided, they found that FDI does have a significant impact on developing-country growth. However, their estimation techniques employ an ordinary least squares (OLS) estimator with panel data and using this—Carkovic and Levine argue—might lead to what amounts to a "false positive."

Marc Melitz attempted to reconcile these two investigations by pointing out that the Carkovic and Levine rejection of the FDI-growth relationship arises when they introduce controls on trade openness. When changes in trade and FDI occur simultaneously, the evidence in both studies, Melitz argues, shows a strong positive impact on developing–host country growth.

The "reconciliation" of these two major research studies would clearly benefit from further investigation. Carkovic and Levine note the concerns about mixing rich and poor countries in empirical studies of FDI and growth, but they indicate that limiting the data used to developing countries did not alter their own results. They also disagree with Melitz that it was inappropriate to control for trade openness in assessing the relationship between FDI and growth; Carkovic and Levine argue that it is important to know whether an independent relationship between FDI and growth exists. However, to do so one would have to sort out the complex interdependence between trade and FDI that is noted in the literature, and it is not clear that simply including a measure of trade openness as an independent variable achieves this. Also, it is worth noting that a forthcoming article by Pradeep Agarwal (forthcoming 2005) using an Arellano and Bover and Blundell and Bond estimator but a somewhat different specification than Carkovic and Levine shows a robust relationship between FDI and growth in a sample of developing countries.

The Carkovic and Levine results emerge after they introduce a country-specific variable that is assumed to be time invariant and then eliminate it by first-differencing independent variables in the time dimension. This is appropriate if country-specific effects are fixed (time invariant) but could go awry if these effects are not—e.g., if the country-specific effect proxies for policy toward FDI, which certainly has changed for some countries in their sample over the time range of the data.

Melitz uses the case studies introduced in part II of this volume to contrast how FDI in import-substitution strategies may reduce trade, while FDI as part of a corporate integration strategy may expand trade, reducing host country growth in the first scenario and increasing host country growth in the second. But he concludes—like Robert Lawrence—that more extensive research is needed to confirm empirically that the combination of restrictions on FDI and on imports is behind the subaverage performance of developing countries that attract FDI without concurrently increasing their level of trade.

A puzzle emerges in the trade-and-FDI-generate-growth relationship, however, because Blonigen and Wang fail to find a robust relationship between FDI and growth among developed countries, where trade barriers would appear to be lower than for developing countries in general. One explanation might be that FDI among developed countries is heavily populated with mergers and acquisitions rather than greenfield investment, which may not lead to a boost in growth. Alternatively, FDI as a percent of gross domestic product (GDP) has been higher to developing countries than to developed ones, even if the absolute magnitude of the flows to developed countries has been large. Thus, the result for developed countries could be that FDI's contribution is simply lost in the noise—i.e., the data are just not good enough to enable econometric "filters" to discern the effect even if such an effect is present.

The Human Resource Threshold for Benefits from FDI

Many statistical studies have found that FDI positively affects growth in developing countries only if the country has a minimum threshold stock of human capital. The results reported by Borensztein, De Gregorio, and Lee (1998), for example, suggest that for a given level of human capital, an increase in FDI raises the growth rates of per capita income, except for economies with the lowest level of schooling. Blonigen and Wang likewise find that FDI has a significant impact on per capita growth only after education levels in the less developed country (LDC) are at a high enough threshold level.

However, Mauritius illustrates how "ideas" introduced via FDI can alter a host country's development path 10 to 20 times more powerfully than trade liberalization alone. Mauritius was a nation so poor it was used by British economists to illustrate the concept of "Malthusian economics" (Romer 1992, 1994). Moran adds Madagascar, Lesotho, the Dominican Republic, and the Philippines to the country case studies in which low-skill FDI operations create tens of thousands of jobs and hundreds of millions of dollars in exports. Dani Rodrik and Ricardo Hausmann point out that FDI provides the best prospect for El Salvador to upgrade the country's export base from footwear and garments to higher value-added manufactures (Rodrik and Hausmann 2004).

While "sweatshop" abuses are a grim reality in many low-skill–intensive plants, foreign direct investors have consistently been shown to pay more than domestic employers, controlling for plant size and worker skill level, in poorer as well as richer developing countries.[10] In Madagascar, for example, Mireille Razafindrakoto and François Roubaud (1995) found export processing zone (EPZ) workers earning 15–20 percent more than other workers with comparable education level, work experience, and length of tenure. In fact, Edward M. Graham (2000) has found that compensation for

---

10. In addition to Lipsey and Sjöholm in this volume, see Brown, Deardorff, and Stern (2002).

host country workers in foreign manufacturing subsidiaries is greater as a multiple of average compensation per worker in the manufacturing sector for lesser and least developed countries than for middle-income developing countries. In middle-income developing countries local workers in foreign-owned plants earn 1.8 times the average manufacturing compensation; in lesser and least developed countries local workers in foreign-owned plants earn 2.0 times the average manufacturing compensation.[11]

Moreover, there is intriguing evidence that FDI in poor countries is not without externalities. When Mauritius launched its export-led growth, virtually 100 percent of the export firms were foreign-owned. Then, after gaining experience in the foreign plants, managers and workers left to start locally owned firms, representing 50 percent of total equity capital in EPZ firms within 15 years (Rhee, Katterback, and White 1990, 39). In the Dominican Republic the comparable figure for indigenous firms establishing operations alongside MNC plants was 35 percent, and 20 percent in the Philippines, both over a shorter time period. While human resource movements are well documented, flows of technology transfer—either explicit or inadvertent—require further investigation.

Thus, alongside a multitude of cases in which poorer countries have been unable to attract much FDI or to use FDI effectively for development, examples exist of poor LDCs achieving much greater (relative) success. Discovering the ingredients for turning the first into the second should be a priority area for future research.[12]

Enlarging the Prospects for Spillovers and Externalities

Given the importance of spillovers and externalities for host country development, it is surprising that more investigation of the conditions that are most conducive to the emergence of spillovers and externalities has not occurred.

As Moran points out, country studies have found that host economies that afford business-friendly treatment to both indigenous firms and foreign investors are more likely to find indigenous firms becoming suppliers to the MNCs (Rhee, Katterback, and White 1990, 39; Hill 2004). Local companies need an operating environment that enables them to operate on a competitive basis no less than foreign investors. As Beata Smarzynska Javorcik and Mariana Spatareanu report in part I of this volume, and Todd J. Moss, Vijaya Ramachandran, and Manju Kedia Shah report in part III, well-functioning financial institutions that provide credit on reasonable

---

11. Graham (2000, table 4.2, 93–94) eliminates salaries for foreign managers and supervisors from these calculations.

12. For initial steps along these lines, see Moran (forthcoming 2005).

risk-adjusted terms to small and medium-sized domestic firms are particularly important to creating a strong indigenous business community.

As Javorcik and Spatareanu as well as Blalock and Gertler show, the level of technological and managerial capabilities among local businesses determines whether they are likely to be able to qualify as suppliers to foreign investors, or to respond positively to the "productivity shock" created by the foreign presence. Other research has discovered the same phenomenon. Ari Kokko (1994) found that spillovers between foreign affiliates and local firms in Mexico varied as a function of the productivity difference between them; if the local firms had much lower levels of productivity, there was little evidence of spillovers. Ari Kokko, Ruben Tansini, and Mario Zejan (1996) uncover similar results among manufacturing firms in Uruguay (also see Blomström and Wolff 1994).

Country studies show that as host economies become more developed, what started out as relatively small and weak backward linkages into the host economy become thicker and more complex (Siew-Yean 2004, 225). A growing pool of trainable and trained workers helps indigenous firms just as it does MNCs. The length of time an individual foreign investor operates in a host country also affects the breadth of backward linkages, with new investors having few connections to the domestic economy and more experienced investors having a more extensive network.

Host country policies also play a role in facilitating backward linkages and spillovers. As Moran notes, studies undertaken under the auspices of the United Nations Conference on Trade and Development (UNCTAD) argue that the Economic Development Board of Singapore might serve as a model (UNCTAD 2001; McKendrick, Donner, and Haggard 2000). The Board offered to reimburse the salary of a manager from each MNC affiliate who had responsibility to invite local firms to participate in the affiliate's own training programs and identify which firms showed promise of qualifying as suppliers. The affiliate would recommend specific machinery for these firms to purchase to upgrade their performance, for which Singapore's Small Industry Finance Program would provide loans, which would be paid back from sales to the affiliate. The affiliate managers—or their human resource counterparts—would be asked to help design the curricula of vocational institutions adjacent to the industrial parks where the affiliates were located.

This "vendor development" model thus used foreign investors as *talent scouts* to sort through potential suppliers, and then helped the most capable or the most trainable to finance the improvements recommended by the investors. The model has relied on light-handed facilitation by host authorities, rather than regulations that obliged the MNCs to purchase specific amounts of supplier products or to form joint ventures with the supplier firms. The expenditure of host resources has been modest.

Programs to encourage spillovers and externalities cry out for further research. Should they be directed only toward smaller local firms or toward all local firms independent of size? How can they be designed to avoid the cronyism that so often plagues government-backed financing schemes in the developing world?

Should initiatives in finance and training be fashioned to encourage "clustering" or be spread uniformly across the economic landscape? Should vocational training programs be focused on meeting the needs of foreign investors and their local suppliers, or on forms of training most needed by workers in the economy at large? All these questions lay the groundwork for future research.

References

Agarwal, Pradeep. 2005. FDI in South Asia: Impact on Growth and Local Investment. In *Multinationals and Foreign Investment in Economic Development*, ed., Edward M. Graham. London: Palgrave/MacMillan. Forthcoming.

Aitken, Brian, Gordon H. Hanson, and Ann E. Harrison. 1997. Spillovers, Foreign Investment, and Export Behavior. *Journal of International Economics* 43, no. 1–2 (August): 103–32.

Akerloff, George. 1970. The Market for 'Lemons': Quality Uncertainty and the Market Mechanism. *Quarterly Journal of Economics* 84, no. 3 (August): 488–500.

Alonso, Eduardo. 2001. Trade and Investment Promotion: The Case of CINDE in Costa Rica. Presentation at the Inter-American Development Bank, Washington, September 18.

Altshuler, Rosanne, Harry Grubert, and Scott Newlong. 2001. Has US Investment Abroad Become More Sensitive to Tax Rates? In *International Taxation and Multinational Activity*, ed., James Hines. Chicago: University of Chicago Press.

Blomström, Magnus, and Ari Kokko. 2003. The Economics of Foreign Direct Investment Incentives. In *Foreign Direct Investment in the Real and Financial Sector of Industrial Countries*, ed., H. Herrmann and R. E. Lipsey. Berlin and New York: Springer Verlag.

Blomström, Magnus, and Edward N. Wolff. 1994. Multinational Corporations and Productivity Convergence in Mexico. In *Convergence of Productivity: Cross-National Studies and Historical Evidence*, ed., William Baumol, Richard Nelson, and Edward N. Wolff. Oxford: Oxford University Press.

Borensztein, E., J. De Gregorio, and J. W. Lee. 1998. How Does Foreign Investment Affect Growth? *Journal of International Economics* 45.

Brown, Drusilla K., Alan V. Deardorff, and Robert M. Stern. 2002. *The Effects of Multinational Production on Wages and Working Conditions in Developing Countries*. Discussion Paper 483. University of Michigan Research Seminar in International Economics (August 30).

Dixit, Avinash K., and Robert S. Pindyck. 1994. *Investment Under Uncertainty*. Princeton: Princeton University Press.

Feinberg, Susan, and Michael Keane. 2004. *Accounting for the Growth of MNC-Based Trade Using a Structural Model of US MNCs*. Working Paper. College Park, MD: University of Maryland.

George, Alexander L., and Andrew Bennett. 2004. *Case Studies and Theory Development*. Cambridge, MA: MIT University Press.

Graham, Edward M. 2000. *Fighting the Wrong Enemy: Antiglobal Activists and Multinational Enterprises*. Washington: Institute for International Economics.

Graham, Edward M. 2004. Do Export Processing Zones Attract FDI and Its Benefits: The Experience from China. *International Economics and Economic Policy* 1: 88–103.

Hill, Hal. 2004. Six Asian Economies: Issues and Lessons. In *Managing FDI in a Globalizing Economy: Asian Experiences*, ed., Douglas H. Brooks and Hal Hill. New York: Palmgrave Macmillan.

Katayama, H., S. Lu, and J. Tybout. 2003. *Why Plant-Level Productivity Studies Are Often Misleading, and an Alternative Approach to Inference.* NBER Working Paper 9617. Cambridge, MA: National Bureau of Economic Research.

King, Cary, Robert O. Keohane, and Sidney Verba. 1994. *Designing Social Inquiry: Scientific Inference in Qualitative Research.* Princeton: Princeton University Press.

Kokko, Ari. 1994. Technology, Market Characteristics, and Spillovers. *Journal of Development Economics* 4: 279–93.

Kokko, Ari, Ruben Tansini, and Mario C. Zejan. 1996. Local Technological Capability and Productivity Spillovers from FDI in the Uruguayan Manufacturing Sector. *Journal of Development Studies* 32 (April): 602–11.

Larraín, Felipe, Luis Lopez-Calva, and Andres Rodriguez-Clare. 2001. Intel: A Case Study of Foreign Direct Investment in Central America.

Levinsohn, Jerome, and Marc Melitz. 2002. *Productivity in a Differentiated Products Market Equilibrium.* Working paper. Ann Arbor, MI: University of Michigan.

McKendrick, David G., Richard F. Donner, and Stephan Haggard. 2000. *From Silicon Valley to Singapore: Location and Competitive Advantage in the Hard Disk Drive Industry.* Stanford, CA: Stanford University Press.

Moran, Theodore H. 2005. *Foreign Direct Investment and the Development of Low Income Poorly Performing States.* Washington: Center for Global Development. Forthcoming.

Mutti, John H. 2003. *Taxation and Foreign Direct Investment.* Washington: Institute for International Economics.

Razafindrakoto, Mireille, and François Roubaud. 1995. Les Entreprises Franches à Madagascar: Economie d'Enclave ou Promesse d'Une Nouvelle Prospérité? Nouvel Esclavage ou Opportunité pour le Développement du Pays? *Economie de Madagascar,* no. 2.

Rhee, Yung Whee, Katharina Katterback, and Jeanette White. 1990. *Free Trade Zones in Export Strategies.* Washington: World Bank, Industry Development Division (December).

Rodrik, Dani, and Ricardo Hausmann. 2004. Discovering El Salvador's Production Potential. Photocopy (August).

Romer, Paul. 1992. Two Strategies for Economic Development: Using Ideas and Producing Ideas. *Proceedings of the World Bank Annual Conference on Development Economics.* Washington: World Bank.

Romer, Paul. 1994. New Goods, Old Theory, and the Welfare Costs of Trade Restrictions. *Journal of Development Economics* 43.

Shah, A., ed. 1995. *Fiscal Incentives for Investment and Innovation.* New York: Oxford University Press for the World Bank.

Siew-Yean, Tham. 2004. Malaysia. In *Managing FDI in a Globalizing Economy: Asian Experiences,* ed., Douglas H. Brooks and Hal Hill. New York: Palmgrave Macmillan.

Spar, Debora. 1998. *Attracting High-Technology Investment: Intel's Costa Rican Plant.* Foreign Investment Advisory Service Occasional Paper 11. Washington: World Bank Group.

Thomas, Kenneth P. 2000. *Competing for Capital: Europe and North America in a Global Era.* Washington: Georgetown University Press.

UNCTAD (United Nations Conference on Trade and Development). 2001. *World Investment Report 2001: Promoting Linkages.* Geneva: United Nations Conference on Trade and Development.

Wells, Jr., Louis T., and Alvin G. Wint. 2000. *Marketing a Country: Promotion as a Tool for Attracting Foreign Investment,* rev. ed. Washington: The International Finance Corporation, the Multilateral Investment Guarantee Agency, and the World Bank.

About the Contributors

Garrick Blalock is an assistant professor in the Department of Applied Economics and Management at Cornell University. His research focuses on firm strategy and emerging markets.

Magnus Blomström has been a professor of economics at the Stockholm School of Economics since 1990 and president of the European Institute of Japanese Studies, Stockholm School of Economics since 1997. He was an assistant professor in the department of economics, University of Gothenburg (1985–87) and a research fellow at the Institute for International Economic Studies, University of Stockholm (1982–84). He is a research associate at the National Bureau of Economic Research and research fellow at the Centre for Economic Policy Research. He is coauthor or coeditor of *Scandinavia and the EU* (Stockholm: SNS Förlag, 1994; in Swedish), *Foreign Direct Investment: Firm and Host Country Strategies* (MacMillan, 2000), *Topics in Empirical International Economics: A Festschrift in Honor of Robert Lipsey* (Chicago University Press, forthcoming), and *Japan's New Economy: Continuity and Change in the 21st Century* (Oxford University Press, forthcoming).

Bruce A. Blonigen is the Knight Professor of Social Science in the economics department at the University of Oregon. His research interests include empirically examining international trade issues from a microeconomic and political economy perspective, especially with respect to multinational corporations and antidumping policies. His work has been funded by the National Science Foundation and has been published in journals such as the *American Economic Review, Review of Economics and Statistics, Journal of International Economics,* and the *Canadian Journal of Economics.* He is also on the editorial boards of the *Journal of International Economics, Journal of International Business Studies, Canadian Journal of Economics,* and *North American Journal of Economics and Finance.* He is a research associate with the National Bureau of Economic Research.

Maria Carkovic is a senior fellow at the Carlson School of Business, University of Minnesota. She has also taught at the University of Virginia's department of economics. Her areas of interest in teaching and applied research include the determinants of economic growth, dollarization, international capital flows, and the characteristics of business cycles. Prior to teaching, she spent 12 years as an economist at the International Monetary Fund, where she focused on economies in Latin America, Africa, and Europe.

Asim Erdilek is a professor in the department of economics at the Weatherhead School of Management, Case Western Reserve University. His research interests include FDI and the Turkish economy.

Susan E. Feinberg is an assistant professor of international business at Rutgers University. Her work examines the location and operating decisions of US multinational firms. Her research on the intrafirm trade of US multinationals was the subject of testimony before the United States Trade Deficit Review Commission.

Paul J. Gertler is a professor of economics at the Haas School of Business, University of California, Berkeley. He is also a professor of health services finance at the university's School of Public Health, faculty director of the Graduate Program in Health Services Management, and associate director of the Center on the Economics and Demography of Aging. He is a faculty research associate at the National Bureau of Economic Research; an affiliated professor at the Institute of Global Health, University of California, San Francisco; research fellow at the Bureau for Research in Economic Analysis of Development; and scientific adviser, National Institute of Public Health, Cuernavaca, Mexico.

Holger Görg is a lecturer in the School of Economics at the University of Nottingham. He is also a research fellow at the university's Leverhulme Centre for Research on Globalisation and Economic Policy (GEP). He is an external research director at DIW (German Institute for Economic Research), Berlin. His research interests include empirical international trade and industrial organization focusing on the activities of multinational companies, FDI, and outsourcing.

Edward M. Graham, senior fellow at the Institute for International Economics, was associate professor in the Fuqua School of Business at Duke University (1988–90), associate professor at the University of North

Carolina (1983–88), principal administrator of the Planning and Evaluation Unit at the OECD (1981–82), International Economist in the Office of International Investment Affairs at the US Treasury (1979–80), and assistant professor at the Massachusetts Institute of Technology (1974–78). He is author or coauthor of a number of studies on international investment and technology transfer, including *Reforming Korea's Industrial Conglomerates* (2003), *Fighting the Wrong Enemy: Antiglobal Activists and Multinational Enterprises* (2000), *Global Competition Policy and Competition Policies in the Global Economy* (1997) with J. David Richardson, *Global Corporations and National Governments* (1996), and *Foreign Direct Investment in the United States* (3d ed. 1995) with Paul R. Krugman.

Gordon H. Hanson is a professor of economics in the Graduate School of International Relations and Pacific Studies and the Department of Economics at the University of California, San Diego. He is also a research associate at the National Bureau of Economic Research and coeditor of the *Journal of Development Economics*. His current research examines the economic consequences of Mexican migration to the United States, how and why multinational firms globalize their production activities, and the factors that shape countries' export capabilities. In his recent work, he studied the impact of globalization on wages, the fiscal and labor market consequences of immigration, and the implications of trade reform for regional economies. His most recent book is *Immigration Policy and the Welfare System* (Oxford University Press, 2002).

Beata Smarzynska Javorcik is a senior economist in the Development Research Group at the World Bank. She served as a country economist for Azerbaijan and did extensive work on transition countries, including her native Poland. Her research interests focus on factors affecting inflows of FDI, including rule of law, environmental standards, and protection of intellectual property rights. Her ongoing work examines productivity spillovers from FDI, particularly those taking place through contacts between multinationals and their local suppliers. Her research has been published in economic journals such as *American Economic Review, European Economic Review, World Economy,* and *Journal of Economic Integration.*

Michael P. Keane has been a professor in the department of economics at Yale University since August 2000. He was a professor in the department of economics at New York University (September 1998–July 2001) and the University of Minnesota (July 1996–August 1998), associate professor (September 1993–June 1996) and assistant professor (September 1988–August 1993) at the University of Minnesota's Industrial Relations Center and department of economics, and visiting assistant professor in the department of economics at New York University (January 1993–May 1993) and the department of marketing at the University of Alberta (January 1991–March

1991). His research interests include labor economics, empirical microeconomics, applied econometrics, and consumer choice behavior.

Robert Z. Lawrence, senior fellow, is also the Albert L. Williams Professor of Trade and Investment at the John F. Kennedy School of Government at Harvard University. He served as a member of President Clinton's Council of Economic Advisers from 1999 to 2000. He held the New Century Chair as a nonresident senior fellow at the Brookings Institution between 1997 and 1998 and founded and edited the *Brookings Trade Forum* in 1998. He was a senior fellow in the Economic Studies Program at Brookings (1983–91), a professorial lecturer at the Johns Hopkins School of Advanced International Studies (1978–81), and an instructor at Yale University (1975). He has served as a consultant to the Federal Reserve Bank of New York, the World Bank, the OECD, and UNCTAD. He is the author or coauthor of more than 100 papers and articles on international economics and of several books, including *Crimes and Punishments: Retaliation under the WTO* (2003), *Globaphobia: Confronting Fears about Open Trade* (Brookings Institution Press, 1998), and *Building Bridges: An Egypt-U.S. Free Trade Agreement* (Brookings Institution Press, 1998).

Ross Levine is the Curtis L. Carlson Endowed Chair of Finance at the Carlson School of Management, University of Minnesota. Before joining the university, he was with the Board of Governors of the Federal Reserve System, the World Bank, and the University of Virginia. At the World Bank, he conducted research on financial-sector policy issues and contributed to operational missions on a range of topics. He continues to investigate the linkages between financial-sector policies and economic development.

Ping Lin is an associate professor at the department of economics, Lingnan University of Hong Kong. He is also a research fellow at the university's Center for Public Policy Studies. His research interests include industrial organization, competition laws/policy in East Asia, economics of innovation, and FDI and technology transfer. His articles have appeared in the *Journal of Industrial Economics, International Journal of Industrial Organization, Review of Industrial Organization, European Economic Review, Journal of Economic Theory, Canadian Journal of Economics, Oxford Economic Papers,* and other academic journals. He has also provided proposals on establishing competition laws in China to the State Council of China and written articles on FDI-related merger control.

Robert E. Lipsey is professor emeritus of economics at Queens College and the Graduate Center of the City University of New York and a research associate and director of the New York office of the National Bureau of Economic Research. He has written books and papers and edited volumes on FDI prices in international trade, the history of international trade, national balance sheets, and the measurement and international comparison of prices, income, output, and saving.

Guoqiang Long is a senior fellow and deputy director-general of the department of foreign economic policy, Development Research Center (DRC) of the State Council of the People's Republic of China. He has extensive experience in studying China's foreign economic policies and industrial, urban, and regional development policies. He has received a number of awards, including the National Prize for Excellent Research on Foreign Economics and Trade and the Prize of China Development Studies. He was a visiting fellow at the Center for Northeast Asian Policy Studies (CNAPS) of the Brookings Institution (1998–99), visiting scholar in the department of economics, George Washington University (1999), and senior lecturer and assistant chair of the department of urban and regional science, Peking University (1987–93).

Marc Melitz has been an associate professor in the department of economics at Harvard University since July 2004. He was an assistant professor there from July 2000 to June 2004. He is a faculty research fellow at the National Bureau of Economic Research, a faculty associate at the Weatherhead Center for International Affairs, and research affiliate at the Centre for Economic Policy Research. He is associate editor of *Economic Journal* and is on the program committee of the 9th World Congress of the Econometric Society.

Theodore H. Moran holds the Marcus Wallenberg Chair at the School of Foreign Service at Georgetown University. He is the founder of the Landegger Program in International Business Diplomacy at the university and serves as director there. He is on the executive council of the McDonough School of Business at the university. His most recent books include *Reforming OPIC for the 21st Century* (2003), *Beyond Sweatshops: Foreign Direct Investment, Globalization, and Developing Countries* (Brookings Institution, 2002), *Parental Supervision: The New Paradigm for Foreign Direct Investment and Development* (2001), and *Foreign Investment and Development* (1998). In 1993–94, he was senior adviser for economics on the Policy Planning Staff of the Department of State. He returned to Georgetown University after the NAFTA and Uruguay Round negotiations. He is a consultant to the United Nations, governments in Asia and Latin America, and international business and financial communities. In 2000, he was appointed counselor to the Multilateral Investment Guarantee Agency (MIGA) of the World Bank Group. In 2002, he was chairman of the Committee on Monitoring International Labor Standards of the National Academy of Sciences.

Todd J. Moss is a research fellow at the Center for Global Development, specializing in African economic policy, financial-market development, and global economic relations. He taught at the London School of Economics'

Development Studies Institute and worked at the World Bank, the Economist Intelligence Unit, and the Overseas Development Council. He has published many articles on African finance and is the author of *Adventure Capitalism: Globalization and the Political Economy of Stock Markets in Africa* (2003) and coeditor (with Sam Mensah) of *African Emerging Markets: Contemporary Issues, Volume II* (2004).

Vijaya Ramachandran is an assistant professor of public policy at the Georgetown Public Policy Institute and a visiting fellow at the Center for Global Development. She is a survey specialist, and her areas of expertise are private-sector development, entrepreneurship, and foreign investment. She was recently a senior economist at the World Bank, managing the work of the Regional Program on Enterprise Development, including private firm surveys in 12 African countries. She served as a senior economist in the Executive Office of the Secretary General of the United Nations and taught at the Sanford Institute of Public Policy at Duke University. She has written articles on FDI and private-sector development in Asia and Africa. She is the author of *Investing in Africa: Strategies for Private-Sector Development* (2000) and coeditor (with Nicolas van de Walle and Nicole Ball) of *Beyond Structural Adjustment* (2003).

Kamal Saggi is a professor and director of graduate studies in the department of economics, Southern Methodist University. He has done extensive research in the theory of international trade and investment, international technology transfer, and economic development. He has published many scholarly articles on these subjects in leading economic journals such as the *Journal of International Economics, Journal of Development Economics,* and *European Economic Review.* He was also a consultant to the World Bank's Development Research Group and International Finance Corporation.

Manju Kedia Shah has served as a consultant to the World Bank for the past decade, working on a variety of investment climate issues. She has carried out firm surveys in East Africa and has published papers on firm growth, firm networks, and the determinants of productivity.

Fredrik Sjöholm is an associate professor in the European Institute of Japanese Studies at the Stockholm School of Economics. He was previously with the National University of Singapore. His main research interests include international and development economics. He is currently engaged in several projects on host country effects of FDI.

Mariana Spatareanu is a researcher in the Development Research Group at the World Bank. Her research focuses on measuring the productivity spillovers from FDI as well as on factors affecting the inflows of FDI, including labor market regulations and environmental standards. Her research interests also include modeling the investment decisions of firms and the way they respond to changes in monetary and fiscal policies.

Eric Strobl is an associate professor at the University of Paris X. His research deals primarily with empirical issues in international trade and industrial economics, focusing on questions concerning multinational companies and firm subsidization. He has also worked on various issues in development economics, including the impact of climate change and labor market imperfections.

Miao Grace Wang is an assistant professor of economics at Marquette University, Wisconsin. Her research interests include international trade and FDI with a focus on the macroeconomic impacts of FDI, such as the impacts on the host country's economic growth and domestic investment. She has been a manuscript referee for academic journals such as *Journal of Regional Science, Review of Social Economy*, and *International Regional Science Review*.

Index

Carr, Markusen, and Maskus (CMM) empirical
framework, 226–28, 230, 231, 232*t*, 233
Chad, 340
chemical industry, 269*n*, 291, 296, 299, 301*b*
Chile, 111, 380, 384
China, 16–17
advanced technology, 327–29, 329*t*, 330*t*
automotive industry, 289, 333–35
balance of payments, 335
cooperative enterprises, 316, 316*n*, 318*t*
crowding out versus spillovers in, 333–35, 368
Deng Xiao Ping "reformist" faction, 378
economic policies, 370
economic policy factions, 378
enclave-featured economy, 334
export and foreign-invested enterprises, 328*t*
export tendencies, by enterprise types, 325*t*
FDI distribution, by industrial sectors, 317–18
FDI inflows, 223, 319*t*, 367
FDI policies, 318–22
FDI sources, 317, 319*t*
foreign-invested enterprises, 316, 317, 317*t*, 318*t*,
320*t*
foreign trade, 322, 323*t*; import substitution
strategy, 324; policy goals, 324
high-performance electronics industry, 290–91
Hong Kong and, 317
information technology clusters, 324
investment promotion, 378–79
Japan and, 317, 319*t*, 324
Japanese multinational corporations in, 301
joint venture enterprises, 316, 316*n*, 318*t*
Li Peng faction, 378
mobile communications industry, 331, 331*t*
performance requirements, 315, 321
processing trade, 325–27
R&D centers, 329–31
"round ripping," 367
solely foreign-owned enterprises, 318*t*
special economic zones, 378–79
"swap market for technology" strategy, 17, 334
Taiwan and, 317
tax system, reform of, 326
technology spillovers, 327, 329–35, 331–32
Trade Related Investment Measures (TRIMs)
Agreement, 335
US and, 317, 319*t*, 324
vocational training, 332
World Trade Organization and, 315, 322,
325–26, 335, 370
Chrysler Corporation, 285, 383
Cobb-Douglas production function, 180
colonialism, economic. *See* imperialism
Compaq, 285, 383
Costa Rica, 302, 379–80
Abbott Laboratories and, 380
Baxter Healthcare and, 380
FedEx and, 380
high-performance electronics industry, 291
Intel and, 379–80

Motorola and, 380
Procter & Gamble and, 380
credit availability, 8, 12, 52–53, 64, 73, 76
Indonesian financial crisis and, 85–86, 89, 100,
102, 104
Czech Republic, 6–7, 46
assistance to suppliers by MNCs, 63*t*, 65*t*
competition and the entry of MNCs, 54*t*
distribution of MNC suppliers, 60*t*
employee training and entry of MNCs, 58*t*
horizontal spillovers, 48
knowledge transfer and entry of MNCs, 57*t*
local firm's employee loss and entry of MNCs, 56*t*
local firm's market share and entry of MNCs, 55*t*
marketing strategies and entry of MNCs, 59*t*
sourcing by MNCs, 58–62; intermediate inputs,
61*t*; from North America, 59; patterns,
62*t*
spillovers as compared with Latvia, 51–54, 53*t*
spillovers as compared with Romania, 40, 46,
49, 50*t*

Daewoo, 288
DaimlerChrysler, 288–89
Deng Xiao Ping "reformist" faction, 378
dependency theory, 342
developed countries, 391–92
crowding in versus crowding out, 238, 241
economic growth, 233–38
investment patterns, 222–23
versus less developed countries, 12–13, 18,
221–22, 224*t*–25*t*
pooling with less developed countries, 238, 242
R&D internalization in, 110–11, 118, 133
Trade Related Investment Measures (TRIMs)
Agreement, 384–85
developing countries, 45, 195, 197–98, 297–98
development. *See* host economies; less developed
countries; *specific countries and regions*
Dominican Republic, 305, 391, 392

East Asian financial crisis, 76–77, 89, 90*t*, 100, 102,
104
El Salvador, 305, 391
endogeneity of factor inputs, 180–81, 184, 186,
385–86, 388
Equatorial Guinea, 340
Ethiopia, 345
European Bank for Reconstruction and
Development, 383
European Union (EU), 112, 149, 222, 228, 251, 381–82
Association Agreements, 68
Hungary and, 289, 300
incentive packages, 381–82
Romania and, 68–69
export processing zone (EPZ), 305, 391–92
externalities. *See* spillovers

FedEx, 380
FIE. *See* foreign-invested enterprises (FIE)

import substitution (IS), 3, 284–85, 290–92, 294, 296–97
India, 2n, 66n, 111, 297, 301, 384n
  high-performance electronics industry, 290
  import substitution, 290
  productivity spillovers, 32
Indonesia, 4, 7, 8, 25, 74, 380, 388
  automotive industry, 288
  data sources, 90
  East Asian financial crisis and, 76–77, 90t
  FDI inflows, 223
  financial crisis and credit availability, 85–86, 89, 100, 102, 104
  fixed-effect estimation, domestic and exporting establishments, 103t
  foreign and domestic firms, descriptive statistics, 92t
  foreign investment policy, 88–89
  horizontal technology transfer, 77–78
  International Monetary Fund banking reforms and, 76
  liquidity insurance, 99–101, 102, 83–86
  Lithuania and, 79
  manufacturing growth, 88
  market concentration and price, 98
  measurement of foreign investment, 93–95, 96t
  output and value added, 99
  production function estimation for domestic establishments, 96–98, 97t
  productivity, 93
  productivity spillovers, 33–39, 34t, 39t
  suppliers, 80–81
  technology spillovers, variables affecting, 91t
  technology transfer, 81–83, 83t
  value addition, 82, 82n
  wage spillovers, 27–28, 29t
industrial equipment industry, 291
Intel, 302, 330, 380
Inter-American Development Bank, 383
International Finance Corporation (IFC), 383
International Monetary Fund (IMF), 76, 87, 197, 219
  World Economic Outlook, 202, 206n, 219
International Organization for Standardization (ISO). See ISO 9000
International Standard Industrial Classification (ISIC) industries, 35, 37–38, 90, 92, 96
intrafirm trade, 245–46, 247–48, 253, 256, 256n, 263–64. See also under multinational corporations (MNCs)
  affiliate-to-affiliate, 256, 257t–58t
  affiliate-to-parent, 256–63, 259t–60t
  data sources, 219, 250n
  "deep integration" and, 16
  employment and, 266t
  nature of, 268–70
  parent-to-affiliate, 261t–62t, 263
  property, plant and equipment (PPE) and, 246
  real wages and, 258t–62t
  sample affiliates, 254t–55t

study results, 267–68
trends, 251–53
wages, employment and PPE growth, 264, 265t, 266t
Ireland, 9, 381
  multinational corporations in, 138, 154–55: data sources for, 144n; domestic plant population in, 148t; effects on domestic plant entry, 143, 146t; employment share, 146–48, 147t; indigenous plant entry rate model, 144–45; linkages to domestic suppliers and customers, 139–41; market access spillovers, 143n; plant growth, 153t; plant survival, 148–50, 150t; productivity spillovers, analysis of, 141–43; R&D spillovers, 143n; raw materials purchases, 141t
IS. See import substitution (IS)
ISO 9000, 6, 64n

Japan, 80
  automotive industry, 79, 268n–69n, 288
  China and, 317, 319t
  Indonesia and, 88
  multinational corporations, 7: electrical machinery industry exports, 302; joint ventures, 89; R&D, 109; suppliers and, 79–80; technology transfer, 290, 293; vertical spillovers, 66–67
Japan Bank for International Cooperation (JBIC), 324
Japan External Trade Organization (JETRO), 324

Kenya, 17–18, 291–92, 347–48, 347t, 348–49. See also Africa
knowledge-capital model, 226, 229t–30t
knowledge transfer, 54, 65, 68, 182, 187
  mechanisms, 182
  productivity spillovers and, 46, 48, 50–51, 56–57
  sources, 247, 269

labor, 39, 49, 77, 93, 343
  costs, 80, 86, 324, 345n, 348, 356
  markets, 5, 24, 27–28, 39, 39–40, 77
  productivity, 30, 32–33, 35–36, 118n, 142, 154
  skills, 274, 304
  supply price of, 189
  turnover, 46–47, 53–54, 107, 118
  unit requirements, 165, 167, 180
  Witwatersrand Native Labor Association, 341
Latvia, 46, 51–52, 52t
  MNCs' assistance to suppliers, 66t
  spillovers as compared with the Czech Republic, 51–54, 53t
LDCs. See less developed countries (LDCs)
Lenovo Group, 332
less developed countries (LDCs), 221–22. See also developing countries
  economic growth, per capita GDP, 236t–37t
  economic growth studies, 234–35
Lesotho, 391

Romania, 46, 48, 67–69, 118, 384
    European Union Association Agreements and, 68
    spillovers as compared with the Czech
        Republic, 40, 46, 49, 50t
Russia/Commonwealth of Independent States
    (CIS), 59, 75

Seagate, 290, 302
Siemens, 330
Singapore, 110, 301, 301n, 384
    Economic Development Board of Singapore
        (Board), 393
    FDI inflows, 223
    high-performance electronics industry, 290–91
    Small Industry Finance Program, 393
South Africa, 111, 282, 340
    automotive industry, 288–89
Southeast Asia, 302, 302n
    high-performance electronics industry, 290–91
South Korea, 66, 202, 302, 302n, 324, 369
    automotive industry, 288
    per capita growth rate, 203, 297
    petrochemical industry, 292
Soviet Union, 342. See also Russia/Commonwealth
    of Independent States (CIS)
spillovers, 186–87
    Africa, 369–70
    backward linkages and, policies to promote,
        283–84, 300b, 306–08
    in the Czech Republic and Latvia, 51–54, 53t
    in the Czech Republic and Romania, 40, 46, 49,
        50t
    firm surveys, 50–51
    foreign ownership, degree of and, 65–66
    harmful, 4–5
    horizontal versus vertical, 5, 6, 46, 47–48, 50,
        54–57
    Ireland, 143n
    measurement of, 138, 302
    nationality of investors and, 67–68
    negative productivity, 196
    pecuniary, 9, 138
    positive, 3–4: empirical evidence for, 175–76;
        survey results and, 177–78
    productivity, 4–5, 24, 29–30, 31–39, 34t, 139,
        141–43
    prospects for, 392–93
    R&D, 143n
    Romania and the Czech Republic, 40, 46, 49, 50t
    technology, 24, 30, 74–75: Asia, 29; case studies,
        30–31; China, 331–32; Indonesia, 91t
    wages, 4, 24–29, 40; Indonesia, 27–28, 29t;
        Mexico, 28; South Carolina, 27; United
        Kingdom, 27, 28, 40; United States, 40;
        Venezuela, 28
Standard Industrial Classification codes, 251
sub-Saharan Africa. See under Africa
Sudan, 340
sweatshop abuses, 391–92
Sweden, 109

Taiwan, 109–10, 302, 317, 324
Tanzania, 17–18, 340, 345. See also Africa
    business environment, 350
    FDI inflows, 347–48, 347t
    political environment, 349
    regulatory discretion, 349
    technology and management procedures, leakage
        of , 283
technology transfer, 164, 164n, 165n, 248, 283, 392
    costs and benefits, 170–72, 172n
    horizontal, 77–78
    Indonesia, 81–83, 83t
    joint ventures and, 291–92, 303
    mandates, 292–93, 303, 308, 321
    market competition and welfare effects, 81–82
    speed of, 292
    vertical, 78–81
Texas Instruments, 283
textile industry, 58, 291–92, 296, 321
Thailand, 15, 283–84, 302, 380, 384, 388
    automotive industry, 289
    Japanese multinational corporations in, 268n–69n
total factor productivity (TFP), 6, 8, 32, 49–59, 180,
    219
    domestic firms, 142, 175, 180, 296, 386–87
trade
    governmental policies and, 276
    preferential agreements, 68
    theory, 84–85
Trade-Related Aspects of Intellectual Property
    Rights (TRIPs) Agreement, 112
Trade Related Investment Measures (TRIMs)
    Agreement, 2n, 307, 384, 385
    China and, 335
Turkey
    automotive industry, 288
    background and literature review, 108–11
    Customs Union Agreement with the European
        Union (EU), 112
    data sources, 112–15
    Generalized System of Preferences (GSP) and, 112
    Special 301 Watch (Priority Watch List) and, 112
    Technology Development Foundation (TTGV),
        111–12

Uganda, 17–18, 350–51. See also Africa
    FDI inflows, 347–48, 347t
United Kingdom (UK), 51, 78, 235n, 250, 383, 109
    Annual Respondents Database (ARD), 27–28
    wage spillovers, 40, 27–28
United Nations (UN)
    Conference on Trade and Development (UNC-
        TAD), 3, 23, 393
    Millennium Declaration, 337
United States (US), 32
    Canada and, 14, 41, 138, 190, 247, 386
    China and, 317, 319t
    exports, 85, 100
    foreign investment, 274–75, 277, 290
    locational subsidies, 382

Other Publications from the Institute for International Economics

* = out of print

POLICY ANALYSES IN
INTERNATIONAL ECONOMICS Series

1   The Lending Policies of the International
    Monetary Fund*   John Williamson
    August 1982   ISBN 0-88132-000-5
2   "Reciprocity": A New Approach to World
    Trade Policy?*   William R. Cline
    September 1982   ISBN 0-88132-001-3
3   Trade Policy in the 1980s*
    C. Fred Bergsten and William R. Cline
    November 1982   ISBN 0-88132-002-1
4   International Debt and the Stability of the
    World Economy*   William R. Cline
    September 1983   ISBN 0-88132-010-2
5   The Exchange Rate System,* Second Edition
    John Williamson
    Sept. 1983, rev. June 1985   ISBN 0-88132-034-X
6   Economic Sanctions in Support of Foreign
    Policy Goals*
    Gary Clyde Hufbauer and Jeffrey J. Schott
    October 1983   ISBN 0-88132-014-5
7   A New SDR Allocation?*   John Williamson
    March 1984   ISBN 0-88132-028-5
8   An International Standard for Monetary
    Stabilization*   Ronald L. McKinnon
    March 1984   ISBN 0-88132-018-8
9   The Yen/Dollar Agreement: Liberalizing
    Japanese Capital Markets*   Jeffrey A. Frankel
    December 1984   ISBN 0-88132-035-8
10 Bank Lending to Developing Countries: The
    Policy Alternatives*   C. Fred Bergsten,
    William R. Cline, and John Williamson
    April 1985   ISBN 0-88132-032-3
11 Trading for Growth: The Next Round of
    Trade Negotiations*
    Gary Clyde Hufbauer and Jeffrey J. Schott
    September 1985   ISBN 0-88132-033-1
12 Financial Intermediation Beyond the Debt
    Crisis*   Donald R. Lessard, John Williamson
    September 1985   ISBN 0-88132-021-8
13 The United States-Japan Economic Problem*
    C. Fred Bergsten and William R. Cline
    October 1985, 2d ed. January 1987
                         ISBN 0-88132-060-9
14 Deficits and the Dollar: The World Economy
    at Risk*   Stephen Marris
    December 1985, 2d ed. November 1987
                         ISBN 0-88132-067-6
15 Trade Policy for Troubled Industries*
    Gary Clyde Hufbauer and Howard R. Rosen
    March 1986   ISBN 0-88132-020-X

16 The United States and Canada: The Quest for
    Free Trade*   Paul Wonnacott, with an
    appendix by John Williamson
    March 1987   ISBN 0-88132-056-0
17 Adjusting to Success: Balance of Payments
    Policy in the East Asian NICs*
    Bela Balassa and John Williamson
    June 1987, rev. April 1990 ISBN 0-88132-101-X
18 Mobilizing Bank Lending to Debtor
    Countries*   William R. Cline
    June 1987   ISBN 0-88132-062-5
19 Auction Quotas and United States Trade
    Policy*   C. Fred Bergsten, Kimberly Ann
    Elliott, Jeffrey J. Schott, and Wendy E. Takacs
    September 1987   ISBN 0-88132-050-1
20 Agriculture and the GATT: Rewriting the
    Rules*   Dale E. Hathaway
    September 1987   ISBN 0-88132-052-8
21 Anti-Protection: Changing Forces in United
    States Trade Politics*
    I. M. Destler and John S. Odell
    September 1987   ISBN 0-88132-043-9
22 Targets and Indicators: A Blueprint for the
    International Coordination of Economic
    Policy
    John Williamson and Marcus H. Miller
    September 1987   ISBN 0-88132-051-X
23 Capital Flight: The Problem and Policy
    Responses*   Donald R. Lessard and
    John Williamson
    December 1987   ISBN 0-88132-059-5
24 United States-Canada Free Trade: An
    Evaluation of the Agreement*
    Jeffrey J. Schott
    April 1988   ISBN 0-88132-072-2
25 Voluntary Approaches to Debt Relief*
    John Williamson
    Sept.1988, rev. May 1989   ISBN 0-88132-098-6
26 American Trade Adjustment: The Global
    Impact*   William R. Cline
    March 1989   ISBN 0-88132-095-1
27 More Free Trade Areas?*
    Jeffrey J. Schott
    May 1989   ISBN 0-88132-085-4
28 The Progress of Policy Reform in Latin
    America*   John Williamson
    January 1990   ISBN 0-88132-100-1
29 The Global Trade Negotiations: What Can Be
    Achieved?*   Jeffrey J. Schott
    September 1990   ISBN 0-88132-137-0
30 Economic Policy Coordination: Requiem or
    Prologue?*   Wendy Dobson
    April 1991   ISBN 0-88132-102-8

African Debt and Financing*
Carol Lancaster and John Williamson, eds.
May 1986 ISBN 0-88132-044-7

Resolving the Global Economic Crisis: After Wall Street*
by Thirty-three Economists from Thirteen Countries
December 1987 ISBN 0-88132-070-6

World Economic Problems*
Kimberly Ann Elliott/John Williamson, editors
April 1988 ISBN 0-88132-055-2

Reforming World Agricultural Trade*
by Twenty-nine Professionals from Seventeen Countries/*1988* ISBN 0-88132-088-9

Economic Relations Between the United States and Korea: Conflict or Cooperation?*
Thomas O. Bayard and Soogil Young, editors
January 1989 ISBN 0-88132-068-4

Whither APEC? The Progress to Date and Agenda for the Future* C. Fred Bergsten, editor
October 1997 ISBN 0-88132-248-2

0 **Economic Integration of the Korean Peninsula** Marcus Noland, editor
January 1998 ISBN 0-88132-255-5

1 **Restarting Fast Track*** Jeffrey J. Schott, editor
April 1998 ISBN 0-88132-259-8

2 **Launching New Global Trade Talks: An Action Agenda** Jeffrey J. Schott, editor
September 1998 ISBN 0-88132-266-0

3 **Japan's Financial Crisis and Its Parallels to US Experience**
Ryoichi Mikitani and Adam S. Posen, eds.
September 2000 ISBN 0-88132-289-X

4 **The Ex-Im Bank in the 21st Century: A New Approach** Gary Clyde Hufbauer and Rita M. Rodriguez, editors
January 2001 ISBN 0-88132-300-4

5 **The Korean Diaspora in the World Economy**
C. Fred Bergsten and Inbom Choi, eds.
January 2003 ISBN 0-88132-358-6

6 **Dollar Overvaluation and the World Economy**
C. Fred Bergsten and John Williamson, eds.
February 2003 ISBN 0-88132-351-9

7 **Dollar Adjustment: How Far? Against What?**
C. Fred Bergsten and John Williamson, editors
November 2004 ISBN 0-88132-378-0

8 **The Euro at Five: Ready for a Global Role?**
Adam S. Posen, editor
April 2005 ISBN 0-88132-380-2

VORKS IN PROGRESS

'ew Regional Arrangements and
e World Economy C. Fred Bergsten

The Globalization Backlash in Europe and the United States
C. Fred Bergsten, Pierre Jacquet, and Karl Kaiser

The United States as a Debtor Nation: Risks and Policy Reform William R. Cline

China's Entry into the World Economy
Richard N. Cooper

American Trade Politics, 4th ed.
I. M. Destler

The ILO in the World Economy
Kimberly Ann Elliott

Reforming Economic Sanctions
Kimberly Ann Elliott, Gary C. Hufbauer, and Jeffrey J. Schott

Merry Sisterhood or Guarded Watchfulness? Cooperation Between the IMF and the World Bank Michael Fabricius

Why Does Immigration Divide America?
Gordon Hanson

Future of Chinese Exchange Rates
Morris Goldstein and Nicholas R. Lardy

NAFTA Revisited: Achievements and Challenges
Gary Clyde Hufbauer and Jeffrey J. Schott

New Agricultural Negotiations in the WTO
Tim Josling and Dale Hathaway

Workers at Risk: Job Loss from Apparel, Textiles, Footwear, and Furniture
Lori G. Kletzer

Responses to Globalization: US Textile and Apparel Workers and Firms
Lori Kletzer, James Levinsohn, and J. David Richardson

The Strategic Implications of China-Taiwan Economic Relations Nicholas R. Lardy

Making the Rules: Case Studies on US Trade Negotiation, Vol. 1 and 2
Robert Z. Lawrence, Charan Devereaux, and Michael Watkins

Prospects for a US-Egypt Free Trade Agreement
Robert Z. Lawrence and Ahmed Galal

High Technology and the Globalization of America Catherine L. Mann

International Financial Architecture
Michael Mussa

Germany and the World Economy
Adam S. Posen

Automatic Stabilizers for the Eurozone
Adam S. Posen

Global Forces, American Faces: US Economic Globalization at the Grass Roots
J. David Richardson

Prospects for a US-Colombia Free Trade Agreement Jeffrey J. Schott

Curbing the Boom-Bust Cycle: Stabilizing Capital Flows to Emerging Markets
John Williamson

DISTRIBUTORS OUTSIDE THE UNITED STATES

Australia, New Zealand,
and Papua New Guinea
D.A. Information Services
648 Whitehorse Road
Mitcham, Victoria 3132, Australia
tel: 61-3-9210-7777
fax: 61-3-9210-7788
email: service@adadirect.com.au
www.dadirect.com.au

Canada
Renouf Bookstore
5369 Canotek Road, Unit 1
Ottawa, Ontario KlJ 9J3, Canada
tel: 613-745-2665
fax: 613-745-7660
www.renoufbooks.com

United Kingdom and Europe
(including Russia and Turkey)
The Eurospan Group
3 Henrietta Street, Covent Garden
London WC2E 8LU England
tel: 44-20-7240-0856
fax: 44-20-7379-0609
www.eurospan.co.uk

India, Bangladesh, Nepal, and Sri Lanka
Viva Books Pvt.
Mr. Vinod Vasishtha
4325/3, Ansari Rd.
Daryaganj, New Delhi-110002
India
tel: 91-11-327-9280
fax: 91-11-326-7224
email: vinod.viva@gndel.globalnet. ems.vsnl.
net.in

Japan and the Republic of Korea
United Publishers Services Ltd.
1-32-5, Higashi-shinagawa,
Shinagawa-ku, Tokyo 140-0002 JAPAN
tel: 81-3-5479-7251
fax: 81-3-5479-7307
info@ups.co.jp
For trade accounts only.
Individuals will find IIE books in
leading Tokyo bookstores.

Southeast Asia (Brunei, Burma, Cambodia,
Malaysia, Indonesia,
the Philippines, Singapore, Thailand
Taiwan, and Vietnam)
APAC Publishers Services
70 Bedemeer Road #05-03
Hiap Huat House
Singapore 339940
tel: 65-684-47333
fax: 65-674-78916

Visit our Web site at:
www.iie.com
E-mail orders to:
orders@iie.com